KLEPTOPIA

ALSO BY TOM BURGIS

*The Looting Machine: Warlords, Tycoons, Smugglers and the
Systematic Theft of Africa's Wealth*

KLEPTOPIA

HOW DIRTY MONEY IS
CONQUERING THE WORLD

TOM BURGIS

**WILLIAM
COLLINS**

William Collins
An imprint of HarperCollins*Publishers*
1 London Bridge Street
London SE1 9GF

WilliamCollinsBooks.com

First published in Great Britain in 2020 by William Collins

1

A catalogue record for this book is
available from the British Library

HB ISBN 978-0-00-830834-6
TPB ISBN 978-0-00-830835-3

'Macavity' from *Old Possum's Book of Practical Cats* by T.S. Eliot,
courtesy of Faber and Faber Ltd.

Typeset in Adobe Garamond Pro
Printed and bound in Great Britain by
CPI Group (UK) Ltd, Croydon

MIX
Paper from
responsible sources
FSC™ C007454

For Camilla

CONTENTS

PART II: CHRYSALIS

PART III: METAMORPHOSIS

A NOTE ON TRUTH

This is a true story. Each of the facts of which it is composed comes from an interview or a document, corroborated wherever possible by other sources. Where a character is described as thinking something, that is because they told the author their thoughts or otherwise recorded them. Every character was given a chance to check facts before publication. Where there are conflicting accounts of an event, the version that appears most probable is given in the text, with the dispute discussed in the notes. The notes contain a description of the source of every significant piece of information in the book. In the cases when sources would only speak on condition of anonymity, they are described with as much detail as possible without making them identifiable. Occasionally, all that can be said is that the source of a particular fact is a confidential interview. This is because the source in question could face reprisals for revealing what he or she knew. While anonymous sources are not ideal, especially in a book about the nefarious power of secrecy, it is important for those whom others would wish to silence to have their voice in this way, subject to the author's best efforts to test their credibility. The truth has had a rough time in recent years. The author's endeavour here has been to lay open the foundations on which this story is built in such a way that the reader might both believe it and enjoy it.

CAST OF CHARACTERS

In London

Nigel Wilkins Head of compliance at the London office of the Swiss bank BSI, later on the staff of the City of London regulator, the Financial Conduct Authority

Charlotte Martin Nigel's companion

Trefor Williams Ex-UK special forces, investigator at the private intelligence firm Diligence

Ron Wahid Bangladeshi-American founder of the private intelligence firm Arcanum

Neil Gerrard Lawyer at the City firm Dechert

The Trio

Alexander Machkevitch aka **Sasha** Kyrgyz-born member of the Trio of Central Asian billionaires behind Eurasian Natural Resources Corporation (ENRC)

Patokh Chodiev Uzbek-born member of the Trio

Alijan Ibragimov Kyrgyz-Uighur member of the Trio

Mehmet Dalman British-Cypriot City financier, ENRC director then chairman

Victor Hanna The Trio's man in Africa
Shawn McCormick Ex-US intelligence official hired by ENRC

The khan

Nursultan Nazarbayev Ruler of Kazakhstan since 1989,
    president until 2019 then chair of the Security Council
Rakhat Aliyev aka **Sugar** Nazarbayev's son-in-law, later in exile
Timur Kulibayev Nazarbayev's other son-in-law, billionaire
Kenes Rakishev Kulibayev's protégé

The oligarch

Mukhtar Ablyazov Kazakh ex-minister, tycoon and founder of
    BTA Bank
Peter Sahlas Canadian lawyer retained by Ablyazov
Madina Ablyazova Ablyazov's daughter, in Geneva
Iliyas Khrapunov Madina's husband
Leila Khrapunova Kazakh businesswoman, Iliyas's mother
Viktor Khrapunov Kazakh politician, Iliyas's stepfather
Bota Jardemalie Harvard-trained Kazakh lawyer at BTA Bank

The gangsters

Semyon Mogilevich aka **Seva** aka **the Brainy Don** Moscow's
    premier criminal moneyman
Sergei Mikhailov aka **Mikhas** Boss of the Solntsevskaya Bratva,
    a Russian crime syndicate

In Africa

Billy Rautenbach Zimbabwean businessman, backer of Robert
    Mugabe's regime

Robert Mugabe Ruler of Zimbabwe, 1980–2017

Emmerson Mnangagwa aka **the Crocodile** Mugabe's security chief, then successor

Joseph Kabila President of the Democratic Republic of Congo, 2001–2019

Augustin Katumba Mwanke Kabila's right-hand man, died in 2012

Dan Gertler Israeli mining tycoon close to Kabila and Katumba

In North America

Felix Sater Russian-American fraudster, money launderer, spy and real estate developer

Tevfik Arif Kazakh founder of the New York real estate venture where Sater worked, Bayrock

Boris Birshtein Soviet-era moneyman residing in Toronto

Alex Shnaider Russian-Canadian billionaire, Birshtein's protégé and, for a time, son-in-law

Every man lives his real, most interesting
life under cover of secrecy

Anton Chekhov,
The Lady with the Dog

PART I

CRISIS

The secret of a great fortune with no apparent
cause is a crime that has been forgotten
because it was done properly

Honoré de Balzac,
Old Goriot

1

The Thief

Kensington, January 2008

Moral courage, yes, but it was also mischief, a quality discernible in the creases at the corners of his eyes, that made Nigel Wilkins decide to steal the secrets of a Swiss bank. It was the year when everything changed, 2008, the end of the old days. Forty years he had worked in banking, though he had never really been a banker. Not the way the bankers themselves used the word, nor the way other people had lately started using it. For one thing, he was much too shy. He could shoot a look of granite through his spectacles. Yet behind it lay not simply the stifled arrogance of the cleverest man anyone who knew him had ever met, but also an unbearable awkwardness. No self-respecting master of the universe would be seen dead in one of Nigel's frilly shirts. Nor would they yield to baldness as gamely as Nigel had, consigning the last of his once voluminous locks to a small cardboard box labelled 'Nigel's hair' that he displayed on a shelf in his flat. They probably wouldn't have thought about money as much as Nigel had. Thought about it, as opposed to just multiplying it. In his teens, Nigel had been enthralled by the Labour prime minister Harold Wilson, who terrified the establishment with his long Yorkshire vowels and his way of explaining in a straightforward way the meanings of money: who had it, how they got it and why the great many who lacked it might have a decent claim to a bigger share of it. Nigel had started investing his pocket money, as others experimented with a chemistry set or crueller ones held a magnifying glass over a slug. Mathematical ideas that made practical sense, that was what he liked. He thought about becoming an engineer but his temperament needed a discipline that had more room for disagreement and debate. He found economics: the art of telling money's stories.

Nigel was freer than many in his world because, although he had made plenty of it and parted with little of it, money had no hold on him. The things that others were compelled to buy were for him an encumbrance: mobile phones, televisions. He preferred his old radio and the antediluvian three-piece suite a friend had given him. During the war, his father, Arthur Wilkins, had worked in a factory making armoured vehicles in Basingstoke, a humdrum town west of London. Afterwards, he became a Methodist lay preacher. Nigel Charles, his second and final child, was born on the hinge of the century, March 19, 1950, into a generation for whom frugality, after it ceased to be the only option, became either a penance for others' greater sacrifices or a curse to be lifted with material excess. Nigel's great treat would be a first-class ticket for a long train ride, mainly to savour the complimentary scrambled eggs. Perhaps a bit of cake later, after listening to an edifying talk. At his flat – four floors up in Kensington, a brisk walk from Buckingham Palace or the royal parks, less brisk when his chest gave him trouble – he would repair rather than replace. On the mantelpiece stood a photograph of him on a rare holiday, aboard a canal boat. The bookshelves were full of economics, finance, international law. *Behind the Corporate Veil*, *Infectious Greed*, *What is Sarbanes-Oxley?*. If these were the tools of his vocation, the Thomas Hardy novels were his solace. He turned to them so often that the titles on their cracked spines were scarcely legible. *Jude the Obscure* was his favourite. Perhaps he saw himself in Jude. Perhaps he felt the meaning of all those heavy books about the functioning of wealth when he reread the passage about the three children. They are found hanging beside a note that reads, 'Done because we are too menny.' Nigel had a single self-help volume, too: *Overcoming Depression*. It looked as though it had never been opened.

Nigel had been a quiet child. But with adulthood had emerged a distrust of authority that could approach contempt. For university, he had moved to the ideal place to indulge this antagonistic streak: Manchester, a city whose inhabitants made a joyful art of insubordination and were prepared to suffer for it. They spoke of the Peterloo massacre as if they remembered it. They took pride in the workers who had accepted destitution as the price of standing against the slave-owning Confederate suppliers of the cotton for their mills. It was Manchester that had engendered the Industrial Revolution and all that flowed from it, including the Labour Party, whose branch in Kensington, where the average income was the highest in the land, would have in Nigel an unwavering candidate in its quixotic campaigns to win control of the municipal council. His comrades noted his effectiveness as a needler of the powerful and called him the Exocet, a missile that is hard to detect until it detonates.

Nigel would joke – a half joke, it seemed to those who heard it – that he couldn't say what he did for a job because it was secret. He had studied criminology as well as economics, but for most of his career had done nothing more cloak-and-dagger than economic research. Bankers would hire him to suggest what the next chapters of money's stories might be and he would sketch the scenarios, projecting himself into the mind of the classical economist's stock character, rational and law-abiding. Then he had taken a position in the enforcement division of the Financial Services Authority, the body that oversaw British banks. Here, he thought at first, he had finally found his natural habitat. Nigel was a stickler, the sort who never let you get things done the easy way. At the FSA, he had soon despaired of what he felt was a reluctance to go after financial crime.

Happily, at just that moment there appeared an opportunity for mischief, the sort that brought forth Nigel's flat, tight-lipped smile. But Charlotte Martin was anxious. She knew Nigel better than anyone did. They had met through one of the campaigns Nigel conducted against those he perceived to abuse their power, in this case the landlords of London's leaseholders. As far as Nigel was concerned, the landlords were using feudal rights to blackmail their tenants, Charlotte among them. He learned letting law inside out, and bombarded the property barons with their own subclauses and small print, marshalled in letter after excoriating letter. Charlotte was tall and slender. Her voice carried a hint of her Essex roots. She had a smile that emerged slowly to illuminate her whole face. They became a couple for a while, thereafter platonic soulmates. Even to her, Nigel was often inscrutable. She felt she was constantly trying to read him, to decipher him. But when he told her that he had taken a job as something called a 'compliance officer' at the London office of a Swiss bank, she was sure it would bring him no good. Swiss bankers would 'push his buttons', she warned him. Nigel was having none of it. This was his chance to get on the inside: he would be a watchdog in sheep's clothing. Compliance officers had been around for a while but following a procession of corporate scandals – Enron, WorldCom and the rest – they became ubiquitous, the designated conscience of big business. In practice, what compliance officers at banks usually did was attempt to swathe the organisation in a veil of rectitude without restricting bankers' moneymaking in any meaningful way. Nigel's approach would be precisely the opposite. 'I can force them to comply,' he told Charlotte. His eagerness did nothing to put her at her ease. She told him again: don't go to BSI. But he went and, for a while, no ill came of it.

That had been two years ago, back before everything changed. But Nigel could see what was coming now. Finance – making money from money – was collapsing, for the moment at least. Twenty-two days into 2008, the US Federal Reserve made emergency cuts to interest rates. On every surface of Nigel's flat lay a clipping from the business pages or a lengthy proposal to constrain financiers. He had positioned one of the wheezy armchairs with its back to the large window, so that the clear light before dusk would stream over his shoulder as he sat down, opened a single bottle of ale – Old Speckled Hen, usually – and commenced the evening's reading. Naturally, he understood the mortgage-backed securities and the credit default swaps. He grasped that the many would be sacrificed for the few. He knew that after the panic, the search for the past would begin, to discern the tale that could be traced from the wreckage of money. Plenty of people, some almost as clever as Nigel, had fathomed this much. But what Nigel started to realise as 2008 got going was that everyone would be digging for the past in the wrong place.

Nigel's father used to say that anyone who did wrong would get what was coming to them. His son thought that principle needed some enforcing. In a battered old notebook with '1970s-style laptop' on the cover, he recorded the suspicions he had formed as he shuffled daily to and from BSI's office in the City of London. He had, he wrote, stumbled upon the world's biggest fraud. And there was something else, something deeper – Nigel sensed it faintly, with a shiver – connected somehow to what was happening to money: far away, the screams of the tortured, the silence of the dead.

2

A Feast

Whitehall, February 2008

In February 2008, while it was just about still possible to pretend the crisis wasn't happening, a tall, lean billionaire with a thin face and receding hair made his way to the Banqueting House on Whitehall. Around the corner, in Downing Street, the chancellor of the exchequer was nationalising a failed bank, Northern Rock. Here, as across the West, the bailout of the financial system had begun, a transfer of public wealth to private pockets that ranked in scale alongside the one that had made this and many other billionaires' fortune the previous decade. Crisis was all around, but the chamber of rare beauty into which the oligarch now stepped was a place apart. It stood a half-hour walk along a bend in the Thames from the City, as it had since James I commanded from the architect Inigo Jones somewhere to indulge his love of masques, the lavish performances at which the royals could move among their subjects in disguise. James's heir, Charles I, commissioned Rubens to paint for the ceiling nine panels in homage to the divine right of kings to rule with absolute power. In January 1649 those images were among the last things Charles saw when, wearing two shirts so as not to shiver in the winter chill, he was led through the feasting hall to the scaffold erected outside the building, condemned as a traitor by Parliament. Now the cherubs and the lions, the swirling triumph of the Virtues over the Vices, of Wisdom over Ignorance, looked down on places set for seven courses and a Kazakh string quartet playing their counterpoints and harmonies.

The oligarch's name was Alexander Machkevitch. His many, many friends called him Sasha. For all his wealth, Sasha retained something of the academic he used to be, albeit one with a gaudily expensive wardrobe. Perhaps it was the spectacles, or the precise thatch of his moustache. When he spoke English, it was with what an undiscerning Westerner would hear as the standard Thick Russian Accent. Sasha did hold Russian nationality, and had spent stints of the tumultuous nineties in Moscow, but he was in fact Kyrgyz. His mother had been a distinguished prosecutor back when Kyrgyzstan was a province on the Asian fringe of the Soviet empire. Young Sasha had been bright. He developed a mastery of language and secured a position at the university in Bishkek teaching philology. A life of obscure lecturing lay ahead of him. Then capitalism happened. Suddenly, there was a new thing to be: a businessman. Not just any businessman: Sasha wanted to be a superstar businessman. He would liken himself to the author trying to write a bestseller. He wanted money because he felt the power it would bring him.

It was three years since Sasha's name had first appeared on the Forbes list. Next to it, his 'net worth', as they called it: $1 billion. He was, along with Bill Gross, Martha Stewart, Michael Milken, Wilbur Ross and sixty-six others, the joint 620th richest person in the world. That was a triumph, for sure. And now, a greater one: here he was among the money kings, in the flesh, welcoming luminary after luminary to the Banqueting House. Ivan Glasenberg was there. He ran Glencore, a commodities trading house based in Switzerland, and probably exerted more influence over the flow of the global economy's raw ingredients than any man living. Beny Steinmetz, a diamond baron from Israel, had shown up too. Sasha liked precious stones: he wore shoes encrusted with them.

But Sasha, like the monarchs in whose place he now sat, knew, as they had learned, that even apparently boundless power is never absolute. He and his two partners, both fellow Central Asian billionaires, were known collectively in the City as 'the Trio'. They drew their fortunes from the wondrous rocks beneath an expanse of steppe and mountain ten times the size of the United Kingdom. Kazakhstan was a land of nomads and horsemen (and, to its proud rulers' intense vexation, Borat). Neither Sasha Machkevitch nor his partners had been born there, yet they were said to control as much as 40 per cent of the economy. What a bounty it was that had passed from the Soviet state to those, like Sasha, with the skill to learn the language of capitalism in a few short years. There was uranium, more of it than anywhere on Earth except Australia, where the stocks had long ago been divvied up. To the west, under the Caspian Sea, there was oil, measure-less caverns of it. As long as humanity wanted electricity, be it from splitting atoms or burning hydrocarbons, Kazakhstan would have buyers. Likewise for copper to make the wires to carry the charge to keep civilisation's lights on. The biggest buyer, these days, lay next door: China. Then there was the chromium, the iron, the bauxite, the zinc. China needed those too, as did anyone who wished to make anything that flew or shone or lasted.

The blessings were abundant. Abundant, and one man's to bestow.

Nursultan Nazarbayev had been Soviet Kazakhstan's last Communist Party boss, and then, without interruption to his rule, independent Kazakhstan's first capitalist leader. Loyalty was all he demanded. That and a share of the booty commensurate with his position as father of the nation. Gaining and retaining Nazarbayev's favour was a delicate undertaking. His daughter's erstwhile husband, a chubby and peculiar former intelligence officer called Rakhat Aliyev but known as Sugar, had recently fled to Europe. One of the secret documents Sugar claimed to have swiped before he departed was a psychological portrait of the president prepared by the KNB, the Kazakh successor to the Soviet KGB. 'He has a tendency to classify people according to groups, "his" group and the "others". Those who agree with and accept his opinions and stick to the rules are in "his" group. Anyone who does not accept his opinion is one of the "others" and thus an enemy … If the enemy does not surrender, he must be destroyed.'

One of Sasha's partners had witnessed a display of Nazarbayev's psyche. Patokh Chodiev, blue-blooded Uzbek and product of the prestigious Moscow school of international relations attended by the children of the communist elite, had served as a Soviet diplomat before switching to business. He made Nazarbayev's acquaintance, growing so close to him that he was invited to accompany the first family on a holiday to the French Riviera in 1995. Their host was Behgjet Pacolli, a Kosovan businessman angling for Kazakh contracts. One day he arranged an outing to a restaurant near Monaco. When they arrived at Le Pirate, the party surveyed the establishment with mounting alarm. Wooden benches, beams thick with soot from the open fire, no crystal: this was not the manner in which a latter-day khan was accustomed to dining. Chodiev took a seat at the edge of the group, near the door. Waiters dressed as pirates laid out plates that reminded one guest of prison crockery. 'Where the hell have you brought us?' the president snarled at Pacolli. Pacolli paled. Nazarbayev seized a plate and smashed it to the ground. A dreadful silence. Nazarbayev grabbed another plate and flung it. 'This is not what I call a vacation, dammit!' he screamed. His wife, Sara, was close to tears. 'Nursultan, Nursultan, calm down,' she pleaded. 'If you don't like it here, we'll go somewhere else. Stop it, please, and calm down.' Nazarbayev would not be quieted. He hurled a wooden chair into the fire. By now the owner – in pirate captain outfit – was losing it. He too picked up a chair and slung it into the fire. Nazarbayev threw another, and the two of them continued to immolate the seating until, suddenly, their expressions changed. They started to laugh. Then Pacolli started to laugh. The three men laughed together. Delighted, they revealed to their bewildered audience that the whole thing had been a lark. The restaurant's specialty was arranging such violent spectacles for the amusement of those in on the joke. All the khan's jokes were funny, so the rest of the party at once joined in by shattering the remaining crockery.

Chodiev, Sasha and the other oligarchs of Kazakhstan understood that the president giveth and the president taketh away. One of their number, Mukhtar Ablyazov, had had the temerity to demand democratic reforms. His businesses had been confiscated and he had been sent to a prison camp. Sugar had furnished Nazarbayev with three grandchildren, descendants with which to build a dynasty. Not even that could save him when he challenged the boss. A former minister who joined the opposition was found dead. According to the official account, he had committed suicide by shooting himself three times.

For an oligarch seeking safety there was one option so bold that you might have thought it would be difficult. First, turn yourself into a corporation: one of the most powerful fictions in which Westerners chose to believe, endowed with privileges and protections, and yet blissfully easy to create. Second, add to that corporation the assets Nazarbayev had allowed you to acquire – mines, banks, whatever. Then sell a share of your corporation for Western money. It was the successful completion of precisely this gambit that Sasha, his partners and their hundreds of terribly important guests now gathered at the Banqueting House to celebrate. Sasha and his fellow founders of the Eurasian Natural Resources Corporation had sold a chunk of their shares to the public, who could then trade them on the London Stock Exchange. For the Kyrgyz philologist, the Uzbek diplomat and Alijan Ibragimov, the canny Uighur trader who was the third member of the Trio, here was a dream made reality. Better still, the shares were trading so well that ENRC was on its way to inclusion in the FTSE 100 list of the most valuable British companies. The money managers of endowments and pension funds would now as a matter of course invest in this formidable corporation, yoking their fortunes to Sasha's.

Not that it had been cheap. Marrying into the City took a lot of ushers. Deutsche Bank, Credit Suisse, Rothschild, Morgan Stanley and ABN Amro: their bankers charged $118 million. On top of that were the lawyers at Jones Day and Cleary Gottlieb. Another $30 million to PwC, the auditors ('professional services firms', they called themselves these days). All the personages who agreed to sit on the board would cost hundreds of thousands too, year after year. You needed the names, though. 'City grandees', that was the shorthand in the business pages. They helped put everyone at their ease. There were two knights: Sir Paul Judge used to be director general of the Conservative Party, Sir Richard Sykes chairman of GlaxoSmithKline and rector of Imperial College. Ken Olisa had been high up at IBM. Roderick Thomson was a 'venture capitalist', a particularly favoured epithet. Gerhard Ammann had served as chief executive of the Swiss arm of Deloitte, like PwC one of the Big Four audit firms that rotated between every FTSE 100 corporation and the government departments that stood beside the Banqueting House.

They had earned their money, though. The vital thing was for Sasha and his partners to shape the story that was told about them. 'The past ambushes you in the present,' went a saying Kazakhs liked to quote. There had been an awkward moment ahead of the listing when the London Stock Exchange's regulators had found out about the Trio's troubles in Belgium. Years before

his fall, back when he still worshipped his father-in-law, the
hapless schemer Sugar had been looking for a way to weaken the
Trio's position in Nazarbayev's court and improve his own. He
attempted to achieve this by claiming to the Belgian authorities
that the Trio, among others of his enemies, were using bribes
they had extracted from Western investors in Kazakhstan to buy
splendid properties in the West, specifically Brussels. Investigators
in Europe followed Sugar's lead further than he had meant them
to; they discovered Nazarbayev's own secret bank accounts. The
Belgians opened a case against the Trio on suspicion of laundering
money: the offence of making the proceeds of crime look like
everyday money. It dragged on for so long that it was still going
as the proposed listing of ENRC in London approached. But if
the Trio feared they might be deemed undesirable as a result,
they had underestimated the City's thirst for their money. A
cordial agreement was reached. ENRC shares would begin to
trade as planned but the Trio themselves would refrain from
sitting on the corporation's board, even though they would still
own almost half the stock. And the authorities went further still
to make them feel welcome. A Credit Suisse banker, James Leigh-
Pemberton, persuaded the regulator to bend the rules and allow
the Trio, the Kazakh state and another oligarch who between
them owned ENRC to place just 18 per cent of the company's
shares on the market, sacrificing a minimal portion of control to
attain the sanctity of a London listing.

Just in time, too. The perceptive in the City could see that
their long run of ever more perfect freedom, beginning with
Margaret Thatcher's big bang and advancing, to their pleasant
surprise, under Tony Blair's New Labour, was facing a prolonged
interruption when the masses worked out that they had been left
with the bill for the incipient crisis. The new moneymen of the
former Soviet Union shared with the libertarians of the City a
loathing for the state. They had done splendid business together,

the industrial triumphs of the proletariat laid out in lavish stock market prospectuses. At the exchange there were handsome bonuses for bringing in listings. One executive there concluded: 'Why wouldn't ENRC or anyone else come to London? We invited them. They did not have to knock too hard.' The London bankers' and lawyers' private pursuits matched those of the oligarchs and their retinues. 'The finest of the finest prostitutes. Any drug you want. Different batches of girls. Limitless money. Limitless.'

No one could tell you the hour or the day when it happened, but that time had ended and another had begun. The crisis was the obvious reason: everybody was talking about it every minute, you couldn't get away from it. And yet changes more profound were taking place far beneath, in the black aquifer of secret money. Here and there, those shifts rippled to the surface, causing disturbances whose meanings were hard to discern. When police in Moscow detained a corpulent sixty-one-year-old Ukrainian called Sergei Schneider in the evening of January 23, 2008 on suspicion of tax dodging, some thought it was a message, others an almighty blunder. A spokesman for the Russian Interior Ministry claimed that it was only after fifty-odd officers in balaclavas had arrested the portly fellow during a raid on his business partner that they realised Sergei Schneider was just one of his many aliases. The man they had in custody was Semyon Mogilevich, arguably the most powerful criminal operating in the globalised economy. All the mobsters could make money; you would have had to have been a lousy crook not to get rich in the lawless nineties. They could all counterfeit, extort, traffic. Mogilevich's unique talent was to slink that money around the world incognito, transforming it as it went so that the stain of its origins disappeared. In the former Soviet Union, this was a skill prized above all others: the ability to turn the filthy lucre mined from the ruins of the collapsed empire into valid currency of the capitalist world, currency that could buy what they sold there: property, security, legitimacy. Mogilevich had studied economics, both at university in Ukraine and in practice in Moscow during the transition that began in the late 1980s. The Brainy Don, that was what they called him, banker to the underworld. Despite the Americans having charged him with forty counts of racketeering, fraud and money laundering allegedly committed in dozens of countries – and further accusing him of ordering murders – he had been living quite happily in Moscow before his arrest. Stories soon circulated that the police commander who picked him up had received a severe reprimand. Mogilevich's detention had put Vladimir Putin's regime in an awkward position. They could hardly just let him go: he was on the FBI's most wanted list. And yet they had no desire to incarcerate the Brainy Don. For the sake of appearances, he had to be described in public as though he were an enemy of the state. In truth he was an ally of the kind of state Putin was constructing, a gangster state. All the same, maybe this had not been entirely an accident, or if it was, it was at least one that the new order could exploit. The crisis into which the democracies were descending was an opportunity for the kleptocrats, those who ruled by theft. Perhaps Putin had chosen this moment to demonstrate to the lord of criminal money that the nineties, that bacchanal of looting, were over, that theft now had a greater purpose, a hierarchy to which even the Brainy Don would be obliged to submit. In that he was not alone. The unctuousness of the City of London's welcome for rich ex-Soviets was no longer being reciprocated.

The same month that the Trio threw their banquet on Whitehall – February 2008 – an American and a Brit met late one evening at the Hyatt hotel near Marble Arch. The Brit, a cerebral bean-pole called John Lough, had a job at TNK-BP, a fractious joint venture between the British oil company BP and some Russian oligarchs. It was fascinating work for a fluent Russian-speaker who had spent years studying the Soviet Union and what followed, first for a British military think-tank, then while running Nato's office in Moscow. BP's geologists mapped Russia's reserves of oil and gas: there were few larger, fewer still that Western companies were allowed to buy. Lough and his colleagues tried to navigate the politics. His superiors valued his work. Nonetheless, he was pretty sure he was about to get fired. The feeling deepened when the American arrived, looking agitated.

Normally, Shawn McCormick was a picture of confidence. In his early forties, he wore good suits and administered bone-crushing handshakes that Lough always took to be an assertion of authority. Unlike Lough, McCormick had not learned Russian. He was, however, proficient in what Lough called 'American corporate-speak', occasionally travelling from Moscow to the US to acquire the latest 'management bollocks'. The businessman vibe was a recent development. McCormick had started off at an intelligence think-tank in Washington, then served in Bill Clinton's National Security Council, where he held top-secret clearance. In 2003 he had joined TNK-BP to set up a government relations team. He knew Lough from BP projects they had both worked on in London, and recruited him over lunch to join the team. The one proviso was that, to keep staff numbers down, Lough would work as a consultant. That suited Lough fine: his children were in school in the UK. He could keep his family at home and nip over to Moscow for a week or two every month or so.

In his new job Lough met Bob Dudley, a career oilman from Mississippi who BP's bosses had sent to Moscow to run TNK-BP. Lough would prepare briefing books for Dudley and write speeches for him, capturing his cadences so well that Dudley found reading them was like speaking in his own voice. Lough got on better with Dudley than he did with McCormick, though he had nothing against McCormick, finding him intelligent and

perfectly professional. Then, in the summer of 2007, when Lough
was on one of his trips to TNK-BP's expansive open-plan office
in Moscow, McCormick drew him aside to a corner near the
coffee machine where they would not be overheard. 'Just be
aware,' he said, 'you are being watched by the FSB.'

Lough was not surprised that his work might attract the FSB's
attention. It had retained much of the character of its Soviet
antecedent, the KGB. Putin, a KGB veteran, had made the agency
a central cog in his system of power. Less than a year had passed
since Russian agents poisoned their former confrere Alexander
Litvinenko in London. Anglo-Russian relations were awful. Lough
knew he had been watched back when he was in Moscow for
Nato. Now he was working for TNK-BP, he had been careful to
keep his contact with the British embassy to a minimum. He
stayed in touch with some old contacts – the Austrian defence
attaché, for instance – with whom he could discuss Russian
politics. But having any dealings with British intelligence could
mess up his professional work, he realised, and in any case, they
never approached him. All the same, Lough knew he was working
on matters close to the heart of Putin's regime. TNK-BP held
rights to some of the richest reserves of gas anywhere in the world
but could only extract it with the blessing of Gazprom, the state
company that Putin had appointed an old ally to run. Lough
had been assigned to a team trying to figure out how decisions
were made at Gazprom.

A few weeks after McCormick's warning, Lough was on his
way back to London. He didn't like going to the airport by car
– Moscow traffic could be as hard to predict as the Kremlin – so
he took the train. It was usually a chance for a pleasant snooze
before flying. This time, a fellow passenger sat down opposite
him and struck up a conversation. The man was in his forties,
burly, wearing a T-shirt and travelling with a long bag. Unusual,
Lough thought. He was a gangly Englishman with the bearing

of an Oxford don, so conspicuously foreign that Muscovite strangers never attempted to chat. The man asked Lough about his family, his job, his life in the UK. At one point, he asked: 'Are you afraid of flying?' When the train pulled in, the man picked up his long bag. It was obviously empty. The man hurried away into the terminal. Lough checked in and headed for security. As he approached, an official beckoned him over to a group of customs agents. They went through his documents and carry-on bag. One of them asked if he was transporting anything he shouldn't be. He said he was not. His checked bag appeared. They went through that too. They produced forms for him to sign, consenting to a search of his person, whereupon he was led to a room that was bare but for a bench and a sink. Lough braced himself, thinking he might be confronted with a wrap of some narcotic or other that had been planted in his luggage. The agents carefully inspected his clothes and looked closely at his shoes. After a while, they told him he could be on his way. As he was gathering his belongings one of the agents chit-chatted with him. Then he said: 'Last question, Mr Lough. Are you afraid of flying?'

Lough knew he had been warned. He took the message to be: you are in our sights, you should be careful about coming to Russia. He reported the incident to his bosses. A colleague with FSB contacts asked them what was up, and was told that while Lough might be under surveillance, nothing sinister should happen. It was the *should* that stayed with Lough. Nonetheless, he returned to Moscow for a few days in January 2008. When he left, he was once more pulled aside at customs and searched. This time he called Bob Dudley, the head of TNK-BP, as soon as he got through passport control. He wanted to communicate a message to the Russian intelligence officers who would doubtless be listening in to Dudley's phone: 'I deal with the CEO, so don't screw around.' Once he was out of Russia, he told McCormick: until we get to the bottom of this, it's not safe for me to go back.

It was around then that something changed in McCormick's manner. When they met up in Brussels soon afterwards, he seemed to Lough impatient, confrontational, nervous. He told Lough they would meet again soon. Two weeks later they took their seats at the Hyatt in London. Speaking in a disconcertingly friendly way, McCormick told Lough that, because the Brit could no longer go to Russia, he was being made redundant. He would receive three months' pay, but McCormick wanted him to stop working instantly, abandoning all his commitments. Bob Dudley had sanctioned his dismissal, McCormick said, neglecting to mention that he had led Dudley to believe that Lough wanted to quit. Lough was staggered. As they parted, he offered his hand, an English reflex. But to his horror – he was, as he put it, 'not a huggy kind of person' – he found himself enveloped in McCormick's embrace.

A month passed. Lough grew convinced that something strange was going on. And then, in Moscow, dozens of armed FSB officers stormed into TNK-BP's offices a few blocks from Red Square, where they drilled open the safes. A few days earlier, the FSB had detained Ilya Zaslavskiy, an Oxford-educated Russian-American who had worked alongside Lough on the Gazprom research, along with his brother. They were accused of espionage. It was soon apparent to Zaslavskiy what was afoot: a scheme to cast him as a mole who was passing state secrets to his handler, the dastardly British spy John Lough. Such a narrative would advance the Russian oligarchs' efforts to wrest more control over TNK-BP from their British partners. It would also help Putin's regime strike back after the Brits accused his agents of committing murder on UK soil. From the safety of the Russian parliament, of which he was now a member, Andrey Lugovoy, the prosperous former FSB officer who had left a trail of polonium around London before apparently slipping some into Alexander Litvinenko's tea, declared his support for the espionage

investigation. It mattered not that the main document Zaslavskiy
was accused of stealing – Gazprom's anodyne strategy blueprint
– had in fact been formally sent to TNK-BP by the Russian
authorities. No, this document was declared a secret of scarcely
estimable value, the loss of which into Western hands, a
pro-Kremlin newspaper reported, would have cost Russia billions
of dollars.

Two weeks after Zaslavskiy's arrest, FSB officers interviewed
Shawn McCormick. The venue, Lefortovo prison, had pulsed
with terror since Stalin's purges. Dissidents and traitors to the
motherland from Alexander Solzhenitsyn to Litvinenko had been
incarcerated there. McCormick had told American diplomats in
Moscow that he was relaxed about the FSB's request that he come
for an interview, saying he had been assured he was seen not as
a suspect in their espionage investigation but as a witness. A lesser
man might have been more concerned: one prominent Russian
newspaper had reported that, as well as Zaslavskiy, 'the FSB
suspects Shawn McCormick, head of the international relations
department of TNK-BP, who may be deported from Russia'. And
the FSB had told the press that its team found business cards of
CIA officers during the raid of TNK-BP's office. It did not reveal
where they had been found. But the person in the office with a
past in intelligence was not Lough or Zaslavskiy but McCormick.
In his time at the White House, McCormick had enjoyed
top-secret clearance to read the reports produced by America's
spies. Now he sat before their Russian counterparts. Over
seventeen hours he proceeded to give an account, the distortions
in which, though subtle, played neatly into the FSB's narrative.

'I would like to note an unusual status of John Lough,'
McCormick said. By this he meant Lough's position on a contract
rather than on staff – a banal arrangement suddenly made to
seem suspicious. McCormick made a point of mentioning that
Lough had worked for Nato. Lough knew some wonks at the

Foreign Office, not policymakers, but this became 'extensive ties to the UK government' in McCormick's account. At every turn, McCormick seemed determined to bend the facts to fit the FSB's script, especially when it came to Lough's relationship with the villain of the piece, the Russian-American Ilya Zaslavskiy.

On the occasions when Zaslavskiy and Lough had spoken to each other at work, they had used the polite form of Russian. They never socialised. Yet McCormick – who did not speak Russian – said the two conversed informally and had 'relations that were more than just business ones'. He told the interrogators: 'You can say they were friends.' McCormick said Lough had requested that TNK-BP take on Zaslavskiy as a consultant. Lough couldn't have done that even if he'd wanted to: he wasn't senior enough. Lough and Zaslavskiy had worked together on the Gazprom research team, where both reported to a Scot in charge of the project. Again, McCormick's version did not match reality: he told the FSB Zaslavskiy reported to Lough. He said Lough 'supervised' Zaslavskiy. His interrogators recorded this using the same Russian word one would use for a spy's handler.

The FSB interrogators typed up a summary of McCormick's evidence. McCormick signed it. They added it to their file, alongside similarly helpful testimony they had collected a day earlier from another witness. Sergei Novosyolov had served as a senior investigator on the organised crime beat at the Russian Ministry of Internal Affairs before becoming TNK-BP's vice president for economic security. In his interview, he had claimed that McCormick had informed him that John Lough had been hired on the recommendation of Bob Dudley, a falsehood that could implicate the top BP man in Russia in the espionage narrative. Novosyolov accurately explained some insignificant aspects of Lough and Zaslavskiy's work, but he also furnished the FSB's investigators with several false details that could assist them as they conjured up a spy ring. Their case was taking shape like the best of the KGB's 'active measures' from the Cold War: take a few threads of truth, stitch in the necessary fictions and weave it all together to form the lie you require.

Ilya Zaslavskiy and his brother faced between five and twenty years in prison. Because they held their nerve and refused to confess, the best that a kangaroo court could concoct was a conviction for a failed attempt at industrial espionage. They were given a suspended sentence of a year's imprisonment and two years' probation, with a life of self-imposed exile to follow. John Lough was banned from Russia. Bob Dudley started to feel ill. He took a blood test; some of those around him whispered it showed poison in his bloodstream. He recovered, the story went, once he started avoiding the food provided by TNK-BP. Upon hearing that the authorities were coming to arrest him, he fled the country. Hundreds of other BP staffers were forced to leave.

Shawn McCormick left BP not long afterwards. He had demonstrated a talent for assisting in the creation of an alternative reality that could be used as a weapon. It was a talent that would prove useful for his next employers – the Trio.

Maintaining your alternative reality was more valuable than any oilfield or seam of precious metal. And yet, now and then, in the privacy of, say, a royal palace of masques you had rented for the evening, you could indulge in a moment's delicious contemplation of the original reality, the way things actually were. At the Banqueting House, Ivan Glasenberg of Glencore, the commodities king himself, rose to say a few words in his clipped Johannesburg accent. Those present owed thanks to his homeland, he said. The South African government was struggling with power cuts. That was making life even more miserable than usual for South Africans. It was also curtailing mining, which had pushed up the prices of the metals those mines contained. Glasenberg delivered the punchline: South Africa's troubles were good news for corporations that mined those metals elsewhere, such as

ENRC, the share price of which had doubled. His audience hooted with laughter and banged their fists.

That night, as he sat at the top table, beneath images of the last god-kings, Sasha was beginning to comprehend the extent to which money could be turned into power. 'It's so exciting,' he had told a fellow businessman back in Kazakhstan shortly after ENRC's London listing. 'You just don't understand how provincial we are here. These are new horizons.'

3

Tunnels

Cheapside, February 2008

BSI's London office lay equidistant from the Bank of England and St Paul's, bang in the centre of the City of London, the aorta of the global financial system. The unremarkable building stood on Cheapside, the City thoroughfare laid down by the Romans, where medieval merchants sold sheep's feet and eels. The Stocks Market at its east end became known for the appalling stench of rotting fare. Around the corner was the Lord Mayor's residence, the Mansion House. There Tony Blair had leavened a speech about unjust global trade with a reaffirmation that the City 'creates much of the wealth on which this British nation depends'.

From the start, the Swiss financiers who created Banco della Svizzera Italiana, or Swiss-Italian Bank, saw their task as helping money cross national borders. Construction of what was then the world's longest tunnel, through the St Gotthard massif in the Alps, was under way. It would carry a railway to connect northern and southern Europe. When the work was completed, the Swiss president declared that 'the world market is open'. The Italian-speaking Swiss city of Lugano lay on the new railway's route. It was there that BSI's founders opened a bank in 1873, to capitalise on the new trade route. They did well, expanding in Switzerland

and sending bankers abroad. The bank came through one world war. In the second, BSI's bankers did what many Swiss bankers did: they collaborated with the Nazis. At the same time, they did what they would start to do for their rich clients: they spun a story that reversed the truth. As Swiss bankers and their apologists told the tale, the reason that Switzerland made it a crime to violate bank secrecy was to help persecuted Jews protect their savings. In fact, the law was first drafted in 1932, the year before Hitler came to power. The impetus came not from altruism but self-interest. It was the Great Depression. Governments badly needed to collect taxes. Those of Europe's rich who were disinclined to pay them found that by entrusting their assets to Swiss banks' anonymised accounts, they could dodge their dues. Parisian magistrates were demanding the Swiss cooperate in their investigation of tax evasion by wealthy French. At home, Swiss farmers and workers wanted the banks brought under control. The solution was to build a wall of secrecy around the banks – and then, when anyone asked about it over the years that followed, say it had all been down to the Jews.

Between the wars, foreign wealth managed by Swiss banks increased tenfold. After 1945, banks like BSI started opening offices in strange places, often corners of the crumbling British empire. The City of London had for centuries run the business side of a colonial project that extended from the slave ships of the Atlantic to the gold fields of the Cape and the East India Company's cargoes of teas, dyes and opiates. As British power waned, many of its smaller possessions remained bound to the City, only now in the service of other people's empires. Where once an island produced a particular crop, now it offered a particular flavour of financial secrecy: a type of trust, say, or a species of front company. BSI set up in the Bahamas and on Guernsey. Its bankers also needed to be near some actual rich people – high net worth individuals, as they were to be known

– so they were stationed in New York, Hong Kong, Monte Carlo and of course London itself.

The Swiss bankers didn't do anything clever or original with the money. They just invested it in stocks and bonds like anyone else lucky enough to have a little to put aside. What mattered was that the money moved to a special place, a place beyond the reach of governments, of the law, of society. This place was known as 'offshore'. As the richest 1 per cent came to amass a quarter of all increases in incomes – leaving the bottom 50 per cent with less than a tenth – the amount of money stashed 'offshore' grew to $7.6 trillion. That was, at least, the best guess, because a guess was all anyone was allowed to make. Put another way, of every hundred dollars the world's households held, eight were offshore. When economic crises came, a country's resilience was measured by its reserves, the store of cash, assets and gold upon which it could draw. The offshore bounty was double the single biggest reserves – China's – and more than half the global total. Swiss banks held a third of this bounty. By the time Nigel joined in 2006, BSI ranked in the top ten. It held $48 billion of its clients' money. If it had been a country, it would have had the world's twenty-fifth biggest reserves.

BSI was not a bank like the high-street banks, for people with salaries and mortgages. It was a private bank. In the London office, the chief private banker was Fabrizio Zanaboni. He was an expressive Italian whose father had worked for the bank. Half a dozen bankers reported to him. Between them they took care of about three-quarters of a billion dollars for a few hundred clients. The bankers were in theory constrained in the clients they could take on by Nigel's judgement of the probity of each. On one account, he had been required to decide whether a recently deceased Ukrainian businessman had or had not been poisoned. A background report on another client sketched out his connection to the St Petersburg mafia, but a banker had jotted

on the margin: 'tenuous link, not relevant in my opinion'. Few
clients, it appeared, were beyond the pale. Another of the bankers
wanted to construct a financial labyrinth for a Romanian-born
businessman called Frank Timis. After Ceauşescu had killed his
father, the teenaged Timis fled to Australia, his BSI banker
informed her superiors, where he was twice convicted of possessing
heroin with intent to supply. These early missteps, the banker
explained, should be excused. Timis merely 'fell in with the wrong
crowd'. He had since moved to London and made millions from
mining ventures in eastern Europe and Africa. These days, his
banker reported, he had 'excellent connections'. Accusations that
he had lied to investors about the potential of a Greek oil prospect were, likewise, nothing to worry about. As for what Timis
wanted done with his money, the banker proposed setting up a
foundation in Panama that he would control discreetly through
a power of attorney. The Panama foundation would own two
companies registered in the British Virgin Islands. The companies
in the British Virgin Islands would open accounts with BSI in
Monaco.

Nigel of Basingstoke tried to put himself inside a BSI client's
mind. 'Why would I come to London to set up an account in
Switzerland in the name of a Cayman Islands entity with directors in Panama? Now, it makes absolutely no sense unless there
is something quite underhand going on.'

Nigel tried to keep an eye on one BSI banker in particular.
Khofiz Shakhidi was a thirty-year-old Tajik with dark, lively eyes,
an oval face and a lopsided smile. His father was an acclaimed
composer from Soviet Tajikistan who described his works, which
included a ballet called *Death of Usurer*, as 'attempts to create a
synthesis between East and West'. His Western-educated son's
accent bore only a slight trace of his origins. He could be charming
and was clearly intelligent, but Nigel felt he went out of his way
to wind him up. BSI's bosses in London had poached Shakhidi

and two of the other private bankers from a rival, Crédit Agricole, two years before Nigel joined. They brought a couple of hundred rich clients with them. Many were from the former Soviet Union, so Zanaboni, the senior banker, decided to do some vetting. He hired Martin Flint, who had spent twenty years at MI5. Flint now worked for Risk Analysis, one of the private intelligence agencies that were proliferating in Mayfair, the quarter of London that most knew only from their Monopoly boards, but where a few conduct the business of the rich. Flint was instructed to find out everything he could about Shakhidi's clients. He did his work and filed his report. The decision went up to BSI's bosses in Switzerland, who agreed that the London office could take them on.

Nigel was kept apart from the bankers, in his own office. He was signing off on their requests to open accounts for clients and shift their money around the world but he had little idea who the clients were or where their money was coming from. Outside, the crisis was getting worse. Northern Rock showed you how it was going to go: the enormous losses bankers had run up while enriching themselves would be borne by the public. But Nigel noticed something else that was happening in parallel. The banks seemed to be splitting open, their tricks revealed for all to see. And yet, quietly, more and more money was going to ground. In late February 2008, Nigel read in *The Times* that half of all commercial properties in the UK no longer belonged to named human beings. Instead they belonged to companies, registered in far-off places, the identities of their owners published nowhere. It was as though another tunnel had been dug, one that carried money away to a place of which no one spoke.

4

The Dual State

Moscow, February 2008

In the eleven years he had spent trying to write Russia's laws, Peter Sahlas reckoned he was granted admittance to the Kremlin more times than any other Westerner. Always pristine, hair immaculately trimmed, tie knot and top button joined as if magnetised, he seemed to gleam like his black chrome suitcases. He could have passed for one of the management consultants who pranced into post-Soviet Moscow billing by the hour to install capitalism. But he was not one of them. He had taken upon himself a higher task: to install the rule of law. In February 2008, he realised he had failed.

Peter was a liberal to his bones. His Greek father had been just young enough to avoid being rounded up with the men from his village during the civil war that followed liberation from the Nazis. He had emigrated to Canada, toiling in restaurants until he had his own and could afford to bring over his siblings and his bride. His swankiest establishment was on the ground floor of a tower of bank offices. His children, he decided, should be the ones eating the muffins, not the ones getting up at 5 a.m. to bake them. 'This is a free country,' he told them, 'and you can do what you want. But you've got to be a doctor or lawyer.' First, though, he worked them in his restaurants, so as to be sure they understood that money didn't grow on trees. At school in Toronto, Peter liked nothing more than making a stand for what were becoming his animating principles. He and his friend Vinay – a pair of 'shit-disturbers' as Peter put it – scandalised the Catholic school authorities by running on the front page of their student newspaper an interview with a doctor renowned for performing abortions. When the head summoned them, they delivered a jeremiad on free speech. In defence of this right they were prepared to take risks that older and more celebrated liberals were not. They sought out a copy of Salman Rushdie's *The Satanic Verses* and published a review.

Peter stayed in Toronto for university. During his first year studying international relations, he answered an ad in a student paper for English teachers in Czechoslovakia. In the summer of 1990 he arrived in Pilsen, an hour outside Prague. Václav Havel's Velvet Revolution had toppled the communists six months earlier. No one under forty had ever known freedom, the last Soviet troops had yet to depart and Czechs seemed unsure as to their new relationship with the state. At the end of one of Peter's lessons, one of his students, a Czech soldier named Pavel, came up to him. He explained that he had devised a small act of rebellion against the lingering old order. He planned to sneak a Westerner into his barracks without authorisation. No one would ever know except Pavel and his fellow conspirators, but they could feel the thrill of defying a power that not long ago had seemed total. The Westerner he had in mind was Peter, who thought it a great idea.

Pavel supplied Peter with a set of scratchy khaki fatigues, complete with army-issue underwear, and told him to come to the spot in Pilsen where a bus collected servicemen who had spent a few hours' leave in town and took them back to the base. When the bus arrived at the barracks, the soldiers and their disguised infiltrator got off outside the gate. Pavel muttered to

Peter not to meet the guards' eyes. 'I'll walk ahead. Your job is to follow me. And look casual.' The mission suddenly seemed less appealing to Peter. 'I'm so fucked if I get caught,' he thought. But he kept his eyes down, and made it to Pavel's unit's block. On the wall was a world map with the Soviet Union at the centre. Peter shared a meal of slop with his brothers in arms. Then it dawned on him that he had made a crucial error: he had planned the crime, but not the getaway. There was only one way out: midway between two sentry posts, where soldiers who missed the bus would slip back over the wall after dark. At 4 a.m., Pavel guided Peter to the spot. 'Don't worry,' Pavel said, 'you won't get shot. But don't look back.' As Pavel gave him a boost up the wall, Peter had visions of being arrested and charged with espionage. He jumped. No shots, no shouting. He landed in a farmer's field and scuttled away.

That summer, Peter's hosts, Czech lawyers, took him to Auschwitz, to the courtroom at Nuremberg, to Berlin to chip chunks off the wall. He travelled across what had recently been the Eastern Bloc. He felt he was witnessing history – participating in it, even.

Peter and his friend Vinay decided to take the English-teaching programme to Russia. They worked extra shifts as waiters until they had made enough money for tickets on a British Airways flight to Moscow in the summer of 1991. Their command of the language extended to *da* and *niet*. Upon arrival, they threw themselves on the mercy of a taxi driver called Oleg. He found them a room and a meal – an emaciated chicken washed down with fermented milk that caused alarming black flora to bloom on their tongues overnight. The next morning, Oleg saw them onto the train to Leningrad. In the old tsars' capital, soon once more to be called St Petersburg, Peter and Vinay had arranged to teach English to journalists. They lodged in a hotel and, clean-living Canadians both, resisted the manager's ceaseless attempts to introduce prostitutes to their beds. The journalists kept Peter abreast of events when, while he was away on a trip to Paris, communist hardliners attempted a coup against Mikhail Gorbachev. He returned the following year, and this time his students taught him Russian.

Back in Canada, he started training to be a lawyer. Deploying his gift for polite persuasion, he secured Canadian government funding to examine aspects of the Russian legal system. At spring break, when other students would go to Florida, he would go to Russia and take five professors with him. When an opening arose on a project to help the Russian government draft a civil legal code for the post-communist era, Peter was selected. He went home and told his girlfriend about a 'crazy idea' to move to Russia. They had met in Paris, her home city, two years earlier. Peter had been in town for a month to improve his business French. At a house party one hot summer night, he had found his path to the fridge blocked by two French women in conversation. As he made his way past, he got chatting to one of them, and carried on until the early hours. Cécile worked for a bank. When, soon thereafter, it ran into trouble, she switched to a literary career, and moved to Canada to join Peter. She had been there less than a year when the prospect of moving to Moscow came up. To Peter's delight, she was keen. They arrived in 1996. Soon Peter was visiting the Kremlin as many as forty times a year. A state of laws was taking shape. Boris Yeltsin had succeeded Gorbachev, and Peter moved among the mandarins of the new Russia. Once, in an airport lounge, he was introduced to an official from St Petersburg who handed him his business card. Peter chuckled to see the man's name sounded like the Québecois dish of fries, cheese curd and gravy, *poutine*.

In the late nineties, towards the end of Yeltsin's tenure, Peter grew frustrated. The president, he knew, was 'basically drunk or comatose', making it impossible to get anything done. And the reformers were indulging in the very behaviour they were supposedly rooting out. Even Boris Nemtsov, their charismatic man of the people, was caught on film luxuriating in a hot tub full of bankers with teenage strippers for entertainment. The *siloviki*, figures from the military and the old KGB, were accumulating influence. In the Kremlin, there was no one with the authority to arbitrate between the factions. When Putin took over in 2000, Peter was unsure what to expect. His work on the new legal codes could have been stymied at any stage if the new president had turned against reform. But time and time again, decisions would percolate up to Putin and he would do what Peter hoped he would. Putin, as prime minister under Yeltsin, had been the Butcher of Chechnya. But as president, despite granting Yeltsin lifelong immunity from prosecution, he declared 'a dictatorship of law'. Peter was pleased. He continued to be pleased until Putin's people took a man, a young lawyer Peter's age, and slowly put him to death.

Yukos was an oil company, the biggest in Russia. Its owner, Mikhail Khodorkovsky, was a nerdy-looking, top-of-the-class engineer whose childhood dream had been to manage a prestigious Soviet factory. Instead, he was one of the first to make a success of private business, a decriminalised but still disreputable activity in the last communist years. He understood the value of personal connections in a system without any binding rules and began his experiments in the market economy with the authorities' blessing. Khodorkovsky imported computers and dabbled in currency exchange. He soon realised that the most profitable role in the new Russian capitalism was that of financial middleman, advancing funds to factories and other government agencies, claiming the money back from the treasury and taking his cut. That gave him the cash to spend on the bargain privatisations that Yeltsin's reformers embarked on with the enthusiastic backing of the West. Those reformers dreaded more than anything else the return of the communists, so as the 1996 presidential elections approached, they were desperate to prolong the rule of their sozzled protector. For that, they would need the support of the newly minted tycoons. The reformers 'had come to power to create a fair, equitable law-abiding market economy; to keep it, they sponsored one of the world's sleaziest insider deals', wrote Chrystia Freeland, one of the most astute correspondents in Russia at the time. A handful of businessmen carved up the oilfields, mines and factories that had been the engines of the Soviet empire. In exchange for loans to the undernourished treasury and political backing for the Yeltsin regime, they gained the right to take over the management of these prime state enterprises and then to buy them for a fraction of their value. This sell-off gave birth to Russia's oligarchs: Vladimir Potanin, Boris Berezovsky, Roman Abramovich and the rest. Khodorkovsky and his partners paid $350 million to buy a three-quarter stake in Yukos, with its 100,000 employees, its oilfields and its refineries. Two years later, in 1997, the company was valued at $9 billion, and by 2002, $12 billion. Khodorkovsky became the richest man in Russia.

Khodorkovsky turned Yukos into one of the best-run Russian corporations. Western oil executives courted him. It seemed there was nothing he couldn't do. Convinced that he was the man to bring true democracy to Russia, he started to fund civil society groups and opposition parties. In doing so, he violated a rule that Putin had instituted to subjugate the oligarchs: if you want to keep your money, stay out of politics. In October 2003, armed agents boarded Khodorkovsky's jet while it refuelled at a Siberian airport and took him away. He was charged with fraud and tax evasion. Yukos's accountants used the same rules to prepare its books as all the other oil companies. But shortly after Khodorkovsky's arrest, the tax authorities produced a bill for $3.3 billion.

The Yukos defence team had hired a Toronto law firm and heard about the young Canadian who was intimately involved in designing Russia's legal architecture. Peter Sahlas was invited to a meeting. When he arrived, there were fifteen people in the room, including a former Canadian prime minister. Peter passed on what his contacts in Moscow had told him: that Putin was tightening his grip on the judiciary. Soon, Peter's phone rang again. It was Bob Amsterdam, a pugnacious Bronx-born Canadian commercial lawyer working for Yukos. Amsterdam wanted Peter on the team.

Khodorkovsky was entering his third year in jail. He was an unlikely totem for a campaign to defend the rule of law. Ruthless despite his nervous giggle, he owed his riches in significant measure to his ability to hobble rivals by exploiting legal technicalities and loopholes. Such tactics had included rewarding with a place on the Yukos payroll the former official who, while in government, had written ambiguities into Russia's commercial legislation to be put to precisely these uses. But this case was far more important than the seizure of an oil company, Amsterdam told Peter. 'This is the rule of law in Russia. This is geopolitical stability. And this is energy security for Europe. Russia is still a nuclear state. We need Russia to be law-based and stable. And when there is security of property, security of contract, rule of law and human rights in Russia, then it's in everyone's interests.'

Part of Bob Amsterdam's approach to the case was to get deep into the legal theory. He read incessantly. One day he handed Peter a copy of a little-known work of German legal scholarship, *The Dual State: A Contribution to the Theory of Dictatorship*. Its author, Ernst Fraenkel, had survived the Western Front in the First World War and gone to law school in Frankfurt. He prac-tised labour law in Weimar Germany, becoming fascinated by questions of how the law serves the interests of the wealthy and the powerful. He became a prominent commentator and, during Hitler's rise, a defender of the rule of law. Soon he was living a double life. In public, he continued to practise law, having successfully argued for an exemption from the Nazi ban on Jewish lawyers due to his military service. In secret, he was at work on what would be called 'the ultimate piece of intellectual resistance' to the Nazis.

The dual nature of the Hitler regime dawned on Fraenkel in 1936 in a Berlin court. He was representing employees of a union who claimed that their in-house wage agreement should be honoured even though the Gestapo had reconstituted the organisation along Nazi lines. The secret police sent along a lawyer who argued that 'any action the Gestapo required or deemed necessary was lawful', whether it be dissolving a social organisation or dissolving a marriage. Nonetheless, the judge found the German legal code was in the workers' favour. A few days later, Fraenkel received a copy of a new Gestapo order. The court's judgment stood, but Fraenkel's clients' compensation had been seized for the benefit of the regime.

While others fled Germany, Fraenkel remained, trying to fathom 'a regime whose defining attribute is to disguise its true nature'. Digging up legal records in the main library in Berlin, he would request all manner of unrelated works to throw Nazi spies off the scent. Fraenkel found what he believed to be 'a key to understanding the National Socialist system of rule'. It was the 'concurrent existence of a "normative state" that generally respects its own laws, and a "prerogative state" that violates the very same laws'. In other words, Nazi Germany was not a straightforward totalitarian system. It retained some vestiges of the rule of law, chiefly in matters of business, so that the capitalist economy had the basic rules it needed to keep going. But the prerogative state – Hitler's political machinery – enjoyed what Fraenkel called 'jurisdiction over jurisdiction'. It was itself beyond the law, and it could strip the protection of the law from any individual or group as it pleased.

Eventually the prerogative state turned its gaze on Fraenkel himself. The authorities had failed to rumble his clandestine literary activities, but his legal defences of fellow Jews marked him out. In September 1938, his phone rang with a tip-off: the Gestapo were finally coming for him. Fraenkel and his wife fled, six weeks before Kristallnacht. An early version of *The Dual State* departed separately, in the diplomatic bag of a sympathetic official at the French embassy. Author and manuscript were reunited in New York, where the book appeared in 1941 in English. It was widely reviewed, but within ten years had fallen out of print. Yet the book always had admirers among those seeking to understand the relationship between dictators and the law. As Bob Amsterdam and Peter Sahlas absorbed Fraenkel's work, they said to themselves: 'Eureka.'

Peter could see a dual state like that Fraenkel had depicted emerging in the post-Soviet combination of capitalist economics and authoritarian politics. He understood that the parallel was inexact. 'The goals of the prerogative state in the Third Reich were uniquely horrific,' he wrote as he collected his thoughts. But as he watched Khodorkovsky's defenestration, he grasped what he called 'the utility of legitimacy' to kleptocrats. The state was unable to find anything from the privatisation process – gargantuan rip-off though it was – on which to hang a criminal conviction. 'You don't nail somebody with lies to punish them for something else that they did,' he thought. 'If he did something illegal, nail him for what he did that was illegal.' But that was not what Putin's state was doing. This was, Peter concluded, a political takedown on a grand scale, perhaps the biggest ever if you measured it in money.

Khodorkovsky had been convicted on the initial fraud and tax-evasion charges, but by 2007 he would be eligible for parole.

His incarceration had made him a liberal icon; his imminent release could be dangerous for Putin. Fresh charges were required. The prerogative state had to act.

Rangy and gaunt with penetrating eyes, Vasily Aleksanyan had studied at Harvard before returning to Russia to practise law, eventually becoming counsel to Khodorkovsky's oil company, Yukos. In March 2006, with Khodorkovsky in prison, Aleksanyan was named the corporation's new boss. His task was to fight off the bankruptcy that Putin's regime was engineering. Two days after his appointment became public, Aleksanyan was summoned to the prosecutors' office and told to 'stay far away' from Yukos's business. He responded that he planned to ignore this suggestion. 'This,' the official delivering the warning replied, 'is the first time I have seen a person volunteer to go to prison.' Two weeks later police seized Aleksanyan from an apartment in Moscow. They took him to Matrosskaya Tishina prison, a dungeon for enemies of Russia's rulers. He was charged with having used his professional skills to 'legalise' shares in Yukos oil projects that the company's executives were supposed to have embezzled. His lawyers argued in court that, as a single parent to a young son and sole support to his aged parents, Aleksanyan should be released while he awaited trial. The prosecutors told the judge they had unspecified 'operative information' that Aleksanyan was planning to flee. The judge ruled that he should remain in detention, in part because his 'personality' might lead him to 'take measures to destroy evidence and objects and documents which are important for the investigation but which have not yet been found by the investigative bodies'.

Bob Amsterdam gave Peter Sahlas the task of helping to get Aleksanyan out of prison. Peter had seen how the Russian state was struggling to fulfil its basic duties under Yeltsin. 'The whole emergency response system was non-functional,' he remembered. 'Car accidents, people that fell from windows, or people that were shot – bodies were just not cleaned up.' Four or five times a week he would happen upon a corpse in the street. It felt like an absence of power. In fact, power had been hoarded. Now it was being unleashed.

Aleksanyan had damaged his right eye as a child. In prison the sight in his left started to fail as well until, by the time the prison doctors examined him, he was struggling to see. They took blood and did tests. The results came back: Aleksanyan was HIV positive. The virus was attacking hard, but the doctors who conducted a medical assessment at the prosecutors' behest concluded that Aleksanyan was fit to be detained and well enough to assist the investigators in their enquiries. Soon he was suffering severe headaches and pain in his throat. His sight was almost gone. He needed the cocktail of antiretroviral drugs that, under careful supervision of specialist doctors, could keep HIV at bay and protect a weakened immune system from what would otherwise be lethal infections.

After nine months in prison, Aleksanyan told his lawyers on the outside that he had been taken to the prosecutors' office. When he got there, he said, he had found himself sitting opposite a senior investigator called Salavat Karimov. Karimov was not involved in his case. His job was to find evidence that could be used to secure a fresh conviction of Mikhail Khodorkovsky when his current imprisonment ended. Karimov told Aleksanyan he understood that his medical situation was grave. He might even need treatment outside Russia. Karimov said he could help, could ensure that Aleksanyan was released. All he would need to do was spend a couple of weeks in a discreet isolation unit to devise testimony that would 'suit the leadership' in their campaign against Khodorkovsky. In exchange for Aleksanyan's signature on a statement, Karimov would put his own on an order relaxing his detention. Aleksanyan informed him that he was never going to sign. He was taken back to prison.

As Aleksanyan's immune system started to collapse, he was kept in a cell the walls of which were fetid with mildew and fungus, teeming with bacteria that he felt were consuming him. The prosecutors again and again petitioned the court handling the matter to extend Aleksanyan's pre-trial detention, warning that if he were released he would conspire with other Yukos insiders to frustrate justice. The court complied. When Aleksanyan had been locked up for a year, an investigator on his case told one of his Russian lawyers that if he admitted his guilt and agreed to cooperate, he would be let go. His cell was horribly cold. He was kept hungry. He needed to go to a hospital to receive antiretrovirals. Instead a prison medic came to his cell with some packets of pills. Unable to check what he was being asked to swallow, the near-blind man refused to take them. His feverish body lost a tenth of its weight. He developed anaemia, shingles and oral thrush. He struggled to swallow, and showed signs of encephalopathy. There were lesions on his liver, his gallbladder was inflamed. His eyeballs were sinking into his skull. A consultant from the Chelsea and Westminster Hospital in London to whom Aleksanyan's lawyers sent his medical records concluded that there was 'imminent threat to his life'. They applied once again to the prosecutors' office for his release on grounds of ill health. An official there agreed and sent a motion to the judge requesting bail, only for a representative of the same office to argue against his release at the hearing. The judge ruled that it was up to the investigator to decide whether a suspect should be released. The investigator declared that it was up to the prison authorities. The prison authorities determined that Aleksanyan should remain incarcerated. Another official from the prosecutors' office visited him, Aleksanyan told his lawyers. She made the offer a third time: give us the false testimony we need to fit up Khodorkovsky and you will have your treatment. Again, he refused.

On January 22, 2008, hunched, swaying and barely able to stand, Aleksanyan appeared before the Supreme Court to appeal the latest extension of his detention. He addressed the court by video link from a cage in his prison. When Peter Sahlas watched the footage, he was mortified. It felt like watching a murder.

After apologising for coughing, Aleksanyan said that now 'even the doctors look upon me with horror'. He described the offers that had been made to him to buy his liberty by falsely incriminating Khodorkovsky. The Supreme Court dismissed his appeal. His trial began a week later. The following day he was diagnosed with lymphoma related to what was now full-blown AIDS. The court ruled that, if released, he might 'thwart the establishment of truth'. So, when on February 8 he was at last taken to a civilian hospital to begin treatment with antiretrovirals for the AIDS and chemotherapy for the cancer, he was shackled to his bed. Guards accompanied him to the toilet and declined to wear sterile uniforms. The court agreed that Aleksanyan's relatives could visit him, but his captors decided otherwise.

In London, Paris, Berlin and Washington, Peter Sahlas was trying to orchestrate an intervention to save Aleksanyan. In Aleksanyan's pitiful form, Peter glimpsed a man whose fate he might have shared had he been born in Moscow instead of Toronto. The case, Peter had realised, was not fundamentally about the law. It was about geopolitics. His job, as he saw it, was 'to understand the depth of depravity that the prosecutors and the court have sunk to and translate that into English and explain why this was important'.

When the European Court of Human Rights, to the jurisdiction of which Yeltsin had submitted Russia, finally ordered Aleksanyan's unconditional release, he left prison to live out the couple of years his devastated body could give him. A fresh prosecution and conviction of Khodorkovsky proceeded without him. With him and the rest of the original oligarchs jailed, exiled or otherwise diminished, a new crop was emerging, who owed everything to Putin. Igor Sechin, a former intelligence officer and secretary to Putin, became chief executive of Rosneft, the state-owned oil group that gained control of Yukos's assets. As Peter watched this unfold, a passage from Gogol's *Dead Souls* came to his mind: 'our country is perishing, not now from an invasion of twenty foreign armies, but from ourselves: that beyond the rightful administration, another administration has been formed, much stronger than the rightful one.'

5

Silhouette

Cheapside, July 2008

From behind the screen, the silhouette began to speak. 'Good morning,' said a Central European voice. 'I swear that the testimony I am about to give will be the truth, the whole truth and nothing but the truth, so help me God.'

The silhouette used to be one of the IT guys at a bank in Liechtenstein that provided anonymous accounts to its clients. To the outside world, the identities of these clients were concealed behind what the silhouette called 'high-grade camouflage'. But the bankers themselves needed a record of which account belonged to whom. It had been the silhouette's job to index the documents recording these details. As he read file after file, the silhouette realised that he was looking at a system for corruption, circumventing embargoes and tax evasion. When he asked his bosses about, say, their clients' connections to dictators, the answer was always the same: 'None of your business, just stick to your designated job.' Instead, the silhouette made off with copies of 12,000 of the bank's records. The bank, LGT, belonged to Liechtenstein's royal family. The silhouette – back then he was still Heinrich Kieber, now he had a new name, a secret name – was declared one of the principality's most wanted fugitives. He began to disseminate the files. On February 14, 2008, German authorities launched raids on tax evaders identified in the LGT records. A dozen other countries followed. Kieber was taken into a witness protection programme, from where he recorded his silhouetted appearance before a committee of the US Senate.

As he watched a feed of the Senate hearing, something clicked in Nigel Wilkins' head. The mysteries that swirled around him in BSI's office on Cheapside began to make sense.

Nigel had taken an interest in the work of Carl Levin, a senator from Michigan. Levin had deployed powers of the Permanent Subcommittee on Investigation that Joe McCarthy had once used to hunt communists, to pierce bank secrecy. Nigel was watching online as that work reached a climax in July 2008. Levin had a kindly manner, but from the dais of the hearing room he peered at his witnesses over the glasses on the end of his nose and never released them from his gaze until he had what he needed. His investigators had spent months piecing together how banks had helped Americans hide their wealth from the tax authorities. They had interviewed the silhouetted Kieber and a braggadocious New Englander called Brad Birkenfeld. Birkenfeld had been a private banker at Union Bank of Switzerland. UBS held more wealth than any other bank – $1.8 trillion. It was enough to buy the three most valuable corporations of the day, PetroChina, ExxonMobil and General Electric. Birkenfeld's services for UBS's American clients had included transporting diamonds inside a tube of toothpaste. A combination of righteousness and a thirst for revenge after having been made redundant led Birkenfeld to unburden himself to the tax authorities and to Levin's investigators.

Levin had his evidence, but he was not a judge, just a politician. As Nigel watched the feed, one after another the bankers who had deigned to obey the committee's summons invoked their Fifth Amendment constitutional right against self-incrimination and respectfully declined to answer the senators' questions.

Then, after more than two hours, the committee's chairman called the day's final witness. Mark Branson had flown in from Zürich, where he worked as a senior executive at UBS. An Englishman in a grey suit and sober tie, he stood to swear his oath. His tone was assured. But as he sat down he clasped his right wrist in his left hand and fidgeted with the papers in front of him. Rather than plead the Fifth, he started to read from a prepared statement. He explained that he had worked for UBS since 1997, and five months ago had been put in charge of 'maintaining a strong compliance framework for our wealth-management business worldwide'. He said he had read the report that the committee's investigators had prepared. 'On behalf of UBS,' he said, 'I am apologising. I am committing to you that we will take the actions necessary to make sure that this does not happen again.' A crackle went through the room. The world's richest private bank was confessing. One of Levin's investigators slipped him a note that just said: 'Wow.' Branson admitted that UBS bankers had set up sham companies to hide money from tax authorities. Caught red-handed, the bank would henceforth turn away Americans who came asking to stash their money abroad. Not only that, said Branson, the bank's bosses would agree to violate the cardinal rule of Swiss banking: they would help the US authorities identify those of its 19,000 American clients who had evaded tax.

Nigel had printed off a single page of Levin's investigators' report. It was headed 'Tax Haven Bank Secrecy Tricks'. He scanned the list. Avoiding talking to clients on office phones; using foreign shell companies and credit cards; ensuring that mail came to the bank, not to the client's home – all were techniques used daily at BSI. 'These structures are used in order to conceal ownership from the authorities,' Nigel wrote in his notebook. 'These are structures deliberately designed to hide the proceeds of crime.' And under the law, the person who was most responsible for them was Nigel Wilkins. As the compliance officer, he was the registered employee with a duty to report any suspicion of money laundering. If he failed to do so, he could be prosecuted.

Shortly before Levin's hearing, the UBS banker Brad Birkenfeld had been arrested as he disembarked from the overnight flight from Switzerland to Boston. American prosecutors had figured out that he had failed to reveal his own role in concealing a billionaire's wealth. Birkenfeld had sensed what was coming: he had spent the flight reclining in his business-class seat with a stiff drink watching Harrison Ford in *The Fugitive*. For the rest of the Swiss banking fraternity, his arrest was terrifying. Carl Levin had likened financial secrecy to Russian Matryoshka dolls: 'shells within shells within shells … which in the end can become impenetrable to legal process'. Now the law was encircling the bankers and their clients.

6

Mr Billy

Harare, September 2008

On September 15, 2008, the day the talks to save Lehman Brothers were abandoned and the bank was left to expire, and that Sasha Machkevitch bought six Damien Hirsts for $22 million at Sotheby's, Robert Mugabe appeared before his people and signed a deal that would allow his rule to endure. More than twenty-eight years had passed since he vanquished Ian Smith's white-supremacist Rhodesians. For the liberating hero, the scene today at the Rainbow Towers hotel in Harare was beneath his dignity. Still, he managed a smile as he shook hands with Morgan Tsvangirai, the hulking trade unionist who would have won the election a few months back had Mugabe's operatives not so thoroughly brutalised anyone they suspected of intending to cast a treacherous ballot for the opposition. Tsvangirai had agreed to form a power-sharing government over which he and Mugabe would jointly preside. He looked delighted as the cameras flashed, evidently oblivious that he had walked into a trap. With the foreign statesmen who had brokered the deal, he had just legitimised the theft of an election. The thieves had used power to steal money, then used that money to steal more power. It was the work of a master.

Growing up the son of a wealthy Rhodesian, the unpredictable, uncontrollable, irascible Billy Rautenbach's principal pastime had

been rally driving. His father, Wessels Rautenbach, had maintained a haulage enterprise despite the tightening economic
blockade on Smith's regime. When times changed in 1980,
Wessels changed with them. The white trucker made a friend of
Emmerson Mnangagwa, despite Mnangagwa having been tortured
by the Rhodesians for fomenting their downfall. The Crocodile:
that was how Mnangagwa was known. 'He will size you up,' a
spy who studied him concluded, 'and decide if he's going to eat
you.' The Crocodile was security minister at the time the regime's
forces massacred ethnic rivals in Matabeleland. Some of the
thousands who died began their eternal rest with relatives dancing
at gunpoint on their fresh graves, chanting slogans in praise of
Mugabe. The Crocodile moved on to other positions in the
regime, but could never quite manage the popular touch. The
opposition politician who dared to defeat him in a parliamentary
election only avoided death because the young thugs who had
doused him in fuel failed to light the match. No matter, the
Crocodile knew his true and enduring role: to bring in money.
And in Wessels Rautenbach's boy Billy, he found a candidate for
a particularly sensitive mission.

Zimbabwe had plenty of buried treasure: fat seams of platinum,
gold and diamonds. But to the north there lay a still greater
bounty. Mobutu Sese Seko had controlled access to these riches
since taking power in Congo with the CIA's assistance in 1965.
The wealth of this land the size of western Europe – a state,
previously pillaged by the Belgians, in little more than name –
proved insufficient to satisfy Mobutu's appetite. At his palace in
the rainforest where less fortunate Congolese endured starvation
and Ebola, 10,000 bottles of champagne were consumed each
year. But now the Cold War was over and the hot wars were
beginning. A pledge of ideological allegiance to the capitalists or
the communists used to earn a dictator licence to loot in the
comfortable expectation of superpower support should the

plundering prompt any mutinous rumblings from the populace. No longer. Ferdinand Marcos had sent Filipino troops to join the Americans in Vietnam. But when Filipinos rose up in 1986, salvation failed to materialise from the West and he was forced into a hurried escape bearing only what he could stuff into a couple of planes: sixty-seven racks of clothes, seventy pairs of bejewelled cufflinks, a silver-mantled statue of the infant Jesus in ivory, a few million freshly printed Philippine pesos of spending money and twenty-four gold bricks. Augusto Pinochet, Henry Kissinger's man in America's backyard, had spent decades bolstering Chile as a Pacific sandbag against the red tide. He had overthrown Salvador Allende – a particularly dangerous leftie, having been elected. Chileans Pinochet deemed subversive were taken to a converted cultural centre outside Santiago, stripped, strapped to a set of bedsprings known as 'the grill', and then, in many cases, were 'disappeared'. And yet, after a referendum deposed him, all that emerged from Washington was news that he had used a bank there to stash a stolen fortune. In Congo, Mobutu experienced a similarly stomach-turning abandonment. As a rebel army advanced, the Americans told him to go. There wasn't even time to hire the customary Concorde for the journey into exile, just an old cargo plane.

Mobutu's fall offered a once-in-a-generation opportunity for an ambitious kleptocrat like the Crocodile. The new boss in Congo was a rotund authoritarian, Laurent Kabila. He had been judged by his confrère in an earlier rebellion, Che Guevara, to lack 'revolutionary seriousness, an ideology that can guide action, a spirit of sacrifice'. Even before he deposed Mobutu, Kabila had set up a company through which the assets of the state would be transferred to the benefit of him and his entourage. When a lawyer questioned the propriety of this arrangement, Kabila replied, 'But this law you are talking about, it is man who made it, no?'

Soon Kabila would need the money for more than just his own enrichment. When his alliance with erstwhile backers in Rwanda fractured, they invaded, beginning five years of war that would end millions of lives. Kabila found that the Zimbabweans and other allies who had helped him topple Mobutu were unwilling to kick in again while their debts from the first conflict remained unpaid. He would have to do what the rulers of ex-Soviet states were doing to monetise their positions: sell off his nation's natural wealth.

The day Mugabe promised Kabila Zimbabwean troops, a new boss of the Congolese state mining company was named. Kabila soon took to referring to him simply as 'Mr Billy'. They had a double arrangement. Some of the profits from copper and cobalt sales would go to the Zimbabwean government to pay for the soldiers. But in parallel Rautenbach would send monthly payments, said to be as much as two million dollars a time, back to the Crocodile, to be divided among those in the Zimbabwean regime Mugabe deemed deserving. Kabila's people received their share too. So did Rautenbach himself: shortly before his appointment, the Congolese authorities assigned to his private company the rights to an expansive terrain groaning with minerals.

Rautenbach had a short fuse, but he could be pleasant when it suited him. 'He knows how to say the right thing,' an associate said. 'He knows how to read people. He can connect with people. He can put himself on whatever level: dealing with a border guard or a president, he knows how to make his pitch.' At first, his masters were satisfied. Extracting the minerals that lay under Congo's copperbelt – much of the planet's copper, required for the wires that carried electricity, and most of the cobalt, required for the batteries that stored it – took highly technical skills. This expertise Rautenbach entirely lacked. For a time he could have his miners grab the easy ore that lay close to the surface, then sell the copper to Marc Rich, a sanctions-busting trader holed up in Switzerland, and the cobalt to the commodity house Rich had founded, Glencore. Those sales helped Mr Billy satisfy Kabila, who called weekly wanting more money for his war. But once everyone had been paid, there was no money left to invest in excavating the deeper seams. By the start of 2000, production was falling and creditors were seizing shipments. In March, Kabila fired Rautenbach.

That might have been the end for Billy Rautenbach. Might have been, had he not understood that dirty money's true value is not measured in numbers. It is measured in names – knowing the names of those it has corrupted.

In July 2000, four months after Kabila ditched him, Rautenbach learned that some of the most senior members of Kabila's and Mugabe's regimes were to gather at the Elephant Hills in Zimbabwe. The hotel, all pools and palms and room service, stood beside the Zambezi River at the point where it tips into the cauldron of Victoria Falls. Rautenbach turned up and set about his mission: lobbying to restore his position in the Congolese mining game. But no sooner had he started schmoozing than he was summoned to see Nicholas Goche, the head of Zimbabwe's Central Intelligence Organisation. We know what you are up to, he told Rautenbach. We know you threatened to kill Bruce Jewels.

Bruce Jewels was a banker, one of HSBC's best-connected in Africa. It was he who had safeguarded the bank's interests in Congo as Kabila replaced Mobutu. His protégé, a sharp-minded son of the copperbelt called Augustin Katumba Mwanke, was rising fast through Kabila's regime, part of a new clique that was starting to influence who got what in the mining province. A rumour had reached Jewels' boss at the bank that Rautenbach wanted him dead. The bank had hired a private investigator, a gluttonous former British Army officer known as Captain Pig, who was acquainted with the spooks of southern Africa. He had discussed the threat with his contacts at the top of Mugabe's regime, including Nicholas Goche, the intelligence chief. Now Goche had Rautenbach in front of him at the Elephant Hills, he explained that the Zimbabwean government did not like this sort of thing. Particularly because Rautenbach's association with the Crocodile meant the name of a senior official was being dragged into it. Rautenbach protested his innocence. Yes, he had no love for Bruce Jewels. But the enmity was Jewels' own fault: he was conspiring to blacken Rautenbach's reputation and drive him from Congo. Besides, why would he do something like put a contract out on a banker when he was already in so much trouble with the South Africans? His Hyundai franchise there was in debt, and the economic crime squad had raided his mansion in Johannesburg, carrying off three truckloads of documents. They were preparing charges of fraud, theft and corruption. A prosecutor in Pretoria had claimed Rautenbach had had a hand in the murder of a Korean rival. And South African intelligence had him on a list of the country's top twenty organised crime suspects. Rautenbach had told the media it was all a 'witch hunt', but Goche was unmoved. He gave a stern instruction: pull your horns in, behave yourself, or you will pay dearly.

Rautenbach saw the threat, and he called it. To the Congolese, he let it be known that he had documentary proof of how much he had paid Kabila personally for his mining concession. To the Crocodile and the others he had enriched in Mugabe's court, he made the same threat: as one minister put it, to 'spill the beans on the lot of them'.

Over the years that followed, in various foreign and international courts, Rautenbach asserted his claims to Congolese mining rights, winning back some of what he had lost. Zimbabwe continued to give him safe harbour. He prospered even as Mugabe commanded the seizure of white farms. Western powers imposed sanctions on Mugabe and his circle; Mugabe and his circle blamed those sanctions for the nation's immiseration, while they themselves devoured the economy. The currency grew worthless, no matter how often the central bank removed a few zeroes. A land of farmers ran out of food. Millions fled.

On March 29, 2008, Zimbabweans voted in a general election unlike any other since Mugabe had taken charge in 1980. This time, he was not certain of victory. He still had his partisans, but the pride and promise of his earlier years had so decayed that many of the rest of the population obeyed only because of the atrocities in which, with the 'degrees in violence' he boasted of holding, he was now expert. And yet there was no stifling the new mood of defiance. Zimbabweans voted in their millions for the opposition candidate, Morgan Tsvangirai. The polls closed, but the results did not appear. Tsvangirai said his party's tally showed he had won. Still no results appeared. A month passed. Then the electoral authorities declared that, while Tsvangirai had indeed received the most votes, he had fallen short of the majority needed, under Zimbabwe's election rules, to avoid a run-off against Mugabe.

In an African election – or, for that matter, an election almost anywhere else – $100 million will change the course of history. And even at his darkest hour, there was still a place to which Mugabe, scourge of British imperialists, could turn for salvation: London.

In Mayfair, the domain of the hedge funds, a pair of moneymen, one Australian and one American, had designs on Africa. On March 16, 2008, two weeks before the Zimbabwean election, the Australian prepared to set forth in furtherance of this endeavour. Two days earlier, Bear Stearns had died. Wall Streeters were mostly horrified. But Vanja Baros was brimming with possibilities. He emailed his boss, Michael L. Cohen, with the latest. Cohen was a young buck of Mayfair. He had not passed thirty when Daniel Och, the New York superstar financier, had sent him to London. Cohen had recently advanced his Anglofication by adding to his Bentley a $28 million country estate in Hampshire once owned by the Duke of Wellington and where Nigel Wilkins' father used to preach in the nearby village chapel. He sought what all the hedge fund managers sought: opportunities to turn money into more money faster than conventional investment would allow. To this end, Baros had packed his bags for a trip to Africa. He emailed Cohen to say they should speak before he set off, 'coz I'm back in jungle for a couple of days and maybe no reception'.

The way to accelerate the multiplication of money was to be closer to power than others could get. London was full of moneymen who knew how to do that, how to spot the places where power was suddenly exposed, like a seam of ore torn open by some tectonic shift. Of course, where the earth could shake once, it could shake again. Just look at Bill Browder. He had made plenty in St Petersburg back when the city had been Putin's territory only to be chased out in 2007. Things could go awry in Africa too, but it was trebly tempting nonetheless. One, they knew how to maintain power there: a thirty-year reign was perfectly doable. Two, the heat and the fevers, the pitted roads and plunging planes, the jumbled languages, the juju and the sheer insignificance of the moneyless masses: these were all excellent prophylactics against scrutiny. And three, while the rest of the global economy was beginning its descent down the shitter, the bit that Africa did – supplying raw materials – was booming. The Chinese economy was doubling in size every eight years. The economies around it were doing something similar. Never before had the basics been in such ferocious demand: copper to wire, iron to gird, coal to fire, uranium to split. The Soviet empire's stocks had been claimed in the nineties. The treasure of Australia and the Americas was thoroughly tied up. But Africa: in Africa what was spoken for one day was available the next.

In Zimbabwe, Baros met Andrew Groves, the son of a
Rhodesian policeman who had knocked around the African
mining scene for years, raising money from investors in London
with his partner, a retired England cricketer called Phil Edmonds.
Their most recent venture was called Central African Mining &
Exploration, or Camec. They had a Zimbabwean shareholder,
too, and Baros made his acquaintance as well – Billy Rautenbach.
Rautenbach had taken a stake in Camec in exchange for some
of his Congolese mining concessions. Cohen and Baros had
already put some of the Och-Ziff hedge fund's millions into
Camec. After Baros's Zimbabwe trip, they put in a few more,
taking the total to $150 million. They might have been less
enthusiastic had they established what that money would be used
for.

Billy Rautenbach was embarking on his latest manoeuvre. The
scheme began with Mugabe's people leaning on the giant mining
house Anglo American to surrender a choice platinum prospect,
in order that it might be deemed to have met its obligations
under an 'indigenisation' policy. The stated aim of this policy
was to reunite ordinary Zimbabweans with some of the mineral
wealth that had for centuries been carted off by colonisers. In
this case, after Anglo American gave in, the ordinary Zimbabwean
selected to receive this redress was Billy Rautenbach. The mine
came with a commitment to furnish Mugabe's government with
$100 million, ostensibly as a loan. But Rautenbach would not
put up the money himself. On April 11, while Zimbabweans
were waiting to learn the election results, Camec bought the
platinum mine from Rautenbach and paid over the hundred
million to the regime. On May 2, the electoral commission
announced that the election would go to a run-off. The moneymen
had their deal. Mugabe had his warchest.

Over the weeks that followed, Mugabe's goons conducted
Operation Makavhoterapapi ('Where did you put your vote?').

Those who had cast their ballots for Morgan Tsvangirai – the gangs said they had lists – were rounded up and punished. 'It's your own fault, voting for the opposition,' one contingent of thugs told an activist as they pummelled him and beat his brother to death. 'That's why we are doing all these things to you. When we have the run-off, you will know how to vote.' More than a hundred died. Thousands were detained and tortured. With five days left until the run-off, Tsvangirai pulled out of what he called a 'violent, illegitimate sham of an election process'. On June 29, Mugabe was inaugurated for a fresh term, surrounded by troops in dress uniform and yellow berets. Such was the outrage abroad and the chaos at home that Mugabe submitted to peace talks with the opposition, hosted by his South African counterpart, Thabo Mbeki. It took the best part of three months, but by mid-September Mugabe had secured a deal that allowed him to stay in power, albeit with Tsvangirai appointed prime minister until the next election.

Billy Rautenbach had proved his worth again. Now it was time to make a return on his investment. London was the place for that: a *bureau de change* for converting power into money. As luck would have it, three rich gentlemen had recently arrived who were looking to broaden their horizons.

7
Shutdown

Cheapside, September 2008

The Wednesday after the weekend that Lehman Brothers collapsed – the first Wednesday of the new days – Nigel Wilkins' boss fired him. This did not come as a surprise. It wasn't simply that every bank everywhere was firing everyone it could. Nigel had known it was coming since June, when a letter had arrived from BSI headquarters in Switzerland informing him that the London office would shortly be closing. BSI's management offered Nigel $30,000 to accept redundancy, about a quarter of his annual salary and much more than they were obliged to under his contract. But, being Nigel, he had no intention of going quietly. After he realised that his colleagues were using some of the secrecy techniques Senator Levin had identified, he emailed his superiors to say that 'compliance shortcomings involving Swiss banks' had come to his attention. As a result, he went on, he had arrived at 'the provisional conclusion that BSI should also be making disclosures to the relevant authorities. In the circumstances I consider that, as compliance officer, I should be free to deal with these issues in the absence of an immediate threat of dismissal.'

Nigel was convinced that the reason BSI's bosses in Lugano wanted to get the bank out of the UK was to avoid the increased scrutiny of the City that was bound to follow the crisis. He knew that BSI's London office had already received a private warning from the Financial Services Authority that it was conducting insufficient checks on the origins of its 'high risk' clients' money. That was back in 2004, before he joined the bank. On September 11 he wrote to his bosses again, suggesting that he be kept on because he had worked at the City regulator, which 'is being obliged to supervise firms more closely in the aftermath of Northern Rock and the credit crunch'. To no avail: after the Lehman weekend, Nigel's boss wrote to him to confirm that he was being dismissed and that there was no job for him elsewhere at BSI. His last day would be a fortnight hence.

Still Nigel did not relent. He explained that most of the bank's London clients were using the same techniques – creating sham companies, avoiding paper trails – that had come to light in the UBS scandal. That was serious. In an industry accustomed to seeing corporations take the punishment when wrongdoing was discovered, real people – actual human bankers – were going to jail; there was good reason to think Brad Birkenfeld might not be the last. BSI bankers in the London office were still taking clients' instructions, despite the accounts ostensibly having been moved weeks earlier to other BSI offices overseas. Nigel's superiors in Switzerland told him he lacked 'reasonable suspicions against any of the clients'. He refused to let it lie, even once he had left the office and set off home along Cheapside for the last time. 'My abrupt dismissal on Tuesday prevented me from completing my list of clients about whom I have suspicions, and submitting the necessary report to the authorities,' he wrote in an email. 'The fact that nobody else in BSI supports my suspicions is irrelevant.'

Maybe no one had been looking, but if they had, they might have detected mischievous crinkles at the corners of Nigel's eyes as he departed.

8

The Fallen Oligarch

Astana, January 2009

The crisis spread outwards from the money capitals. In the early hours of Thursday, January 29, 2009, a withering Siberian wind coursed in off the steppe and engulfed Astana. Snow cloaked the old town, its paved riverbanks where lovers strolled on milder evenings, its restaurants serving pilafs of steaming rice slick with melted butter, the beer halls with fires stoked by the descendants of the German-Russians Stalin carted off to the wilderness when he turned on Hitler. The blizzard swirled onwards into the new city, the part Kazakhstan's rulers had erected for themselves. Its skyscrapers were monuments to wealth bestowed by geology and handshakes, its fine hotels appointed to the standards of the international commercial classes. In one of these, Bota Jardemalie was fast asleep when the phone beside her bed rang. Blearily she checked the time: 4 a.m. 'What the fuck?' she thought. She pulled the receiver to her ear and heard her boss's voice, calling from his suite a few floors up. 'Bota, could you please take your computer and come to my room?' Something in his tone was too controlled, too ordinary. Bota dressed swiftly, threw her belongings into her suitcase, grabbed her laptop and jumped in the lift.

Mukhtar Ablyazov opened the door to his suite. He was wearing a suit. Despite his seniority in years and within the bank, he used the polite form of Russian with Bota, as she did with him. 'I've been putting things together,' he said, 'and I think they are going to arrest me this morning.'

The expression on Ablyazov's oval face, with its pointed chin and expansive forehead, remained oddly calm. He called room service and ordered her tea with milk, then began to explain his reasoning. They had travelled to Astana to discuss the Kazakh government's plans to do what practically every government was doing, if they hadn't already: bail out the country's banks. Ablyazov was the owner of BTA Bank, one of Kazakhstan's biggest. He had started to sense something was off the previous afternoon, when he bumped into the chief banking regulator. She had blushed and hurried away without speaking to him. He was due to meet Karim Massimov, President Nazarbayev's prime minister, later that day but Massimov's office had called to say the meeting would be delayed. Ablyazov sensed a trap. He was sufficiently alarmed to activate an arrangement with a well-placed contact. The contact could not risk alerting Ablyazov directly if there were a plot against him. But years earlier he had agreed that, should he get wind that Ablyazov was to be seized, he would indicate as much by neither answering nor returning his calls. Ablyazov had called him and received the silent signal in reply.

Bota, lively and irreverent by nature, black hair flowing down her back, sat quietly and listened. She knew Ablyazov had been sent to a prison camp, years ago, for a few months, but she had been out of the country at the time, studying law at Harvard. Now she was back home, one of the young Westernised executives trying to make BTA a credible international bank. She knew that in Kazakhstan you expected intrigue and backstabbing over valuable assets. Indeed, she had assumed that Nazarbayev would have demanded a secret stake in Ablyazov's bank. Money was power, and banks dealt in money. Timur Kulibayev, the president's son-in-law and Kazakhstan's richest man according to Forbes, already owned one of BTA's main competitors. Bota had worked hard to make BTA an institution to which Royal Bank of Scotland, the biggest bank in the world, had lines of credit. She was convinced it was solid, even against the shockwaves emanating from Wall Street and the City of London. With fellow members of the Kazakh elite, she would argue the merits of state intervention in the banking system, but these disputes would always end with drinks or a friendly shisha pipe. Now, sitting with Ablyazov as the snow billowed outside, she started to see that there were graver forces at play. The crisis had presented Nazarbayev and his court with the pretext they needed to seize BTA from Ablyazov and make it look like a rescue rather than robbery. She felt a surge of frustration.

Ablyazov's bodyguard had a jet on standby at the airport, but the snow kept them trapped at the hotel. They waited, not knowing when there might be a knock at the door. Bota opened her laptop and took notes as Ablyazov recounted the events that had led up to this moment. He handed her some SIM cards. If he were arrested, each was to be used to reach a different contact. Among them were some of the few journalists the regime had not yet bought or terrified into submission. Bota had heard talk of Ablyazov's clandestine links to the opposition, but had dismissed it as gossip. Now she took the SIM cards and hid them in a candy wrapper. Everything felt surreal. Ablyazov handed her his watch.

'Take it,' he said. 'You will give it back to me when you see me.'

'You'll need it,' Bota said.

Ablyazov smiled. 'If they arrest me they're going to take it anyway.'

The snowstorm passed. As he made the dash to the airport, Ablyazov was certain he would be caught by the KNB. But the congenital paranoia of the Kazakh ruling class seemed to have come to his aid. Everyone knew everyone. So anyone hatching a plot was loath to bring others in on it for fear of being double-crossed. 'Even if you are the prime minister,' Bota understood, 'you don't know who you can trust.' None of those who wanted to lay hands on Ablyazov had sufficient confidence in their colleagues in the regime to send instructions that a roadblock be erected to stop him en route to the airport or that, if he got there, his plane be kept on the ground. He arrived and boarded but the aircraft could not take off: there was too much ice on the wings. He waited as the mechanics doused the plane in de-icer. Then, at last, the engines roared, the pilot accelerated down the runway, and they were in the air. Before long, the plane had crossed the border.

Bota emerged from the hotel onto the space-age boulevards of Astana's new city. It was a metropolis of discordant glam, as though Kubla Khan had slipped Isaac Asimov a tab of acid and told him to dream up a capital to sit at the fulcrum of a new order, with China to the east, Russia to the north and, from the west, approaching as once they walked the Silk Road, suitors seeking oil, uranium and customers for their skills in transforming tainted money. At one end of the main thoroughfare the Khan Shatyry, or royal marquee, swerved woozily skywards. An immense pleasure dome designed by Norman Foster, it had opened on Nazarbayev's seventieth birthday. Halfway down the promenade stood the headquarters of the sovereign wealth fund, sponsors of the Astana cycling team, to which Lance Armstrong, the greatest athlete ever to straddle a saddle, had recently been recruited. At the other end, before the presidential palace, rose the Bayterek Tower, the sacred egg of the mythical Samruk nestled in the upper branches of the tree of life. Towards the top of the tower, visitors could place a hand into the golden imprint of Nazarbayev's in supplication to the father of the nation.

With Ablyazov's watch clasped under her sleeve, Bota went to BTA's office in Astana. But she realised there wasn't much she could do, so she decided to return to her home in Almaty, the commercial capital among the mountains far to the south. When her flight landed, she turned her phone on to see several messages. A strange fax from the banking regulator had arrived after she left the Astana office. The fax contained an order that the bank's management make provision for what the regulators declared to be huge impending losses by setting aside $3.5 billion. It was Thursday evening. The fax gave a deadline of Sunday to assemble the impossible sum, seven times BTA's annual profits. Bota had no doubt what was happening: Nazarbayev's regime was manoeuvring the bank into a position where it would have violated the regulator's instructions. That would give him a licence to snatch it.

When Bota reached her home in Almaty, she told her husband what had happened. Like her, he was a corporate lawyer. Immediately he was reminded of a landmark expropriation case in Russia – the seizure of Mikhail Khodorkovsky's Yukos. 'You remember the way they treated the lawyers?' he said. 'There is no fucking way we are staying.'

Bota thought through her options for an instant evacuation on a Kazakh passport. She had lately been making trips to the UK with a view to preparing BTA to follow ENRC and list its shares on the London Stock Exchange. Her visa was still valid, so London it was. She expected to be away for a week, until everything calmed down.

Ablyazov had made for London too. Bota went to his hotel and set to work on his claim for political asylum. This was hardly her field, but she was far more familiar with the West than her Soviet-trained boss, and spoke perfect English. The British asylum lawyer she hired listened to her account, saw the resemblance to the Khodorkovsky case, and put her in touch with Bob Amsterdam. Bob Amsterdam called Peter Sahlas, who was living in Paris. After an initial chat with Bota on the phone, in May

2009 he took the Eurostar to London. It was a beautiful, warm spring day, and he made his way to the restaurant Bota had chosen, not far from Buckingham Palace. He had plenty on, but this meeting sounded intriguing: a woman on the run from the Kazakh dictator.

As they ate, Bota explained that the Kazakh authorities who had seized Ablyazov's bank were trying to turn the tale on its head. They were saying that Ablyazov had looted BTA so greedily that, when the financial crisis struck, it would have collapsed had the state not stepped in to nationalise it. In this account, the scheming oligarch was no ordinary crook. He was the Bernie Madoff of the steppe.

Immediately Peter thought back to Putin's first moves against Khodorkovsky. He remembered how Yukos's auditors, the British firm PwC, had, after encouragement from the Kremlin, withdrawn ten years of the company's accounts. That had helped the prosecutors to manufacture their narrative that Khodorkovsky had stolen billions. Of course he had made his fortune through the filthy privatisations. But so had everybody else. The authorities needed an accusation specific to him, the oligarch who had dared to enter politics. Getting PwC to withdraw accounts they had previously certified created a vacuum for an alternative reality.

Peter soon returned with Bob Amsterdam. They headed to Tower 42, the tallest in the City, on the other side of the Bank of England from Nigel Wilkins' office at BSI. As they rocketed upwards in the lift, Ablyazov's innocence was still an open question. Perhaps he was what his enemies said he was: a fraudster scarcely rivalled in scale and guile. Peter knew that the world in which he now moved was an information battleground. Every word could be true, every word could be a lie; the cleverest storytellers took a few truths and spun them together into a big lie. All there was for it was to meet the eyes that met your own and make a judgement of character.

The lift climbed above the City, rising beside the wall that marked its medieval limits. Peter and Amsterdam stepped out to behold what might have been the offices of some funky start-up. There were wires dangling from the ceiling, and a stack of servers in the middle of the floor. People were running back and forth. Bota greeted them, and sat them down in a meeting room with a glass door and glass walls.

When Ablyazov appeared, he was wearing a shirt and tie. He spoke no English. Amsterdam listened through an interpreter, but Peter knew enough Russian by now to hear Ablyazov in his own words. Quickly he discerned a deep intellect, articulately expressed. This man, it seemed to Peter, had obviously been through a lot in life from the very beginning, and had learned a lot the hard way. Ablyazov launched into an explanation of his problems. Amsterdam stopped him. 'This is not how we are going to do this,' he said. 'I want to know everything about you. What's your earliest memory?'

For the next four days, Ablyazov unfolded the narrative of his life. He recounted how he had earned a gold medal upon graduation from high school, how he had been permitted to collect it only once his parents had paid a bribe to the headteacher, how he remembered the money being passed across the table. He described his gift for physics, especially underground nuclear explosions – an emotive subject for Kazakhs, under whose wide plains the Soviets had conducted theirs. His talents should have been the ticket to Moscow that he craved after his first child, the tiny Madina, caught pneumonia in Soviet Almaty. But instead the local apparatchiks, affronted by this ambition, evicted the family from their little room. This was the late eighties: capitalism was seeping in through the cracks, and with it came marvels such as photocopiers and fax machines and personal computers. He found people who wanted these devices, he found people who wanted to sell them, and he collected his commission. In half a year he had bought a house. Soon he was making so much money he didn't know what to do with it. It could not have been illegal: no one had written any laws governing the conduct of business.

Now the call came from the institute in Moscow, the chance to fulfil his dreams of scientific luminescence. But no: life had given him the opportunity to do business. The future was a vast unanswered question, he should stay and make all the money he could. He roped his extended family into his enterprise as it grew and grew, trading anything. He lost everything, then made it back in three months. After a swindler sold him a consignment of apples, all of which were rotten except those on top, he began to enforce ironclad contracts. Then came the privatisations – if you talked about them the way the capitalists talked about them, an exercise in freeing the animal spirits of the new entrepreneurs from the dead hand of the state. He bought a bank, BTA, with a partner. Billions of dollars, he was worth. He went into government – by now he was one of the foremost figures in the new Kazakhstan – in charge of power supply, then as minister of energy, industry and trade. He alone stood up to the president, denouncing the promotion of Nazarbayev's relatives and the creeping establishment of what he called a 'clan-ocracy'. When he refused to continue in the cabinet, Nazarbayev demanded to see him. 'You don't respect your president,' he ranted, 'you don't respect me as a person, you're not loyal to me.' He calmed down and asked again: 'Come back and work for me.' Again Ablyazov refused. 'Well, in that case, you're going to have to give me a chunk.' They would be partners. The president would take half of BTA Bank. It would be a guarantee against disloyalty. Ablyazov stood firm: no. He knew change was coming. He wanted it, and found that others did too. Together, these reformers founded a political party, Democratic Choice of Kazakhstan. Nazarbayev, their enlightened ruler, crushed it.

In the prison camp, it was thirty-five below outside. Thieves whose code prohibited submission to their jailers slashed open their own bellies with razors and nails; prison rapists who got you alone threatened to fetch their vaseline. The beatings went on so long that the pain stopped. *I no longer existed. This was just a body. But I was not in this body – I was standing off to the side.* Pummelled legs locked straight so you had to shit standing up. While he was inside, Nazarbayev took everything, out of greed, of course, but also – even mainly – to eliminate him as a political threat in a system now controlled by force of secret money. Everything except what Ablyazov had managed to hide. He had entrusted his stake in BTA to a partner who, although he was forced to hand over a slice to Nazarbayev's people, managed to hang on to most of it.

It was a lie that got him out, after almost a year in camps and prisons. He promised Nazarbayev that he would stop organising the opposition. He moved to Moscow, shipped his children to the West and began to build the bank back up. He hired bright young things like Bota. They were making BTA a proper bank, a Western-style bank that could, in time, list its shares in London, protected from the grasping president. For as he discovered when he returned to Kazakhstan, Nazarbayev's covetousness had not abated. Ablyazov's shares were well concealed, held by his partner's widow, his partner having died in a hunting accident. But again and again Nazarbayev summoned him, again and again demanded that he give him a stake in the bank – and not just a chunk, not any more. Now the president wanted a majority share, control. For which Ablyazov would be paid, if anything at all, a sum far less than the market price of $4 billion or so. At the palace in Astana, under the tower of the sacred bird's sacred egg, Nazarbayev told him on January 4, 2006: 'I am afraid of you and afraid of your billions, that you can turn them against me, they are in the bank that you are controlling and that is why I need to control the bank with you.' Nazarbayev's courtiers came to Ablyazov with schemes to cut him in; so did the president's frontmen and spymasters. On February 23, 2008, as Kazakh banks like banks everywhere grew shaky and vulnerable, Nazarbayev spoke to him while both were in Moscow. They met at what had once been a residence for members of the Soviet Central Committee, now the home of one of Nazarbayev's fixers. This was the final warning, the president said. The BTA shares were to be transferred to the designated frontman by April 1. If not, Ablyazov would be arrested and imprisoned. The bank would be taken by force. Ablyazov strung out his resistance for eleven more months. Then came the night of the blizzard, and the silent signal from his contact that the time had come to run.

Peter Sahlas believed him. The level of detail, the spontaneity of his delivery. Here was a fellow shit-disturber. As Ablyazov recounted his first forays in business, hauling photocopiers on a bus, Peter was transported back to his old Russian days in the tempestuous nineties. He could smell the diesel. I knew those guys, he thought, the guys who were hawking those machines.

At any moment, he thought, the police might appear at Tower 42. Kazakhstan would have issued a Red Notice through Interpol requesting Ablyazov's arrest. Peter filled page after page with notes. He counselled Ablyazov to fight back, hard. Lawsuits, PRs, lobbyists. But Ablyazov preferred caution. He would sit tight and see how far Nazarbayev's reach extended into the West.

9

Top Secret

London, April 2009

Nigel Wilkins was due at the employment tribunal near the Thames in London's legal quarter on April 2, 2009, for a hearing in the case he had brought against BSI for wrongful dismissal. That day, the prime minister, Gordon Brown, was convening the leaders of the world's twenty biggest economies. They had gathered to pledge public money in the sum of $5 trillion – equivalent to the entire annual output of the second biggest economy, Japan – to try to prevent the bankers' crisis ruining too many other people. Nigel had already received his own payout. The tribunal hearing was cancelled because, three days earlier, BSI's bosses had agreed to double his redundancy money to $70,000, more than half a year's pay, and he had withdrawn his claim.

The point, for Nigel, was not the money. The point was not letting them get away with saying they had been right and he had been wrong. In his submission to the tribunal, Nigel had enumerated the techniques his colleagues had been using to anonymise their clients' money. He was losing his job, he argued, because the people who controlled BSI in Switzerland wanted to sweep away all trace of the bank's activities in London before the Financial Services Authority, the City watchdog, and Her Majesty's

Revenue and Customs, the tax agency, started tightening up in response to the crisis.

As part of the settlement, Nigel undertook not to repeat these claims on pain of having to give his payout back. But Nigel was a student of jurisprudence. He knew that no contract could override the law. There was a particular statute he had in mind: the Proceeds of Crime Act (2002). That statute – clause 330, to be precise, and Nigel could quote the clauses from memory – made it a crime to know that money laundering was taking place and fail to report it. You didn't even have to know for sure to be guilty, just have 'reasonable grounds for knowing or suspecting'. Moreover – clause 331 – there was a special duty on the officer each bank had to nominate to be on the lookout for laundering. BSI had nominated Nigel. And anyway, as Nigel knew but his former colleagues on Cheapside did not, all this was moot. Because Nigel had already tipped off the City regulator and the tax authority. Six days before he left BSI, he had sent letters telling them what was going on at BSI's office. And he was ready to back up his claim with the contents of the three red boxes that now sat in his Kensington flat bearing the handwritten label 'top secret'.

As part of BSI's preparations to vacate its London premises, Nigel had been moved from his lonely office into the main room where the private bankers and their secretaries sat. The bankers, seemingly convinced that a code of silence protected the whole office, maybe even the length of Cheapside or the entire City of London, had left papers lying around on their desks. In the evenings, when they departed to champagne bars and airports, Nigel had started shuffling through the documents. Then he had begun to make photocopies, and to take those copies home. Thoughts of what might happen to him if he was caught had crept into his head. Not just the formal sanction from his superiors but the enmity of clients who guarded their money so jealously. He kept going all the same, and told no one, not even Charlotte.

10

Paying Your Dues

Pretoria, September 2009

On Friday, September 18, 2009, Billy Rautenbach boarded a plane in Zimbabwe. It took off and flew south. As it cruised through the diamond skies of a southern African spring, Rautenbach could savour his liberation. For years this trip had been impossible. Ever since the Scorpions, post-apartheid South Africa's crack police unit, had started digging into his affairs a decade back. They had put out a warrant for Rautenbach's arrest on charges of corruption, theft and fraud – an international warrant, confining him to places, such as Zimbabwe and Congo, whose authorities could be persuaded not to honour it. He could not even go to London to see his son. The international warrant he had dealt with four years ago. It was a simple matter of making the acquaintance of a South African drug trafficker, Glenn Agliotti, and handing him a hundred grand. Agliotti slipped at least $30,000 of it to Jackie Selebi, South Africa's first black police chief, who was proving himself just as corruptible as his apartheid-era predecessors. Selebi cancelled the international warrant. He took down the Scorpions too, as it happened, before his influence trading was discovered and he was arrested himself. It had been a good bit of business for Rautenbach. He was even able to say he hadn't known that Agliotti would use the money to bribe Selebi. But that still left the charges in South Africa. They were the matter in hand today.

Rautenbach's plane touched down at a private airport outside Johannesburg. From there he made the short trip up to Pretoria, where he presented himself in court. The worst things imputed against him – those claims that he had had a hand in the death of a Korean competitor – had never made it as far as formal charges. There were other charges, though: 326 of them, related to economic crimes. Rautenbach pleaded guilty to every one. Or rather, his haulage company did. In exchange for a $5 million fine, the South African prosecutors had agreed a plea bargain under which Rautenbach himself would be charged with nothing.

It was a most satisfactory use of the windfall Rautenbach had received that very day. His benefactors were three businessmen from Central Asia: Sasha Machkevitch and his partners.

While Rautenbach was resolving his legal trouble before the court in Pretoria, the Trio's corporation, ENRC, was making an announcement to the London Stock Exchange. It was spending nearly $1 billion to buy Camec, the mining company that had acquired a Zimbabwean platinum prospect by agreeing to send Robert Mugabe's regime $100 million just when he needed funds to steal the 2008 election. Rautenbach's stake in Camec entitled him to a payout of $124 million from ENRC. The $5 million fine that was the cost of exoneration in South Africa was small change.

11

The Informant

Brooklyn, October 2009

The US unemployment rate passed 10 per cent in October 2009. Christmas was approaching, and half a million Americans were losing their jobs each month. In a Brooklyn courthouse, one American was pleading for a second chance. A third chance, if you counted the time he stabbed that guy as well as the mafia-backed stock fraud he was up for today. Felix Sater was forty-three. Today he would learn whether a judge would take the next twenty years from him. His mother and his sister were in court. Elsewhere, his three daughters awaited news.

The Honourable I. Leo Glasser commenced proceedings at 10 a.m. on October 23. He had seen plenty of life: won a Bronze Star fighting in Europe, came home and studied law in Brooklyn, named district judge by Ronald Reagan in 1981. It was he who John Gotti had loudly described as 'that faggot' at the start of his murder and racketeering trial. At the end of it, Glasser had sentenced Gotti to life without parole. He wore bow ties and spectacles and thought profoundly about the meaning of the law.

Felix himself was not short of material from which to compose the autobiography he would place before the judge. After public school in Brooklyn he had put himself through college at Pace University on Manhattan, studying accounting. A few blocks south of the campus lay Wall Street. This was the 1980s, the Wall Street of Gordon Gekko. Greed was good. Felix qualified as a broker and was soon making money at Bear Stearns, then at Lehman Brothers. He was still only twenty-five when, one night in 1991, as men of Wall Street do, he went out to a bar in Midtown – El Rio Grande – and drank too much. A fellow drinker got into an argument with Felix about a woman. Felix seized a margarita glass and smashed it into the man's face. He went down for a year. His broker's licence was revoked, so when he got out he had no legal way to get paid for his financial knowhow. A boyhood friend offered him the chance to come in on a scam. It was a pump-and-dump: you acquired stock in bullshit companies, talked some suckers into driving up the price by spending their savings buying the shares, then sold your own. Felix knew how to set up front companies to launder the proceeds. Soon the racketeers had made and washed $40 million.

'I'm not proud of what I have done,' Felix told Judge Glasser. With his paunch and his fleshy face, the dark hemispheres under his eyes, he looked as though no day of his life was easy. He could also flash a smile of unencumbered glee, but this was a solemn occasion. 'I felt I was trapped at the time I agreed to do it. I had a bar fight and went to jail, which is something I never thought I would ever do. Nobody ever thought I would go to jail for a bar fight. I had to find money for an appeal that my lawyer was trying to file and I didn't have a job. I had a four-month-old daughter at that moment, legal bills mounting, personal bills.' In time, Felix told the judge, he came to despise himself for his part in the scam. 'My parents did not sacrifice what they sacrificed to have me come to this country and become a criminal.'

This was a stretch. Crime ran in the family. Felix's parents left Moscow in the early seventies when Felix was six. The family followed the same route as many other Soviet Jews: Israel first, then the States. Brighton Beach, at the southern tip of Brooklyn, drew in ex-Soviets. Borscht joints sprang up along the shore. Soviet criminals seized the opportunity to expand into the capitalist world. Vyacheslav Ivankov was the most fearsome of them all. He was a *vor v zakone*, a thief-in-law, initiate of the highest circle of Soviet organised crime. Before Ivankov departed for the new world, Semyon Mogilevich, the Brainy Don, chief of the post-Soviet criminal moneymen, was said to have sprung him from a Russian prison. In Brighton Beach Ivankov developed one of the violence-to-finance networks that were taking shape, overseeing a diverse commercial conglomerate in which he supplied the savagery and left the business side to less heavily tattooed New York Russians. His group specialised in credit-card fraud and extortion. It washed millions of dollars through US banks and front companies, setting up its own or blackmailing legitimate enterprises into cooperating. Real estate was so perfect, it might have been built to launder. Typically, the idea was to own a property for a while then sell it on, thus transforming the original tainted money into the proceeds of a common-or-garden real estate deal. But one such property so took Ivankov's fancy that he moved into it: an apartment in a gilded skyscraper on Fifth Avenue, a couple of blocks down from Central Park, next to Tiffany's.

Ivankov, psychopath though he was, was careful to form alliances with the locals. He recognised an alignment of interests that had first been forged at a meeting in 1983 in Huntington, Long Island. A delegation of Russian gangsters from Brighton Beach had sat down with representatives of the Colombo organisation, one of the five Italian families that had run crime in New York since the Depression. They had come to discuss a fabulously successful scam concocted by Lawrence Iorizzo, a genius fraudster from Queens. Iorizzo was six feet tall and thirty stone. Fat Larry, they called him. It was said he could eat nine pizzas at a sitting.

Each of the two wives with whom he fathered a total of eight children remained, for a while at least, unaware of the other, despite living only fifteen minutes apart.

Fat Larry displayed a similar gift for duplicity in matters of commerce. He owned a growing chain of unbranded fuel stations on Long Island. Like all other filling station owners, he would add state and federal taxes to the prices he charged customers. But then he would shuffle the income along strings of offshore companies, ensuring that the final one went bust before the taxman got his share, the money having been siphoned off, like so much bootleg fuel, through Larry's pipeline of phony firms. Because they paid no taxes, Fat Larry's filling stations could charge less than his competitors. They were so successful that a pair of West Coast mafiosi resolved to snatch them. Fat Larry needed protection. For this he turned to the most frightening gangster on Long Island, Sonny Franzese. On paper, Franzese was merely the proprietor of a humble dry cleaners in Brooklyn. In truth, he was a senior figure in the Colombo family, making money from clubs, restaurants, strip bars and the music business. He put the fear of the Almighty into those who crossed him. The West Coasters thought better of their putative takeover, and in 1981 Fat Larry welcomed as a silent partner Franzese's stepson Michael, along with all the muscle his enterprise might require in future. Between them, Fat Larry and Michael Franzese super-charged the filling station scam. Their masterstroke was to bring in the Soviets.

The particular Soviet who joined the gathering in Long Island was Michael Markowitz. Of Romanian origin, he had arrived in the States via Israel in 1979, and now operated a fuel scam similar to Fat Larry's. The Italians could simply have dispatched Markowitz, perhaps in some colourful, cement-lined fashion that would have emphasised their territoriality. Instead they opted for a merger. Times were changing in the underworld; the Soviet arrivals could not simply be ignored or intimidated. Many of them had done time in labour camps. Some had connections to the KGB. There was little for them to fear in America, certainly not an FBI that kept doing soft deals with leading organised criminals. Nor, these days, even the five families, their leadership increasingly disrupted by rats and the occasional crusading prosecutor. Markowitz's boss, Evsei Agron, had arrived in Brighton Beach from St Petersburg and established his position with the help of an electric cattle prod.

The multinational fuel scammers reaped, by Fat Larry's estimation, $1 billion in their first year from filling stations across New York. Their rivals – oil companies whose bosses felt obliged to pay at least a portion of their taxes at home, not to mention the tithes due to Nursultan Nazarbayev and others who controlled their access to crude abroad – quietly signed up for racket fuel. The gangsters' tankers would refill stations belonging to Texaco, Chevron and Shell under cover of night.

Michael Franzese and Fat Larry bought yachts, planes and a $350,000 mobile home down in Florida, where Franzese would be named an honorary police commissioner. The fuel racket was the crowning enterprise in a portfolio that made him the biggest mafia moneymaker since Al Capone.

Fat Larry found the situation more stressful. He seemed to understand something that did not always dawn on those who came into illicit riches: that tainted money was easier to get than it was to hide, easier to hide than it was to clean, and that if it spilt out into the open, it sat there like a crude slick on the ocean surface, attracting an awful lot of attention. Running a fuel scam meant getting paid by customers scrabbling together a few grimy dollar bills to buy half a tank. Cash. Larry was drowning in cash. The Russian-Italian scammers would fly suitcases of it to Austria, where bankers didn't ask questions. Even so, it appeared the world could not absorb the volume of cash that Larry needed to unload. In the end he decided on radical measures: he burned the singles. He contemplated burning the fives. But in 1984, just a year after the merger with the Russians, Fat Larry got busted. He tried to cooperate with the FBI but ended up fleeing to Paris, a mafia contract on his head. There, despite some concerted dieting, he died. Michael Markowitz, the Russian mob's man in the scam, also spent his final years in fear. Like Larry, he turned informant when the racket was discovered. In 1989 he was shot dead as he drove his Rolls-Royce through Brooklyn.

Fuel scams proliferated, and with them the interconnections between America's Italian and Soviet criminal networks. At least four of the five families were involved, sometimes acting as an industry regulator overseeing the various competing Soviet operations. Soon Russians and Italians could be found arm-in-arm in assorted criminal ventures. In 2000 the police arrested a Soviet immigrant called Michael Sheferovsky for an extortion scheme that involved a kidnapping. Sheferovsky's partner was Ernest 'Butch' Montevecchi, a soldier in the Genovese family under the eccentric leadership of Vincent Gigante, who for decades deceived the authorities by shuffling around in bathrobe and slippers like a nutjob while maintaining a mind of such cunning that the Oddfather, as he became known, was regarded as the paramount don of the Cosa Nostra. With the Muscovite Sheferovsky, Butch spent the nineties going up and down Brighton Beach extorting the owners of restaurants, food stores and a clinic. Butch had been arrested in 1999 after a tap on his phone caught him participating in a stock fraud. Now Sheferovsky had got caught as well. He struck a deal with Loretta Lynch, the prosecutor in Brooklyn. For six years he assisted the FBI in their efforts to disrupt organised crime before, on the morning of June 20, 2006, he was brought before the court of the Eastern District for his lawful present to be weighed in the balance against his lawless past. His lawyer painted a piteous picture. Sheferovsky was in a poor state: bouts of cancer, heart trouble, depression. He drank, though that was, his lawyer said, 'based upon a factor in his upbringing and cultural issues and what has been going on lately in his life'.

A lawyer for the government had given the judge a report on Sheferovsky's endeavours as an informant, which included wearing a wire. Now he added that Sheferovsky had also tipped off the FBI about a $2 million Medicaid fraud among Brooklyn's Poles. 'To the extent that his cooperation was not more productive,' the government lawyer continued, 'it was largely the result of the fact that he was out of the game, so to speak, by the time he was arrested.'

His own lawyer chimed in. 'Mr Sheferovsky is now sixty-one, he has five grandchildren. He fortunately has a very supportive family. For someone that got involved in doing the things that have been described in the Russian community, mainly he regrets that. And to that end determined rather early on in the game to assist the government, not only to help himself but also to make amends for what he had done.'

Now his lawyer came to the sticky part. The crimes to which Sheferovsky had confessed carried a custodial sentence of between seven and nine years. 'I don't believe that the government objects at all to what we are asking for,' he said – namely, for Sheferovsky to be spared jail. It was, he accepted, 'quite a departure' from the norm. As for restitution, the government's lawyer informed the judge that 'the victims are either unidentifiable, dead or were extorted of money which was itself the proceeds of criminal activity'.

'All right,' said the judge. 'Mr Sheferovsky, is there anything that you would like to say before I sentence you?'

'Yes.'

'Please.'

'Honourable Judge, I am very sorry for all my life. I apologise to the government, to you, to my family. I never go back to criminal activity. This was a mistake in my life. I grew up in a tough country. My grandfather was shot like he was fighting the communism. I don't know, but I think if you give me a chance, don't go in jail, I think I will be a good citizen. I am really sorry, is what I am saying. I am sorry.'

'Thank you. All right. Are you ready to be sentenced?'

'Yes, sir.'

The judge read out his sentence. Three years' probation, a full financial disclosure, treatment for substance abuse and mental ill health. No drinking, no drugs. At the government's request, the record of the case was sealed from public view. 'Michael Sheferovsky' was the name on the docket, but the judge had to check, because the defendant seemed to have two names. His lawyer explained that he was known by both. 'In the Russian community he is known by Sheferovsky and the Americanized version is Sater. In his relationships with American people, it is Sater.'

Now, three years on, in the same court, under the same prosecutor, it was Sater's son's turn to plead his case.

'The acts I committed were despicable,' Felix Sater told the judge. 'They weren't just financial fraud. I took ability and opportunity and flushed them down the toilet.' He left the pump-and-dump scam, he said, because he did not want to be involved in criminal activity. To get away from it, he went to Russia, the land of his father, and worked in telecoms. And there began his next chapter, richer even than the earlier ones in material from which he could spin his story for the judge.

One night in Moscow, an American defence contractor got talking to Felix over dinner. When Felix went to the bathroom, the contractor followed him. In the safety of the gents, he surreptitiously arranged a rendezvous for the following day at an Irish

pub. There he proceeded to recruit Felix for US intelligence. Felix
was well suited to the task. He spoke fluent Russian, and wanted
thrills. Moreover, for reasons he did not expound in the letter
his lawyers had sent Judge Glasser before the hearing, he knew
people in Russian intelligence, too. Knew them sufficiently well,
in fact, that when an American spy asked him to help gather
information on an anti-missile system, he was able to get inside
the military installation where the Russians kept it. Somehow,
he could sidle up to the Americans' most prized targets. He
helped them track down a batch of Stinger anti-aircraft missiles
that the CIA had provided to the Afghan *mujahideen* back when
the US supported their cause against the invading Soviets. Islamist
terrorism was fast becoming a priority for those charged with
securing America: in 1998 al Qaeda blew up the US embassies
in Kenya and Tanzania, killing more than two hundred people.
The FBI was trying to trace its leader, Osama bin Laden. When
the pump-and-dump scam was discovered and Felix flew home
to face the consequences, he handed over a piece of paper on
which he had written five of bin Laden's satellite-phone numbers.
He pleaded guilty to racketeering, a crime that carried a twen-
ty-year prison sentence, for his part in what the police
commissioner called 'Goodfellas meet the Boiler Room'. But,
apart from forfeiting a house in the Hamptons, he was allowed
to remain at liberty, with his court file sealed, while he endeav-
oured to prove his worth as a law enforcement asset. He kept up
his intelligence work, now under the auspices of the FBI. After
the September 11, 2001 attacks, he once again demonstrated his
miraculous ability to win the confidence of America's enemies.
He cultivated the personal assistant to the Taliban leader Mullah
Omar and identified some of al Qaeda's American money launderers. He posed as a money launderer himself so convincingly
that he was able to infiltrate two transnational crime networks,
jetting to Cyprus and Turkey to play his roles. And there was

little he did not know about Russian organised crime. He fed the Americans information on the Red Mafiya, the oligarchs' criminal connections, even a scam involving accident insurance claims in the US.

Today in court it was his FBI handler, Leo Taddeo, who addressed the judge. Taddeo, a former Marine, was effusive. Felix had shown himself willing to turn on his criminal comrades. Like his father and the rest of the Soviet-born criminal cohort in New York, he had teamed up with the Cosa Nostra. Then he had shopped them. Taddeo explained to Judge Glasser that Felix had been instrumental in bringing down Frank Coppa. Coppa, a captain in the Bonanno family, was the king of the stock scams through which the mafia was penetrating Wall Street. But the FBI had struggled to nail him for any one scam – until, Taddeo explained, Felix joined their cause and incriminated Coppa. Soon Coppa himself was singing, helping to snare the top ranks of the Bonannos, a family so tight it had survived infiltration by the FBI agent who went by Donnie Brasco. Members of two of the other families had been involved in Felix's pump-and-dump scheme, providing the muscle that encouraged loyalty from corrupt brokers and saw off rivals. They had gone down too. One was Danny Persico, whose uncle, Carmine 'The Snake' Persico, ran the Colombo family from inside a federal penitentiary. The other was Ernest 'Butch' Montevecchi – the Genovese family soldier who had been Felix's father's accomplice back in their days extorting up and down Brighton Beach.

While helping to incarcerate this assortment of mobsters, Felix had been a model asset, his handler Taddeo told the judge. 'He answered every single phone call I made to him. He answered every question honestly. He did his best to be truthful and not exaggerate.' The FBI had spent the nineties struggling to stop criminal infiltration of Wall Street. 'Between success and failure for us is often an effective cooperating witness.' Felix Sater was that cooperating witness. 'I'm here today on his behalf,' Taddeo said. 'I hope that his family can get on with their lives and he can go on to be prosperous and a good dad and husband. I know he is.'

Felix's lawyer took up the story. Two moments of weakness, one when drunk and the other at the behest of an old friend, should not define a life, he argued. 'He made a stupid mistake in a bar fight and again that had a ripple effect which caused him to make another stupid mistake. But really since 1996 he has been working legitimate jobs, cooperating since 1998 with the government.' The lawyer said he hesitated to use the word 'redemption', then used it anyway. 'I think he has redeemed himself. He has made many, many amends.' He knew the request he was about to make was extraordinary, but nonetheless he asked the judge to give Felix no prison time at all, not even probation. The government's lawyer agreed: Felix, he said, had 'prevented far more financial fraud than he has caused'. His only known infraction since the pump-and-dump scam had been a couple of weeks earlier when, driving home after dinner out with his wife, he had narrowly failed a breath test.

Felix now spoke himself. He told the judge he could have ended his cooperation years earlier, but had chosen to keep going. 'I was asked many times by various agents, by various prosecutors, "Is it time to get sentenced yet?" I said, "No, I'm willing to continue working." I did it all because I want some redemption. Yes, I am a criminal. Yes, I am guilty of the things I have done.' His redemption had already suffered a grievous setback. 'I went into real estate development and I built a very successful real estate company,' he said. But then a reporter at the *New York Times* had discovered that this new figure on the real estate scene was in fact a brawling swindler, and that the Feds were covering up his past crimes in return for his cooperation. 'I had to leave my company,' Felix told the judge. 'The company that I built with my own two hands, otherwise the banks would have said, "There's a criminal involved." I had to get out.' The *New York Times* story had mentioned one of his ruses as a US intelligence asset: an offer to buy a dozen missiles that Osama bin Laden had put up for sale on the black market. A week later, Felix informed the judge, his daughter came home and told him the kids at school were saying her dad was a terrorist. 'I guess the worst thing that is going to happen and is happening is the blight I put on my children and I will now, in the past and in the future, try to do good deeds, try to be a positive member for my family and for my community, to in some way hopefully balance out the mountain of garbage I heaped on my own life.'

Mountain, Judge Glasser clearly thought, was the right word. The pump-and-dump conspiracy, he said, had been 'a massive series of securities frauds, which were conceived by a cadre of callous, corrupt villains'. He had often wondered how such crimes come about. 'I have been able to answer that question by assuming and believing that most of us have a little voice inside us which speaks to us when we think of or are about to do something wrong. It says to us, "Don't do it, it is wrong." And there were times that I have come to know that there are some persons who don't have that little voice. They never hear it, never listen to it. And there are some who do.' Felix Sater, the judge thought, had heard the voice but declined to listen to it when his old friend offered him in on the scam. And this was no petty crime. Most people, he said, define serious offences as those that 'inflict serious physical harm: murder, rape, burglary, assault. But the offence with which you were involved was also extremely serious.' Hundreds of people had lost money they had saved for their retirement or their children's education. In some respects the harm from such 'white-collar crime' was worse than those other offences, Glasser continued. As he was unable to administer 'a credible injection into your head and instantaneously instil respect for the law', the judge would just have to try to convey 'an understanding that when the law makes certain conduct illegal, it means it. That's what promoting respect for the law means. Believe what the law means when it says securities fraud is a crime. Don't do it. And the arm of the law is pretty long. It eventually will catch up to you.'

Glasser was approaching his decision. 'I sometimes like to think of a question that somebody said was asked about God. Somebody asked whether God prays. And the response was, "That's a remarkably silly question. God prays! What would God pray for?" And the answer was that God prays that his sense of mercy will overcome his desire for justice.' Yet Glasser faced a dilemma, the same one every judge dealing with an FBI informant had faced since 1994, when the Whitey Bulger scandal broke. An Irish mobster from south Boston, Whitey had helped the FBI catch the local Italian mafia boss – conveniently, Whitey's chief rival. This was back in the seventies, a time when the mafia embodied the anxiety that wholesome America had lost control of its cities. Thanks to the endeavours of his childhood friend and FBI handler John Connolly, Whitey went on to enjoy a couple of untroubled decades running the Boston drug trade and throttling anyone who threatened to expose his bargain with law enforcement. All along, he presented himself as a bulwark against the very scourge he was visiting on the city. Connolly took Whitey's money and fended off any attempt to go after him, portraying his thuggish pal as a gold-plated informant. Mostly, Whitey's intel was either worthless or had simply been recycled by Connolly from other sources. But that scarcely mattered. As any vaguely competent criminal strategist knew, co-option is even more powerful than fear. Yoke a cop, a businessman or a politician to your enterprise, as Whitey had done with Connolly, and suddenly they were not just protecting you, they were protecting themselves. The truth was yours to dispose of as you saw fit.

Felix Sater, as the court had heard at length from his lawyers and handlers, was on a different path, a straight path, the path of an upstanding New York real estate man, striving onwards even when the horrors of his past reappeared like a body discovered in the foundations of some redeveloped property. Still, although he did not refer to Whitey's case by name, Judge Glasser had evidently recognised that informants like the Boston gangster – or Felix Sater – who had been involved in complex crimes had an unjust advantage. 'The more sophisticated and knowledgeable the criminal, the more valuable is his cooperation and the more benefit he can obtain and offset the punishment which might otherwise have been imposed. We see that all of the time. Low-level drug dealers, couriers, have no information they can give to the government which would provide any assistance, so they suffer the sentence which the law requires.' To what extent, the judge asked himself, did Felix's efforts in the service of the law offset the twenty years it demanded be taken from him? 'I would suspect you had gone to bed every night or every other night sleeping a little restlessly and wondering what your sentence is going to be. Then, when the day of punishment comes, what will be my fate? For a period of eleven years – and it's true of cooperating generally – there is a kind of psychological imprisonment and burden which they carry over that long period of time.' Felix and his fellow racketeers were thieves, that was the word for it, but 'your cooperation over all of those years clearly manifests that you have a very sincere and deep respect for the law'.

The moment Felix had waited for through those eleven years had arrived. 'I'm going to impose,' began the judge who had sent John Gotti away for life without parole, 'a fine of $25,000.' That was it. The court file would remain sealed. Glasser had one final admonition. 'Next time you go to dinner with your wife,' he told Felix, 'drink more modestly.'

12

The Real

London, May 2010

The crisis of banks became a crisis of states on May 2, 2010. The financial calamities of 2008 had started to damage what was called 'the real economy', causing recessions worldwide. Governments that had spent fortunes to rescue banks saw the public purse deprived of tax revenues as businesses sacked their workers or closed altogether. Sovereign borrowing that had seemed manageable before the crisis was now impossible to repay. After a weekend of negotiations, European leaders agreed to loan Greece $146 billion to prevent it defaulting on its debts. In exchange, the government in Athens consented to reduce public spending dramatically, the better to service its creditors. This would be achieved by consigning a great many Greeks to destitution.

The reckoning was surely at hand. Nigel Wilkins had just turned sixty. At last, the time had come for him to strike his blow.

Not long after he alerted the authorities before departing BSI, someone from Her Majesty's Revenue and Customs had called. Nigel had offered to come to HMRC's offices, but was instead told to be outside the branch of WHSmith at Hammersmith station at 10 a.m. There he should look out for a man in a khaki jacket carrying a khaki bag, and when he saw him, should follow him. Nigel had waited as instructed, spotted the khaki man and walked after him for a mile until he heard a voice calling his name. He looked round and saw another man beckoning him into a hotel. 'We did this just to make sure that no one else knew where you were going and to make sure you weren't being followed,' the tax agent explained.

Nigel had talked to the agent and his partner for four hours, and handed over a list of BSI clients. 'You probably won't hear from us again,' the agent had said.

Each day, Nigel waited to open his newspaper and see that the Swiss bankers he had exposed had been brought to justice. Maybe even their clients too. Either that, or some accident might befall him the way it had befallen other whistleblowers from inside the financial secrecy industry. They are bigger than you, Charlotte had warned him when he decided to take them on, they will squash you. She knew it wasn't vanity that drove him on, even if it sometimes looked that way. The plunderers might try to spin their own histories, but Nigel knew what he had seen with his own eyes, the sheets of paper in his red boxes, the records of where money had come from, where it had gone and the disguises it had worn. That was what Nigel insisted on: the past – the past was real.

PART II

CHRYSALIS

'You are a slow learner, Winston,'
said O'Brien gently.

'How can I help it?' he blubbered. 'How can I
help seeing what is in front of my eyes?
Two and two are four.'

'Sometimes, Winston. Sometimes they are five.
Sometimes they are three. Sometimes they are
all of them at once. You must try harder. It
is not easy to become sane.'

George Orwell,
Nineteen Eighty-Four

13

Beginnings

London, December 2010

Of the Trio, it was Sasha Machkevitch who most enjoyed the spotlight. But he liked his public life to be choreographed. Lately, it had been distinctly freeform. Others had been far more embarrassed by the WikiLeaks cables, but still, it hardly sat well with the munificent, cosmopolitan image Sasha was busily cultivating to be sniggered at as a penny-pinching hick. 'It is not clear what Machkevitch is spending his billions on,' went the cable from the US embassy in Astana to Foggy Bottom, 'but it is certainly not culinary talent. On all four occasions the Ambassador has eaten at one of his houses, the menu has been similar.' Sasha's cook had served beshbarmak, a dish of boiled meat with noodles, and pilaf. 'The wait staff appeared to be graduates of a Soviet cafeteria training academy. The wine, at least, was somewhat upscale with reasonably good French vintage bottles uncorked for the guests. The Astana residence has wooden plaques on the doors that would fit in nicely in a Wyoming hunting lodge but are somewhat out of touch with the upscale "Euro-remont" that is so popular among the Kazakhstani elite.'

Those Westerners could sneer all they liked. Just look at the latest Forbes list. After three years as gentlemen of the London

Stock Exchange, Sasha, like his partners Ibragimov and Chodiev, came in at $3.3 billion in 2010. More than Lauder, more than Spielberg. He was worth three Tom Barracks or T. Boone Pickens. And yet you didn't want too much attention. Anything worth knowing about money was worth keeping secret, except how much of it you had. Which was why the email that arrived in ENRC's inbox on December 20, 2010 was unsettling. The sender was anonymous, described only as an engineer at Rudny.

Rudny: the huge iron mine carved from the punishing expanses up by Kazakhstan's border with Russia. It was a fountain of money for the Trio, one of the prime assets that formed their corporation, ENRC. The engineer wrote that he had felt compelled 'to report certain facts of corruption and malpractice' at the mine, and listed them. Contractors inflated their costs in exchange for kickbacks. The company budget was being used to pay for work on a boss's farm. Farhad Ibragimov, nephew to Alijan Ibragimov, Sasha's partner in the Trio, was alleged to be on the take. As the engineer described it, Rudny was being run as a racket for the benefit of a handful of its managers, leaving everyone else to contend with shitty equipment.

The email appeared to have been copied to Kazakhstan's intelligence agency and chief prosecutor. No problem there: both answered to Nazarbayev, the Trio's patron. But these days ENRC was a UK public company, one of the most valuable. It had a London headquarters beside the royal park at St James's. It had directors and legal compliance officers. They read the email and resolved to follow standard procedure for a major listed corporation: hire a big City law firm to look into the allegations. That way you could control the investigation, decide who, if anyone, would be handed over to the authorities, and what those authorities would be told. On the face of it, this was a case of fraud against the company rather than anything more serious like, say, bribery. But for the Trio there was a danger. If someone began digging at Rudny, perhaps they would start to unearth the past. If they dug deep enough, maybe they would get all the way to the beginning.

*   *   *

Back when Moscow was still the capital of an empire, Boris Birshtein would alight from his twenty-eight-seat private jet and sweep through customs like a dignitary to where his motorcade awaited with a police escort to accompany him up to Lenin Hills. At the entrance to his magnificent villa on Kosygin Street, some of the armed guards wore military uniform; others were in plain clothes and carried KGB identity cards. Round of face with a bushy moustache, Birshtein would emerge from his limousine dressed like wealth personified in a sable-lined coat adorned with a diamond brooch.

'I'm for many years in business with Soviet Union,' he once told a reporter. 'I started with Brezhnev and, you know, somehow I manage to get in some way unique position and I met lot of people and made friendship with a lot of very powerful people.' Born in Lithuania, he had departed first to Israel, settled in Toronto in 1982, then begun commuting from Canada back to the USSR. 'I spent a lot of time, step by step, meeting a lot of people, building connections and relations. These connections led me to the top.' But now, with Gorbachev in power and the Soviet empire changing day by day in unthinkable ways, the question was whether those who occupied the top today would occupy the top tomorrow. 'Boris always wanted more than money,' one of the managers of his trading business in Moscow concluded. 'He wanted influence. Money was just a tool for this.' There were two crowds you needed if you were going to retain your influence through the coming transformation: the spooks and the crooks. Boris Birshtein had ways in with both.

Across town from Lenin Hills, at a four-storey peachy-beige building around the corner from Red Square, the incipient capitalism with which the name of Birshtein was growing synonymous was dismaying a servant of the Party called Anton Volkov. Volkov had been away from KGB headquarters for years, posted in the West. Now he was back, and had been assigned to the First Chief Directorate, the body that oversaw foreign operations. Vladimir Kryuchkov, the head of the directorate from 1974 until his recent promotion to KGB chairman, had impeccable totalitarian credentials. As a young diplomat in Budapest in 1956, he had displayed fierce opposition to the Hungarian revolution that was put down by Soviet forces. But he had also had the misfortune to accompany Gorbachev on his trip to Washington in 1987 to sign the arms control treaty that spelled the end. Back in Moscow, Gorbachev gave orders that the Party work out how to turn power into money before the former ran out. 'The top priority,' Volkov recalled Kryuchkov decreeing, 'should be developing the KGB banking and business empire.' Henceforth, the First Chief Directorate, for decades devoted to destabilising capitalism, would adopt the ways of the Main Adversary. Volkov would go to work in the morning and someone would call and ask, 'How is our venture with the Koreans going?' After lunch someone else would call. 'How is our venture with the Americans going?' No one was talking about national security. Everything was business; there was no time for intelligence work. Volkov thought: the country is dead.

The Party already had a business manager, Nikolay Kruchina, who was in charge of assets including a property portfolio alone that was worth $9 billion. In August 1990, with the union already disintegrating, Kruchina's superior, deputy general secretary Vladimir Ivashko, sent a secret memorandum to Gorbachev. He proposed a major expansion of the party's joint ventures with international businesspeople as a means to hide its riches and maintain influence abroad. That was all well and good, but seventy-three years of communism had left the regime short of capitalist acumen. Everyone was talking about the market economy, Volkov noticed, but no one knew anything about it. No one except the likes of one of Volkov's colleagues in the KGB's First Chief Directorate, Colonel Leonid Veselovsky. He had served in Portugal and Zürich, assigned to one of the most delicate international missions: distributing financial support to communists in the West. During the Cold War, hundreds of millions of Soviet dollars had passed through companies known as 'friendly firms' to organisations around the world that supported the cause. The firms would purchase Soviet raw materials cheaply and resell them in the West at the far higher market price. The difference would be deposited in the bank accounts of sympathetic organisations operating in those Western states. It was a delightful use of capitalism against itself. Now, Volkov learned, Colonel Veselovsky had been tasked with a similar mission that had a different purpose: hiding the Soviet regime's wealth before whoever might take over could get their hands on it. Veselovsky elaborated his plan in a memo to the Central Committee. He would move Party funds abroad by setting up companies to receive them in Western countries – places with what he called a 'mild taxation system', such as Switzerland. There was no question that the authorities in those places might object to the arrival of these new riches. As Volkov knew from his time in the West, nobody there cared about money laundering.

The Party gold: that was what they called the money that was smuggled out of the dying empire. How much departed? A billion dollars, some calculated. Volkov reckoned that much had been shifted out through one bank alone. One KGB defector put the figure at $50 billion.

At Boris Birshtein's villa in Lenin Hills, KGB men would come and go. He appointed a veteran of the KGB unit that protected the most powerful politicians as his head of security. His company signed up to business ventures planned by a Russian academic, Georgi Arbatov – better known within the KGB by his codename, Vasili. And Birshtein also found work for the architect of the KGB's money-laundering system: Colonel Veselovsky. The two had met when Veselovsky, during a brief promotion to the Communist Party's Central Committee, had negotiated Birshtein's lease of the Lenin Hills villa. The mansions were usually reserved for visiting statesmen – Kissinger, Castro – but Birshtein got his way. Soon afterwards, he gave Veselovsky a contract to work for his company with the title 'economic adviser'. Veselovsky returned to the city where he had once been posted for the KGB: Zürich, the global capital of clandestine money. Birshtein furnished him with lakeside accommodation and a silver Mercedes. Zürich was full of ex-Soviets making like bigshots. 'A lot of Russians are coming saying we have millions – and at the end, it's nothing,' a Swiss accountant who worked with them observed. Veselovsky, by contrast, 'seems to be for real – he comes with money with a government stamp'.

Around the time he recruited Veselovsky, Birshtein's fortunes experienced a sudden change for the better. Previously, he had been struggling with creditors. But the half-dozen joint ventures his company, Seabeco, formed with Russian firms in 1991 and 1992 were highly profitable. Seabeco's annual turnover reached half a billion dollars. Eight hundred employees across the globe were engaged in the fabulously lucrative trade between the collapsing communist empire, where for a pittance you could buy chemicals or fertiliser or metals from some woebegone factory, mine or stockpile, and the capitalist world beyond. Birshtein branched out from Russia into the other new ex-Soviet republics: a casino in Moldova, steel in Ukraine. The transition to capitalism would open the odd wormhole: during Birshtein's project to transport Kyrgyz gold, $4 million went missing. He opened offices

in Switzerland and in Europe's ancient trading city, Antwerp.
And he became acquainted with the new force that was injecting
some entrepreneurial flair: the gangsters.

Boris Birshtein met Mikhas at a reception thrown by the
Moldovan president. They got talking. Mikhas – Sergei Mikhailov
was his real name – had grown up in a dingy corner of nineties
Moscow inaptly called Solntsevo, or Sunnyside. In his youth he
had travelled the Soviet Union deploying his mountainous
physique in Greco-Roman wrestling tournaments. Back in
Moscow, he took a job managing a hotel for apparatchiks, but
with the coming of capitalism embarked on a career in business.
The commercial climate was one that could be termed hostile:
Mikhas would come to consider that his greatest success in business was staying alive. He would also breezily deny that he had
anything to do with the organisation he had founded: the
Solntsevskaya brotherhood, named after his home district. Putting
his faith in God, Orthodox superstitions and associates who
helped him open bank accounts abroad – including, naturally,
in Switzerland – he oversaw the brotherhood's international
expansion. His people arrived in America on visas sponsored by
IBM. After a while, the FBI drew up a list of the brotherhood's
commercial activities: drug trafficking, visa fraud, bribery, murder,
money laundering and extortion. Mikhas was arrested in Russia
for the latter offence in 1989, but was not convicted. The brotherhood grew into Moscow's foremost mafia. It had two thousand
members, operating in franchises. For muscle, it drew on the
vory, tattooed thieves such as Vyacheslav Ivankov, forged in the
communist gulags. But its leaders, Mikhas in particular, belonged
to a new type of capitalist criminal, the *avtoritet*, or business
gangster.

Trust was important in business, Mikhas believed, and he felt
Boris Birshtein trusted him. When both of them took houses in
Switzerland, Birshtein would invite him round; he introduced

Mikhas to Alex Shnaider, the son-in-law he was grooming as his heir. Mikhas and Birshtein made plans. The most ambitious was to get in on the biggest of all the money-spinning trades between East and West: by reviving a gas pipeline running from the Central Asian fields to Ukraine, the doorway to Europe, with all its insatiable hobs, radiators and power stations. Mikhas was planning to invest $150 million. But then, in 1996, he was arrested as he landed in Geneva and charged with organised crime, unlawful residence and buying Swiss property illegally. Two years later – after a key witness was murdered by unknown assailants, Russian prosecutors working with the Swiss were suddenly fired, and promised evidence failed to arrive – Mikhas was cleared of the charges. Nonetheless, businessmen such as Boris Birshtein who were keen to preserve their status in the overworld wanted nothing more to do with him. And by then, Birshtein had problems of his own.

In the summer of 1993, Boris Yeltsin's government had been on the verge of collapse. Moscow's criminal moneymen were universally in favour of Yeltsin's rule, permissive both by inclination and inebriation. Corruption, the use of public office for private gain, was not some threat to the system; it was the system. And that meant politics became something new: a game of secrets, in which your money was power, but so was knowing where your enemy hid his and how he had made it. That was the game Boris Birshtein lost.

Yeltsin was desperate to neutralise the threat from his deputy, a nationalist former fighter pilot called Aleksandr Rutskoi who had taken to calling Yeltsin's policy of 'shock therapy' – the attempt to turn Russia capitalist in a hurry that caused a collapse in living standards – 'economic genocide'. A corruption inquiry provided the means. In late August, the lawyer Yeltsin had appointed to run the inquiry called a press conference in Moscow. He alleged that millions of dollars had been diverted from Russia's sorely depleted coffers by way of a deal in which Russian cotton worth $20 million had been traded for baby food worth just $10,000. From the huge profit on the trade a kickback had been deposited into a Swiss account. A further $3 million, from the sale of farm machinery, had arrived in another Swiss account. Both accounts were secretly controlled by Rutskoi. Yeltsin suspended his vice president, 'pending clarification'. One of Yeltsin's senior officials warned that 'corruption has penetrated into the top echelons of power, and if the situation remains unchanged, the state itself will become criminal'. The company at the centre of the affair had, the official said, been created by the Communist Party in the last years of the Soviet Union to smuggle state money to the West. This company was likened to an 'octopus that enveloped the Russian economy'. It was called Seabeco – Boris Birshtein's corporation, its name emblazoned in gold letters on the side of his private jet.

Birshtein had boasted of knowing Rutskoi, a repeated visitor to the Lenin Hills villa. When Rutskoi was jailed after a failed rebellion, Birshtein was finished in Moscow. Yeltsin would recall with disgust the sole time he met him, in the company of a minister who appeared to be Birshtein's puppet. 'A country can't be rich if it has no rich people in it. There is no real human independence without private property. But money, big money (which is actually a relative concept) is always, under any circumstances, a seduction, a test of morals, a temptation to sin … In order to cross that ethical line, in order to run that red stoplight, under Russian conditions you don't necessarily have to peddle pornography, sell drugs, or deal in contraband cheap goods. Why fool around with such nickel-and-dime stuff? It's easier to buy one government official after another. Birshtein tried to get to the very top – and he almost made it.'

The Rutskoi Affair left Boris Birshtein incensed. 'It's not a secret for anybody that there is corruption in Russia, but I'm not

a policeman,' he said. 'I never in my life did anything illegal.'
He retreated to Switzerland. Seabeco would soon be no more.
But Birshtein had helped to start something much larger. Anton
Volkov, the KGB man, kept a close eye. 'Seabeco,' he saw, 'was
the nest that gave birth to a lot of little birds.' An immense
transfer of resources from the state to private interests would
soon be under way, creating new kleptocracies from the Baltic
to the Pacific. Birshtein's fledglings were circling overhead. Among
them were three ambitious Central Asians: a diplomat, a trader
and a philologist.

14

Big Yellow

Finchley, February 2011

Back in his university days in Toronto, Peter Sahlas would listen riveted to his international relations professor, Janet Stein. She would interpret history through psychology, from the First World War to the Bay of Pigs, then apply her techniques to the old men in Moscow playing out the endgame of the Soviet empire. Peter came to believe that the events that shaped the world happened the way they did because powerful people made choices based on their own interests and foibles. Listening to Mukhtar Ablyazov speak for day after day at Tower 42, he saw just that: for all the great forces at play in the former Soviet Union, for all the economic shockwaves of the financial crisis, here was a corrupt dictator pursuing an honest businessman because he wouldn't pay him off.

But where Peter felt the truth of Ablyazov's story, Trefor Williams detected lies.

Williams was an athletic Welshman, a champion rower who had served in the British special forces. Now his talents were available to paying clients. Diligence, the corporate intelligence firm that employed him, was known as one of the most effective in London. Williams had a reputation for being able to hunt down pretty much anyone or anything, with a particular knack for finding money. He loved his work, loved the chase. He had decorated Diligence's offices in a skyscraper at Canary Wharf with his collection of James Bond posters. But he spent much of his life on the road – Cyprus one week, a Caribbean island the next – seeking out the human beings behind front companies. Today, February 11, 2011, the quarry was a little closer: a Big Yellow storage facility in north London.

Williams and his teams of bloodhounds had been tracking Ablyazov and his associates for months. They watched them as they came and went from Tower 42 and from Ablyazov's residence in Highgate. Williams was convinced they were hiding something. Four months ago his team had watched the oligarch's brother-in-law, Salim, load up his Lexus with crates of documents. They followed him as he drove to the Big Yellow opposite a BP garage on the North Circular in East Finchley. Salim went in, returned without the crates and drove off. Williams' team hired a storage unit so they could get inside and observe Salim each time he visited. But the warehouse was vast, row upon row of padlocked doors. To avoid arousing his suspicions, they had to keep their distance. They saw that he was going to the second floor, then taking the first right and the second left. Finally they had got close enough to see the precise unit: E2010. There was no time to lose. If Salim realised he had been rumbled, whatever was behind the door of E2010 would vanish. Williams sent word to Chris Hardman, a top lawyer at Hogan Lovells, the City law firm. Hardman had, like Williams, been retained by BTA, the bank Nazarbayev's regime had seized from Ablyazov. Hardman had brought a suit in London against Ablyazov accusing him of looting BTA and stashing the money abroad. He swiftly persuaded a judge to grant permission for a search of the Big Yellow unit, then, as Williams waited outside, looked on as the manager snipped off the padlock with bolt cutters.

Inside unit E2010 were twenty-five crates of documents and a hard drive. They revealed a web comprising thousands upon thousands of front companies. Money that belonged to BTA Bank had passed through this web – as a loan to build an aquarium in Moscow, say, or a port on the White Sea – and ended up with companies apparently under Ablyazov's control. BTA had had auditors signing off on its accounts – EY, one of the Big Four – but now the new owners sent in PwC, who looked at the books and told a different story. Billions of dollars were missing, the bank's new owners alleged. Ablyazov had an alternative explanation: BTA went bust because Nazarbayev had first destroyed confidence in it with slanderous announcements, then expropriated it. Bollocks, thought Trefor Williams. He was convinced Ablyazov was no dissident, just playing to the gallery of Western liberals to disguise what he really was: a master thief.

*   *   *

Upon arriving in London, Ablyazov had considered hiring some private spooks himself, to counter the intelligence operation he was sure Nazarbayev had launched. He arranged to visit a firm called Arcanum in Knightsbridge, next to Hyde Park. In its offices a silver chessboard stood on a mounting shaped like a fist. Arcanum's founder, Ron Wahid, was a portly Bangladeshi-American. He mostly wore a suit and loafers, no tie, a spray of stubble on his chin. He could be genial. But he could also turn, with a temper some who knew him attributed to insecurity, so much so that he seemed to some to have a dual personality. Depending on who you believed – not an easy decision in such matters – Wahid was either one of the most sophisticated espionage mercenaries or a con artist who made a lot of money by masquerading as one. In the nineties, he had noticed that the neoliberal vogue for outsourcing public services had spread to the state's most sacred duty: security. If Erik Prince of Blackwater could make a fortune providing guns for hire to do America's fighting, Ron Wahid could make money doing its spying: a third of the workforce of the US intelligence agencies were contractors. And the trend was not confined to the land of the free. As globalisation disconnected corporations from nations, private security firms could adopt a business model like that of Glencore or the other stateless commodity traders, catering to all regimes and accountable to none. Indeed, some became intelligence traders, extracting information one day for a client to whose enemies they would offer their services – and what they had learned – the next.

Wahid and his people met Ablyazov and his people three times, first at the Arcanum offices, then at smart hotels nearby. Bota Jardemalie went along. The week she had thought she would have to spend away from Kazakhstan had turned into months. Her role was changing, without her having much say in it, from jet-set corporate lawyer to lieutenant in a campaign of resistance to a dictator. The first time she saw Wahid, Bota was struck by his look: sapphire cufflinks, custom-made alligator shoes. 'I've never seen rich people trying so hard to show how rich they are,' she thought. Wahid would arrive with an entourage. They would produce gadgets to jam any eavesdropping devices that might be nearby. Bota didn't know what to make of the fast-talking, name-dropping Wahid. He would say things like, 'Meet me at the new bar of the Berkeley Hotel at midnight.' She would go, and he would order champagne. She had the impression he considered everyone but himself an idiot. He gave her a Sony laptop with a fake alligator-skin cover. She never opened it.

Wahid boasted to Bota that he knew everyone in the Kazakh elite. There seemed to be some truth in that. He knew Sugar had worked for the Trio too. He liked to drop hints that he was some sort of CIA man, swanning in and out of Langley. He made much of his Washington connections. On the walls of Arcanum's office hung signed photographs of three US presidents: Bushes senior and junior and Bill Clinton.

Wahid described to Ablyazov the capabilities he could offer. Ablyazov found him pushy, pitching Arcanum as a super-service that had enormous resources at its disposal. He didn't buy it. The relationship lapsed.

Ablyazov's life in exile was rather more comfortable than that of the typical human flotsam that washed up in the UK. His residences rivalled even the president's. The Bishops Avenue in Highgate was known as Billionaires' Row: Ablyazov's mansion was a couple of doors down from the one Nazarbayev owned through a front company. Ablyazov's country pile, set in a hundred acres just west of London, was not far from Sunninghill, the estate that Nazarbayev's son-in-law Timur Kulibayev had bought from Prince Andrew.

Ablyazov's family, like his fortune, was gradually transitioning from East to West. While he was in a Kazakh prison camp, his first child, Madina, set off to boarding school in Hertford. She already spoke more English than her parents, thanks to the month's course they had sent her on in Edinburgh. When, after Ablyazov's release, her parents came to Europe, Madina would serve as driver, translator and fixer, shuttling them between the weddings, birthdays and holidays to which the Kazakh establishment decamped more or less en masse. On a trip to Nice in 2006, she had been required to do even more shepherding than usual. Her mother had morning sickness, evidence of the rather surprising incipience of Alua, a fourth child nineteen years after the first. Her father had an appointment at some hotel to meet another Kazakh politician, Viktor Khrapunov; Madina accompanied him. Relations between the two men were frosty. Khrapunov had never adjusted to life after communism. Under the Soviets he had risen from technician on the Almaty grid to a senior boss running the city's power. The electrical system meant a great deal to him – he bore the scars from the third-degree burns he suffered trying to staunch a burst boiling water pipe at a power station. By the time he was serving as Almaty's mayor, capitalism had arrived, personified by the likes of Ablyazov, and it wanted to take things away. Ablyazov said Almaty's power should be privatised so he could buy it himself. Khrapunov believed the state should not surrender such a vital asset. Unpleasant articles about Khrapunov appeared in Ablyazov's newspaper. Nonetheless, they were now on speaking terms, and Ablyazov wanted to rent a property from Khrapunov.

Madina delivered her father to the meeting. Khrapunov's stepson Iliyas was there. He had long, gelled-back hair and appeared to be going through a hippy phase. Madina was petite, sparky and winsome, with enormous brown eyes. She took one look at Iliyas and thought: not my type. Still, they chatted and, out of politeness as much as anything, offered to show one another round their respective towns, should they ever pass through. Iliyas had been in Geneva since he started boarding school there in 1998. Madina was living in London, embarking on a business and media degree. They exchanged numbers. Later that year, he came to London and called. He had cut his hair. Madina upgraded her opinion to: he's all right. He looked kind. And he was bubbly, unlike those uptight Kazakh boys she had dated. After a few months, by the time they sat down for dinner at the Dorchester with their parents in February 2007, she was madly in love. When Iliyas produced a ring, everyone behaved very properly. His parents had been reluctant at first, but Ablyazov at least seemed no longer to be in open conflict with Nazarbayev. The dinner and the proposal passed cordially.

The next day, as he set off back to Geneva, Iliyas opened a note from Madina. *I've been stupid, I'm too young, I'm not ready, the ring is in the suitcase.* When he called her, she sobbed. Ablyazov had made her do it. They agreed to continue their romance in secret. She would buy phone cards so the calls from London to Geneva would not show up on the bills her father paid. The next summer, 2007, both families were back on the Riviera – Cannes this time. Iliyas sneaked into Madina's hotel to see her, but ran into Ablyazov, who confronted Madina. She refused to break it off again. I can't break his heart any more, she told her father angrily, I love him. It's him or me, her father replied. He was hatching plans – plans that for now had to be clandestine, because of the promise to stay out of politics with which he had secured his freedom – and Madina marrying Iliyas would not help. Cool off, Madina told him, let's talk later. My father, she thought once she was alone, is never going to change his mind. She packed her bags. Before leaving, she texted Ablyazov the time of the dinner he was due to attend that night, and when the bus would leave the hotel, then turned off her phone.

Iliyas had recruited his sister's fiancé to help with the escape – Dimi, the son of Gennady Petelin, once a big fish in the Kremlin. Dimi parked his Jaguar outside the lobby. Madina and Iliyas jumped in. But before they could set off, one of Ablyazov's business partners emerged from the hotel. He owned car dealerships back in Kazakhstan, and approached the Jaguar to admire it. The lovers cowered on the back seat, shielded by the tinted windows. A porter had placed Madina's suitcase beside the vehicle. It was large, red, and bore a big yellow sticker with her name on it. Dimi seized the suitcase, stuffed it in the boot, started the engine and drove away. Madina was shaking. What am I doing to my mother and father, she thought. They went straight to where Iliyas's parents were staying. When she turned her phone on the next morning, there were a great many missed calls. Her mother Alma rang again and told Madina of the havoc she was causing. Upon being told that his big sister had eloped, one of her brothers had said: Who's going to pack my luggage? Alma was losing it, shouting down the phone. Madina was crying. Standing over her, Iliyas's mother, Leila, could listen to this no longer. She took the phone from Madina. Alma, she said, stop making her cry, they are going to get married, and it's up to you: either you are going to see the grandchildren or you're not.

The wedding took place in Almaty three weeks later. Viktor Khrapunov invited Nazarbayev. The president replied: 'I am not coming to a party that my political enemy is organising.' Ablyazov was still refusing to hand over a stake in his bank. Nazarbayev had let it be known that attendance was discouraged. Most of the guests were from Ablyazov's side, and thus already out of favour by dint of their relationship with him. The following week, the couple threw a party in Geneva. The father of the bride was stressed: apparently a crisis was coming that would be dangerous for banks, including his. Unlike the wedding, all sorts came to this celebration. Tevfik Arif flew in. Back in Kazakhstan, he had explored some money-making opportunities with the Khrapunovs, and they had made investments worth millions with Arif's company, Bayrock. He was in New York these days, making it big in real estate. That was the game young Iliyas wanted to get into. In fact, Arif's partner was going to help him get started. He rolled up at the wedding party in Geneva too. A Russian-American, very New York, name of Felix Sater.

*   *   *

While Trefor Williams' sleuths were staking out Big Yellow, on January 29, 2011, Mukhtar Ablyazov received an urgent message from the Metropolitan Police. An Osman Warning, they called it. Ablyazov 'may be subject of a kidnap or physical harm, which may be politically motivated', the message said. 'The Police cannot protect you from this threat on a day-by-day, hour-by-hour basis.'

Desertion from Nazarbayev's regime was not tolerated. Zamanbek Nurkadilov, a jittery former mayor and minister who had joined the opposition, was found on the floor of his billiards room. The police declared his death a suicide – a particularly dextrous one, given that two bullets had entered his chest and a third his head. Altynbek Sarsenbayev, formerly Nazarbayev's information minister and ambassador to Moscow and a friend of Ablyazov, had always had a liberal streak. In government he had quarrelled with the president, but when he finally broke with the boss, the opposition party he helped to found was relatively mild. He wanted reform, compromise. Two months after the 2005 election, in which Nazarbayev was declared the winner with 91 per cent of the vote, Sarsenbayev was shot in the back of the head on a suburban street in Almaty. The hands of his driver and bodyguard had been bound before they too were executed. Initially, the authorities intimated that the killers had held a business grudge against Sarsenbayev. Then they switched the blame to what they said were five members of the KNB's specialist Tiger unit who had gone rogue.

There was an alternative theory. It was put about by Sugar, the president's own son-in-law. Sugar had received intelligence that implicated Nazarbayev himself in Sarsenbayev's assassination. Or so he claimed, once he too had joined the ranks of the traitors.

Sugar. They called him that because a swathe of the Kazakh sugar industry formed part of the extensive portfolio of business interests that he had used his position to grab. Nazarbayev had granted this man, Rakhat Aliyev, access to the two most sacred places in his domain: his intelligence agency and his daughter's bed. Sugar had been twenty when he married Dariga, in 1983. He trained first as a surgeon, then as a lawyer. His wife's father, rising towards the apex of power, was entrancing. 'He would call me his son,' Sugar would recall, 'and I regarded him like a father.'

Once he was ruler and Kazakhstan was independent, Nazarbayev appointed his pudgy son-in-law to key positions in his dual state. Sugar was named head of the tax police, a body, as Mikhail Khodorkovsky learned in Russia, that was useful for reining in overmighty businessmen. Then he became deputy head of the KNB. As he gained power, an ambition stirred in Sugar's breast: he wanted to sit one day in the biggest chair of all.

In the late nineties, an opportunity presented itself. He could simultaneously score points with the old man and damage two sets of rivals at once. The first, Akezhan Kazhegeldin, was due his comeuppance. He had resigned as prime minister to challenge Nazarbayev for the presidency, an affront that could not go unpunished. Kazhegeldin spoke fluent Western. He had presided over privatisation and was now in exile, hailed as thwarted reformer. Sugar thought he could smear Kazhegeldin by claiming he had enjoyed a taste of the kickbacks that the Belgian company Tractebel had paid, via the Trio, to win a Kazakh power contract. Both the exile and the oligarchs denied any such illicit enrichment. But Sugar's idea was less to seek the truth than to destabilise competitors.

Sugar survived the sensational backfiring of this scheme, which inadvertently alerted law enforcement agencies across the West to the secret bank accounts into which Nazarbayev received bribes. He was banished from the presidential court for a while, dispatched to Austria as Kazakhstan's ambassador in 2002. But three years later he was called home. Nazarbayev needed his skills as a schemer to help rig the presidential election.

It was after his victory in that election that Nazarbayev began to prepare a constitutional amendment that would allow him to remain *elbasy* ('leader of the nation') for life. Sugar decided he did not have that kind of time. As he would tell the story: 'I directly confronted him on this change and told him that I would be running for president in 2012. The confrontation was highly charged and prompted the avalanche of conflict that exists between me and President Nazarbayev today.'

Sugar's downfall was immediate. No sooner had he resumed his ambassadorship in Austria in February 2007 than he learned that he had been accused of abducting two managers at a Kazakh bank he owned. Other charges followed. He was alleged to have run a mafia-style network inside Kazakhstan, to have been laundering illicit income through front companies in the Middle East and Europe in heroic quantities, sometimes $10 million a day. In the US, the president's lobbyists spread word that it had been Sugar, not Nazarbayev, who had ordered the death of Sarsenbayev, purportedly because Sarsenbayev had informed the president of Sugar's coup-plotting.

Kazakh investigators searched for *kompromat* on the fallen prince. They found what they needed when, shortly after Sugar's break with Nazarbayev, a woman alerted the authorities to the fate years earlier of her daughter, Anastasiya Novikova. Young, blonde and beautiful, Anastasiya had been a newsreader on Sugar's television station. The investigators discovered that she had also been Sugar's lover, with whom he had been two-timing the first daughter. She had lived in Austria during Sugar's posting there until, heavily pregnant, she moved to Lebanon. Her daughter was not a year old when Anastasiya's body, dressed in pyjamas, was found impaled on railings five floors below an apartment belonging to a relative of Sugar's. The Kazakh investigators, supported by the dead girl's parents, developed a theory that Sugar had forced Anastasiya into a sham marriage to conceal their affair, and then, when he suspected her of infidelity, instructed his henchmen to drug her, repeatedly rape her and, when she died, fake her suicide.

Such evidence as they could muster for the more baroque parts of the tale was inconclusive, but this and the other accusations of depravity and venality were sufficient ammunition for the

campaign against Sugar. He was stripped of his ambassadorship
and the diplomatic immunity that went with it. Kazakhstan
formally asked Austria to send this criminal home. A court in
Vienna refused the extradition request on the grounds that Sugar
was at risk of persecution if repatriated. But the law at home
exhibited no such stubbornness. Sugar was convicted, in his
absence, of kidnapping, forgery, embezzlement, running an
organised crime group, abuse of office, coup-plotting, arms
trafficking and the illegal disclosure of state secrets, including
espionage on behalf of Austria and the US. A civil court and a
military tribunal each sentenced him to twenty years in a penal
colony. His assets were confiscated, as were some belonging to
his allies.

Sugar was sitting on the terrace of his Austrian residence in
conference with his lawyers one summer day in 2007 when a
bodyguard approached bearing a document that had been
hand-delivered by a diplomat from the Kazakh embassy. It bore
Sugar's signature – forged but notarised – consenting to the
dissolution of his twenty-four-year marriage to the president's
daughter Dariga. A judge had granted the divorce four days
earlier. Sugar called Dariga, who told him her father had threatened to take away all that the family owned. Thereafter Nazarbayev
forbade her to take Sugar's calls, and changed her son's name to
Nazarbayev. Venera, the youngest child, was told that her father
had gone abroad on a very long business trip.

Sugar moved from city to city and eventually to Malta, an
island that offered the benefits of European Union membership
while also enjoying a reputation as a haven for the dubiously rich
in their time of need. When a Kazakh minister sent word that
the president was ready to make peace if only the prodigal
son-in-law would board a charter flight to meet him, Sugar, who
had tried to use precisely such a ploy to ensnare the exiled reformer
Kazhegeldin in London, declined.

Not only was Nazarbayev failing to neutralise Sugar, Sugar was setting himself up, with jaw-dropping chutzpah, as some sort of freedom fighter, telling tales of his struggles to turn back the tide of corruption that issued forth from the despot he had once adored but whom he had come to learn was consumed by greed and the lust for power. To help paint this picture, he revealed a dossier of secret documents outlining something called 'Project Super Khan'. Some of the documents were clearly genuine; others were harder to authenticate. They showed that Nazarbayev was determined to bring the oligarchs to heel, as Putin had in Russia, to make the state itself the oligarch-in-chief, harnessing its powers to his private ambitions. Against any oligarch who failed to submit to this new order, Nazarbayev's servants would use 'active measures', just as the Soviets had. They would turn the protections the exiles sought in the West against them by passing to Western law enforcement agencies evidence of the improper origins of the recalcitrant tycoons' fortunes.

Nazarbayev had reason to be disquieted. In his world, there were only two elements to power: money and, when that was insufficient, fear. Popular consent had nothing to do with it, even if you had to go through the occasional sham election so that you and your allies at home and abroad could pretend your rule was legitimate. There were very few major repositories of Kazakh money that were not in thrall to Nazarbayev: after all, they could only have been amassed at his pleasure. But those few that were beyond his control were showing signs of uniting. Sugar was in touch with other former insiders living in exile. Most alarmingly, after Ablyazov had fled through the Astana snowdrifts to London, Sugar had made contact with him. They had known one another since they were teenagers. Ablyazov's aides found the former first son-in-law something of an oddball, with his erratic moods and his psychopath's laugh. At times he would seem friendly, at others he would come across all Kazakh crime boss. Newly divorced and with little prospect of seeing his children and first grandchild, Sugar seemed lonely. He was afraid, too. Twice, he claimed, the Kazakhs had planned to have him killed. Ablyazov was similarly in peril. In Moscow after his release from prison in 2004, he had announced at a press conference that he had discovered Nazarbayev's plot to assassinate him. Sugar, then still part of the regime, called to insist that he had had nothing to do with any plotting. Now that they were both on the outside, Sugar disclosed more. He told Ablyazov he had been at a breakfast in Vienna with Nazarbayev when the idea of bumping Ablyazov off had come up. The president had expressed concern about his political activity. His advisers had told him that if he were to order a hit, it would have to look like just another of the growing list of commercial disputes in the former Soviet Union settled with a gun.

From his first days in London, Ablyazov had been preparing his application for political asylum in the UK. His narrative was the one he had recounted to Peter Sahlas at Tower 42: the brilliant businessman who nurtured a dream of democracy for which he was mercilessly hounded by a despotic kleptocrat. On July 7, 2011, his application was granted. He was officially a refugee from persecution. Any hope Nazarbayev had of extraditing him – Kazakhstan lacked a treaty with the UK to do so, but the Russians had one and could have obliged their ally – was extinguished. The president had shown himself ready to forgive, for the right price. He had sent an emissary to London with an offer: hand over BTA Bank's Russian assets to Nazarbayev, chuck in another $50 million, and maybe things will be easier for you. Ablyazov demurred. So Nazarbayev was left with no choice. He would have to attack what mattered most: the money. The Kazakh state – an instrument Nazarbayev treated as his personal property – could use Ablyazov's own bank against him. Having seized BTA, Nazarbayev's regime could make out that it was the aggrieved bank, not the state, that sought redress against the fugitive.

It was one of the privileges granted to corporations that they could go to court. And if they violated the principles of justice, they could not be incarcerated, for they were made of paper and ideas, unlike any flesh-and-blood creatures who might oppose them. To pursue its missing billions, BTA retained Trefor Williams' private intelligence company Diligence, Portland, a PR consultancy founded by Tony Blair's old media strategist Tim Allan, and a firm of the finest London lawyers, Hogan Lovells, where the flinty and brilliant partner Chris Hardman took up the case. As far as they were concerned, any political dimension to the dispute was irrelevant. It was about Ablyazov's money: did it belong to him, or to the bank? If they could show it was the latter, that made Ablyazov a thief. BTA would pursue him in the commercial courts, a civil suit with no jury to hear the bleatings of the ersatz dissident, just a judge versed in fraud. Better still, with a bit of spin Ablyazov could be cast as that most reviled of villains: a perpetrator of the banking crisis for which everyone apart from the bankers was now beginning the long and miserable labour of paying. In the years before the crisis, the bosses of Royal Bank of Scotland had embarked on a megalomaniac acquisition of ABN Amro, a Dutch bank that had extended credit to Ablyazov's BTA. Not long afterwards, Royal Bank of Scotland required the single largest bank rescue ever performed, swallowing public money equivalent to a third of the annual budget of the National Health Service. The British press made the connection. London commuters opened the *Evening Standard* to see a picture of Ablyazov looking shifty in pinstripes under the headline, 'Does this Kazakh banker know the secret of RBS's missing billions?' A peer of the realm declared: 'We taxpayers are on the hook for 83 pence of every pound lost by RBS. Its management must pursue the foreign billionaires as diligently as they do struggling British businesses and homeowners.'

15

Watchdogs

London, March 2011

On a Saturday morning in November 1983, six thieves wearing balaclavas and carrying handguns entered the Brink's-Mat high-security warehouse near Heathrow Airport. A guard in league with the gang helped them get in; once inside, they soaked another guard in fuel, lit a match and demanded the combination to the vault. They made off with three tonnes of gold ingots and two boxes of diamonds, booty worth $20 million. The papers called it the crime of the century, the most valuable robbery ever committed in Britain. But something else also set it apart from previous crimes. The ringleader's lover moved from a council flat off the Old Kent Road to a listed farmhouse in a verdant London suburb worth close to $1 million, paid for from a Swiss bank account. A pair of Rottweilers guarded the entrance. They were called Brinks and Mat. 'The Brink's-Mat trials have revealed a new style of criminal, skilled in laundering money and investing it profitably,' wrote *The Times*' crime correspondent in 1988. 'Unlike the Great Train Robbers, most of whom ended up broke, the bullion robbers had contacts with professional advisers, property dealers and US crime syndicates.'

Launderers for the Brink's-Mat gang used the proceeds to invest in the redevelopment boom in London's derelict Docklands and to convert part of Cheltenham Ladies' College into flats. 'Purchases were carefully constructed,' *The Times* reported, 'so that investigators would find themselves trapped in blind alleys created by banking and legal conventions, claiming client confidentiality.' The gang melted down the gold, reconstituted it with a different purity and sold it back into the market in such quantities that, if you wear gold jewellery that was made in Britain after 1983, chances are it contains metal from their haul. Something similar happened to the cash proceeds from selling the gold. The launderers' shell companies and anonymous accounts were scattered through Switzerland, Liechtenstein, Jersey and the Isle of Man. With exceptions such as the farmhouse – discovered by a detective cross-referencing an underworld tip with back issues of *Country Life* – and the Docklands developments, the money was spun through the laundry so many times that the stain vanished.

As Nigel Wilkins pondered what he had seen at BSI's office on Cheapside, he came to a conclusion. 'Activities of the Swiss banks,' he wrote in his notebook, 'make bank robbers look like petty crime.' Financial secrecy, he believed, was concealing 'the world's biggest fraud'. The bankers who supplied that secrecy were engaged in 'facilitating the plundering of exchequers round the world'. That plunder, its origins erased, was then pouring into Western economies, where it would enjoy the protection of property rights and the rule of law. As far back as 1999, Senator Carl Levin had published an estimate for the total amount of criminal money – the proceeds of everything from bank robbery to bribery – laundered worldwide of up to $1 trillion each year. Half of that laundering was done in the US, equivalent to twice the budget of the most powerful organisation on earth, the American military.

Suddenly, spontaneously, some of the plunderers were encountering resistance. In March 2011, shortly after Egyptians had forced Hosni Mubarak to cede power, a young Syrian took a can of spray paint and wrote on a wall: 'It's your turn, doctor.' The physician he had in mind was the ophthalmologist who controlled Syria, Bashar al-Assad. When the youngster and friends were arrested and tortured, the Syrian revolution began. Assad ruled by theft and fear – like Mubarak, like Ben Ali in Tunisia, who had fallen after Mohamed Bouazizi ignited himself and began an uprising, like Muammar Gaddafi and the king of Bahrain, both of whom deployed troops to uphold kleptocracy.

Whichever of them would topple, whichever of them would endure, Nigel understood there was a machine that would continue to ensure that either they or whoever succeeded them could turn power into money and smuggle it out. The machine was both corrupted and corrupting. Nigel knew where its master cog lay: the City of London. Like a soldier addicted to war, he couldn't stay away from it. After BSI fired him, he took a job at the City of London Corporation, the arcane, opaque, half-private, half-public body that ran the financial district's affairs. For three years he worked there, until a better opportunity arose. On July 1, 2011, he received a letter from the 'HR Transactions' department of the City's regulator. It confirmed the offer of a job at the Financial Services Authority. Nigel would finally wield the powers to interrogate the stories moneymen told about themselves.

16

The Savarona

London, May 2011

Sir Paul Judge put it as delicately as he could. Sasha taking over as chairman of ENRC would not, he wrote, 'help to redress the governance deficit'. Sir Paul had seen scandal before: he was running the Conservative Party during the sleaze years of the early nineties under John Major. Now he was once more watching the swirl of money mixing with power. He and his fellow non-executive directors of ENRC were supposed to be the counterweight to the Trio, standing up for the multibillion-dollar corporation's other shareholders: the pension funds, the small investors, the nest-eggers, the punters. But ENRC plc was not working as public companies were supposed to. The City body that assessed such things gave ENRC the lowest governance rating it had ever issued. MPs were asking questions about how the company made acquisitions. In May 2011, three and a half years after ENRC's flotation on the London Stock Exchange and with its annual general meeting just a fortnight away, Sir Paul emailed his fellow non-execs.

'Our objective,' Sir Paul wrote, 'must be to maintain and grow the business so that all of those involved can benefit.' But first they had to decide what to do about Sasha Machkevitch. Because Sasha had let it be known that he desired to be chairman. Even if the Financial Services Authority could be persuaded to agree to something it had refused to sanction when ENRC arrived in London, having Sasha in the chair could hardly be expected to end the dysfunction, Sir Paul wrote. Since the previous summer, the share prices of other London-listed mining companies had gone up by 15 per cent; ENRC's had gone down by 15 per cent. Everyone was losing money – the Trio themselves were each down $1 billion. Worse, if Sasha became chairman, the press would pry into his past. Every story, Sir Paul warned, would include a sentence along the lines of: 'ENRC, whose Chairman is Sasha Machkevitch who has been embroiled in a number of difficulties with his tax affairs and was caught last year on a boat carrying underage prostitutes, has announced …'

A few months back, on September 28, 2010, a yacht called the *Savarona* had been at anchor in the Mediterranean, off the coast of Antalya. At 450 feet, it was more than half the length of the *Titanic*. Another delectable morning at sea was unfolding when those aboard detected the sound of rotor blades. Amid a roar of swirling air, a helicopter set down on the deck. Turkish police officers disembarked and commenced a search of the vessel and its sixteen luxury suites. They found condoms. They found girls: nine of them, from Russia, whom they arrested for prostitution. And they found the man who had hired the *Savarona* – Sasha Machkevitch.

The case had caused a stir. The *Savarona* had once belonged to Kamal Atatürk, father of modern Turkey. But Sasha had been allowed to go on his way without facing any charges. And Sir Paul's concerns about the girls being underage had been misplaced: happily, the youngest was eighteen. In any case, they were not going to tell tales of what had happened at sea. After their arrest, the girls had received a text message from the woman who had been giving them their orders. 'Shut up,' it said, 'and sign nothing.' They obeyed.

No, the danger that the *Savarona* scandal created for Sasha was subtler than Sir Paul could grasp. It was the kind of danger that emanated from kleptocracies, where the price of prosperity was complete loyalty to the boss. Sasha knew how it worked. In December 2010, a few weeks after the *Savarona* unpleasantness, Sasha had travelled to Switzerland to see Viktor Khrapunov. Once a senior official in the khan's government, Khrapunov had been cast out, undone by young love. His stepson Iliyas's marriage to Madina Ablyazova had hitched the Khrapunovs' fortunes to those of her father, Nazarbayev's bitterest enemy. Viktor was in Geneva, where Iliyas and Madina lived, recuperating from high blood pressure. As he told the story, Sasha had come to deliver a terrifying message.

They met at the airport. 'I'm sorry to have to address it,' Sasha began, 'but I've heard that you are now working against the president as allies of Mukhtar Ablyazov.'

'I'm not a traitor,' Khrapunov replied. 'If the president chooses to believe this malicious gossip, I can do nothing but regret it.'

'Is that the message you want me to give?'

'Exactly.'

'So it's a declaration of war?'

'You've been asked to repeat my answer word for word,' Khrapunov said. 'Just do that.'

Sasha wanted to be sure Khrapunov understood the consequences of perfidy. 'You do know that the entire state machinery will be mobilised against you?'

Khrapunov replied that, if attacked, he would defend himself and his family.

There was one more matter to discuss. As a boy, the Khrapunovs' son Iliyas had marvelled at the bejewelled shoes of kindly Uncle Sasha. But that was back when the Khrapunovs were still welcome at Nazarbayev's court. Since marrying into Ablyazov's family, Iliyas had imbibed some of his father-in-law's habit of making trouble

for Nazarbayev's clan. Ablyazov had learned about some assets
that the president's own son-in-law, the billionaire Timur Kulibayev,
kept in Switzerland. Iliyas had hired a private detective to find
them. Then he had learned the first lesson in the game of secrets:
trust no one. The private detective snitched on him to Nazarbayev's
people. So now, as they sat together at Geneva airport, Sasha
produced a document and showed it to Viktor Khrapunov. It was,
Sasha explained, the letter Nazarbayev required Iliyas to sign.

Nazarbayev, everyone in his court knew, was obsessed with
these letters. They were a pledge of allegiance that, in Nazarbayev's
mind, gave him the moral right to destroy you if you broke it.
The one Sasha had brought was wildly over the top, but when
his father showed it to him, Iliyas thought it best not to send
nothing at all. He wrote his own version.

> Dear Mr President
> I was raised based on the best Kazakh tradition and with
> respect for my fatherland and my ancestors. Recently, I have
> read reports in various media which indicate that I have been
> involved in cowardly intrigues against Kazakhstan. I assure you
> that these assertions are false and that I have not and will not
> do anything against Kazakhstan or you.

The following month Sasha and Viktor Khrapunov met again,
in Courchevel, the Trio's favourite French ski resort. This time
Khrapunov brought his wife, Leila. As Viktor recounted the
meeting, Sasha brought along the second of the Trio, Patokh
Chodiev. Chodiev sat there in silence while Sasha spoke. Iliyas's
letter had failed to placate the president. Investigations into his
activities would commence.

'If we find anything,' Sasha said, 'we'll find him wherever he
is in the world to hold him accountable.' The penalties he would
face, Sasha added, could include 'physical elimination'.

Viktor couldn't speak. Leila had been a successful business-woman and had fought battles of her own against Nazarbayev's cronies. She erupted.

'Yesterday you were on good terms with us. You even called Viktor your big brother. Why are you now threatening us? We moved away so we could have a quiet life, we're not concocting any intrigues, we're not attacking anyone. Why don't you explain that to the president? What's stopping you from helping your big brother?'

'I understand,' Sasha said. It seemed to the Khrapunovs he did not want them to make a scene. 'Just tell Iliyas he shouldn't do anything wrong. The boss doesn't appreciate it when people act up without his permission.'

In case the Khrapunovs were in any doubt about the gravity of their situation, before they departed Courchevel, the Trio had, as Viktor would recount the scene, introduced them to some associates: gangsters from Ukraine and Chechnya. The gangsters happened to mention how good they were at handling delicate situations efficiently.

A delicate situation: you could say that again. On the chess-board of international kleptocracy, Sasha was struggling to guard all his pieces. Yes, according to Viktor Khrapunov, he had done Nazarbayev's bidding and carried his threat to Iliyas. But he had also been left badly exposed because of something the Turkish police had found on the *Savarona*. Not the girls, not the condoms, but an old friend called Tevfik Arif.

Arif and Sasha went way back. Both owed their fortunes to the hasty sell-off of Soviet industry that followed Kazakhstan's independence. A Kazakh-born ethnic Turk, Arif had worked for the local arm of the Soviet Ministry of Commerce and Trade and then, like the economy itself, switched to private enterprise in the early nineties. He was one of four business-minded brothers. In 1993, perceiving that their Kazakh enterprise was becoming entwined with organised crime, he left for Turkey. But the family retained sufficient connections in Kazakhstan – one brother had a job at the Ministry of Industry – to prosper. In the privatisations, Sasha and his partners in the Trio picked up an almighty chromium mine. The Arifs snaffled the adjacent plant that made products from chromium. As Arif continued westwards – by the early 2000s he had set himself up in a mansion on Long Island – he dug a tunnel for money to follow him.

In New York, Arif had founded a real estate venture, giving it the good solid name of Bayrock. One of the financial managers he hired believed he channelled at least $10 million of the family's Kazakh revenues into the company. And money begat money, which was to say, if you wanted people to give you theirs, you had to look like you had plenty already. Handy, therefore, to have some billionaire comrades. A Bayrock presentation trumpeting the company's $2.5 billion of real estate projects included in a list of its 'sources of financing' a name becoming synonymous with riches: Sasha Machkevitch. His corporation was described as Bayrock's 'strategic partner'. Sasha would burnish Arif's credentials in money circles. A Forbes-certified tycoon with a FTSE 100 company, he would appear at meetings like an angel of wealth. Like the time at the Lanesborough, one of those Knightsbridge hotels where moneymen congregated when in London. Arif had been there, along with Bayrock's deals man, the Brooklyn fraudster-spy Felix Sater. They were talking with some investors who came from Iceland but seemed to have Russian funds behind them. In waltzed Sasha, for all the world just there by chance, a walking demonstration of Arif's and Felix's status among the new money kings. The Icelanders duly entrusted $50 million to Bayrock.

There had been one other person at that Lanesborough meeting. Younger than the rest, just starting out in the money game. Iliyas Khrapunov. The Khrapunovs had been doing business with Arif and Bayrock for years, since long before their excommunication on account of Iliyas marrying into the Kazakh opposition. For Sasha, hanging out with a business partner of Nazarbayev's enemy in the privacy of a superyacht shouldn't have caused any bother. But now, after the raid on the *Savarona*, his relationship with Arif was in the newspapers, all the way through the trial at which Arif was acquitted but his aide and a pimp went to jail. A jealous khan might see it in simple terms: Arif is in business with the Khrapunovs. The Khrapunovs are in league with Ablyazov, my enemy above all others. Arif holidays on yachts with Sasha and declares Sasha backer of the very venture that moves millions with the Khrapunovs. And that leaves Sasha ... where? That psychological portrait of Nazarbayev, the one Sugar had taken with him into exile, made it perfectly plain how the boss considered questions of fealty. There was his group, and there were the others. That classification was not just some tactic. It was 'essential to him', according to the profile. Fall from his group to the other and you were among the enemies. If the enemies did not surrender, they had to be destroyed.

17
Off the Books
Rudny, May 2011

Project Maria: that was to be the codename for ENRC's internal investigation into the suspicious goings on described in the email from the anonymous engineer at the Rudny mine in Kazakhstan. To run it, ENRC's directors in London selected Neil Gerrard. He had a reputation as one of the premier white-collar lawyers in London, a man who could both get to the bottom of shifty financial dealings and, thanks to his excellent connections at the top of the Serious Fraud Office, manage the fallout if you ended up having to inform the authorities. Gerrard, the son of a soldier, was not one of the obsequious City types. He swore, he stared, he asked more questions than a three-year-old. He was tough, too. As a police cadet, he had fractured his spine trying to make the high hurdles team for the Olympics. Six months later he was out of hospital, out of the Olympic team and out of the police. He started again with a law degree in Manchester, where he demonstrated an early disrespect for big business: his thesis detailed how tobacco companies were subliminally advertising to children. But at the white-collar crime firm he joined they needed defence lawyers. That's what he started to do: defend those accused of complex fraud. The job, like the frauds, was not straightforward. The best way for a corporation to avoid the full force of the law was to investigate itself, unburden itself to the authorities and maybe, if a sacrifice were required, offer up a rotten apple or two to the prosecutors. Gerrard became one of the hotshot lawyers boards would call in to establish the details of skulduggery and to handle negotiations with the Serious Fraud Office. He grew to know the SFO well; so well that, when the top job there came up, he was shortlisted.

Gerrard's brief was to test the allegations from the anonymous engineer and similar rumours about other aspects of ENRC's business in Kazakhstan. First, though, he needed to figure out his new client. He knew next to nothing about the Trio – so little that a better-informed colleague was startled that he had taken on an investigation into their affairs. Immediately, Gerrard perceived that any notion that the Trio had surrendered control of ENRC when they floated a chunk of their shares on the London Stock Exchange was illusory. In theory, ENRC had become a British public company, controlled by a board acting in the interests of all its shareholders, among them a great many august investment firms and British pension funds. But as Gerrard and his team got to work, he saw that the Trio were still in charge. When ENRC's executives wanted to know what to do, they turned not to the board, with its independent City grandees, but to the oligarchs.

Gerrard discovered he was not the first lawyer to look under the corporation's bonnet. Five years earlier, in 2006, as the Trio's bankers were preparing ENRC for its listing on the London Stock Exchange, they had hired a team from the City law firm Herbert Smith to investigate some iffy paperwork. ENRC's auditors had discovered that the documents purporting to verify sales of the output from the company's mines to Russian buyers were fake. The team from Herbert Smith started sifting through the files and interviewing the ENRC employees involved. Soon they discovered something they called the Russian Trading Scheme.

It was, they came to believe, a system for keeping some of the prodigious revenues that ENRC's mines generated off the books. Ores from ENRC's Kazakh mines and alloys from its smelters were sold across the border in Russia via a string of front companies. ENRC would get paid – but only a third of the profits. The rest was siphoned off as cash payments, the lawyers concluded, 'for the benefit of' Sasha and his partners Chodiev and Ibragimov. Over three years the scheme had diverted $870 million. The Trio seemed to be defrauding their own company to ensure a flow of clandestine money. The lawyers wondered why. To facilitate the payment of bribes, the witnesses they spoke to speculated, though the lawyers found no evidence of this. Days before their forensic data experts were due to start trawling through the computers in ENRC's Moscow office, substantial amounts of information were wiped. In any case, the two managers who had run the scheme said that they 'deliberately did not seek to retain any documentation' relating to it. The man who was alleged to have collected the Trio's cash – a relative of one of the oligarchs – insisted he was never told the identity of the individuals from whom he received it, nor of those to whom he was instructed to disperse it to meet the Trio's 'various commitments'. None of this had got in the way of ENRC's initial public offering in London. Indeed, it may have helped: the Herbert Smith lawyers learned that staff in the corporation's Moscow office had been instructed to leave their computers switched on 'so that information could be deleted due to the impending IPO'.

It was clear from Herbert Smith's report that Neil Gerrard would have one opportunity to secure evidence of the shady dealings the anonymous engineer had alleged. He assembled a team of technical and legal experts and arranged to fly them to Kazakhstan. He knew they would be left to flap in the Siberian winds unless the local staff understood that the interlopers enjoyed the support of the Trio. So he had written to the ENRC directors who would be overseeing his investigation and warned them that, while his work would be expensive – well over half a million dollars, more if his team received less than full cooperation or came across more suspicious goings on – it was preferable to the alternatives, which included the corporation being ejected from the stock exchange and its directors facing criminal charges for false accounting. Or, potentially, something worse.

In May 2011, Neil Gerrard and his team prepared to travel to Rudny. Of the dozen mines, smelters and industrial factories that collectively generated $7 billion of revenues for ENRC that year – a sum slightly greater than the budget for the city of Los Angeles – Rudny was the biggest. Its mines cleared $1 billion in profit. ENRC generated two-thirds of all local taxes, provided Rudny's central heating, restaurants, nightclub, cinema, bowling alley and hotel, and employed one in two men of working age. This was the Trio's town. What Potosí had been for the Spanish and Bombay to the British, Rudny was for them: the engine of an empire. Only theirs was a private empire, built on the ruins of states.

In 1988, the last Soviet days, Patokh Chodiev had been making two hundred bucks a month at the Ministry of Foreign Affairs in Moscow when a diplomat from the North American section introduced him to a visiting businessman. That was how he had met Boris Birshtein, the flamboyant Lithuanian-Canadian with the villa in Lenin Hills and the contacts book full of Soviet bigwigs. Chodiev helped Birshtein get a vital loan, then joined his company, Seabeco. It was a place where people spoke in whispers or went outside to confer. Birshtein dispatched Chodiev to Belgium. There he met a fellow recruit to Seabeco, a sinewy Kyrgyz academic-turned-businessman, Sasha Machkevitch. The source of Birshtein's influence was overly apparent, Chodiev thought: his operation 'stank of the KGB'. So the duo, having added the trader Alijan Ibragimov to their number, had found new backers. The Bombay-born Reuben brothers had cornered Russian aluminium, an industry built to serve the USSR's military and left stranded by the end of the command economy. Into that vacuum the Reubens inserted their commodity trading house, Trans-World. It grew into a state within a state, victorious in the 'aluminium wars'. Already on their way to becoming the richest men in Britain, the Reubens looked to expand their interests from Russia into the rest of the former Soviet Union.

The once proud industries of Kazakhstan, of the new ex-Soviet republics second only to Russia in natural riches, were approaching collapse. Mines, refineries and smelters were close to laying off tens of thousands of workers because of the economic disaster that the new capitalism had brought. In this moment of crisis, Oleg Soskovets, a Kazakh in Yeltsin's Kremlin, commended to his old comrade, Kazakhstan's ruler Nursultan Nazarbayev, three partners from neighbouring Central Asian countries. The Trio were offering to take over the management of the stricken mines, refineries and smelters. And they had money – the Reubens' money. The Reuben brothers put some of their fortune behind the Trio as Kazakhstan began to privatise at what informed observers deemed 'frightening speed'. Kazakhs said of the auctions: 'Going once, gone!' The Kazakh authorities' own adviser called the sales 'filthy cheap'. In a closed tender, against no serious competition, the Trio and their British backers acquired a chromium mine in western Kazakhstan and the smelters that went with it for a third of what they made in a year. Ten per cent of the shares at KazChrome were allocated for employees. Their bosses told them: 'Do you want to keep working here? If you do, you have to give up your shares.' When they realised they had been paid a fraction of what their stock was worth, the workers tried to sue. Their lawyer was arrested over a faked hit-and-run and warned to drop the case. He buried his files in the ground and left them to decompose.

The Trio and the Reubens captured more prizes. They paid less than $100,000 for two more enterprises that would turn over billions in the years that followed. An aluminium business – and the iron mine at Rudny.

In the years of privatisation, ownership was a shifting concept. Alter the past and your present could be superbly enriched or instantly impoverished. The Trio double-crossed their backers, the Reubens, claiming the swathe of Kazakh industry they had acquired together for their own. The Kazakh supreme court ruling that blessed the Trio's hold on the assets was, one of the Reubens' lieutenants declared, a 'pantomime'. The Reubens sued in other courts and extracted a 'substantial payment' from their former partners, but it was the Trio who emerged in control of the money-spinning Kazakh mines. As for where all that money was going, that was now the question that preoccupied Neil Gerrard.

From the moment they arrived in Rudny, Gerrard and his team were followed by armed men. The settlement had been built in defiance of the steppe's extremes. The mines were immense, silver-grey peach cores whorled into the earth. Little else was as it seemed.

Kazakh law required that ENRC's subsidiary at Rudny, as a condition of its mining licence, educate some Kazakhs each year at its own expense. In 2010 the subsidiary's 'children programme' funded study for twenty-six offspring of its employees. This endeavour might have retained its apparent unblemished worthiness had not someone in ENRC's internal audit department cast an eye over the list of beneficiaries. Sixteen of them were studying at the local institution in Rudny, eight more elsewhere in Kazakhstan, and another in Russia. One fortunate student, however, was pursuing his education all the way across the sea at Michigan State University, springboard to greatness of billionaire businessman Eli Broad, pioneering botanist William J. Beal and superstar basketballer Magic Johnson. The children programme's annual budget was supposed to be $6,000. But the Michigan student alone had been allocated $38,000. The students' parents acted as guarantors for the scholarships, and their units and job titles were listed. But for the Michigan student's father, only a name was recorded. The internal auditors had made some enquiries and ascertained his job title: he was a regional police chief. If ENRC money was being used to curry favour with a public official, that went beyond false accounting – that was bribery.

After they landed in Rudny, it did not take Gerrard and his team long to see that someone was trying to throw them off the scent. They asked to visit a particular office. This building was owned by ENRC's subsidiary but also served as the registered address of a mysterious company. That company owned a Soviet farm – the one the anonymous engineer had claimed was owned by one of the mine's bosses and tended on the company dime. On arrival at the office, Gerrard's team's translator overheard a manager telling the receptionist not to speak to the investigators. They asked to see the second floor, which was supposed to house the ENRC office: if this really was a company building, rather than the headquarters of an agricultural moonlighting operation, it would be in use on company business. The staff refused. The investigators went away, complained to a local ENRC boss and returned later that night, assured that they would be allowed into the office. Instead they were taken to the first floor, which was furnished with three desks with empty drawers, two chairs, no pictures, a laptop and a printer that had not been connected to one another, and an accountant who, asked why she was still at work five hours after the end of her shift, explained that she had lost track of time.

Rudny employees had been tipped off as to which computers were to be searched, giving them time to download and use sophisticated data-deletion tools. When Gerrard's team asked about the Michigan scholarship granted to the police chief's son, senior staff in Rudny warned them that they were asking 'political questions'. There had been plenty that might have attracted the police's attention: eight fatal incidents in the past two years, two caused by heart attacks, one by a drunk miner setting off detonators. Gerrard's team couldn't identify any favours that had been bestowed on the company in exchange for the scholarship. But when they were shown documents purporting to authorise the award, they could tell that they were fakes. The team returned to London convinced there was more to be discovered. In August, a private investigator they had sent to Rudny was attacked in his hotel room. His car was set on fire and his laptop damaged. His assailants told him they were teaching him a lesson for asking about matters that were none of his business.

Nonetheless, Gerrard's team went back to Kazakhstan in October. When they went to examine the computer of Farhad Ibragimov, nephew to Alijan Ibragimov of the Trio and one of those named in the anonymous engineer's email, they discovered that all the emails had been deleted the previous day. They tried to interview four other employees who appeared crucial to the various schemes, but were told that they were ill, unavailable or had left the company.

Despite the obstruction, Neil Gerrard felt he was piecing together a picture of how the operation in Kazakhstan really worked. And he was starting to suspect that there was something altogether more sinister going on in the other part of the ENRC empire – in Africa.

18

God's Kingdom

St Paul's, October 2011

Nigel Wilkins was a devoted reader of *Private Eye*. He shared the magazine's insatiable urge to expose hypocrisy. On October 15, 2011, a group of protesters were prevented by the police from staging the demonstration they had planned outside the London Stock Exchange. They proceeded instead to the square overlooked by St Paul's Cathedral. There they remained, erecting an encampment of 150 tents. The City of London police issued a warning. It was headed, 'Terrorism/Extremism update for the City of London Business Community'. The force had intelligence that the Occupy London camp contained 'individuals who would fit the anti-capitalist profile'. Upstanding capitalists in the area were warned to be on the lookout for 'suspected activists'.

Nigel had recently finished his three years working for the City authorities. 'I share the concerns about the way the City of London Police endeavour to brand protest groups such as Occupy in the same group as extremist and terrorist groups,' he wrote in his notebook. 'This is the same police force that did nothing to tackle the large-scale market manipulation taking place within the banks located in the City. Nor did their political masters, in the shape of the Corporation of London, do anything to protect the millions of consumers conned into buying services that were of no value to them.'

Three years had passed since the collapse of Lehman Brothers, three years since Nigel extracted a thousand pages of confidential documents from inside the financial secrecy industry and alerted the agencies entrusted with preventing abuses of money to what appeared to be glaring examples of such abuses taking place in the heart of the City. Apart from that one furtive meeting with agents from the tax authority, nothing had happened. He was a few months into his new post at the Financial Services Authority, assessing requests from banks, hedge funds and anyone else who sought authorisation to operate in the City. As it happened, fifth on the list of Occupy London's demands – after 'an end to global tax injustice and our democracy representing corporations instead of the people' – was the rather geekier: 'We want regulators to be genuinely independent of the industries they regulate.' From his seat within the City's regulator, it was increasingly obvious to Nigel that the watchdog was not policing the moneymen but protecting them. It was funded by the banks, its headquarters among theirs at Canary Wharf, the outcropping of skyscrapers that formed a second City of London to the east along the Thames. 'Most people in the organisation,' he observed, 'their contact is with the industry. And all these people are looking for a job in the industry.' His colleagues saw their task as removing obstacles to the transportation and multiplication of money. 'You end up in the ambiguous situation where you are helping a firm out of a difficult situation. I think that's completely wrong.' This was the body that had issued BSI with a private reprimand in 2004 for failing to check where its clients' money came from, then four years later received Nigel's tip-off that he believed that bank was handling the proceeds of crime, and appeared not to have deemed this behaviour unbecoming to the City.

What mattered, Nigel reflected in his notebook, was the story that was told, the story that was projected onto the world. That was what made the clouds angry rather than some other mood, what determined who was Jekyll, who was Hyde. The vocabulary of the stories about money served those who had lots of it: the quantity was described as their 'worth'. And the stories about money, the important ones, weren't really stories about money. They were stories about power. But money was something you were allowed to just take, whereas power was supposed to be bestowed. You didn't want to be a character who hoarded power. One who hoarded money, on the other hand – that made you a star.

In Nigel's 'top secret' red boxes were page after page of the raw material for stories that showed money was really power in disguise. Many of BSI's clients were labelled as 'PEPs', or 'politically exposed persons'. As well as a few Brits, there were Europeans, Russians, Lebanese, Central Asians, Arab royalty. Some were 'oligarchs', another word for someone very rich who had become so thanks to the favour of a political ruler. BSI's bosses were perfectly aware of where these clients' money was coming from. Nigel had taken a report prepared for the bank by Boston Consulting Group on how to find and serve clients including oligarchs and 'federal and municipal functionaries, officers in the military, security organs etc.' who are 'highly dependent on personal political network', and who demand 'high confidentiality ... in order to prevent negative publicity and avoid pressure'.

Nigel contemplated the meaning of his discovery. His mind wandered to religion, and the echoes between the two. Nigel's father had so embraced Christianity as to become a lay preacher. Nigel, never one to follow a path laid out for him, despised organised religion. He had followed the news reports on the rape of innumerable children by priests. 'The issue is not whether

Christians might be flawed,' he wrote in his notebook, 'but concern that the Churches as institutions have covered up serious wrongdoing by their clergy to the detriment of its victims.' Writing up an idea for Swiss banks to be made to compensate poor countries whose taxes they had helped to fleece, he drifted into a parallel with Jehovah's Witnesses. 'This is not about evangelising and converting the heathen to their beliefs; this is rather about preserving their position as what they say is a small elite guaranteed entry into God's Kingdom at Armageddon. They believe there isn't enough space.' Struggles in this world, he wrote, were 'not between religions, but over economic power, between the corrupt and the not corrupt'.

19

Fear

Zhanaozen, December 2011

It was when she saw the yurts that Roza Tuletayeva felt the first twinge of unease. For six months, she and a few hundred fellow workers at OzenMunaiGaz had maintained a vigil in the square. They took shifts, day and night. Their strike was just, they felt sure of that, and they would not be moved. Roza was approaching fifty. Her face could transform in an instant into an enormous smile partly composed of glittering gold teeth. She could also arrange it into the stern expression of a woman with whom it would be unwise to trifle. She had never wanted to be one of the leaders of the strike. Her nature just led her to the front. She had never particularly wanted to work in oil at all. Growing up in Turkmenistan, she initially studied pump mechanics but retrained as a teacher and took a job in a nursery while she raised three children by a feckless husband she had married too young. When, after the dissolution of the USSR, she moved back to her Kazakh mother's homeland, she had come to Zhanaozen.

Before the Soviets started pumping oil from the underground reservoirs that extended inland from beneath the Caspian Sea, few but Sufi hermits braved the desert. But the immense drills needed guidance and maintenance, so, eighty miles into the steppe along the lone road from the shore, the village of Zhanaozen grew to a town of a hundred thousand. Rings of breezeblock bungalows connected by unpaved streets surrounded the town square. In a row across the top of the square stood the *akimat*, or mayoralty, the hotel for visiting dignitaries and the offices of OzenMunaiGaz, or OMG, the local arm of the national oil company. In 2010, OMG's nine thousand employees, along with their counterparts in the neighbouring stretch of wilderness, extracted from the desert oil and gas worth $4 billion, piping it out through their godforsaken spigot of the global carbon economy. The square's tidy formations of fir trees were stunted and offered little protection from the elements. Nonetheless, on the morning of December 16, 2011, it was bustling. A stage stood ready for patriotic performances to celebrate the twentieth anniversary of Kazakhstan's independence. Yurts had been erected on the neat hexagonal paving stones to serve horsemeat stew with dumplings, camel milk and other traditional delights.

When Roza arrived in the square and saw the yurts, she knew they were a provocation. Kazakhs never put up their yurts on stone. Someone must have ordered them to be placed there, close to the strikers' spot. Roza went over to talk to the yurts' owners. They should be ashamed of themselves, she told them. Some apparently were; they prepared to strike their yurts and leave. But the nearby police officers stopped them and the yurts stayed put.

Roza had run a little trading business when she first came to Zhanaozen. Soon the post-Soviet economic crisis put paid to that and she found a position servicing the rigs out in the desert. It was hard work and dangerous. That was not her objection to how things went at OMG. What made her blood boil was the way even the lowliest bosses treated ordinary workers like Roza as chattels. Bring this, they would bark, do that. She observed that the children of the wealthy or those who enjoyed their favour would be appointed to senior posts. This was maddening, especially when the demands became more demeaning. Down by the Caspian, at a resort called Kendirli, there was a presidential mansion. When Nazarbayev wanted to use it, workers from the oil companies would be sent to rid the place of bugs and to clean the pools and saunas. The first year, Roza went along with it. The second, she refused. When you take up any job, she argued, it has a job description. Housekeeping for the president was not part of hers. Roza encouraged others to adopt the same stance. If bosses are stupid, she reasoned, they should be taught sense.

In Soviet times, mid-level specialists in the mines or the oilfields enjoyed foreign travel, spa vacations, a certain prestige. After the dawn of capitalism, the same workers still earned more than most – outside the kleptocracy, anyway – but life was considerably more constricted. Hardship pay, once guaranteed by the state for those who toiled in the desert oilfields, was now, the workers were informed, to be dictated by market forces. Other forces also were at play. The workers discovered they were being paid only about half of the salaries recorded on the forms their bosses were submitting to the treasury. The difference was presumably supplementing the bosses' own income. This was all the more vexing because you had to pay to get a job in the first place. As with any formal position in Kazakhstan, securing employment at the state oil company required a bribe. Low-level oil workers had to pay three months' wages to the head of human resources. So the workforce at OMG were down before they even got paid, and when that pay arrived half of it was missing. 'Money,' observed an activist who took up their cause, 'is the only river that flows upwards.'

Meanwhile, the poverty rate in the region around Zhanaozen had reached one in five, the highest in Kazakhstan. In the good years, Kazakh banks had taken some of the money that had overflowed from Western banks and doled out credit to anyone who wanted it. The oil workers of Zhanaozen had wanted it. They bought houses and fridges and cars they couldn't afford. The interest rates were 15 per cent, 18 per cent. When the crisis came, these workers – each supporting extended households of a dozen or more – began to feel the suffocation of unpayable debt. Staff meetings at OMG grew heated. You are a *vor*, workers shouted at the bosses, a thief. Most of the workers belonged to a union, but its leaders seemed subservient to the management. So, in May 2011, thousands of them walked out of their own accord.

Almost immediately, the strike was declared illegal. The Zhanaozen City Court ruled that the OMG workers had failed to follow grievance procedures set out in the labour code. In any case, strikes by staff at any site deemed a 'hazardous production facility' were prohibited. Rather than fold, a score of strikers upped the ante. They began a hunger strike. Roza was one of them.

Roza's children begged her not to starve herself. But she had been thinking. She had been pondering the transition from the Soviet empire to capitalism. She read Kazakhstan's constitution from beginning to end. It declared that all resources – land, water, forests, lakes, seas – belonged to the state. Roza was minded to give the president the benefit of the doubt: clearly he was unaware that everything was being stolen.

If Nazarbayev did not know what was afoot in the oil industry, he had grown decidedly myopic. It was controlled by a member of his own household, his daughter's husband, Timur Kulibayev. By the time the Zhanaozen workers went out on strike, Timur and his wife were each worth $1.3 billion, a combined fortune equal to that of Malcolm Glazer, the owner of Manchester United, or Oprah Winfrey. This wealth Timur had gathered by operating at the intersection of the market and the state. Nazarbayev appointed him to run the national oil and gas company, KazMunaiGas, of which OMG was a major subsidiary, then promoted him to chairman of the sovereign wealth fund that owned KazMunaiGas and the rest of the assets the state acquired or seized, such as Mukhtar Ablyazov's confiscated bank, BTA. While Timur was stewarding the Kazakh state's commercial interests, he had amassed his own private ones; the line between the two could appear vanishingly thin.

Roza knew that oil could make people stupendously rich. It was just a question of which people, and how many of them. She had seen a documentary on Dubai. A land of Bedouins on sand dunes had become an oasis of plenty. She envied them. Why, she wondered, have we lived in the Soviet Union for seventy years and then in Kazakhstan for twenty-five more and we have fuck all, we have nothing? I don't want to live to see something sometime. I want a decent life here and now. If we have everything right now, all the wealth, all the resources, why can't I live decently? Why do I need to ask someone's permission? She took the decision to go on hunger strike not because she wanted to but because she had no choice. No one was listening to what she and her comrades were saying.

When the police broke up the strike at the OMG facility in early July, Roza was already in hospital. The workers regrouped in the main square of the nearest town, Zhanaozen. As soon as she was able, Roza joined them.

The months on the square were trying. The summer was stifling. Winter brought rain, snow, subzero winds. The bosses started firing people for participating in illegal industrial action, which prompted some of the strikers to go back to work. But the hundreds in the square remained resolute. Drunkenness was kept to a minimum to avoid giving the authorities an excuse to remove them. From a minibus parked at the edge of the square, KNB agents kept an eye on the strikers. Kazakh media, loyal to Nazarbayev, largely ignored them. When journalists did show interest, they mostly worked for foreign groups – the BBC or Al Jazeera. The reporters found the loud and forceful Roza made for a good interview. She hoped her words would reach the president, so he could hear of their plight. She also sensed that she was taking a risk. 'All this talking,' she thought to herself. 'One day I'll be punished for this.'

The morning of Independence Day was bitterly cold. Normally, the celebrations in the square were derisory. Today, Roza noticed with indignation, teachers had brought their pupils. The singing started on the stage towards the bottom of the square. It seemed to Roza to grow louder and louder.

There were a hundred or so strikers in the square. As usual, many were wearing their thick company-issue hooded jackets, half blue, half red and bearing the OMG logo on the breast. After years under the unforgiving sun, their jackets were worn and faded. But that morning the strikers noticed dozens of people they didn't know wearing new jackets, the colours fresh and brilliant.

The set-to about the yurts had got everyone riled up. A large contingent of police had been deployed to the square. They began to edge forward, encircling the strikers. Towards the end of the morning, scuffles broke out. A group of about thirty men in bright new OMG jackets rushed the stage. They trashed the sound equipment, throwing speakers to the ground. Yurts were torn down, the festive tree tipped over. An old bus behind the stage was set alight. Soon the strikers noticed smoke rising at the top of the square. The *akimat* was on fire. Then they saw plumes from the next building along, the hotel. When smoke started to billow from OMG headquarters, some of the strikers rushed towards it in hope of dousing the flames: the basement contained the records of their labours, medical cards and other official paperwork.

As the discord mounted, many of the townsfolk rushed from the square. Teachers herded pupils away. Roza encouraged the nearby strikers to leave too: no good could come of this, she thought. But they refused to move, so Roza decided she couldn't either. She looked around and noticed another detachment of police approaching.

From the middle of the square, Nurlibek Nurgaliyev watched the police approach with his usual calm. He had worked the oilfields for more than twenty years. A big leathery rapscallion with bloodshot eyes, he was fond of a gently inebriated afternoon doze. His luxuriant snores would punctuate the conversation in fellow workers' living rooms. But when it came time to be counted, he had joined Roza in the hunger strike and then taken his shifts in the square. He was as slow to startle as the dromedaries that plodded the wastelands outside town, his voice a robust baritone deepened by incessant smoking. The oncoming police provoked no alarm in him. Even when he heard the tinny crack of gunfire, he assumed they were firing rubber bullets, as they had on occasion before. He glanced to his right, where three men were squatting and looking up at the smoke rising from the *akimat*, the hotel and OMG headquarters. One of them clapped his hand to his eye. He screamed. A spurt of blood gushed down his face. What the hell, Nurgaliyev thought, it's real bullets? He felt a thump on the right side of his jaw, just by the chin. He stepped towards a group of his colleagues but had not reached them when he collapsed.

Nearby, a group of women wailed. A bullet had passed through the head of a child, aged about twelve, killing her instantly.

Torekhan Turganbaev had no idea anything was amiss in the square. He was at home, a few blocks away, out of earshot. He was a few weeks shy of his fiftieth birthday, had done all right for himself from a career in oil, and kept going to work when the others went on strike. His round-shouldered portliness retained a hint of a bullish strength that carried through to his firstborn, in whom it was magnified to the point that the shy young Amanbek had grown into a formidable wrestler. Topping off Amanbek's magnificent frame were gleaming teeth, a sculpted jaw and jet-black hair cut in a neat fringe over his forehead, the total effect resembling a fifties American sports star. Now twenty-seven, Amanbek and his wife had two young daughters. He had followed his father into the oil industry as a machinist. Because neither had joined the strike, there had been no call to attend the demonstration on the main square, but that morning Amanbek had headed over anyway to take in the Independence Day celebrations. The first Turganbaev knew of the trouble was when he saw someone running down the street outside his house. He called his son's mobile. There was no answer. He waited an hour and called again. A woman answered. She said she was a nurse. 'If you're looking for the owner of this phone,' she said, 'you should come to the hospital.'

Inside the hospital, blood covered the walls and the floors. Not just a spattering, but thickened pools, mixed with dust and sand. Somewhere, doctors were struggling to remove the bullet that had passed through Nurlibek Nurgaliyev's leathery jaw and lodged in his shoulder. Medical staff were running in every direction. Turganbaev began to search for his son. He went to the wards on the ground floor and then upstairs. Eventually he came to a room where three human shapes lay under shrouds. He pulled back the first. It was a face he did not know. The second, too, covered a stranger. He lifted the shroud over the third corpse and saw the face of his son, a bullet hole in the centre of his forehead.

At first, Roza had been perplexed when she saw people falling to the ground around her in the square. She heard *sspt sspt sspt* but could not tell where the sounds were coming from. A young man ran up to her. 'Aunt Roza,' he called. He told her a bullet had killed one of the strikers. Roza looked at him. 'What do you mean, killed?' Two ambulances arrived. Roza and four other women formed a shield around a paramedic as she tended to the fallen. Roza noticed a group of men – bosses, they looked like – standing near the wrecked stage, watching the scene unfold. Then someone grabbed her by the scruff of the neck and shoved her into a car. It was her son. He drove to Roza's sister's place. When the car stopped, Roza went to get out. But her feet wouldn't move. She crawled inside. There she discovered she had pissed herself.

For a while afterwards, Roza found her memory of what had happened was disturbed. When she tried to call to mind the events in the square, it was as though she was looking at a ripped-up picture. She would glimpse people running, then they would disappear. All she could conjure up of the stage was one blue edge. Noticing these holes in her recollection would give her a surge of anxiety. When she ate, the food had no taste.

Zhanaozen was placed under a state of emergency. Telecommunications were jammed in the city and much of the internet blocked nationwide. The prosecutor general's office announced that twelve deaths had occurred on the square, with two more resulting later from injuries and one caused by fire. Some said more had perished. But they had not died in vain. To her delight, six days after the shooting, Roza heard that the president himself had come to Zhanaozen. Never mind that he addressed only the town bigwigs rather than the strikers, and that he spoke not in the square but in an official building some way away. Never mind that: what mattered were the words he spoke. 'The workers' demands were, in general, justified,' Nazarbayev declared. 'Even if the workers had violated labour discipline, the employers should not have forgotten that those were our citizens. They didn't come from the moon. They should have listened to them and, as much as possible, supported them.

Unfortunately, this was not done.' He seemed to accept what the strikers already knew: that infiltrators had been sent to the square to cause disturbances that would serve as a pretext for the massacre. 'Persons,' the president said, 'who have nothing to do with this work dispute took advantage of the complicated situation and organised mass disorder.'

Roza heard on television that a commission had travelled from Astana to establish the truth. She was thrilled: the country would see that the strikers had simply been demanding their rights, day after day, through scorching heat and intense cold. At 10 a.m. on December 27, she presented herself at the local prosecutor's office, assuming that was where the commission would be found. The officials on duty initially declined to let her in, but she insisted on being heard. Eventually a young man ushered her onto a bus.

The bus made the short drive to the office of the KNB. Roza was taken inside, led to an interrogation room and told to sit on a chair. She asked for a lawyer but none materialised. A KNB officer called Yerzhan came up to her.

'You are done,' Yerzhan told her. 'You burned down the yurts. We put up twenty-two yurts and you burned them down. I will burn down your house like those yurts. You have a fourteen-year-old daughter who is at School Number Seven. I will kill her. I will kill all your relatives. You are done now.'

Roza replied: 'You put up the yurts?'

Yerzhan stopped speaking. Another man moved behind Roza, holding a machine gun. He pressed the muzzle into her back.

'If anything happens,' Yerzhan said to him, 'just shoot her.'

A succession of KNB men came and went from the interrogation room. 'You've been caught,' they said, 'you are guilty.' Hours went by, then they sent her home. But a week later they came for her again. Police this time. She was at her parents' house when they found her. It was the evening. Her father came outside and watched as they took her away.

Roza had heard the whispers of what was going on in the detention centre. Out the back, in a building known as 'the garage', detainees were being stripped and forced to crouch in unbearably cold water. In the basement they were beaten with truncheons and warned that if they told anyone they would be jailed. Already one detainee had died. Bazarbai Kenzhebaev had come into town from his village to visit his daughter and newly arrived grandchild. The police had grabbed him as he walked to the maternity unit. They took him to the detention centre and slung him in the garage. Then they laid him naked on the ground and walked up and down on him, smashing his head into the floor and rupturing his intestine. He died at the hospital four days later.

Men in plain clothes walked Roza into the detention centre and down a corridor with doors leading off on each side. They led her to what she took to be a commander's office. There she was shown a list of her relatives. She was questioned again and again, men shouting at her, but she didn't understand what answers she was supposed to give. One of the men had a scar on his face and a malevolent air. Ruslan was his name. He came towards her carrying a plastic bag. He whipped it over her head and pulled it tight. She gasped for air, but none came. At last Ruslan released the bag. Roza felt her head swim. Then suddenly the bag was back on, her body writhing in panic. Again Ruslan asphyxiated her, and again and again. When the bag split, he went off to find another. His colleague took over. He slapped Roza's face, grabbed her neck. He seized a fistful of her hair and dragged her from her seat. When they took her back to her cell, she tried to tidy herself. As she composed her hair, a clump of scalp came away in her hand.

They had other techniques. The interrogators were sodomising the men with truncheons and metal bars. Roza told her fellow prisoners little of what was being done to her when the doors of the interrogation room closed. But they understood that she was being abused 'as a woman'. She felt ashamed. Her tormentors sketched a hellish future. They said they would send her to a women's prison at the far end of the country, where she would be consigned to the harem of one of the boss inmates. They complimented her on her tongue, all the better for performing her prison-bitch duties. 'No one will find you,' they told her.

Even when the interrogations stopped, the ghosts were still with her. Since the massacre on the square they had been there, the dead. They were in her head and in front of her eyes, but also they were far away, and she was numb to them.

The moment arrived when fear took Roza completely. In the interrogation room, they crowded round her and spoke her daughter's name. Confess, they said, or we will bring her here. We will bring her here and undress her. We will undress her and a gang of men will rape her. They will rape her and you will cry tears of blood.

She would have done anything to protect her daughter. She wanted to protect everyone. Others could betray her if they needed to, if it would keep them out of here. By any means, by truth or lie, let them not end up here, she thought. She would have done anything, but she did not know what it was she was supposed to do, to say. What had happened had happened, she thought.

The courthouse in Aktau, the regional capital at the end of the desert road to the Caspian shore, was too small to accommodate all thirty-seven defendants, so the city's youth centre was given over to the trial. The defendants, half of them OMG strikers, were divided into four groups. Twelve were charged with participating in disorder, eleven with joining an illegal strike, six with taking advantage of the chaos that followed the shooting to loot shops and offices. Eight defendants, including Roza, were accused of the most serious crime, that of being organisers of the unrest. They were placed in a special glass box in the makeshift courtroom.

By the start of the trial on May 27, 2012, Roza had been in detention for nearly three months. She had discovered facets of existence that had hitherto been hidden from her. 'I didn't know,' she thought, 'that one's personality could be destroyed to such an extent, so humiliated.' Variations were added to the fugue of her suffering: the denial of sleep, a sudden blow with a big plastic bottle filled with sand or water, solitude. They said they would throw her in a cell with a tubercular prisoner. They convinced her that it had all been her fault, that those who died on the square died because of her. One night, at about 4 a.m., she had resolved to hang herself using a pillow case. Only the presence of a cellmate in the bunk above hers stopped her. She realised that if she killed herself, her cellmate would be blamed and punished.

Gulnara Zhuaspaeva, the lawyer for Roza and six other defendants, knew full well what the outcome of the trial would be. She had only taken the brief after some hundred other lawyers had refused it, and had only persuaded Roza to accept her representation after convincing her that she was not a KNB plant. On the second day of proceedings, some well-connected friends in Astana phoned Zhuaspaeva to say the decision had already been taken that the eight defendants charged as ringleaders were to be jailed, and not briefly.

The judge, a man in his sixties, spent the entire case mopping sweat from his brow. The accused were of course guilty – why else would they be before him? – but nonetheless a two-month performance of due process had to be enacted. Justice must be seen to be done. When Roza and five other defendants alleged that they had been tortured, the judge instructed the prosecutors to investigate. A few nights later, hours before the judge's deadline for the prosecutors to report back, police interrogators approached the detainees who had alleged torture. Faced with the prospect of chronicling the offences of the very men now standing over them, they declined to commit pen to paper. The prosecutors returned to court to inform the judge that 'there was no evidence of a crime in the actions of the law enforcement agents that responded to the mass unrest on December 16'. The trial resumed. The evidence against Roza, contained in ninety-three binders, had been compiled primarily from tapped phone calls and messages from which the prosecutors made her out to be the ringleader bent on violence. Some of her fellow strikers had incriminated her under interrogation. One of them sought to retract his statement by telling the court that his interrogators had beaten him with a chair and threatened his son.

The trial went on until June 4, 2012, when the perspiring judge read out his verdicts. One by one, he found all but three of the accused guilty. Twenty-one of those convicted were released, either under suspended sentences or amnesties. That left thirteen. He condemned them all to terms of imprisonment starting at three years. The sternest punishments he reserved for those who had dared to spread word of the strikers' cause by speaking to the media. Two who had addressed press conferences in Poland and Moscow got four and six years respectively. He gave Roza the longest term: seven years.

20

Stability

Cambridge, July 2012

Nursultan Nazarbayev was not going to let the events in Zhanaozen detract from his moment of glory, the moment he would stand before the West, legitimate and vindicated, a modern khan for a new world order. There was less than a month to go before he was to deliver a speech in Cambridge. Mercifully, he had at his disposal a master communicator, who had written to him with some advice.

> Dear Mr President
> Here is a suggestion for a paragraph to include in the
> Cambridge speech. I think it best to meet head on the
> Zhanaozen issue. The fact is you have made changes following
> it; but in any event these events, tragic though they were,
> should not obscure the enormous progress that Kazakhstan has
> made. Dealing with it in the way I suggest, is the best way for
> the Western media. It will also serve as a quote that can be
> used in future setting out the basic case for Kazakhstan.

Some draft passages followed. 'I love my country ... essential religious tolerance ... strong ally of the coalition ... progress and openness ...' Then a little false modesty: 'But as the tragic events of Zhanaozen last December showed, there is much for Kazakhstan still to do … I understand and hear what our critics say. However, I would simply say this to them: by all means make your points and I assure you we're listening. But give us credit for the huge change of a positive nature we have brought about in our country over these twenty years …' Move on to a catalogue of reforms under way, then build to the climax: 'All of this will take time; it has to be done with care and with stability uppermost in our minds. This is not to preserve the power of politicians but to preserve the hard won gains of the people.'

The final words of the letter were handwritten:

With very best wishes.
I look forward to seeing you in London!
Yours ever,
Tony Blair

There had been a moment – years, in fact, sickeningly uncertain years – when Nazarbayev had lost control of his image abroad. In exile, his renegade former son-in-law Sugar told a reporter about a family dinner at which Nazarbayev had mentioned having $15 billion in his personal accounts. To another journalist – Glenn Simpson, an investigative reporter at the *Wall Street Journal* with an interest in post-Soviet kleptocrats – Sugar had imparted a bounty of dual-state secrets. Simpson wrote that Sugar 'painted a picture of a Kazakh economy in which the president not only routinely takes illicit commissions but also holds hidden stakes in the copper, uranium and hydrocarbon industries, and maintains a network of offshore bank accounts'. But the worst thing Sugar had done had been his attempt, back when he was loyal, to incriminate his rivals in Nazarbayev's court: the Trio and the former prime minister Kazhegeldin. Following his tip about dubious Kazakh money flowing through Europe, the Belgian police had alerted a magistrate in Geneva, who had found Nazarbayev's Swiss bank accounts. Eighty-five million dollars they had in them. The magistrate had spotted that some of the money had come in from the US, so he alerted American prosecutors. They had at their disposal something called the Foreign Corrupt Practices Act, which meant you could go to jail for paying bribes abroad or accepting them. An absurd piece of legislation, Nazarbayev might have opined: how did anyone think business was done? Especially oil business.

The Americans had wanted the oil under the Caspian, in the Tengiz field. In 1996, Nazarbayev had given it to them. Mobil paid Kazakhstan $1 billion for a share of the Tengiz. Then Mobil had sent another $41 million to an account at Citibank in New York belonging to James Giffen. And Giffen, a Californian banker who had cultivated the Soviet elite during the Cold War, sent some of it on to Nazarbayev's Swiss accounts. When the FBI arrested Giffen in 2003, Sugar's cascading ineptitude left Nazarbayev in what his advisers said was 'direct jeopardy' of prosecution. 'Kazakhgate', the US press called the affair. For seven years the American prosecutors tried to nail Giffen. They hoped to flip him, Nazarbayev's spies in the US warned, in order 'to net the big fish'. Thankfully, Giffen had been a friend not only to dictators. He had also been a friend to the CIA, where he was regarded as holding 'the keys to the kingdom' of Kazakhstan. Giffen testified that he had told his intelligence contacts about the money he was paying into Nazarbayev's Swiss accounts. They had, he said, 'repeatedly told him to stay close to the president and continue to report'. The CIA caused interminable delays to the trial by taking forever to hand over documents. One after another, the prosecutors on the case concluded that life was too short and moved on. When it became clear that the exasperated judge might simply dismiss the whole case, the prosecutors cut a deal. Giffen's company pleaded guilty to one count of corruption, namely providing the Nazarbayevs with snowmobiles. It paid a $32,000 fine. Giffen also pleaded guilty to one charge: that he had failed to inform the US tax authorities of his Swiss accounts. His penalty was $25.

But despite Giffen's escape, for Nazarbayev the fundamental problem remained. Globalisation meant that rule by theft and the rule of law were co-existing. It was like China and Hong Kong: one country, two systems, only global. Such tension could not be maintained indefinitely. One system would have to dominate, leaving the other as a façade.

Nazarbayev's court would continue to operate as it always had, regardless of the occasional flurries of anti-corruption hypocrisy in the West. What belonged to Kazakhstan – or, for that matter, to Kazakh moneymen, or to Kazakh corporations – belonged to Nazarbayev and his circle. And they treated them accordingly, even huge multinationals like Kazakhmys, the corporation that mined Kazakhstan's copper. Kazakhmys had floated its shares on the London Stock Exchange two years before ENRC, and likewise made so much money from the ores it sold that it qualified for the FTSE 100. But while it might have looked for all the world like a British public company, it still had its duties to the khan and his courtiers. On July 1, 2011 – the very day a new law against bribery came into force in the UK – an aide to Karim Massimov, Nazarbayev's prime minister, sent an email to Eduard Ogay, a senior executive at Kazakhmys. The email was written as if addressed not to an important business executive but to a travel agent. 'The chief' – by which the aide meant Massimov – 'has assigned me to work with you on the departure of his family of 4 people to Paris.' The aide had spoken to Massimov's wife to ascertain her wishes. For the trip, a top-notch plane – a twelve-seater to be sure it wasn't too small. Then a couple of days at Disneyland Paris and four or five nights at the George V off the Champs-Élysées. And a car, probably a minibus. Functionaries at Kazakhmys duly made the arrangements. Staff at a company with shares on the London Stock Exchange were organising the Kazakh prime minister's family's luxury European holiday. It wasn't clear from the emails who was paying, but at any rate Kazakhmys employees were spending company time in the service of one of the Kazakh dictator's top lieutenants.

Not to worry, though. Those emails were safely on a private server, and no one was looking into Kazakhmys's affairs. Everyone, by contrast, was looking into ENRC, along with its founders: Sasha Machkevitch and his two fellow oligarchs, the greatest beneficiaries of the new khan's rule.

Neil Gerrard's internal investigation was no longer confidential. Someone inside either the law firm or the corporation had leaked it to *The Times*. Upon reading about Gerrard's investigation, the Serious Fraud Office's top brass wrote to ENRC's bosses in London threatening to start one of their own. If the Trio's secrets started to spill out, some of the khan's own might spill with them. He was close to the Trio personally. Chodiev had been with him on the plate-smashing holiday. Sasha travelled with him too, and bought him outfits from Versace in London. The Trio had set up an entire political party to support his regime, and listed all their employees and their families as members. For his 1999 campaign, Sasha had acted as the 'secret treasurer'. In Nazarbayev's court it was held as fact that he shared in their riches. Sugar said his father-in-law had an interest in the Trio's business. Viktor Khrapunov, the banished former minister, said the same. One of his own spies said ENRC 'had four partners, not three': Sasha, Chodiev, Ibragimov – and the president. His exiled former prime minister, Akezhan Kazhegeldin, the man who had overseen the privatisations in which the Trio amassed their empire, suspected they were mere frontmen for Nazarbayev.

The Trio were ideal courtier-moneymen. In the West, they could blend in with the local billionaires. But none of them had been born Kazakh; they could never entertain ambitions to replace Nazarbayev. And yet perhaps they could ditch him, as they had ditched Boris Birshtein, ditched the Reuben brothers. Perhaps they would be fronts no more, become their own moneymen. Maybe Nazarbayev would ditch them first, before the embarrassment they were starting to cause him with their boardroom scandals in London became anything more dangerous. Or perhaps they could go on as they had before. To do that, though, they would need, Nazarbayev and the Trio, to exert some jurisdiction over jurisdiction, to suborn the rule of law, bend it to their will. Nazarbayev was already succeeding in doing just that when it came to the pursuit of his enemies.

In February 2012, a British judge had found Mukhtar Ablyazov to be in contempt of court. After Chris Hardman at Hogan Lovells had lodged the nationalised BTA Bank's lawsuit against Ablyazov, he had been required to disclose his assets. All of them. Instead, in a witness statement the length of a novel, he had tried to show how he had been playing a game by one set of rules but now found himself judged by another set, the rules of the West. 'It is a fact of life in Kazakhstan that, because of the suppression of political opponents by Nazarbayev through the seizure of their assets, most high net worth individuals such as myself have no alternative other than to hold as many of their assets as possible through a structure of nominees and trustees based outside Kazakhstan. In other words, even those high net worth individuals who are not active opponents of the regime seek to protect themselves by holding their assets in this fashion so that Nazarbayev and his coterie of kleptocrats cannot simply seize them, in the event that they come to the attention of Nazarbayev and his regime. He has now moved up from petty strong-arming of individuals, and instead wants to own and control the whole Kazakhstan economy.' But the fugitive businessman was not in Kazakhstan. He was in London. Hadn't it been Ablyazov himself who had dared to demand 'reform', that Kazakhstan adopt the West's rules of capitalism? Well, he'd certainly got to experience those rules now. Ablyazov had not attended court for the judgment, nor would he be there to hear the sentence: twenty-two months' incarceration. Instead he had vanished. Trefor Williams of Diligence was after him. Everyone in Nazarbayev's court knew that Ablyazov was the ultimate prize. They were sending out their own bloodhounds to hunt him, their own spies to trap him. And not just him: anyone connected to him – Bota, Peter, his bodyguards, his offspring – would be valuable if they could be ensnared, perhaps even turned.

As a fugitive Ablyazov was barred from defending BTA Bank's suits. The court could return default judgments in the bank's favour. Its lawyers had a blank page on which to write the story. Never mind that Nazarbayev's entire system of power was based on theft. Ablyazov would be named a thief, a master thief, a thief for the ages, by Western courts, the most respected arbiters when parties came before them with contradictory accounts of the past.

Nazarbayev had always known what to do with those who departed from the narrative he ordained. Directly or indirectly, he controlled almost all Kazakhstan's newspapers and broadcasters. A few obdurate journalists insisted on disrespecting the khan by, among other outrages, reporting on the Kazakhgate affair. *Respublika*, founded by an impish muckraker named Irina Petrushova with money from Ablyazov, was the worst; it was dealt with accordingly. Its printers were persuaded to quit, one upon delivery of a human skull. Petrushova herself received an ornate funeral wreath. She persisted in defaming her betters, even publishing stories that referred to Nazarbayev's Swiss accounts, so the message was put more clearly. Her staff arrived at *Respublika*'s office to find the decapitated corpse of a dog hung from a window. A screwdriver had been sunk into the animal's

flesh, affixing a note that read, 'There will be no next time.'
Petrushova found the dog's head the following morning outside
her door. Two days later, the office where the newspaper's edito-
rial board met was firebombed, followed by the newsroom. The
Ministry of Information brought criminal charges – against
Petrushova. In August 2002, civility in public discourse prevailed
and she left the country.

But controlling the narrative abroad was more difficult.
Petrushova and others kept writing from exile. The Western press
seized on the fuss about Nazarbayev's Swiss accounts. They ran
stories about how James Giffen had personally shipped in the
presidential Viagra supply. That was a lesson. Henceforth, his
communications strategy would be more sophisticated. Propaganda
specialists, black PR, dark arts – all of it.

Adjusting the public record in the West was certainly more
complicated than it was at home, and vastly more expensive.
Tony Blair guarded the financial details of his consultancy work
as jealously as Nazarbayev guarded the details of his kickbacks,
but the three-term prime minister's services were said to cost
Kazakhstan $13 million a year. Blair understood when to use
light, when darkness. Back in 2006, investigators from the Serious
Fraud Office chasing down bribery related to the sale of British
fighter jets to Saudi Arabia had tried to inspect the middlemen's
Swiss accounts. The House of Saud had sent word that such
interference in their affairs would cause them to cancel the next
multibillion-dollar batch of planes from BAE Systems, formerly
British Aerospace. Blair's government halted the SFO investigation, on the grounds of Saudi Arabia's invaluable assistance in
heading off attacks by adherents of the jihadism the kingdom
itself sponsored. For Sir Dick Evans, a lifelong arms dealer who
had risen to the chairmanship of BAE and been questioned by
the SFO's bribery investigators as they homed in on their targets,
this represented a bullet dodged at the last second. His next

profitable course would lead to Kazakhstan, to set up an airline, Astana Air.

These Brits who had had brushes with the law seemed to understand what Nazarbayev was trying to achieve. Sir Dick assisted another of them, Jonathan Aitken, in his composition of a biography of the leader. Aitken had served as a Conservative cabinet minister before doing a stint in jail for perjury and perverting the course of justice when he was caught lying about the Saudis having paid for him to stay at the Ritz in Paris while he was in charge of Britain's defence procurement. Sir Dick flew him round the country and helped him to craft the picture of Nazarbayev that emerged in 2009 as *Nazarbayev and the Making of Kazakhstan: From Communism to Capitalism*. 'He is a shrewd tactician,' Aitken wrote of his subject, 'a charming conversationalist, a persuasive speaker and a charismatic leader of vision and courage, particularly when facing difficult situations.'

Nazarbayev had learned that Westerners could be just as adept as he was in turning money into power and power back into money. Some, like Dick Evans and Jonathan Aitken, went about it from positions at the top of business and government. Others had to wait until they had left office to monetise their access and influence. They had to get theirs from what they called 'consultancy'. Blair was said to have made $1 million from Ivan Glasenberg's Glencore for three hours spent talking the Qatari prime minister out of blocking its merger with a mining company. JP Morgan, the Wall Street bank that had won the financial crisis, retained him too, as did a Swiss insurance company, the government of Kuwait and Abu Dhabi's investment fund. Some days he was a business consultant, others a philanthropist, or a governance guru, or a peacemaker. His money sat in a web of companies that almost rivalled the complexity and opacity Nazarbayev's Swiss bankers had devised. By one estimate, less than a decade after he resigned as prime minister, his fortune stood at $90 million.

Nazarbayev found that he and his regime had a certain chemistry with figures from Blair's strand of Western politics: the Third Way. It was a system that purported to wed the humanity of the left to the dynamism of the markets. Its proponents possessed, as Tony Judt put it following Blair's election, 'blissful confidence in the dismantling of centralised public services and social safety nets'. They felt themselves to be part of a new, transnational elite that would harness the miracles of globalisation. Peter Mandelson, Blair's strategist, announced the end of the left's anxieties about the hoarding of wealth. 'We are intensely relaxed about people getting filthy rich,' he said. (He added, 'as long as they pay their taxes', though the caveat was often forgotten, perhaps because they did not.)

It was to Blair that Nazarbayev turned for counsel at this delicate moment. The information blackout on Zhanaozen had been insufficient to prevent the basic details leaking out. It was as though someone had spoken aloud a forbidden truth: for the kleptocrat, ruling by licensing theft rather than seeking consent, money can achieve most of what needs to be done. For everything else, there is violence. And so, as he arrived in Cambridge, Mecca of the rational, to deliver his speech, Nazarbayev resolved to follow Blair's advice. For these Westerners, anxious after years of war and terrorism and, lately, the financial crisis, he would be the bringer of stability to a troubled world.

As he sat before his audience of academics and worthies, Nazarbayev's features moved so little that, unless you kept your gaze on his mouth, you might think some disembodied voice were delivering his speech. The whitening hair, augustly side-parted, gleamed above the tanned dome of a forehead, improbably smooth for a man who had just hit seventy-two. The forehead arched down to owlish brows and a snub nose on the end of which perched a pair of svelte reading glasses. The president's eyes mostly followed his text, but every few words they flicked up to inspect his audience. The lips were almost motionless, as though the jaw had been calibrated to open just enough for the sounds to depart. Dressed in a royal blue suit, brilliant white shirt and electric blue tie, he sat forward in his seat, an enormous and antique leather-backed wooden throne. Now and then he added a kindergarten finger-wag of emphasis. From the wall behind him a portrait of Elizabeth I looked on, similarly expressionless.

His small audience was seated around an oval of desks at the centre of a six-hundred-year-old chamber in a building that had over the centuries housed Cambridge's schools of divinity and law.

'The turn of the twentieth century represented a time of extensive and profound change across the vast, geostrategic territory of Eurasia,' he began. 'Over a short period of time, we witnessed global changes on an unprecedented scale; earlier, they would have taken centuries to unfold. New, independent countries appeared on the political map of the world.' The president reminded those present of the pinnacle of history at which he had accomplished all that he had achieved. 'Kazakhstan celebrated its twentieth anniversary of independence in December last year. This period has been the ultimate test of endurance for our young country.' The Soviet authorities, among whom Nazarbayev apparently did not include himself despite three decades in the *apparat*, had bequeathed the new nation 'nothing but systemic financial crisis, a non-competitive economy and an ineffective government system'. Statistical proof: 'By 1992, 40 per cent of the population was living below the poverty line and inflation was almost 2,000 per cent.' The task ahead had been unimaginably vast. 'We had to create a new type of state from scratch: implement new reforms, change the economic system from a centrally planned economy

to a free market and introduce democracy instead of totalitarianism.'

His audience nodded deferentially as they listened through
their translation headsets.

'Taking into account the instability of the surrounding region,'
he continued, 'our priority is to keep a strong state and to maintain the security of our country. That is why we always
concentrate on carrying out gradual reforms, where economic
liberalisation is of prime importance, followed by political liberalisation.'

As Blair had suggested, Nazarbayev gave a cautious commitment to allowing a little more freedom. Then he said:

Unfortunately, the notion of democracy all too often suffers
from a biased interpretation in post-Soviet countries; it is seen
as an opportunity to be beyond the law. This, in turn, has
triggered internal conflict and interethnic clashes. A lack of
political culture and previous experience has engendered
disrespect towards state institutions and a movement towards
violence – this is a slippery slope for any country.

   To see the effects, one need only look at the mass violence
in Osh, the conflicts in Andijan which have claimed the lives
of hundreds of people, as well as the events in Zhanaozen
where, under the instigation of extremists, a labour
disagreement gave rise to havoc on the streets.

A dire warning indeed. At Andijan in 2005 the Uzbek authorities had opened fire, killing hundreds, to put down an uprising.
Following the Kyrgyz revolution in 2010, dozens had died in
riots in the southern city of Osh. Zhanaozen should be seen in
the same context: an intolerable threat to stability that, regrettably,
required the shortening of a few lives to negate. Indeed,
Nazarbayev explained, at Zhanaozen the threat had been still

more menacing. It had comprised that category of ne'er-do-wells Westerners had learned to dread in the past decade: extremists.

Nazarbayev and the West were already united in the fight against extremists. Following Blair's script, Nazarbayev reminded the room that he was and would continue to be a 'stable partner for coalition forces' in Afghanistan. In Zhanaozen, however, it was not an Islamist extremist that Nazarbayev had in mind but a bald, imposing and highly caffeinated former journalist called Vladimir Kozlov.

Kozlov had grown up in the oil region, then worked there as a reporter. He understood the loyalties and rivalries, the history, the oil business. By his thirties he was living in Almaty running a TV channel. He signed up with Ablyazov and the rest of the liberal businessmen, politicians and officials who formed Democratic Choice of Kazakhstan, becoming head of the party's political council. After Nazarbayev declared Democratic Choice illegal and its leaders were jailed or intimidated into surrender, Kozlov founded his own party in 2005. Alga! he called it – Forward! Through all that followed, while others in the opposition were assassinated, exiled or succumbed to anxiety and paranoia, he remained phlegmatic, frequently letting forth his big, wheezy laugh.

Kozlov knew the oil workers of western Kazakhstan from his journalist days. Labour disputes were common, and when they arose Kozlov and his Alga! comrades would try to help out, mainly finding lawyers who would agree to represent the strikers. When OMG's bosses responded to the 2011 strike by firing workers, a delegation came to Almaty and told Kozlov what was going on. At first, he could do little more than try to use the remaining TV channel and newspaper that were not allied to the regime to counter the state-media portrayal of uppity oil workers driven by greed. When winter began to descend on the strikers, Kozlov's party sent tents and blankets, only for the Zhanaozen police to seize them. As the strikers ran out of money, Kozlov instructed that the party budget be used to help them meet loan and mortgage repayments. When that money ran out he turned to the party's exiled benefactor, Mukhtar Ablyazov. Knowing that the KNB would try to trace his funds, Kozlov made arrangements to receive the money in secret. He would get a message to be at a rendezvous in Almaty at a certain time. Given the danger, he would go himself. At the designated spot, a stranger would hand him a bag containing between ten thousand and thirty thousand dollars. He refused to believe the allegations that Ablyazov was a mere thief. But by connecting the Zhanaozen strike with Ablyazov's money, Kozlov had handed the regime a crucial ingredient for the narrative it would tell about the strike and the massacre that followed. Kozlov himself was already technically a criminal. The authorities had refused to register Alga! as a political party and had banned him from contesting the 2011 presidential election. Nonetheless, Alga! would stage public gatherings, and it was at one of these in an Almaty square that Kozlov was to be found on the morning of December 16, 2011. A distressed comrade rushed over and handed him a phone. He put it to his ear and heard: 'They are killing us. We are being killed.'

Nazarbayev's initial comments about the incident at Zhanaozen – the ones that had led Roza Tuletayeva to present herself at the prosecutor's office – had blamed 'bandit elements', rather than the strikers, for the unrest. But quickly, it seemed, his advisers had seen an opportunity. The official account of events started to change. By January 25, the prosecutor general was announcing that 'one of the causes of the mass disorder were the active efforts of some individuals to persuade fired workers to continue their protest action and violently oppose the authorities'. Among those named as having 'incited social discord' was Kozlov.

Kozlov was in detention awaiting trial by the time Nazarbayev gave his Cambridge speech. His conviction was assured: it would be proof that extremists had incited the violence, that they, not Nazarbayev's security forces, were ultimately responsible for the bloodshed.

Having spoken the name of Zhanaozen, the president now hammered home his point:

> The world has recently faced a number of serious threats,
> namely, religious extremism and terrorism, and we are no
> exception. It is vital for us to maintain the same pace of
> development without sacrificing our main value – stability,
> which is the bedrock for progress in our state and society and
> is a vital ingredient in resolving the considerable challenges
> posed by modernisation.

Nazarbayev ploughed on through his text. His achievements were numerous: the economic growth figures, the investment numbers, the membership of a multitude of important multilateral organisations.

> Ladies and gentlemen!
> It would be no exaggeration to say that mankind has literally
> come to the next milestone in its history. The global financial
> crisis of 2008–2009 has come to represent the final watershed
> between an outdated and new format for the future.

In this new future, the West would understand that its interests were aligned with his – that is, with Kazakhstan's. 'There is a saying that an Englishman will even carry a tea kettle to the top of the highest mountain. Well, Kazakhs never go to bed without drinking tea. We are also united by the fact that English people and Kazakhs prefer to drink their tea with milk.'

And united by something else. Nazarbayev had understood that there were Westerners – Westerners at his level, the level of the khan – who shared his great undertaking: the privatisation of power.

21

Too Big to Jail

London, September 2012

The logic of the City was retuning. Yes, impunity had allowed bankers to detonate their banks and destroy the economy. But now it was important that banks were prevented from failing again, even if the cost of that was impunity. And not just impunity for cooking up bullshit derivatives or the other nonsense that had caused the crisis – impunity for everything.

In Washington, Senator Levin's investigative committee had established that what he called a 'pervasively polluted' culture at HSBC had allowed bankers to launder money for drug cartels, terrorists and despots. Founded in 1865 to finance transnational commerce, HSBC's headquarters occupied an entire tower in Canary Wharf. It was the most valuable bank in Europe. In September 2012 George Osborne, the British chancellor of the exchequer, wrote to his US counterpart, Treasury Secretary Tim Geithner, and Ben Bernanke, chair of the Federal Reserve, urging the Americans to go easy on London-listed banks caught laundering money. If HSBC were convicted of a crime and barred from dealing in dollars, Osborne wrote, 'very serious risks for financial and economic stability' would ensue. Three months later, HSBC settled the charges by paying a fine.

The prosecutors at the Department of Justice were not, however, minded to let all banks off the hook. There was one thing you couldn't get away with: welching on American taxes. The prosecutors had extracted billions in fines from UBS and Credit Suisse, the two biggest Swiss banks, for helping their clients do precisely that. But they, like HSBC, avoided conviction. Then, in a Manhattan court in January 2013, lawyers for Wegelin & Co., the oldest Swiss bank, older even than the United States, entered a guilty plea on behalf of the institution itself to charges of using secret accounts to abet tax evasion by Americans. As a result of being a criminally convicted corporate person, the bank would no longer be able to conduct its business. Its management announced that it would close permanently.

Nigel Wilkins thought: if one Swiss bank can be broken, one guardian of money's secrets, then perhaps others can be, too.

22
Sasha and Seva
St James's, March 2013

In the bitter spring of 2013, Sasha Machkevitch descended on ENRC's headquarters in London. The offices stood in St James's, the rectangle of discretion and refinement between Fortnum & Mason and the royal parks, full of brokers and vintners and gentlemen's clubs. They were pretty ordinary on the inside. But they contained too many secrets for disloyalty to be tolerated. The City had wanted the Trio, courted them, invited them in with open arms and bank accounts. And yet now London was turning on Sasha and his partners, threatening with a straight face to impose its laws. In the wake of a financial crisis, suddenly the outsiders were to blame for everything. What was it they had said, those apparatchiks from the Serious Fraud Office, when they had first sat down with ENRC's solicitors back in 2011? Stuff about wanting to 'ensure that ethical UK businesses are not undermined by non-UK corporations with extensive operations abroad who employ unethical practices'. Tell that to 2007; tell that to the Banqueting House.

As for Neil Gerrard, he seemed to be confused about where he owed his allegiance. Evidently he had not understood the world in which his clients operated. They were subject to Nazarbayev's rules: you are ours or you are theirs. The notion of being loyal to an abstract, loyal to the law – to the point, even, of placing that loyalty above your obligations to those who paid you, those who had bought you – this was so preposterous it could only be a cover for darker motives. Gerrard had been pushing and pushing for ENRC to help the SFO do its job – to 'self-report'. That would involve keeping the SFO top brass posted as he undertook his investigation, convincing them every inkling of skulduggery had been explored, then letting them have the evidence he found. 'If I don't deliver – and I've repeated this fucking hundreds of times – if we don't deliver fraud or corruption,' he had once said, 'we've got no deal.' If one of the Trio's people at ENRC objected to any expansion he proposed to the investigation, Gerrard would remind them that he had worked with the SFO's most senior officers on countless cases. If they believed ENRC was failing to cooperate, Gerrard would say, they would order raids not just on ENRC's offices but on the homes of ENRC employees. On the other hand, if they were convinced ENRC had made a clean breast of it, then the corporation itself – an idea, incorporeal, a thing that could not be impoverished or incarcerated – would carry any punishment.

Gerrard had been regularly sketching out for the SFO brass what he had been finding, first on Kazakhstan, then on Africa. That was, he thought, part of the job he had been hired to do. The Trio's loyal soldiers within ENRC had managed to distract or delay much of his work on Africa. Nonetheless, Gerrard had ferreted out some of what had been going on, and from him some of that information had passed to the SFO, whose senior officers now presumed to think for themselves. On January 21, 2013, a year and five months since that first letter had arrived from the SFO, Patrick Rappo, its head of bribery and corruption, wrote to ENRC complaining that the delays had become unacceptable. 'You will appreciate that if we cannot progress these matters with your assistance, we have no alternative but to progress

them without your assistance,' he warned. The SFO could tolerate
a few more weeks. After that, they would have no option but to
open a criminal investigation. And they had been asking questions
about 'board awareness' – a sign that ENRC's sins might be
deemed to have been committed not merely by the corporation
itself but by the flesh-and-blood individuals who controlled it.
Sasha had not, in the end, gone through with his idea to assume
the chairmanship, so neither he nor either of the other members
of the Trio sat on the board. But their people did. If the SFO
came for them, could they all be trusted to keep the Trio's secrets?

Already, too many of those secrets had slipped from their
control. Gerrard knew about Shawn McCormick, knew that, at
some point after he left BP following his strange dealings with
the FSB in Moscow, he had taken up a role for ENRC in Africa.
He knew, too, about the Trio's other American in Africa, their
principal envoy, the stocky former soldier who otherwise seemed
to have no past, Victor Hanna. Worse, in recent days Gerrard
had been saying Hanna should be suspended for obstructing his
investigation. And Mehmet Dalman, the ENRC chairman,
seemed minded to agree. Dalman, the British-Cypriot City
moneyman, had been on the board ever since the listing. A year
ago, as the grandees fell away, he had become chairman and made
all sorts of noises about being the man who would clean up this
scandalous corporation. Clearly he had now lost his mind, or at
least forgotten that ENRC's status as a public company was only
ever meant to be a charade. It belonged to the Trio.

And then there were the secrets not yet disinterred but which
were now perilously close to the surface.

No one was sure when Sasha had first encountered Semyon
Mogilevich, the enormous, ingenious, dryly witty, ceaselessly
smoking criminal mastermind known as the Brainy Don or simply
Seva. Both had known Boris Birshtein in his pomp, before the
Rutskoi Affair brought him down; both had been granted

citizenship by Israel, part of the wave of ex-Soviets whose arrival hastened the corruption of the Jewish state. Money trails connected them, too. Trans-World, the Reuben brothers' company that had backed the Trio as they captured Kazakh mines and factories, did tens of millions of dollars of transactions with two of the Brainy Don's front companies. This was, the Reubens said, all in the course of normal, legal business transactions, and done without any knowledge of the gangster's presence behind the front companies.

Their careers had mirrored one another's: Seva's in the underworld, Sasha's in the overworld. Both saw that there was a gap between East and West through which money could be drained into a black aquifer beneath.

Born in the brutalised Ukraine of 1946, Seva had started out in Kiev. Before he was known for his brain, he was known for his brawn. He was a wrestler: big body, big head. Soon he put the latter to more use. He saw the opportunities for manipulating money. The points where currencies intersected were especially vulnerable. These were not simple exchanges of goods and services: through the value of currencies, the rulers of nations sought to express their strength, dispense patronage, humiliate rivals. There was already plenty of illusion here, rich soil for a fraudster to cultivate his scams. It took Seva a while to learn how to turn the law to his advantage. He was jailed in 1977 for dealing currencies on the black market, got out after eighteen months but was soon back in on a four-year sentence for the same offence. Undeterred, upon moving to Moscow he resumed his career falsifying money, this time the coupons the Soviet authorities issued in exchange for foreign currency.

One day in 1982, Seva met a gigantic fellow wrestler at the gym. It was Sergei Mikhailov – Mikhas – foremost of the new generation of business-gangsters. So began Seva's association with Mikhas's Solntsevskaya brotherhood. Mikhas admired Seva. A very talented businessman, he called him. They embarked on international trade enterprises together. Mikhas would tell those who asked that he and Seva dealt in shoes and spare parts. The FBI believed they also shifted counterfeit jewellery and antiques looted from Russian museums.

Seva could move anything across borders: art, crude, clothes, bootleg vodka and the belongings of emigrating Soviet Jews, gems, girls, gas, guns, heroin, nuclear material, hitmen and, naturally, himself. But he was best of all at smuggling money. He was swift to grasp the changes wrought by the triumph of liberal capitalism. Money could be seized by force and made to look like any other money. Cleansed of its past, it became what all the other money was: 'a formal token of delayed reciprocal altruism', as another brainy don, Richard Dawkins, had put it, a token denoting that you had done society a service and society owed you something in exchange. With those tokens you could buy anything. Better still, money had gone electronic. It could move with the speed of an idea – faster, perhaps, because you didn't even need to put it all that convincingly. Seva turned himself into a criminal banker – *the* criminal banker. With the end of the USSR, the globalisation that had stalled since the world wars broke the old colonial powers was resuming with delirious pace. Western economies were so relaxed about the properties of money – any money, all money – that it was almost too easy to ship it in, easier even than crates of girls or consignments of knock-off booze. A little camouflage and it was as if your cargoes of money were invisible. Better still: the Westerners would provide the camouflage for you.

The island of Alderney, a three-square-mile dependency of the British Crown in the English Channel, became the node of the Brainy Don's conglomerate. Not that he actually did anything there. You didn't have to. There were two lives: the paper life and the real, secret life. In the paper life, Seva was not Seva but

Arigon, a corporate person of PO Box 77, St Anne's House, Alderney. Arigon had bank accounts in Stockholm, London, New York and Geneva. It acquired legitimate businesses, such as the Hungarian national armaments manufacturer, privatised in 1993. It had solicitors in London, a firm called Blakes, just off Chancery Lane. The British police took an interest in Blakes and found that they had moved $50 million through accounts at Royal Bank of Scotland over three years. They had done so at the behest of the Brainy Don, the detectives believed, and the money was the proceeds of extortion, prostitution, arms dealing and drug trafficking from the increasingly multinational enterprise that he controlled from his bases in the former Eastern Bloc. One of the solicitors, Adrian Churchward, was married to a Soviet-born woman, Galina, and raising her son, Yuli. Her ex, the boy's father, was Seva. The officers began an investigation. Operation Sword, they called it. For a year they monitored Blakes. They got in touch with their counterparts in Moscow, from whom they learned of a recent scam. The Russian government had paid in advance for food that had never arrived. Instead the money had found its way to the front companies Blakes appeared to be running for Seva. Someone seemed to be covering their tracks: at least one Russian involved was already dead. On May 16, 1995, three teams from the Southeast Regional Crime Squad assembled at sunrise. They raided Blakes' office and the suspects' homes. They arrested Churchward, his colleague at Blakes, and Seva's ex, Galina. At Blakes' office they found a hundred files detailing the worldwide transactions through which the Brainy Don moved dirty money.

The British detectives' haul was enough to obtain a warrant for the arrest on the charge of conspiracy to handle stolen goods of Seva himself, should he set foot in their jurisdiction. To convict him and his solicitors they would not have to prove his every last criminal endeavour. One crime would do. But the longer they waited for the Moscow police to hand over the evidence, the clearer it became that they were never going to. There was an invisible hand restraining Russian law enforcement from helping the detectives in London convict the Brainy Don and his associates. The charge against Seva was dropped, even though the report of Operation Sword had concluded he was 'one of the world's top criminals who has a personal wealth of $100 million'. A court ordered the Crown Prosecution Service to pay his solic- itors' and Galina's legal costs. The extent of the authorities' sanction was the letter the home secretary sent to the Brainy Don telling him he was no longer welcome on British territory. It was scarcely a punishment for a man who had already seen the changing of the guard at Buckingham Palace and eaten duck in Chinatown, and who in any case preferred to move through the world as a cipher in the financial system.

Seva spent much of the nineties away from the gangland bloodshed of Moscow, residing in the cities on the bleeding edge between East and West – Budapest, Prague. He travelled by bulletproof limousine, commanding a multinational staff of 250, and operated from topless bars – brothels, Western law enforce- ment believed – called Black and White. His reputation as a shadow banker grew. Out in the world, the paper world, he was just a simple grain trader. A reporter asked him if he had ever laundered money. Yes, he replied, once, when I washed a shirt with a $5 bill in the pocket.

In fact, the Brainy Don knew that you could launder money day in and day out for as long as you could maintain a fiction that enough people had a reason to believe – and that the further you got behind capitalist lines, the keener everyone was to believe capitalist stories. For five years, the Canadian business elite, stock market regulators and investors credited the tale that a corpora- tion called YBM Magnex was a successful business that did what its splendid brochures said it did. They believed that it manufactured magnets and had discovered a revolutionary new technique for desulphurising oil, so much so that it was valued at nearly $1 billion. Deloitte & Touche, another of the Big Four auditing firms, vouched for its accounts, allaying any concerns of those who had heard the rumours that YBM Magnex was somehow connected to the Russian mob. Only when an FBI team realised that this supposed vast international corporation was operating from a bit of a disused school in Pennsylvania did the façade collapse. By then, the Brainy Don had sucked in $150 million from investors and laundered more. His executives lived the American dream. One of them, a Russian metallurgy professor called Jacob Bogatin, played the part of the legit entrepreneur leading an exciting start-up as head of YBM Magnex. His brother David was a master of the fuel-tax scam that Fat Larry had pioneered in New York. He bought five condos in the same glittering Manhattan skyscraper where the raging *vor* Ivankov had his.

Or banks: you had to believe in them, or else financial capitalism would have no finance on which to function. Take the Bank of New York, one of America's oldest, a venerable Wall Street institution in which Alexander Hamilton and Aaron Burr had owned shares. It looked as though it was just doing what banks did: taking in deposits, lending them out, investing. But it was also something else: a money laundry, the biggest that at that time had been discovered in the US. Seven billion dollars had departed Russia, passed through Bank of New York accounts controlled by front companies and flowed onwards to be enjoyed in blissful anonymity. The money's past was obscure. But a lot of it had gone through a front company that shared a name – Benex – with one of the fake customers of Seva's YBM Magnex.

Moving money was an art, but from time to time violence was still required. It was to dirty money what the law was to clean – a guarantee that agreements would be honoured. A hitman

arrested in Los Angeles was carrying a business card that gave
his employer as one of the Brainy Don's Hungarian companies.
Those who resisted extortion suffered before the end, their mutilations a deterrent to disobedience in others. The Brainy Don
controlled arsenals, built mortars and missiles. Yet the most potent
weapons came from his armoury of information. Even back in
the Soviet days, when he was just a street fraudster turning forty
in eighties Moscow, he had been in contact with an official from
the criminal division of the Soviet Interior Ministry. The official
knew of his activities and noted them in the files but allowed
him to proceed – suggesting that Seva was playing informant. It
was the same city's police force that would scupper Operation
Sword by withholding evidence of his criminal schemes.

As his enterprise evolved from petty thuggery to transnational
financial services for organised crime, Seva's business had become
the keeping of life-and-death secrets. Keeping them and, as
required, exploiting them. He learned to barter information for
immunity to an extent far greater than even Whitey Bulger
achieved. His deal with German intelligence to supply dirt on
his fellow ex-Soviet gangsters shielded him from law enforcement
there. In the US he danced with Bob Levinson, the FBI's top
man on post-Soviet organised crime. The Brainy Don met
American law enforcement officials to discuss surrendering to
answer the YBM Magnex fraud charges – a proffer meeting, it
was called, where a suspect agreed to speak on condition that he
would remain at liberty and that what he said could never be
used against him. Seva revealed a few nuggets on his friends and
his rivals. No deal came at the end of two days of talks in October
1997, but that was scarcely a loss for the don: he had introduced
information of his own choosing into others' narratives and, that
work done, he was free to slink back into the underworld. In
Israel, his intelligence file disappeared. Such was his own intelligence operation that he could appear a puppeteer. It was said

that, after he and Mikhas fell out over a few million dollars, the Brainy Don had been scheduled for execution at an underworld party he was due to attend in Prague in May 1995. But the police were tipped off and raided the celebrations. As a flock of criminal bosses were carted away, Seva was in a bar nearby, drinking unmolested until daybreak.

And yet the scandals at YBM Magnex and Bank of New York were making Seva famous. Sasha might delight in the glitz of the business scene, but the Brainy Don knew better than to embrace celebrity. It was the last quality clients wanted in an underworld banker. The traces of him grew ghostly once more. When they were detected, however, it was close to the greatest undertakings of the new kleptocratic order.

In February 2006, an American diplomat in Vienna sent a secret cable to Washington. Raiffeisen, an Austrian bank whose executives had expanded its operations aggressively in the former Soviet Union, was acting as the front for anonymous clients who held a stake in one of the most obscure – and most important – companies in Europe. The company's name was RosUkrEnergo. It was registered in Switzerland and it served as the corporate middleman in the gas trade that heated Europeans' houses, fired their power stations, cooked their food and generally maintained them in the manner to which they had become accustomed. The gas came from Central Asia, passed through Russia and arrived in Ukraine, where some of it remained and some of it continued westward. The progress of this commodity along this route – and Vladimir Putin's ability to arrest that progress – ranked among the highest concerns of Europe's leaders. And yet no one knew who controlled RosUkrEnergo. Like a couple of similarly opaque predecessors, it had been granted the precious right to buy the gas in the East, pipe it through Russia and sell it in the West, a transaction from which it earned annual profits approaching $1 billion. Half of RosUkrEnergo belonged to Gazprom, the Russian state gas company run by an old pal of Putin's, curiosity about which could land inquisitive foreigners like John Lough of TNK-BP in big trouble. The other half belonged to whoever was hiding behind the bankers at Raiffeisen. The diplomat was clear in his cable about who the Americans suspected this to be: a son of Ukraine, Semyon Mogilevich, the Brainy Don wanted by the US for the YBM Magnex fraud.

American officials urged the Austrians to make Raiffeisen come clean. Newspapers reported that a mobster was feared to be in charge of Europe's energy supplies. Eventually, a Ukrainian came forward and said he was RosUkrEnergo's secret owner. It wasn't Seva but a businessman of no great renown by the name of Dmytro Firtash. Whether he had been the owner all along, no one could be sure: ownership of RosUkrEnergo resided in instruments called bearer shares, meaning that if you bore them, the stake was yours, and if you gave them to your business partner or your wife or even some stranger you could trust, the stake became theirs, unless they gave them back to you, in which case it became yours again. Another American diplomat, the ambassador in Kiev, recorded Firtash confiding that it was only with Seva's blessing that he had got his start in business. When asked, Firtash dismissed the notion that Seva was behind RosUkrEnergo, as did the Brainy Don's own lawyer. Firtash said his bankers at Raiffeisen had conducted comprehensive due diligence that showed he had no links with any criminal activities. And yet the very investigators those bankers hired discovered buried connections between Firtash's businesses and the Brainy Don's people.

For the American prosecutors, the Brainy Don was the king criminal, personification of the Red Mafiya that was eclipsing even the Cosa Nostra. Most troublingly of all, his interests and those of the Kremlin seemed to be fusing. Either the state was being criminalised or the criminals were taking over the state: the effect was the same. Yes, Seva was detained in Moscow in

2008. But a US extradition request was refused – Seva had taken Russian citizenship, and the Russian constitution forbade the extradition of its citizens. He was released the following year. A spokeswoman for the Interior Ministry – with which Seva had enjoyed a relationship stretching back to Soviet days – announced that the tax-evasion charges against him were 'not of a particularly grave nature'. Soon they would be dropped. The Americans persisted. The FBI put Seva on its top ten most wanted list. Special Agent Peter Kowenhoven, who had worked the file for a decade, declared: 'Through his extensive international criminal network, Mogilevich controls extensive natural gas pipelines in Eastern Europe, and he uses this wealth and power to not only further his criminal enterprises but to influence governments and their economies. With him, it's all about money – money and influence. And the really chilling thing is that he seems willing to work with any criminals, regardless of their ideology.'

The Brainy Don was supposed to have been banned from France. But, using a helpful Belgian diplomat as an intermediary, he had pulled another Whitey Bulger move, arranging to exchange information on politicians and mobsters for clandestine access to the country.

Maybe it was that deal, or maybe some subsequent one, under which Seva travelled to France to see Sasha. Seva was not the only visitor from the underworld: according to the banished Kazakh politician Viktor Khrapunov, it was at Courchevel that Sasha paraded a couple of other ex-Soviet mobsters by way of intimidation. But the Brainy Don was no common crook. For one thing, he let it be known in the 1990s that he was on good terms with the Russian Presidential Security Service, that his contact there was the chief investigator of government corruption. Russian spies who defected revealed that he was also a long-standing agent initially of the First Chief Directorate, the KGB's international division, then of the FSB. And they said that he had, back in the 1990s, struck up a business relationship with another KGB man, one destined for big things – Vladimir Putin.

Seva and Sasha: whatever their true relationship, their currency, like all moneymen, was information. You had to be able to protect your own and harvest your rivals'. Boris Birshtein's downfall in nineties Moscow showed what happened when you lost control of information. And Sasha was operating in the West, where information had been granted its freedom. He had made its markets work for him, its knights and its banks. Now he would have to make its laws do the same. When he arrived at ENRC headquarters in St James's on March 27, 2013, he demanded that Neil Gerrard be fired.

23

The Loving Cup

Canary Wharf, February 2013

On February 11, 2013, a manager in the Authorisations Division of the Financial Services Authority sent an email to all the members of his team with the subject, 'Employee of the Month'. 'With sincere apologies for the delay in communicating this,' he began, 'I am pleased to inform you that we have a joint winner for January.' One of the winners had made a 'significant effort' to complete all the necessary paperwork before the organisation was scheduled to turn into the Financial Conduct Authority in April. Having failed to do so before the financial crisis, it would lose its responsibilities for ensuring banks had enough money. But as the new name indicated, its task would be to continue – or begin – to police behaviour in the City. The second employee of the month had been energetically trying to do just that. 'Nigel,' wrote the manager, 'for demonstrating curiosity and refusing to accept the status quo in respect of Caymans-based funds.'

The status quo, as Nigel saw it, was that about half the money businesses that his colleagues authorised should not have been. His particular concern was the hedge funds, the money houses of Mayfair. They did things like give millions to an ex-cricketer and a policeman's son who spent it currying favour with a

Zimbabwean dictator by paying for him to steal an election. But Nigel's chief concern was where the hedge funds' money came from in the first place. Moneymen would set up a fund in the Cayman Islands: there were ten thousand funds registered there, one for every six inhabitants, collectively holding assets and debt worth $1.4 trillion, enough money to buy Apple three times over. The directors of these hedge funds each sat on tens of boards, sometimes hundreds: they were purely for show. And while the money remained offshore, the people who controlled it were in London. But they only had to secure approval from the regulator to set up as a firm of advisers to the hedge fund, not for the enormous pot of money itself. No one, as far as Nigel could tell, was checking where the money that filled that pot was coming from. Sure, public bodies and pension funds handed over billions upon billions to the hedge funds, swallowing their claims to have special powers to multiply it. But what about all the rest? Nigel concluded that the hedge funds were doing the same thing as the Swiss banks: anonymising money on an industrial scale. Certainly the owners of this money were content to pay hand-somely for the service, even though the returns were meagre. For the six years to 2013, money they entrusted to a hedge fund increased annually by an average of 3.6 per cent, much less than it would have done if invested in a few solid stocks and bonds. Meanwhile, the twenty-five best-paid hedge fund managers earned $21 billion. With that money, you could, say, fund the entire campaigns for the US presidency of both the Republican and the Democratic candidates in every election from the one just passed, Barack Obama's second victory in 2012, to the one in 2092.

Nigel traced the daisy chains of corporate entities that connected the hedge fund managers in Mayfair to the pots of money secreted offshore. Each of the steps might not be illegal, he concluded, but all together they were clearly meant to help people hide money. He mentioned this to one of his superiors. The superior replied: it's only tax avoidance, not tax evasion. Strange that we should be promoting either, Nigel thought. The working assumption among his colleagues seemed to be: that's just how it's done. If they were in any doubt, they could turn to the consultants who worked for the hedge funds and who would visit the FSA's offices in Canary Wharf to give stylish presentations that made the whole thing look thoroughly legitimate.

And yet, there he was, employee of the month. The laurels might have sat a little uneasily on Nigel's rebellious brows. But perhaps times were finally changing. George Osborne had picked Martin Wheatley, a tough former head of the Hong Kong market regulator, to run the new Financial Conduct Authority. His appointment was a departure from the 'light touch' regulation with which Blair's New Labour had sought to prolong Thatcher's big bang. Wheatley's stated approach to the City was, 'Shoot first and ask questions later.'

Still, Nigel could not help but wonder why the warning he had delivered back in 2008 had gone unheeded by the very watchdog to which he now commuted from Kensington every day. After he'd sent his letter explaining his belief that BSI's office in the City was shifting dirty money, an official called Neil from the FSA's intelligence unit had emailed him. 'As I'm sure you'll understand, I can't tell you about any investigation that we will undertake but rest assured, we are taking your information seriously.' Nigel had his thousand pages of documents to hand over. He wrote to Neil: 'I had the privilege of having a front row seat observing precisely how Swiss banking secrecy operates to the detriment of humanity.' The FSA had suspicions about BSI already – that private warning in 2004 over its lax checks on the origins of its clients' money. Now Nigel had offered to explain exactly how offshore accounts were structured to ensure that the real owners of the money that passed through them were completely hidden. One of Neil's colleagues wrote back suggesting a meeting. Nigel agreed, then never heard another word. That was nearly four years ago. Those thousand pages were still sitting in red boxes in his flat, beside the economics textbooks and the Thomas Hardy novels.

These days people had other things to panic about. The beef that Britons were eating turned out to be horse. The comparison was obvious: contaminated meat spreading through supermarkets, like the bad mortgages spliced into the derivatives that had poisoned the banking system, or the dirty money seeping into democracies. Nigel wanted the same attention paid to the third risk as had been to the first two. For now, he would just have to continue his efforts as Trojan horsemeat in the great lasagne of money. He applied to join the Guild of Freemen of the City of London and was accepted. After completing the Ceremony of the Loving Cup – new freemen grasp the goblet with two hands, take a sip, then pass it on, while the guild's wardens guard their backs – he could execute the next stage of his scheme. That was to stand for election to the council that ran the City's affairs. He stood on a platform of 'greater accountability and transparency' and lost heavily. But winning was never the point for Nigel. If you can't beat them, he reasoned, at least annoy them.

24
The Presumption of Regularity

Rome, May 2013

The last light of an Italian evening close to the start of summer had drained from the sky, leaving perfect darkness outside the plane's windows. It was a small aircraft, equipped for luxury. In the cabin, a six-year-old girl watched cartoons. A woman in her forties, with dark eyes, strong cheekbones and a dark bob, looked at the child. With all the energy she had left – she had barely slept or eaten for two days – she suppressed any sign of the fear that was consuming her, lest her daughter sense it. Before the plane had taken off, she had tried to tell them, tell them about how the dictator wanted her husband dead, about what happened to his opponents, about Zhanaozen. Look on the internet, she had said. In the end she had told them she wanted to claim asylum, right there at the airport. But the woman who called herself Laura, the one with the dyed blonde hair who had screamed at her back at the detention centre, she had said, speaking softly now, 'It's already too late, everything is already decided.' They had been in the air for nearly six hours. The mother glanced at the screen that showed the aircraft's progress. They had begun their descent.

* * *

Peter Sahlas was loath to interrupt his barber. It was a question
of respect. Monsieur Dessault had cut his hair for twenty-three
years, from the time Peter chanced upon the establishment on
the Left Bank during a summer in Paris in 1991. Now Paris was
home, and although he travelled constantly – Geneva, it had
been this week, lobbying at the UN for Khodorkovsky – the
barber on Boulevard Saint Germain was a fixed point. Monsieur
Dessault – after more than two decades of forty-five-minute
appointments, it was still Monsieur Dessault, not Joël – had no
time for the amateurs with their electric clippers. He stuck with
scissors. You booked your slot, you turned up and the chair was
ready, without fail. Peter liked the precision. He did not have
time to waste waiting. By the same token, he sought at all costs
to avoid causing any delay. If one of his phones buzzed – Monsieur
Dessault always ribbed him for having two – he would try not
to answer, even if it related to one of the international intrigues
that occupied his days.

It was a Friday afternoon in May 2013, and he was settling
in to the usual badinage with Monsieur Dessault – current affairs
kept safely superficial – when a message arrived.

'Where are you?' It was Bota. It had been four years since they
met for lunch near Buckingham Palace and she had asked him
to come and see her boss, Mukhtar Ablyazov.

Even though Ablyazov had declined to hire him, Peter had
followed the case, frustrated that Ablyazov was being too timid.
Sure, he had been granted asylum, but he had been outflanked
when the Kazakhs brought civil claims against him through BTA
Bank in the High Court. Ablyazov's narrative – the freedom
fighter chased into exile by a despot – had been drowned out by
the Kazakhs': the very terms of the case were about money going
missing in staggering quantities. Vanishing had been a mistake
too, Peter thought. After Ablyazov fled, he could not even offer
a defence. The Kazakhs' lawyers secured default judgment after

default judgment, totting the total he was found to have filched higher and higher and eliciting condemnation after damning condemnation of Ablyazov's character from the judges. Still, Peter had stayed in touch with Bota. Branded as one of Ablyazov's associates, she could not go home. She stayed in London for a while, then moved to Brussels, where she too was granted asylum. When they visited Paris, she and her husband would meet Peter and his wife for a bite.

Another message arrived, seconds later: 'Please call urgently.'

Peter replied: 'Can it wait?'

It could not. He detected from the terseness of Bota's message that something serious had happened. Monsieur Dessault had made sufficient progress that he could continue the haircut on one side of his head while Peter held the phone to the other. He called Bota.

It was the second time he had detected anxiety in her voice. A few months back, just before Christmas, he had been in the dining room at home when she rang. It was early in the morning, and he could hear the strain as she spoke. 'I really need your help,' she said. Ablyazov's bodyguard, Alexandr Pavlov, had been arrested in Madrid on an Interpol Red Notice issued at Kazakhstan's request on charges of conspiring with Ablyazov to loot BTA Bank. The Kazakhs also claimed he had helped Ablyazov concoct a failed terrorist plot to attack Almaty. Peter had whirred into action, locating a Spanish lawyer who managed to slow down the extradition process. Pavlov was still in a Spanish prison, but that was better than being in a Kazakh prison.

'Where are you?' Bota asked now.

'I'm in Paris,' Peter replied, not mentioning that Monsieur Dessault was inches away, snipping.

'You have to go to Rome.'

'What do you mean?' The hair was getting in his collar. 'When do you want me to go to Rome?'

'Now.'

He knew Bota well enough to understand that, if she couldn't spare the time to elaborate, it was because the ten seconds it would take to do so had to be spent moving another piece on the chessboard. He rushed home, showered, picked up his laptop and zoomed to Charles de Gaulle. Only once he was waiting to board did he speak to her again. 'Who am I meeting?' he asked. 'Where am I going?' Bota gave him the name of a hotel. She said he should get there as quickly as he could after his plane landed. Ablyazov's wife and daughter had been kidnapped.

*   *   *

Madina woke at 5 a.m. to feed the baby. She noticed her Skype: lots of missed calls. That was how they stayed in touch. Her father had gone into hiding more than a year ago. She had found it perplexing that you could be sent to prison in Britain for something called 'contempt of court'. She had never believed that her father was a crook. Nazarbayev and his people had been saying he took money from here and there ever since Ablyazov first showed he would not be subservient to the boss; the BTA Bank stuff was just the same thing with bigger numbers. They spoke once a month or so. She knew not to ask where he was, just whether he was safe. At least her mother and her six-year-old sister Alua had EU residence permits. They had gone to Rome, where they could live quietly until Ablyazov's latest political troubles were over.

As she got up to go to the baby, Madina saw not just the missed Skypes but her father's messages: Call me call me call me. She called him.

'Mum's been arrested,' he said.

They had come in the middle of the night. Italian police, dozens of them, armed, had hammered on the doors of the house where Alma was living with her sister and her sister's husband. Alua had been asleep. Madina wanted to get on the next flight from Geneva to Rome and said so. Alma was the emotional one, a contrast to her physicist husband. This was not among the things for which she had prepared herself to cope. But Ablyazov said no, don't, they will let her out. They busied themselves finding lawyers who could make sure. Two days passed. Then more news came from Rome. They had come back and taken the child. 'Go,' Ablyazov told Madina. 'Get them.'

When Madina and Iliyas disembarked in Rome, she spotted a couple of Kazakhs. One of them said something to an Italian official, who scurried after them shouting, 'Documents! Documents!' Documents were shown and they were permitted to pass. They went straight to the office of the Italian lawyer they'd hired. Too late, the lawyer said, they're already on the plane.

*   *   *

Peter Sahlas landed as Friday night in Rome was getting going. He made for the Hotel de Russie next to the Villa Borghese and was waiting by the entrance when Madina and Iliyas walked in. He had never met them, but had heard plenty; it was one of those moments when names became people. Laurent Foucher was with them, a contact of Iliyas's from his property deals, as well as a lawyer and a bodyguard (handshake of steel, Peter noted, the kind of guy you want on your side). Madina's aunt had come, devastated, and her uncle, wearing a black eye administered by the police during the first raid. They set up an impromptu war room right there in the lobby. Guests gawked. The hotel staff roped them off. Bota called in from Brussels, and Ablyazov from wherever he was.

They knew a private jet was in the sky, they knew it was bound for Kazakhstan. Thanks to the tenacious efforts of the Italian lawyers they'd hired, they had a tail number. They put that into an app on Peter's phone, one that tracked flights; the orange, plane-shaped icon on the screen crept eastwards. Iliyas called a contact who knew how to use the number to find the owner. It turned out to be a jet-hire company in Vienna. To the extent that he ever wasn't, Peter had gone into full lawyer mode. Furiously he drafted paragraphs to be faxed to Austria, laying out why the plane must be turned around. Everyone was calling anyone they could think of who might have any scrap of information. Sugar was in Austria – these days he was their friend, or at least their enemy's enemy. But he was in jail, awaiting an extradition decision, so they had to make do with his lawyer. The bodyguard was running around with phone chargers.

The plane was passing over Turkey. Peter looked at Madina. He knew her to be tough as nails, but she was crying. This was never supposed to involve her mother, her sister. This is crossing the line, Peter thought. This is throwing out the rulebook. When it comes to oligarch–regime battles in the former Soviet Union, you don't go after the wife and kid – no one does that. In Russia, through all those years of the Khodorkovsky fight, they never stooped that low. There's an unwritten code of conduct. It can get really dirty and really ugly and you can spend ten years in jail. You can die. But you don't touch the wife or the kid.

Suddenly Peter remembered the smattering of aviation law he had studied. They had been trying to persuade the jet-hire company, but in flight the ultimate authority was the pilot. It was he who made the law on the plane. At 1.23 a.m. Madina emailed the company's lawyer with a message to be passed to her mother, saying that it was imperative she tell the pilot she was an asylum-seeker, that she was afraid for her life and that, as the captain, he had the legal authority to refuse to land in Kazakhstan. The lawyer said he would try. But they had learned something else. Alma and Alua were not the only passengers. Two men from the Kazakh embassy in Rome were aboard too, shepherding them to their destination.

Peter knew what Alma and Alua were flying towards. During the Pavlov affair in Spain, he had read the Human Rights Watch reports on Kazakhstan. He had read about Zhanaozen, heard the name Roza Tuletayeva.

Between frantic calling and faxing, Madina and the others were filling him in on the parts of the story he didn't already know. Alma and Alua had Latvian residency documents that allowed them to live in the EU. Alma had a Central African Republic diplomatic passport too, using the alias she had assumed so Alua could enrol in school without attracting the attention of Nazarbayev's spies. However the passport was acquired, it was genuine. But the Italian officials had insisted otherwise. And so, for the pilot and the airline, it was just another routine deportation, another illegal to be removed from Europe. What was there to question? The instructions came from officers of the state. The law enforcement authorities of the Republic of Kazakhstan had sent a message marked 'very urgent' to the law enforcement authorities of the Italian Republic urging them to visit Villa di Casal Polacco 3, a property in the Roman suburbs. There they might find a fugitive, Mukhtar Kabulovich Ablyazov, wanted under an Interpol Red Notice for serious crimes including fraud, forgery, embezzlement and money laundering. He might have guards, they might be armed. Photographs of the criminal were attached. And even if he could not be found, the investigating officers might come across his wife, using a false name and a false African passport, a crime for which she should be deported.

The airline, the pilot, the stewardess and everyone else enacting the deportation were merely respecting the authority of the state. They were making what Peter had come to call a 'presumption of regularity'. Legitimacy resided in nation states, so if a nation state willed something, it must be legitimate. Never mind if that

state had been hijacked. It was like those participants in the
Milgram experiment. Following instructions by men in author-
itative white coats, they kept turning up the voltage even though
they could hear the screams of their fellow test subjects. Peter
knew that when he tried to tell the story as he saw it – a dictator
pursuing a dissident across Europe, corrupting Western states as
he went – people thought he was crazy. It was outside the realm
of what happens, so incongruous and out of touch with the way
things are meant to be in the world that people would deny and
dismiss and discount anything you said because it didn't fit with
normality.

Now Peter grasped why the propaganda really mattered. It
mattered in these instants when someone from the ordinary
world, just doing their job, needed to come to a decision. The
courtiers Nazarbayev had entrusted with the pursuit of Ablyazov
had certainly prepared the ground. They had hired Tim Allan's
Portland Communications and someone from the agency had
doctored Ablyazov's Wikipedia entry. 'You condition the environment,' Peter observed, 'you create reference points.' The
judgments in London had made Nazarbayev's narrative dominant.
Google his name and you saw 'president'. Google Ablyazov's, and
you would find Lord Justice Kay declaring, 'It is difficult to
imagine a party to commercial litigation who has acted with
more cynicism, opportunism and deviousness towards court
orders than Mr Ablyazov.'

Peter glanced at the flight-tracking app on his phone. Suddenly
the altitude began to tick down. Frantic, Madina called the jet-hire
company again, exhausted, weeping, pleading, begging them to
turn the plane around. This is my mother's life, my sister's life.
The altitude reading kept falling. Down, down, down, down,
zero. Nobody spoke. They're gone, Peter thought, it's finished.
Ablyazov will never see them again. Madina will never see her
mother again, never see her sister again.

Madina fell to her knees. This cannot happen to us, she thought. It happens to people who come on the boats, not people with documents, with a place to live, kids going to school here. She knew what they would do: they would take Alma and Alua somewhere where no word of them could leak out, then ransom them for her father. She felt something inside herself collapse.

The rest of the lobby had emptied. Outside, the quiet before dawn had fallen on the streets.

25

A Legit Shithole

Cincinnati, August 2013

Quite apart from his wife's mother and sister having been abducted, her father being on the run, and his own parents declared enemies of the Kazakh dictator, Iliyas Khrapunov had a new problem: Felix Sater had gone weird. Iliyas had always thought of Felix as having two winning attributes: charisma and storytelling. He was charming – American charming, New York charming. He had the hustler's gift of being persuasive even while advertising that he was a hustler. But he could be considerate, too. When Iliyas had rushed to Rome with Madina and Peter Sahlas to try to save Alma and Alua, Felix had called to offer help. He knew some Italian reporters – Felix knew someone everywhere – who might be useful in getting the story of the kidnapping out. Now more than ever, Iliyas and his family needed people they could trust. Alma and Alua were in Kazakhstan, guests of the regime. Ablyazov was in hiding. And Nazarbayev was making good on the threats that, according to Iliyas's father Viktor, Sasha Machkevitch had delivered. Kazakhstan had formally requested their extradition from Switzerland to face charges that they had conspired to abuse Viktor's public positions to embezzle hundreds of millions of dollars and launder them throughout the West. They were confident they could fend off extradition: the allegations were full of holes. But their lives could never go back to how they were before that day in 2006 when Iliyas and Madina had swapped numbers in a French hotel.

For all the strife, Iliyas still had a career to forge. A few years back, he had been taken by the idea of trying his hand at real estate. His mother had done property deals; his grandfather had been minister of construction in Soviet Kazakhstan. At first Iliyas thought of doing modular housing for students. It was Felix Sater, the loyal old family friend and occasional business partner, who had convinced him that luxury real estate was the way to go, top-end stuff. He was at their wedding party in Geneva in 2007, and he said to Iliyas: find a project and we'll do it together.

Felix was on a roll. He fancied himself as a real estate rain-maker, a big man in the biggest game in New York. Protected from his past by his deals to spy for the FBI and the CIA, he had built a property business with his neighbour on Long Island and fellow transplant from the Soviet Union to the West, the Kazakh moneyman Tevfik Arif. Over on Manhattan, in SoHo, they had raised a skyscraper; in Florida and Arizona, they planned hotels. All told, they said, their company, Bayrock, had cut deals on real estate worth $2.5 billion. And Felix was getting a repu-tation as a man it was unwise to cross. An offending business partner on a project in Arizona said Felix warned him he would send over a cousin who would electrocute his balls, cut off his legs and leave his body in the boot of a car (before later changing his mind and agreeing with Felix that they actually had an 'excel-lent relationship').

Iliyas looked for a project, and found one close to home: an old hotel at the far end of Lake Geneva. He and Felix made plans to convert it into 'ultra-luxury' residences with a Michelin-starred restaurant, cigar lounge, library, wine cellar and swimming pool. Everything was going along nicely until December 2007, when the *New York Times* ran the story revealing Felix's criminal past. Felix had to distance himself from Bayrock. Still, for Iliyas, Felix was a friendly guide in the real estate world. When, shortly afterwards, Iliyas set up his own fund, Swiss Development Group, he asked Felix to help him fulfil his next ambition: to crack America.

In theory, America was closed to undercover money. In practice, it was as open as ever, provided you obeyed the dress code. After 9/11, Congress had sought to restrict terrorist financing. The Patriot Act introduced checks that were supposed to make it harder to launder money through banks or any other business transaction. But lobbyists for certain sectors of the economy successfully secured exemptions from the checks. For real estate, the loophole was so huge you could fit a skyline through it. The market in existing homes alone turned over $1.5 trillion a year, about the same amount as that funnelled through the Cayman-based hedge funds that had aroused Nigel Wilkins' suspicions. On top of that there was commercial real estate and newly built property. If you wanted a mortgage, your lender was obliged to establish who you really were, rather than just the name of your front company. But what money launderer would ever want a mortgage? That would defeat the point. If you paid cash, you could buy American real estate in perfect anonymity to your heart's content. One in three of those who did so saw their transaction go through even though banks had previously flagged them as suspicious. The front of choice was the limited liability company, a corporate person whose controlling human being remained invisible as their money coursed into the US.

New York was the Saudi Arabia of real estate, but there were Dubais and Qatars and Irans too. Florida was popular with Latin Americans and Africans, as well as the usual ex-Soviets. Around Sunny Isles in the south of the state, sixty-three Russians, many of them politically connected back home, spent $98 million on properties in seven luxury towers erected by a single American developer. Pablo Escobar, prime mover of the Colombian drug barons, took a waterfront mansion in Miami Beach, complete with underfloor safe. In steamy Jacksonville on the Atlantic, a young widow called Mamadie Touré arrived in 2009 from the destitute West African state of Guinea. Through LLCs, she dropped more than $1 million to buy three delightful suburban family homes and a restaurant (where diners complained that the fresh strawberries concealed tinned peaches). She had made this money, she eventually confessed, by prevailing upon her husband, Guinea's dictator Lansana Conté, to grant rights to the world's greatest unmined deposit of iron ore to a mining company belonging to the billionaire diamond magnate Beny Steinmetz. Then she hopped it to Florida and invested her earnings in property. Her compatriots back home went on with their short, deprived lives. So did those over in Equatorial Guinea, despite all that oil it sold to Exxon. The US real estate market had a place for their rulers, too. Teodorin Obiang, son of the current autocrat, favoured the west coast. He used one of his LLCs to acquire a mansion overlooking the Pacific in Malibu, California, for $30 million.

Some of the more complex real estate laundering schemes extended into the wider neighbourhood. The money handlers for the drug cartels of Colombia and Mexico had the same dilemma as Fat Larry with his dodgy filling stations in New York. People paid for their cocaine and heroin like they paid for their tanks of fuel: with small bills. To find the safe harbour of real estate, stacks of bills had to be converted into the form with which sellers, lawyers and agents felt comfortable: a bank account whose owners were neatly hidden away behind an LLC. The cartels' dealers in the US sold their product for dollars. You couldn't just wire that kind of money back to Colombia. This was where a strategy called the Black Market Peso Exchange came in. It was one of the biggest laundries the world had ever seen, run by middlemen known as peso brokers. They had clients south of the Rio Grande, who had a lot of pesos. The clients might have been crooks, or just Mexicans or Venezuelans or Colombians who imported goods from the US and wanted to buy dollars at a better rate than the official one, while also avoiding paying taxes on their currency transactions. The peso brokers engineered a swap. A dope dealer in Philadelphia passed his dollar profits to a representative of a Caracas businessman; in exchange, the Caracas businessman gave his pesos to someone from the cartel. None of the money ever needed to run the risk of passing through the international banking system.

The founder of a Colombian marketing company, David Murcia Guzmán, pulled off a classic peso scam. His pre-paid debit-card business brought in torrents of pesos. He arranged to swap them for millions of narcotics dollars in a Merrill Lynch account up in the US. From there, he and his cohorts discovered the delights of moving namelessly through the world behind LLCs. They snapped up ten pieces of Miami real estate and enthused, on tapped phones, that 'we can go out and purchase another twenty properties … without having to expose a single buck'. Before he got caught, Murcia came across a scheme that was arguably even better suited to laundering. It was a property project, a swanky hotel and apartment complex. The apartment prices were to be driven up by appending a flashy American developer's name to the building, but it would actually be built down in Panama, whose rulers courted dirty money the way Costa Rica courted tourists. Murcia found a local fixer who took a million of his dollars and started washing them, paying the deposits on as many as ten of the new American-branded apartments. The physical building itself, the fixer was recorded explaining, the bricks and mortar, was of secondary importance to the money channel it created.

American real estate was the place for Iliyas. With Mukhtar Ablyazov in hiding, he could prove himself as the family's new moneyman. Trading in individual houses or apartments, sure, you could do that. Iliyas recommended to his sister Elvira and her husband Dimi – the driver of the getaway Jag back when Iliyas and Madina had eloped in Nice – that they should spend three million buying and flipping three apartments in the SoHo skyscraper Felix Sater had helped to erect. But Iliyas wanted bigger deals. This time, it was him bringing the money and Felix seeking the right opportunity. He found it in the northern suburbs of Cincinnati, on a state highway, between an Ikea and a grave-yard.

The Tri-County Mall was described by one local with the misfortune to work there as a 'legit shithole'. It was approaching the nadir of its decline, hastened by the Great Recession, and was up for sale. Technically, what was for sale was a note of the mall's debts. On April 16, 2013, the county sheriff conducting the auction received a bid by email from Tri-County Mall Investors LLC, submitted by one of Felix's people. The bid, offering $30 million, made many claims for the investors, though it neglected to mention the source of their funds or the name of Iliyas Khrapunov. Perhaps that was wise: by then his parents and father-in-law had been declared thieves by Kazakhstan. And anyway, that was why everyone in US real estate used LLCs: so you could do your deals in privacy, no questions asked. The bid won. Iliyas arranged payment. The money came from an account at FBME Bank in the name of a front company called Telford International Ltd.

The danger of erasing money's past was that if you didn't record an alternative history, someone else might. Front companies were blank pages: anyone could write on them. Felix Sater understood dirty money. He had made dirty money, moved dirty money, traced dirty money. He understood that, in this arena, things that Westerners saw as contradictory could be simultaneously true. Was Iliyas's father-in-law Ablyazov a crook or a dissident? Both, as Felix saw it. On any given day, he, Felix Sater, could choose the story that suited him best. It was like that pump-and-dump scam he had helped to run, back in his days as a Wall Street fraudster. The truth was irrelevant; what mattered was what people wanted to believe.

After successfully taking control of a Cincinnati shithole, Felix and Iliyas needed to complete the final step: the flip. Felix found a buyer through one of his high-society acquaintances, Neil Bush, younger brother to George W., in the cause of whose War on Terror Felix had spied on jihadis. In August 2013, a group of Asian investors who had appointed Neil Bush as their chairman bought the mall for $45 million. It was a peach of a deal for Iliyas and Felix: money with a past had been replaced with the proceeds of an Ohio property transaction, with a 50 per cent profit to boot, all sorted within four months. The buyers paid their money into an account that Felix controlled, completing a spectacular example of the sort of real estate deal-making on which he prided himself. So much so, in fact, that he considered himself entitled to a greater share of the spoils than Iliyas was willing to pay.

In Geneva, Iliyas received a message from Felix asking him to go to a serviced office building for a telecall. When Felix's face appeared on the screen, Iliyas thought he looked agitated. Then Felix announced: 'I know about the Kazakh stuff.' By this he meant that he knew where Iliyas's money was coming from: his wife's father, Mukhtar Ablyazov, a fugitive certified by London courts as a thief who had stolen billions.

'I'll keep the money safe,' Felix went on.

Iliyas asked him to return the money. Yes, he had once enjoyed a leg-up from Ablyazov. After his wedding to Madina, his mother Leila had given him $10 million to get started in real estate, and had persuaded his new father-in-law to do the same. But Iliyas maintained that the money from Ablyazov had been a loan, and that he had had to give it back when Nazarbayev seized BTA Bank in 2009. The money Felix had been investing for Iliyas in the US did belong to someone who required discretion, but it was not, Iliyas insisted, Ablyazov. It was Gennady Petelin, a wealthy Russian reformer who had joined the opposition, been arrested and fled, and whose Jag-driving son Dimi had married Iliyas's sister Elvira.

'Trust me,' Felix said. 'I know people. I'll keep it safe.'

Iliyas felt betrayed. He wanted to sue. But Petelin had fled Russia and come to the US seeking asylum. He could not risk his name being associated with Ablyazov, as it certainly would be if Iliyas and Felix went to court. Iliyas had no choice but to settle. He accepted defeat in this hand of the game of secrets, and split the profits from the sale of their $45 million Ohio shithole half and half with Felix.

But Felix was not a man to extract anything less than maximum value from an advantage. There were others who liked Iliyas's story the way Felix told it, and would pay for the recounting. What was more, they had just found their lead character. Trefor Williams, the effervescent Welsh bloodhound hired by the nation-alised BTA to hunt Ablyazov and his fortune, had been watching the London courtrooms where the bank's lawyers were securing judgments against the fugitive. One day that summer his team had followed a Ukrainian lawyer who attended the proceedings. His sleuths tracked her to Heathrow, and from there to southern France and to a gated mansion in Nice. A rented white BMW would come and go from the residence. Williams' team, in bikinis and beach shorts, took turns to walk across its path so they could peer through the windscreen as the vehicle slowed. When they spotted Ablyazov's relatives in the car, they felt sure their quarry must be inside the mansion. He switched villas but by now

Williams had him cornered. Word was sent to the French police. On July 31, an armed unit stormed through the gates and ended the oligarch's year and a half on the run.

26

Risk Appetite

Canary Wharf, August 2013

It turned out that Nigel Wilkins' superiors at the Financial Conduct Authority were rather more keen on the status quo than they had appeared when they made him employee of the month for challenging it. He tended to be given the complicated requests for authorisation. When he opposed a particularly sensitive one, Nigel's bosses took him off the case. They started reprimanding him for his own conduct. He failed to clear away his work papers at the end of the day: this warranted a written warning. Another lapse followed, more grievous still. For leaving his laptop on his desk overnight, Nigel received another written warning, a final one. What was more, management informed him, there were 'continuing concerns' about his 'productivity, his communication style' and his failure to adhere to the financial regulator's 'risk appetite'. There was only one thing for it: Nigel needed a 'performance improvement plan'. In August 2013, a doctor was asked to assess if there was a medical reason for his 'performance issues'.

Back in 2005, Nigel had been diagnosed with sarcoidosis. It was a rare condition that caused the tissue of his lungs to swell, leaving him with a hacking cough, short of breath, and taking high doses of steroids. The medication woke him in the early hours, but he had usually been able to doze back off. Now, though, the anxiety of being found unfit by the City's overseers would consume him. He lay awake, his mind racing. By day, he felt exhausted. Charlotte grew concerned. She always worried if he let his campaigning blur with his work. When she suggested as much, Nigel would say, Well, what do you expect me to do? On a shelf in his Kensington flat he placed one of the jokey postcards of which he was fond: 'I've learned so much from my mistakes ... I'm thinking of making a few more.'

27

Doubles

Old Billingsgate, February 2014

Sasha turned sixty on February 23, 2014. For many in Britain, it was a doleful time. They were still earning less than they had been before the crisis. 'We've got to make more cuts,' George Osborne announced. 'That's why 2014 is the year of hard truths.' At Old Billingsgate in the City, the splendour of Sasha's celebrations banished such drab concerns, at least for the chosen three hundred honoured with an invitation. The building itself had been constructed as a fish market under Queen Victoria. Now it was what was called an 'events venue'. And what an event it was. The guests took their seats in the hall among feathers and crystal and roses, and began to gorge. A ballerina entertained them, and acrobats, and a noted bard of the day, Craig David. By the magic of lights and screens a red-carpeted staircase appeared, down which walked their host, the billionaire philologist, recognisable from the tux, aviators and combover. But wait, it wasn't him. It was a double, a dancing double. Doors opened, and out grooved double after double, a score of Sashas, boogying in time to the infectious rhythm of wealth. And then the real thing, the man himself, pressing down on a dummy detonator to launch an indoor firework display.

Sasha still graced London with his presence for occasions such as this. He kept a place around the corner from ENRC's headquarters in St James's. Except they were no longer ENRC's headquarters. When it came to business – as opposed to pleasure – the Trio had tired of the UK, a nation that wanted their money then professed to balk at how they made it. The Serious Fraud Office's top brass had responded to Sasha's decision to fire Neil Gerrard just as he was preparing to hand the results of his investigation over to them by opening a formal criminal case. Relocating their multibillion-dollar corporation abroad was the least the Trio could do to register their dissatisfaction – not to mention making it harder for the SFO's bureaucrats to come meddling in their affairs.

As a new home for their corporate personage, the Trio had selected Luxembourg, a friendly destination for those keen to avoid tax, scrutiny and other encumbrances. To move ENRC from London would be tricky, however. After all, they had sold almost a fifth of the company's shares, which were traded on the exchange. How to get them back without adding ruinously to their corporation's already enormous debts? Yes, the business pages had professed themselves scandalised by ENRC's corporate dysfunction. The Trio combined their votes with those of Nazarbayev's regime, which controlled the state's chunk of the stock, to remove Sir Richard Sykes and Ken Olisa from the board. It was the first time in ten years that a FTSE 100 director had been voted off at a company's annual general meeting. All the same, the longsuffering shareholders were hardly just going to give the Trio back their corporation. Sasha and his partners set bankers to work on the problem. The solution they found was delectable. ENRC's share price had fallen since stories about Gerrard's investigation began to appear, and carried on falling after the SFO announced the criminal investigation in April 2013. Now the shares were trading for about half what the saps

who bought them at the listing back in 2007 had paid. The Trio
would use the corruption investigation into ENRC to subsidise
taking back control.

Better still, they wouldn't even need to part with their own
money. Nazarbayev could not have enjoyed seeing Kazakhstan's
glorious name besmirched in London by association with ENRC.
But neither could he think it wise to resist a plan that would
make it harder for the SFO to follow the money trails of a
company in which he was regarded by his own courtiers as a
secret partner. Money was required to make it work, however.
ENRC had big debts even before all those shareholders had to
be bought out. German Gref, chief of the Putinista financiers,
provided it. Gref's bank, Sberbank, along with another close to
the Kremlin, VTB, agreed to put up a couple of billion dollars
to fund the buyout. A 'take-private', the manoeuvre was called
in the City. Of the new, non-public company, the Trio would
own 60 per cent, the Kazakh state 40. When you added the
new loan to old debts, this company would owe Sberbank and
VTB more than $7 billion, equivalent to three years' profits.
There was a danger in that: the banks could squeeze and squeeze,
and ultimately start seizing the Kazakh mines that pumped out
all that cash. But that was where having a state on the team was
so helpful. It was in Kazakhstan's power simply to confiscate
those mines, invoking some law or other, should anyone other
than those anointed with Nazarbayev's patronage try to lay hands
on them.

That was the beauty of taking over such a swathe of a country's
economy: your interests became the nation's. And nations had
reputations to protect. Peter Mandelson, another of the Blairites
who became consiglieri to the global money kings, had made
that very point. In May 2013, as the plan to take ENRC private
was taking shape, he wrote to his acquaintance Kairat Kelimbetov,
the senior Kazakh official handling the regime's role in the

ENRC delisting. Mandelson warned that the SFO might well in the coming months bring charges against ENRC executives close to the Trio. 'The resulting publicity will be greater and more damaging if ENRC remains listed when the SFO completes its work and I think it must therefore be a priority for all concerned for the company to be de-listed as quickly and as amicably as possible.' The opening offer that the Trio and Nazarbayev's regime had made to those whose shares they wanted to buy was so low the markets might see it as 'confiscatory', Mandelson warned. Raising it to the point that it satisfied those shareholders – an amount that would still be far below the price at which the Trio had sold their shares in London – would, Mandelson counselled, 'be in everyone's reputational interests'.

Mandelson was right: the market saw the offer as a steal. But he was wrong to think the market could not be cowed. The directors representing the minority shareholders could see that there was no prospect of the share price rising again while the Trio remained in charge. And so when the paltry offer came, they moodily concluded that even that was better than holding on to what would be stakes in a private Luxembourgish company over which they would have even less say. By the end of 2013, the Trio's corporation was private once more, safely shifted to the duchy. They had not even had to bother handing over so much as a business plan to Nazarbayev's officials, they retained sole right to appoint the management, and even the Kazakh regime's own bankers knew Kazakhstan was ultimately on the hook for the Russian billions that had bailed the Trio out.

Liberation was at hand for Sasha. He was a celebrated philanthropist now, an Israeli citizen and a leading member of the Euro-Asian Jewish Congress. He had mooted a Jewish Al Jazeera: 'Everybody understands in Israel and the Jewish world today that there is a war not by weapons and military troops but of information.' That was where his own fate would be settled: on the information battlefield. He would need to be sure of his troops.

28

The System

Canary Wharf, June 2014

On Monday, June 23, 2014, as Nigel Wilkins turned the pink pages of the *Financial Times*, a headline caught his eye: 'Past Tax Misdemeanours Follow Private Swiss Banks'. Scanning the first paragraphs of the article, he spotted the name of his old employer. BSI's latest owners – some Italians – were trying to sell it (and its book of $100 billion of clients' money) to a Brazilian bank. But there was a complication. Spurred on by their success, the American prosecutors who had won billions in fines from the two biggest Swiss banks, UBS and Credit Suisse, and terminated the oldest one, Wegelin, had said to the bosses of the rest of them: come in and confess to helping US citizens evade tax and we will let you evade a corporate conviction that would kill your bank. A hundred were now in negotiations with the justice department in Washington. Among them, the *FT* reported, was the eleventh biggest Swiss bank – BSI.

Nigel felt a surge of relief. Back at his flat that evening, he opened up his red boxes. All the time Nigel had been waiting for someone in the City to follow the leads he was offering, the money had been moving. The BSI bankers from the London office that was closed down in 2008 had taken their secrets to places where they could be hidden still deeper. Khofiz Shakhidi, the banker Nigel had had his eye on, had moved to Monaco. That was a good spot for meeting the rich. For clients requiring the utmost discretion, Shakhidi began to send their money to one of the blackest boxes of the global economy: the Bahamas, another former British colony in the Caribbean given over to the service of clandestine money, an industry established there by Al Capone's launderer, Meyer Lansky.

Nigel could not fathom why, six years after he had alerted the authorities, neither BSI nor its clients had faced any consequences. In these times of belt-tightening, of all-in-it-together austerity, the Conservative government had been keen to demonstrate that it was aggressively pursuing those who defrauded the exchequer of precious revenues. There could be no mercy: a mother of four in Margate was jailed for eight months when she was caught cheating on tax. Swiss bankers and their clients received different treatment, however. Britons who had dodged tax by hiding their money in Swiss accounts were offered an amnesty. David Cameron's government struck a deal with Switzerland under which Swiss banks with British clients would have to pay to the British Treasury a proportion of those clients' clandestine deposits, but would not have to reveal their identities. Before a single pound was paid, the clients would have eighteen months to decide whether they would prefer instead to move their accounts to an alternative tax haven. The banks themselves would be immune from prosecution. Asked why, a senior official at HMRC, Dave Hartnett, replied that 'it was very unlikely indeed that we would get evidence against Swiss bankers during the course of this'.

Nigel was interested in systems. The names on his stolen documents mattered less to him. He knew, though, that among BSI's clients were names people lowered their voices to utter. He had once jokingly compared himself to James Bond as he snuck around BSI's Cheapside office after everyone else had gone, photo-copying secrets. But in truth he had no such ego. He wanted the system to kick in, the counter system of institutions and laws, the system that protected the many. He believed in that system, had done all his life. The employment tribunals, the leaseholder courts, the letters pages that from time to time published his insights into the depravities of finance: in these places, anyone could triumph. All you had to be was right.

And yet now, a worry began to nag at him, a queasy feeling that tempered his initial exultation at seeing BSI's wrongdoing confirmed in print. What if the City's watchdogs did at last decide to investigate BSI? What if, as Nigel had always suspected, they followed the money and found it to be filthy? They might reasonably ask whose job it had been to check the money at the time. They could easily find that name in BSI's old regulatory filings: Nigel Wilkins. They could accuse him of having been asleep at the wheel. Good job he had kept his files of evidence: destroying them could have been a crime. And he could point out that, back in 2008, he had offered to hand them over to the authorities for free. Plenty of others in his position had tried to profit by claiming a bounty or blackmailing the banks whose records they had rifled. Even Heinrich Kieber, the whistleblowing silhouette from Liechtenstein, had accepted a $7 million reward from the Germans. Nigel had never asked for money.

While the tourists and trustafarians of Kensington buzzed outside in the warm summer evening, Nigel selected a sample of the BSI documents from his red boxes. A list of some of the clients from the former Soviet Union should do it. If the Swiss account and offshore front company noted beside each of them were not enough, there was the stipulation 'hold mail', an instruction to ensure that no potentially incriminating paperwork went to the client's home. Only a few days earlier, Stuart Gulliver, the boss of HSBC, appearing before Parliament to answer questions about yet another scandal at that bank – this time abetting 'industrial-scale tax evasion' at its Swiss arm – had conceded that there was 'a higher probability' that hold-mail accounts 'indicate areas of concern'.

The next morning, Nigel set off to Canary Wharf. He worked on that day as on any other, but as his colleagues headed home he remained at his desk, composing an email to his boss and his boss's boss. He wrote in his usual way, with economy and precision, but used the vocabulary in which both bankers and regulators spoke. Secret clients were the 'beneficial owners' of 'complex structures', otherwise known as front companies. After learning about BSI's impending admission of guilt in the US, he began, 'I feel obliged to make a statement'. He explained that he had been the compliance officer in BSI's London office for two years up to September 2008. 'While I was there, I became increasingly aware of the bank's activities in assisting clients to hide their assets – taking advantage of both banking secrecy in Switzerland and corporate secrecy in offshore centres. I analysed the complex structures that were set up, and in particular found the key documents linking the beneficial owners to their respective offshore companies.' He attached a scan of the client list. Just before seven o'clock, he sent the email and went home to his flat.

PART III

METAMORPHOSIS

Before mass leaders seize the power to fit reality
to their lies, their propaganda is marked by its
extreme contempt for facts as such, for in their
opinion fact depends entirely on the power of
man who can fabricate it.

Hannah Arendt,
The Origins of Totalitarianism

29

Conquest

Eastern Ukraine, August 2014

Little Green Men, they called them, like invaders from another world. They appeared in Crimea first. Then, in August 2014, they showed up on the mainland, in eastern Ukraine. They spoke with Russian accents, carried Russian weapons. Their green uniforms looked exactly like Russian army ones, only without the insignia. A journalist asked Putin about that at a press conference. 'Take a look at the post-Soviet area,' Putin replied. 'There are many uniforms there that are similar. You can go to a store and find any kind of uniform.' But were they Russian soldiers or not, the journalist asked. 'They were local self-defence units,' Putin said, fixing a look in his eye.

In truth, the covert operation had begun years earlier, the invading force composed not of Little Green Men but of under-cover money.

Ukraine was where Western democracy met the patronage system of the old Soviet Union. Each magnified the other. The only thing more corrupt than a kleptocratic dictatorship was a kleptocratic democracy: there were so many more people who could demand to be bought off, and it was much harder simply to imprison or otherwise eliminate them. From its inception as an independent state, Ukraine was a paradise for moneymen seeking to profit from the privatisation of power. Boris Birshtein was in there right away. He had 'big connections', his gangster acquaintance Mikhas understood, connections that went 'as high as the president'. It was said the first person Leonid Kravchuk met upon assuming the presidency in 1991 was Birshtein, because he was regarded as 'the accountant of the Communist Party'. In 1994 Birshtein funded the victorious campaign of Kravchuk's successor, Leonid Kuchma. European police came across $5 million they believed had passed from Birshtein's companies and associates to the accounts of one of Kuchma's top aides. Birshtein was said to have bragged about greasing Ukraine's KGB chief. Such was the sway he came to enjoy over the newly liberalised economy that one MP considered him 'the real owner' of the country.

For a while, Birshtein was the king of Ukrainian commodities, trading the output of the old Soviet factories. Mikhas hoped that together they might reach even higher, and get in on perhaps the most lucrative trade anywhere in the ex-Soviet sphere: the transport of Russian and Central Asian natural gas westward to Europe. Mikhas's arrest put paid to his ambition for a pipeline venture, but others succeeded, including associates of Semyon Mogilevich, the Brainy Don. Putin and his brother dictators in the other ex-Soviet republics wanted to use control of natural resources to magnify their influence abroad, be it by shaking down BP, listing mining companies in London or turning off gas supplies to Ukraine whenever its leaders leaned overly Westward. At the same time, their primary mission was to divert money from the collective to themselves. If you could figure out a business deal that would achieve both ends at once, there were fortunes to be made.

Before he met Boris Birshtein, Alex Shnaider's life had been on an unremarkable track. His parents, like Birshtein, were Jewish émigrés from the Soviet Union to Canada. Young Alex mopped floors and stacked shelves in their deli. He first encountered Birshtein while studying economics in Toronto. Next to the extroverted Birshtein, Shnaider's awkwardness was evident. He was short and frowned a lot. But Birshtein liked him, and so did his daughter Simona. They married. Birshtein set him up in business, specifically the steel business in Ukraine. Shnaider and his partner, a Ukrainian called Eduard Shyfrin with a PhD in steelmaking, worked the trade like the Reubens in Russia or the Trio in Kazakhstan: ship in supplies, carry off the output of the steel mills, then sell the metal at a profit on foreign markets. By the time the Ukrainian government followed Russia into a programme of selling off state assets in the late nineties, Shnaider and Shyfrin were on sufficiently good terms with both the powers in Kiev and the local bosses to snap up a mill of their own.

The Zaporizhstal steel mill lay 150 miles from Ukraine's border with Russia. One of the greatest steel mills in Ukraine or anywhere else, it employed 50,000 people. Shnaider and Shyfrin spent about $70 million acquiring its shares. A valuation five years later put its true worth at ten times as much.

It would have been Boris Birshtein's greatest triumph: his protégé was becoming a major industrialist in Ukraine, surveying the whole former Soviet Union for more assets to take. Except that poor Birshtein had by now been once more banished in disgrace – this time by his own son-in-law. At first the two had been partners in Midland, the company that would go on to buy Zaporizhstal. But the raid on their Antwerp office in 1996 by Belgian police on the trail of Mikhas's criminal money had left Shnaider shaken. That year, Birshtein left Midland; father- and son-in-law were soon estranged.

Once they had control of Zaporizhstal, Shnaider and Shyfrin spent the next decade getting extremely rich. They bought another mill, the Red October on the Volga, supplier to the Russian military. They bought Moscow real estate. They bought a Formula One team and a 170-foot yacht.

By 2010, Shnaider and Shyfrin each had a fortune of $1.3 billion. They had decided it was time to sell Zaporizhstal. It needed billions of dollars of renovations, the financial crisis had struck, and Russia was destabilising Ukraine by threatening to cut its gas supplies. Rinat Akhmetov, the richest of Ukraine's oligarchs, agreed to pay $690 million for it, and on May 4 they exchanged contracts, with a view to completing the deal by the end of the month. But a couple of weeks later, Shnaider took a call from his partner. Since the Antwerp raid, Shnaider had operated mostly from Toronto, leaving Shyfrin based in Moscow. Shyfrin told Shnaider there would have to be a change of plan: the Kremlin had been in touch.

Two months earlier, Shyfrin had been contacted by an affable Ukrainian moneyman called Igor Bakai, who invited him for lunch. Bakai had made his way from barter trading across the Polish border into the upper echelons of independent Ukraine's flourishing kleptocracy. He was a good-time guy, lavishing cars and watches on the influential, taking them partying and hunting. He was one of those with the nous to come up with a scheme for helping Ukraine's politicians monetise the gas trade for their own ends. He did such a good job that President Kuchma put him in charge of administering the presidency's portfolio of property. Bakai arranged the sale of a storied Crimean dacha to a Russian state bank, for Putin's use. And he was implicated in a scheme to divert money from the state railways towards the election campaign of Kuchma's aspiring successor, the energetically pro-Kremlin Viktor Yanukovych. When Yanukovych's attempt to rig the election sparked the Orange Revolution in 2004, Bakai and the pop star he had married fled the country. After a brief stop in Monte Carlo, they found safe harbour in Moscow, where the Russian authorities refused to send them home to answer the charges brought by the new order in Kiev.

Eduard Shyfrin knew of Bakai as an operator who was very well connected politically both in Ukraine and Russia, with a reputation for facilitating deals for powerful figures. He lived not far from Shyfrin in Barvikha village, a gated enclave of mansions on Moscow's outskirts. They ate lunch at the Avenue, an expensive restaurant nearby. Bakai said he represented parties who wanted to buy the Zaporizhstal steel mill, but not much more. Shyfrin thought little of it. When Rinat Akhmetov made a down-payment on Zaporizhstal, however, Bakai asked Shyfrin to lunch again. This time they met upstairs at the Avenue, in a private room. There was a new note in Bakai's conversation. He mentioned, as though in passing, that a general in the Russian police force had wanted to arrest Shyfrin, but that he had prevented it. Shyfrin knew perfectly well the bigger game that was being played. After five years of pro-Western rule following the Orange Revolution, Yanukovych had finally won power, and he was steering Ukraine back into Russia's orbit. At the same time, depressed demand for steel due to the financial crisis meant eastern Ukraine's mills were going cheap. Russian state banks were putting up money for Russian buyers to acquire them. Their main rival was Rinat Akhmetov, an oligarch far less biddable for the Kremlin.

A day or two later, Bakai invited Shyfrin to his house. There were lots of other guests milling about, including one of Putin's top people. He drew Shyfrin aside and, in very clear terms, told him to do the deal Bakai was proposing. Otherwise, everything he owned in Russia would be at risk. Bakai informed Shyfrin that Zaporizhstal should not be sold to Akhmetov, but to the buyer he represented. That buyer took the form of half a dozen offshore companies using money from a Russian state bank called VEB. Chaired by Putin himself, VEB was the financial arm of his regime, as well as providing cover for spies overseas. The buyer Bakai was fronting for was the Kremlin in camouflage. As with the RosUkrEnergo gas scheme, this Ukrainian deal would have to serve its kleptocratic purpose as well as its geopolitical goal of entrenching Russian economic interests in eastern Ukraine. When Shyfrin called Shnaider in the middle of May 2010, he spelled out how.

On the phone, Shyfrin avoided naming names – he didn't even identify Bakai. But he said the Kremlin saw buying the mill as 'politically strategic'. The new buyers represented the regime, and would have public money at their disposal from VEB. Their offer was exceedingly generous: $160 million more than Akhmetov's. That would be enough to cover the $50 million break fee they would have to pay him, leaving $110 million. Shnaider and Shyfrin would get a sweetener for themselves – but only $10 million. They would have to pass on the remaining $100 million as a 'commission'. They routinely shelled out such payments in Ukraine and Russia, including to managers at ports and factories, to get their business done. But this one was different. It was enormous. A single $100 million commission was more money than the total kickbacks from American oil companies to Nursultan Nazarbayev's Swiss accounts that had been the subject of the largest ever foreign corruption case in the US. It was enough money, in the depths of the Great Recession, to pay that year's wages for twelve thousand Russians – and it was to be channelled from a bank entrusted with the Russian people's money to the private pockets Igor Bakai had been directed to fill.

From Toronto, Shnaider told Shyfrin to go ahead. Putin's regime had acquired another economic forward base in eastern Ukraine. Shnaider, for his part, had decided that his days doing business in the former Soviet Union were over. After receiving their $850 million of the Kremlin's money (and paying the agreed $100 million 'commission'), he and Shyfrin divided up their company. From his share, Shnaider earmarked $40 million to put the finishing touches to a skyscraper he was building in his home town with an American developer, a monument to his transformation.

30

Privacy

Kensington, September 2014

The morning after he emailed his bosses at the Financial Conduct Authority informing them that he had uncovered a dirty money operation in the City, Nigel had arrived at the office in Canary Wharf as usual. The two bosses he had written to asked him to come and see them. He expected a casual discussion, but when he arrived at the designated room, the mood was not casual. They asked him why he had sent his email, and what action he expected them to take. This was information, one of them said, that we should not be privy to: it contained the names of BSI's clients, their account details, things like that. Had Nigel saved any other information on the FCA's systems that should not be there? The senior of the two bosses concluded by saying he would have to seek advice from Human Resources. That was Wednesday. On Thursday, Nigel heard nothing more. On Friday afternoon, as the weekend's boozing was getting under way in the Docklands bars below, he was called to another meeting. His boss had printed out the BSI client lists that Nigel had attached to his email. He pressed Nigel on whether they were definitely genuine. 'This is an exact copy of the document,' Nigel replied, explaining how BSI bankers had left their paperwork lying on their desks at night.

Nigel had brought printouts of his original correspondence with the City watchdog from back in 2008, his first warnings about BSI. He started to take these papers from his folder, but his boss said he did not wish to see any additional documents at present, then briefly left the room. When he came back he told Nigel the conversation would now have to take a more formal turn. As such, Nigel would be allowed a companion. Nigel said he wanted to call in someone from his union. That was not an option at this stage, he was told. Instead he should make use of Errol, a fellow employee with, the boss said, 'experience in dealing with these matters'. Errol was summoned. Nigel's boss produced a script, and said it was important that he read it out verbatim.

'I am suspending you with immediate effect,' he declared. Nigel had, he continued, obtained and circulated within the FCA and without authorisation 'sensitive customer data', which neither he nor the FCA had any right to possess. The matter would now be thoroughly investigated. In the meantime, Nigel should not enter the office, contact his colleagues or speak to any witnesses. He would be informed when he should come in to be interviewed. Once the boss finished reading out the script, Nigel was taken to his desk, told to collect any personal belongings, and escorted from the building.

When Nigel told Charlotte what had happened, she was upset with him. Once again he was pitting himself against power, without regard for his increasingly rickety health. His bosses knew all about his physical condition. One of the occupational health doctors they had told him to see had sent them a report detailing how Nigel grew short of breath when he walked up stairs on account of his sarcoidosis, how he slept badly, how his bowels were irregular and how he suffered from 'workplace stress'. When Nigel explained that this stress was the result of having blown the whistle about the City regulator neglecting its responsibilities, the physician's advice was: Stop banging your head against a brick wall.

Nigel had always sensed that some of the BSI clients whose secrecy he had violated were not the sort of people who would take such exposure lightly. As he waited at home in Kensington to hear the verdict of his superiors at the FCA, he grew preoccupied with the worst that could happen to those who betrayed the confidences of the rich.

He read about Rudolf Elmer, who had worked at the Cayman Islands office of the Swiss bank Julius Bär. Elmer had developed the same suspicions as Nigel: that all the corporate legerdemain his bank supplied to its clients allowed them to evade tax and launder money. He had raised his concerns with his managers, then with the Swiss authorities, then at a press conference in London during which he handed WikiLeaks' Julian Assange two discs containing the account details of 2,000 'prominent people'. The *Economist* story about Elmer that Nigel read described the Swiss authorities' response. They used the banking secrecy law to visit a 'legal hell' on him. He was locked up without charge for 187 days, and he and his family were so hounded by the bank's agents that his daughter was left traumatised.

Nigel researched Kostas Vaxevanis, the Greek journalist arrested when he published the so-called Lagarde List of two thousand Greeks with money hidden in Swiss accounts. Christine Lagarde, while French finance minister, had sent the document to the Greek authorities, who had declined to investigate potential tax evasion or laundering, but were swift to pursue Vaxevanis when he revealed its contents. Those names had come from a far larger list of tens of thousands of clients at HSBC's Swiss unit, the exfiltration of which by Hervé Falciani constituted the biggest leak in banking history. Falciani had worked in the bank's IT department. He fled Switzerland and handed his trove of data to various European governments. Nigel studied his case closely, especially the Swiss authorities' efforts to extradite him to serve the five years in prison to which he had been sentenced in absentia. He took clippings about Antoine Deltour, a twenty-eight-year-old accountant working for PwC in Luxembourg who had exposed an entire industry of schemes to enable multinational corporations to avoid tax. For this he was charged with theft, violating secrecy laws and illegally accessing a database. And Nigel kept a copy of a story from 2006, around the time he had joined BSI, on Andrei Kozlov. As deputy chairman of the Russian central bank, Kozlov had shut down dozens of banks suspected of laundering criminal money. He was killed with bullets to the head and chest outside a football stadium in Moscow.

Ostensibly, Nigel's bosses at the FCA were investigating whether he had violated British law protecting privacy and Swiss law protecting banks' secrets. Nigel concluded that, in truth, he had simply made himself so awkward he could no longer be tolerated. 'They had a problem because they didn't do anything with what I gave them in 2008,' he told an acquaintance. What was more, 'I write in plain English,' a tongue he believed his colleagues deliberately avoided, the better to allow suspect moneymen – or rather, 'customers' – to pass unimpeded between the lines of jargon. And, of course, if the bosses of the regulator were now to start investigating BSI, they would have to face the embarrassment of admitting that Nigel had raised the alarm a full six years earlier. What his fellow regulators still refused to see had never looked clearer to Nigel. BSI was part of an enormous inversion of the rule of law. 'The scale of the money laundering and tax evasion facilitated by the Swiss banks globally makes this activity the largest financial crime on record – and by a very wide margin,' he wrote in his submission to the FCA's inquest into his conduct.

Nigel knew the law. He felt its sanctity. He knew that a banker could be convicted if he suspected a financial offence had been committed and failed to alert the authorities. Why was the FCA not pursuing the many other compliance officers who, everybody now knew, had overseen a rampage of crime before, during and after the crisis, at scarcely calculable cost to society? Nigel had followed the law to the letter, but it was now as though he had taken the Tube to Canary Wharf and disembarked in a Kafka novel. His bosses, the guardians of the City's probity, had suspended him after he told them he had evidence that suggested a crime might have taken place. He had tried to show them that evidence, and they had told him not to. Then, when they called him in to be interviewed, an FCA manager repeatedly asked him: do you have any evidence? He wrote in his notebook that he was up against 'those factions of the FCA who are apologists for the industry – irrespective of how it behaves'. Shutting him up would be 'a victory for those who abuse "confidentiality" in the banking system in order to conceal criminal activity'.

In September 2014, three months after he had been marched from the FCA's offices, Nigel was informed that the investigation had determined 'an inability on your part to adequately respect confidential information'. He was fired for gross misconduct.

31

The Bridge

Moscow, February 2015

Boris Nemtsov strolled past the Kremlin on his way home. It was nearly midnight on February 27, 2015. He had been at dinner with his girlfriend after a long day's agitating. His years in the vanguard of the liberal reformers under Yeltsin were a distant memory. At fifty-five, he was still good-looking, still charismatic, but he was now on the outside. Traitors, Putin's propaganda called Nemtsov and those like him who challenged the leader, fifth columnists, 'aliens among us'. Earlier that evening he had gone on the radio to explain why allowing one man to amass such power would, as he put it, 'end in catastrophe'. He had a knack for revealing telling details of Putin's corruption. His toilet, for instance. Complete with gold fittings, it had cost $75,000, two-thirds of the president's official salary. Lately Nemtsov had been visiting Ukraine, documenting the presence of the Kremlin's Little Green Men. That day he had been handing out flyers for a rally to protest against the invasion.

Nemtsov and his girlfriend were nearing his apartment building, close to St Basil's Cathedral. As they crossed a bridge over the Moscow River, a white car approached. The triggerman fired. Bullets hit Nemtsov in the liver, stomach, heart and head. He died at once, face down in the Moscow night.

There were two possibilities, Nemtsov's fellow dissidents real-ised. Either Putin had ordered the murder, in which case the dictatorship had entered a dramatically more dreadful phase. Or he had not, and some henchman had killed Nemtsov to try to please his master. It was not clear which scenario was more disturbing.

Putin vowed that the FSB's investigation into the murder would spare no expense. And sure enough, the guilty men were found, charged, convicted and jailed. There were five of them, the shooter and four accomplices. They were all from Chechnya. The Russian authorities also indicted the mastermind, another Chechen, but said he could not be located. There was something strange about the story, though. The triggerman was a former deputy commander of Sever, a special forces unit that reported to Ramzan Kadyrov, Chechnya's ruler. Ruslan Mukhudinov, the supposed mastermind, belonged to the same unit – but as a driver. It was peculiar in the extreme that the chain of command would be so inverted. Was it not more plausible that the assassination had been overseen by the man Mukhudinov drove around: Ruslan Geremeyev, a senior officer in Sever? Geremeyev had rented a flat in Moscow for the hit squad, then flew out the day after their work was done, alongside the shooter. Putin's officials had permitted the investigators to indict the hit squad and the missing driver, but refused to allow any charges against Geremeyev. That would have brought the matter too close to the sacred networks of kleptocratic power that stretched between Moscow, Grozny and beyond.

Geremeyev's uncle was Adam Delimkhanov. For Ramzan Kadyrov, Chechnya's despot, Delimkhanov played two crucial roles: enforcer and, the regime's opponents claim, moneyman. The former was vital for any leader who depended as much as Kadyrov did on fear as a source of power, and advertising Delimkhanov's thuggery only helped to magnify its effects. The second role was, by contrast, a quiet one. Putin repaid Kadyrov's success in crushing Chechen separatism with generous federal grants. Kadyrov and his court appeared to see no distinction between this money and their own.

As well as their official duties, Chechen heavies were available for private hire. Viktor Khrapunov claimed that when Sasha of the Trio wanted to demonstrate the seriousness of the threat he was delivering in Courchevel, he paraded a Chechen gangster. When Alex Shnaider and Eduard Shyfrin fell out over how to divide their business following the sale of their Ukrainian steel mill, Shyfrin accused Shnaider of enlisting 'powerful Chechens' by way of intimidation. And when it was decided by those Nazarbayev had entrusted with the pursuit of Mukhtar Ablyazov that they needed some more persuasive allies, it was a Chechen to whom they turned.

In 2014, ownership of BTA, the bank Nazarbayev's regime had seized from Ablyazov, passed to an up-and-coming young member of the Kazakh kleptocracy. Kenes Rakishev, athletic and delicately bearded, had come up under the wing of Timur Kulibayev, Nazarbayev's billionaire son-in-law. But Kenes was very keen to be perceived as a businessman – no, an entrepreneur – in his own right, not some frontman like, say, the Russian cellist whose $2 billion fortune was more likely related to his close friendship with Putin than business acumen. Angry Birds credit cards, that was one idea, or a cryptocurrency venture. He employed PR experts, such as the Etonian who would arrange for Western journalists to interview him and encourage them to seek his views on Brexit or other pressing matters of the day. These efforts failed to convince everyone, however. Executives from one of the companies in which Kenes had invested asked for a loan from the International Finance Corporation, the arm of the World Bank that supported private businesses. The IFC's officials conducted some due diligence on him. After a while a polite email came back to Kenes' people explaining that the IFC would not be putting up any funds, on the grounds that he was 'managing the president's family's money'. Rubbish, Kenes protested. But those entrusted with managing the IFC's money kept it away from him anyway, on the grounds that he had married the daughter of one of Nazarbayev's top officials.

Kenes had a talent for ingratiating himself with the more colourful characters who were concerned with monetising their power, especially those who, like him, owed their position to the previous generation. He was on Prince Andrew's Christmas card list, having helped to arrange the deal whereby Timur Kulibayev bought the Sunninghill mansion that the Queen had given Andrew as a wedding present. Timur paid $6 million over the listing price, thus moving as much of his dubiously acquired fortune as possible into a respectable piece of real estate while simultaneously coopting an influential Western figure. Andrew, theoretically a British trade representative, could then use his connection to Kenes to help a Swiss finance house and a Greek sewerage firm lobby for Kazakh contracts.

Kenes was content to keep less august company, too. His relationship with Ramzan Kadyrov ran deep. Unlike most of their countrymen, both professed to be faithful Muslims. Kenes had money and was ready to deploy it in ways that pleased Kadyrov. Chechnya's ruler used his Instagram account to proclaim himself glad of the 'philanthropic help' that his 'dear brother' Kenes rendered his regime.

While Kenes wanted the West to treat him as an exciting entrepreneur, Kadyrov seemed content to be known as a thug. The one time he met Boris Nemtsov, after listening to him argue in a speech to a gathering of Chechen politicians in 2003 that the republic should have a consensus-based government rather than a president, the office held at the time by Kadyrov's father, he approached him and remarked: 'You should be shot for saying such things.' The air of menace could be valuable. Chechens gained a reputation as the former Soviet Union's most formidable settlers of commercial grievances. You wanted a debt paid, you called a Chechen. Someone like Pavel Krotov. From the Russian business pages, you would know he represented the interests of Kadyrov's prime lieutenant, Adam Delimkhanov. He had even been called Kadyrov's 'personal financial adviser'. When Kenes took over BTA, Krotov became part of the business end of the campaign against Ablyazov. In London, BTA's lawyers had persuaded judges that the vanishing oligarch owed the bank billions, giving the bank the right to seize his assets. In Russia, Krotov joined the effort to encourage those accused of helping Ablyazov steal and launder the bank's money to hand over Russian property ventures worth hundreds of millions. His involvement was mysterious. Kenes would maintain that BTA had never formally engaged Krotov, even though Krotov appeared to have helped draft sensitive messages to top Russian officials on the bank's behalf.

To Westerners, the threatening aura emanating from associates like Ramzan Kadyrov made them anxious not to cross Kenes. When he bought into a London-listed company that controlled a Russian gold mine, other investors found his proposed strategy nonsensical. But as one put it, Kenes was 'not someone I want to be on the wrong side of'. Others were grateful recipients of his largesse: the Clinton Foundation accepted tens of thousands of Kenes' dollars.

And he possessed a power Kadyrov lacked. Kadyrov's Chechen mafia state could enforce silence when required. Nemtsov could no longer disturb Kadyrov's narrative of his own legitimacy. Neither could he contradict Kadyrov's protector, Putin, in his account of the 'self-defence units' operating in Ukraine, or embarrass him with tales of the golden presidential crapper. But eliminating a flesh-and-blood enemy did not scrub him out of the story. Look at Sugar: three days before Nemtsov's death, he had been found lifeless in the Austrian prison cell where he was awaiting trial on charges – fabricated, he said – that he had murdered a pair of Kazakh bankers back in his days as a senior member of Nazarbayev's regime. There had been a makeshift noose around his neck, but his lawyer declared himself highly suspicious that this had been a suicide. No, while sometimes there was no choice but to kill, any competent kleptocracy also needed the ability to rewrite the narrative. That was best done in the forums where disputes over competing stories were settled: courts.

Since Kenes took over, BTA Bank's lawyers had continued their relentless pursuit of Ablyazov's money through the London commercial courts. Now there was a second front: America. That was where Iliyas, the dissident oligarch's son-in-law, was stashing millions. If the US courts could be persuaded to follow the UK ones and declare Ablyazov a master crook, he would at last be running out of safe places to hide his wealth, neutralising him as a menace to Nazarbayev's kleptocracy. It was a job for a proven veteran of putting the law at the service of dirty money: Felix Sater.

32
His Footprints
Are Not Found

Colchester, September 2015

When the Financial Conduct Authority fired him, Nigel
Wilkins did what he had done when BSI pushed him out
six years earlier: he brought a case at the Employment Tribunal.
Not for money. He turned sixty-five in March 2015, and could
then start to draw the seven pensions he had accumulated through
his various jobs. No, if he could secure a payout, that would set
the record straight: it would show who had been right, who had
been wrong. He read that Senator Levin had announced that he
too would soon be retiring. 'You don't get changes without proving
your point,' Levin remarked, looking back on his long years as
inquisitor of the rich. 'It's about the facts.'

At his flat in Kensington, Nigel occupied himself corresponding
combatively with the FCA's expensive lawyers ahead of the
tribunal hearing. His lungs were getting worse. Depression had
always lurked in him. Sometimes it was so bad he had to retire
to bed. Normally he loved a fight, but this time the prospect of
going up against the forces of the City left him not invigorated
but troubled. He was angry, Charlotte could see, and anxious.
He confided in a friend, Robert Barrington, who as head of the
UK chapter of Transparency International lobbied against financial secrecy and the crimes it concealed. Barrington concluded

that Nigel had been treated badly, hung out to dry. He felt friendless in this world, the world of money, in which he had made his professional life. There were some consolations in his private life: long train rides, chocolate, the affection of Charlotte's Burmese cat, Marnie. Nigel printed off Help the Aged's decluttering tips, but his flat showed no sign of his having acted on them. He made a to-do list. It began: 'There isn't very much to do.' Except, of course, for his war with the City. The struggle to be proven right was becoming everything.

A few days after his birthday, he noticed an announcement from the US Department of Justice. BSI had become the first of the hundred Swiss banks negotiating with American prosecutors to settle. It would pay a $211 million fine, three times its profits for the previous year, and agree to a statement of facts admitting precisely the sort of malfeasance Nigel had warned the British authorities about back in 2008. BSI bankers had registered their American clients' accounts to what the prosecutors called 'sham entities' in the British Virgin Islands, Liechtenstein and the like. When the clients wanted to shift money back into the US, the bankers employed subterfuges. Sometimes they sent the client a prepaid debit card with no name on it. When the money ran out, the client would send word back to the bankers. 'Could you download some tunes for us?' asked one. 'Gas tank still running on empty,' said another. BSI's bankers handled nearly $3 billion for 3,500 Americans. Two-thirds of the clients had given 'hold mail' instructions, the same words written against client after client of the London office on the document Nigel's bosses at the FCA had fired him for showing them.

True, the American prosecutors' settlements with BSI and the other Swiss banks could have been much tougher. 'These hundred banks get immunity from prosecution,' Carl Levin fulminated. 'They don't have to disclose names. What they disclose is bits and pieces and they tell us, "You go on a treasure hunt, a wild goose chase.'" Nonetheless, Obama's Department of Justice was extracting billions in fines. It made Nigel wonder: why would the Americans pursue BSI and the other Swiss banks with such fervour while the Brits did nothing? As he marshalled his arguments for his case against the FCA, the answer came to him. After long years tolerating tax evasion by their fellow members of the ruling class, the political leaders of the big Western economies had been forced by the cost of the bank bailouts, the subsequent recession and increasingly widespread hostility to cuts in public services to go after those missing tax revenues. Hence the Americans' pursuit of UBS, Credit Suisse, BSI and the rest. But the City was in a different position. It was not the UK Treasury that the City's clients were primarily cheating. It was everyone else's. And there was one more fact, so huge and so obvious that everyone ignored it the way only problems of such magnitude could be ignored. Tax evasion deprived governments of revenue. Money laundering was the other side of the same coin. Like tax dodging, it was a subversion of money's role as a token of reciprocal altruism that allowed large and diverse societies to function. But while tax evasion sucked money out, money laundering pumped money in. If you could stop yourself thinking about its origins, those inflows of dirty money from around the world were just another source of investment into otherwise declining economies.

That summer, while Nigel was jousting with the FCA's lawyers, George Osborne gave a speech at the Mansion House. He called for the end of 'banker bashing' and declared, seven years on from the crisis, that it was time for a 'new settlement' with the City. He demonstrated what that meant by removing the head of the FCA, Martin Wheatley, whom bankers had deemed excessively keen to actually regulate them. A signal that the UK remained open to dirty money, regardless of the ultimate cost, had been delivered a few months earlier rather more publicly than intended.

When Putin annexed Crimea, David Cameron summoned senior ministers in his government to formulate the British response to the first seizure of European territory since the world wars. One of the officials striding up Downing Street failed to shield his briefing memo from the photographers. It stated that, whatever else the UK did, the City must stay open to Russian money.

And yet Nigel still believed that he might win. You probably won't hear from us again, the spy from the tax authority had told him at the end of their clandestine meeting in 2009. And indeed he had not, not until late in 2014, while he was preparing his employment case against the FCA. He was invited once more to meet HMRC agents, preceded by the same cloak-and-dagger routine to ensure he wasn't followed. This time he arranged to hand over everything. He brought his red boxes; an HMRC spy took them, made copies and gave them back. One of the tax agents thanked Nigel and told him HMRC would look at the UK nationals among BSI's clients and pass details of the rest to their counterparts in other countries. He asked Nigel whether he was prepared to act as a witness if it came to trial. Nigel said yes. The agent warned him not to tell anybody what he had done because it might prejudice any future legal case – and for his own safety. Then silence was resumed.

In September 2015, the City's watchdog reached its settlement with Nigel. He would be paid $64,000 – fifteen grand shy of a year's salary – and two versions of the past would exist. The FCA would still have fired Nigel for gross misconduct. It would not give him his job back. Even though BSI's bosses had now admitted wrongdoing in the US, the City's regulator would not be obliged to launch an investigation into the alleged crimes Nigel believed he had discovered in the BSI office down the road from the Bank of England. But the FCA would furnish him with a reference that would mention none of this, and would state that during his employment 'Nigel was hardworking and carried out his duties honestly and in good faith'. For his part, Nigel undertook not to discuss the agreement with anyone, or to reveal the circumstances of his departure from the FCA.

Summer was fading into autumn when Nigel invited Charlotte and some friends to the Old Siege House, out by her place in Colchester. A lovely old pub, it was; the timbers still showed bullet marks from when parliamentarians had taken the town from royalists. And they did great steaks. Nigel was normally careful with money but today he paid for everything: this was, after all, a celebratory lunch. Charlotte could detect something else, though. This was not victory. Nigel had been exiled from the City, humiliated and silenced. The story of money would be told without him, without what he had found.

At the Old Siege House, Nigel made merry. In the privacy of his battered notebook, he recorded his thoughts. A T.S. Eliot poem came to mind, from *Old Possum's Book of Practical Cats*. He wrote down its title, 'Macavity':

> He's outwardly respectable. (They say he cheats at cards.)
> And his footprints are not found in any file of Scotland Yard's
> And when the larder's looted, or the jewel-case is rifled,
> Or when the milk is missing, or another Peke's been stifled,
> Or the greenhouse glass is broken, and the trellis past repair
> Ay, there's the wonder of the thing! Macavity's not there!

The City's regulator, Nigel believed, should be 'a global policeman to stop people using institutions in London to plunder their fellow countrymen and women back home'. Instead, he concluded, it was 'on the side of the crooks'.

33

Winners

Manhattan, November 2016

Just before midnight on November 8, 2016, Felix Sater called a car to collect him from his home on Long Island. There was a strange energy in the air in New York that night, something new and, for Felix at least, thrilling. His value in the game of secrets was about to go through the roof.

He was already a top-level player. Kenes Rakishev's BTA Bank was paying him a cool million to help with the pursuit of Ablyazov, Iliyas and their money through the US courts. Felix was paid under a secret agreement with Arcanum, Ron Wahid's private intelligence agency. Wahid styled himself as a master of espionage, yet here his people appeared to have made a serious mistake. Paying a witness to testify in your cause was a crime in the US. Except, of course, if you could convince a judge you didn't know you were doing it. Which was where a little corporate secrecy went a long way. The clandestine deal had been agreed not with Felix Sater the living, breathing Brooklyn crook, but with his front company. Wahid's people knew who owned it. But they did not tell BTA's American lawyers, and BTA's American lawyers did not ask, even though BTA was paying $100,000 a month to the front company.

When Felix sat down for his deposition, he declared that Iliyas had betrayed him, not the other way round. He was asked about his Cincinnati shithole shakedown. 'In the middle of the trans-action, Iliyas tried to fuck me and it blew up all our business,' he said. 'I wanted to make sure that I received my just and due entitlement.' Was it now treachery to go over to Nazarbayev's side? Only if you did not understand the new world we were in. All these people whose money he had taken, hidden, laun-dered, commingled – they might look like enemies. Say Iliyas was telling the truth and his dough came from Gennady Petelin, the Russian official who had turned against Putin. Wouldn't that make it a problem that Felix had pulled in millions from Icelandic investors whose money, his own finance director recalled him boasting, came from Russians favoured by Putin? Or say Iliyas really was just a front for his father-in-law, Mukhtar Ablyazov, Nazarbayev's most hated enemy. Surely doing business with him would be incompatible with having for a backer Sasha of the Trio, most loyal of the oligarchs at the khan's court? The Trio had, Viktor Khrapunov claimed, passed Nazarbayev's death threat to Iliyas; Iliyas had told his sister to spend three million bucks on Manhattan apartments Felix's firm had built. Look at it one way and Felix was taking terrible risks, handling fortunes for ruthless fuckers who hated each other. But as Felix was fond of saying, it's a mistake to look through Western eyes. Yes, there were dangers. But ultimately all these characters had more in common than divided them: they were all running from their money's past. Whoever was in the ascendancy today was so because he was the one who had best marshalled the past, inter-ring his own and raiding his rivals', allowing him to designate who was a valiant patriot, who a thief. Tomorrow, the balance of the past could shift – if a Felix Sater or some other dirty moneyman decided to let it shift. For an appropriate fee, Felix had decided to let it shift against Iliyas and Ablyazov.

Felix became part of a team led by Boies Schiller, a New York law firm retained by BTA Bank and the city of Almaty. The bank and the city petitioned various American courts to help them recover the gigantic sums of money they said had been purloined from them by, respectively, Ablyazov and the Khrapunovs, the former when he owned BTA, the latter when Iliyas's father Viktor was Almaty's mayor, the two now united in infamy by Iliyas's marriage to Ablyazov's daughter Madina. The story almost wrote itself. Iliyas had arranged his US real estate investments using an email account in the name of 'Elvis Elvis'. One New York developer referred to him as 'Pedro'. Whenever he moved money, it went from one shell company to another and another and another – sometimes as many as six – in various tax havens and secretive islands. A bank called FBME handled the money transfers. Founded by a Lebanese family in 1982, FBME had been based in Cyprus, then the Cayman Islands, then Tanzania, where its bankers went merrily about their business until intelligence agents from the US Treasury revealed in 2014 that it was a cog in a very large laundering machine used by, among others, drug traffickers, online fraudsters, the son of Equatorial Guinea's ruling kleptocrat and Hezbollah. Iliyas made himself look decidedly shifty in his dealings with the courts, too. He claimed to be unable to remember the passwords to his encrypted email accounts and suffered other lapses of memory that a judge called 'frankly unbelievable'.

The way Boies Schiller told it was the way Felix told it: Iliyas had screwed over Felix and his other partners in 2013 when Ablyazov, discovered in his luxurious Nice hideout, had given an order to liquidate everything and get hold of any and all money that could be mustered for his fight against extradition. Every penny Ablyazov owned was subject to a worldwide freezing order handed down by a British judge in the case brought in London by BTA. If Iliyas's money was Ablyazov's money, then Iliyas had broken the freezing order. He could be found in contempt of court, too, subject to default judgments in which BTA's lawyers could spell out his nefarious part in the saga at their leisure.

Iliyas had the same problem Ablyazov had encountered: the act of hiding money to shield it from a rapacious dictator was indistinguishable from the act of hiding money because you have thieved it. Even if your money was truly clean beneath all the layers of corporate camouflage, if those who wished you harm wrote a story on the blank pages your front companies presented, you were trapped. The only way to refute it would be to peel back the camouflage. And that would give them exactly what they wanted: the secrets of your money. Too late, Iliyas realised he was in a battle not over facts but over narrative.

As well as handling Felix, Ron Wahid's private spies had identified other former allies of Iliyas who could be flipped. Nicolas Bourg, one of Iliyas's deal-makers at his real estate fund, switched sides after BTA's lawyers promised he would not be pursued himself. He gave a statement that Iliyas's money was in fact Ablyazov's. Laurent Foucher struck the same bargain, the lawyer who had worked on Iliyas's real estate projects and who had joined him and Madina in Rome in the desperate hours after Alma and Alua were kidnapped. Now Foucher had made himself useful for the other side. In June 2016 he had arranged to meet Iliyas's former secretary, a Romanian called Alina Zaharia, at a café in Geneva. As she related it afterwards, he had given her the fright of her life, informing her that criminal proceedings were under way against Iliyas in the UK and the US. He told her that, for his part, he was cooperating with the prosecutors to avoid being accused in relation to some stuff that had gone on back when he worked with Iliyas, and counselled her to do the same. She should cooperate as fully as she could, or risk being implicated herself. Alina's circumstances were already precarious. She was broke, out of work and lacked a Swiss residency permit. The prospect of being caught up in a criminal investigation filled her with fear. She agreed to Foucher's request to travel to London and be interrogated. He emailed her a plane ticket for June 24, with a return the same day. In London, Alina was taken to an office. A man introduced himself. African-American, moustache, black-framed rectangular glasses. He spoke in a methodical, precise way. He gave her his business card. It read: Calvin R. Humphrey, executive vice president and chief of staff, Arcanum.

Humphrey was one of the former US government officials Ron Wahid had recruited to his mercenary espionage firm. His biography on the Arcanum website described his 'distinguished career in the US Intelligence Community'. This included a long stint as senior counsel to the House of Representatives' permanent select committee on intelligence. The biography added that Humphrey had been honoured with the Central Intelligence Agency's award for non-agency personnel, the Seal Medallion, and the National Security Agency's Trailblazer Award. It did not mention that he was known as 'Calvin in Action', or CIA.

Humphrey told Alina he worked for a private investigation agency. Iliyas's money laundering, he went on, was the subject of pending criminal cases in the UK and the US. No such cases existed, but Alina wasn't to know that. If she wanted to avoid being implicated in these criminal cases, Humphrey told her, she should answer his questions. She agreed. Humphrey turned on a recorder and asked Alina about Iliyas, his family, his associates and his business affairs. He asked how Iliyas communicated, whether he used encryption software, whether Alina had any of his emails that she could hand over. To her astonishment, Humphrey asked whether she was aware of any plans Iliyas might have to seize power in Kazakhstan following an aerial bombardment waged from helicopters or drones. She said she was not. Finally, Humphrey gave her a forceful warning not to tell Iliyas about their meeting. Iliyas, he said, was under constant surveillance, and she could end up in serious trouble, even be treated as his accomplice.

*   *   *

When it came to picking winners, Felix Sater could be content that he had chosen the right Kazakhs, just like he had grasped how to yoke his own interests to those of the CIA and the FBI. Now an altogether more audacious bet was about to pay off. He wanted to be there to witness the moment in person.

His taxi arrived.

'Hi, how are you?' said the driver.

'Do you know who I am?' asked Felix.

'No, I don't really know you.'

Felix showed the driver a business card, in order, the driver thought, to demonstrate that he was a VIP. They set off towards Midtown, across the bridge that linked his Russian roots in Brighton Beach to the Manhattan moneyman he had become. He and the driver talked a little about the evening's remarkable events, but Felix spent most of the ride on the phone, speaking in Russian. They drove towards Central Park, a few blocks up from the bar where all those years before the margarita glass in his hand had connected with a face that would need a hundred stitches to close its wounds, the moment that had propelled him into this life of secrets. The car pulled up outside the Hilton. Felix had booked a room, but none of those present planned to do any sleeping.

For nearly three hours the excitement in the Hilton's ballroom mounted until the place was humming. It was as though from this boxy chrysalis on Sixth Avenue there was about to burst forth a thing of truth and beauty never before seen. At last, at ten minutes before three, it was done. The metamorphosis was complete.

The ballroom filled with music. A fine American composition, the theme from *Air Force One* – a film scarcely less plausible than the exploits that had brought Felix to this point on this night, in which a crazed Russian nationalist holds a US president hostage. And then, there he was, high up on the gantry, waving down to his people, the winner, the reality star, the man whose name had been the final, crucial ingredient in Felix Sater's magic potion for transforming dirty money: Donald J. Trump.

34
Saint or Sinner

Paris, December 2016

In the chamber of justice, the *juge rapporteur* rose to her feet. Her role was not to reveal the court's decision: that would only come at the end. She would read an account of the evidence the court had heard. But Peter Sahlas knew he would be able to detect from the way she chose to tell the story – which Mukhtar Ablyazov she selected as her protagonist – whether his version had supplanted Nazarbayev's. He looked around the room. It was December 9, 2016. Americans had elected Trump, Brits had chosen Brexit, Russia had stolen a chunk of eastern Europe and no one had done much about it. The liberal order Peter had cherished since he was a boy back in Toronto, fought for by sneaking into a Czech barracks, by toiling to get Vasily Aleksanyan out of prison, by racing to Rome when a Kazakh kleptocrat kidnapped an enemy's wife and child – that order had begun to die. Yet here, today, he was taking his seat on a velvet-cushioned bench in one of the temples of that order. In the hearing room of the *conseil d'état*, the highest French court for matters of government, the walls were royal red, topped with ornate mouldings of the symbols of justice: scales and sword, lamp and hourglass. An inscription read *suum cuique*: to each his due.

Peter looked across at Madina. It was she who was going to speak to her father on the prison phone to tell him the decision. Since Trefor Williams tracked him down to the mansion in Nice, Ablyazov had been held in French prisons, first in the south, then in Fleury-Mérogis, the dreaded hexagon in a bleak suburb of Paris where dangerous suspects were kept, including terrorists. That was what the Kazakhs were making Ablyazov out to be, by issuing vague warnings to European law enforcement agencies that the fugitive was so desperate he was plotting violence. The photographs of Ablyazov being driven to hearings on his extradition with an armed escort had become the stock images of the disgraced oligarch. Now he was entering his thirtieth month of incarceration, eight more than the British contempt of court sentence he had fled.

Back in May 2013, the morning after he had watched Madina crumple in the lobby of that Rome hotel as her kidnapped mother and sister landed in Kazakhstan, Peter had launched himself into the task of getting them back. That would involve somehow disproving the official line that this was just a routine deportation of illegal immigrants. He and some Italian lawyers interviewed everyone who had witnessed the two raids: the first one, to snatch Alma, then the second, when they came back for the girl. The police appeared to have shown little interest in establishing whether any crimes had actually been committed. They had drawn up no inventory of phones, iPads and other evidence they confiscated. That seemed like it might be enough to challenge the legality of the raid, so they filed a claim to do so. A young Italian lawyer working with Peter knew that, when a raid was challenged, the case file was taken from the main police station in Rome to a court office a few floors up in the same building – where lawyers could apply to see it. Brilliant, thought Peter. The young lawyer was dispatched with all haste to the court office above the police station. Not only did he lay hands on the three-hundred-page case file, it was immediately obvious that the police had either forgotten or not bothered to censor it. Some high-octane photo-copying ensued, and Peter had the file in his hands. It was a gold mine, Peter thought, revealing a conspiracy not to deport but to kidnap.

Yet there was no legal mechanism to force Nazarbayev to release Alma and Alua. On arrival in Kazakhstan they had been confined to Alma's parents' place in Almaty under house arrest. From there, Alma was taken for questioning. Afterwards she called Madina and told her what they had said, that she would go to jail and Alua to an orphanage. Either that, or tell us where Ablyazov is. Alma had given the phone to Alua. The girl was crying. She had been a baby when the family left Kazakhstan, and barely knew her grandparents. I don't like it here, she told Madina. She was sad to be missing the end-of-year concert at her school in Rome: she had learned all the Italian songs. She asked, When can I come home? Peter Sahlas knew the law alone would not be enough to achieve that. It's a court of public opinion thing, he decided.

Felix Sater, keen to be helpful to his business associate Iliyas, hooked Peter up with a journalist he knew, a reporter at *La Stampa*. The paper ran a big spread headlined 'They Looked Like Gangsters, They Took Alma Away'. There was a picture of the *bambina* Alua in pigtails. Then Peter fed some of the police file to Guy Dinmore, the Rome correspondent of the *Financial Times*. They met in a hotel. Dinmore put the documents in his backpack and rode his motorbike back to his office. On his way, he realised he was being followed. His tail gave him a menacing look and rode off on a powerful scooter. Once Dinmore started publishing stories on the kidnapping he received angry calls from Portland, the London PR firm the Kazakhs had hired. From his hiding place, Ablyazov gave an interview to an Italian newspaper in which he appealed to the prime minister, Enrico Letta. 'To Mr

Letta, I would say, Think of your own wife and your own children. Could you imagine your wife and children being taken hostage by your political opponents, to be used as pawns in your political battles? That is what has happened to me. Mr Letta, I wish you the courage, conviction and strength to get to the bottom of this sordid affair.'

Peter Sahlas found himself instigating an Italian political scandal. The UN declared the incident a case of extraordinary rendition – the first in Italy since the CIA and Italian intelligence had snatched the imam of Milan, Abu Omar, and flown him to Egypt to be tortured. Five Star, Italy's rising left-wing populist party, leapt on the kidnapping story and used it to attack Letta's coalition. The prime minister declared that the episode had brought 'embarrassment and disrepute' upon Italy. His interior minister, Angelino Alfano, a protégé of Silvio Berlusconi, survived a no-confidence vote but lost his chief of staff after it emerged that he had met Kazakh diplomats before the kidnapping.

Peter was shuttling between his home in Paris and Rome. On the flights he would see people reading in their newspapers about the Kazakh affair. The court of public opinion was forming its account: fifty cops had seized a dissident's wife and her daughter and, with suspicious haste, handed them over to a pair of Kazakh diplomats who had a private plane ready to go, apparently in a grubby attempt to curry favour with an oil-rich dictator. Italy was barely holding it together as it was. The banking crisis had become a recession, which had become a crisis of unpayable national debt. Greece had gone under. Italy, the eurozone's third biggest economy, looked as if it might follow. As the kidnapping scandal engulfed the government, Giorgio Napolitano, Italy's president and one of its few respectable politicians, warned that 'the repercussions to us, in international relations and on financial markets, would be visible immediately, and could be impossible to recover from'. Holy shit, Peter thought, I think I might have broken the euro.

He had not. But the Ablyazov case was becoming a constant emergency that gripped him night and day. After Napolitano's speech, he began to think he was gaining the upper hand in Italy. Then a fortnight later, Ablyazov was captured in Nice. Peter flew to France and met him in the bowels of a prison. It was the first time he had set eyes on the oligarch since he had listened to him tell his life story at Tower 42 in 2009. He told Ablyazov he was glad to see him again, but had never expected these would be the circumstances. He visited Ablyazov frequently from then on, hiring a driver to ferry him to and from the prison.

Peter could see that Ablyazov's arrest had changed the calculus for the Kazakhs. When they were taken, Alma and Alua had been valuable hostages. Now, the cost of keeping them was growing. Ablyazov's chances of escaping extradition to answer for BTA Bank's supposedly missing billions were slim. The Kazakhs had no extradition treaty with France of their own, but Russia and Ukraine did, and both obligingly requested that he be handed over to answer for his purported plundering of BTA's subsidiaries in their countries. The one way he could escape would be to persuade the French authorities that the motive for extradition was not to try him for his alleged financial crimes but to silence an opponent of Nazarbayev, perhaps by simply handing him over to the Kazakhs. What better way to make that argument than by pointing to the kidnapping of his wife and daughter? In December 2013 Alma and Alua arrived back in Italy, where a penitent government granted them asylum.

Still, the Italian kidnapping added grist to Peter's narrative: Ablyazov the Dissident. What was happening in the UK was tilting it back the other way, to Ablyazov the Crook. In April 2014, just as Rome was granting Alma asylum, London was revoking Ablyazov's. He was, after all, a fugitive, deemed by the commercial courts to have made off with $4 billion from BTA. Soon, however, Peter was able to add a little context to the story, thanks to an obscure web page that appeared online in August. Kazaword, it was called, on the Wordpress blog site. It contained a link to a file into which someone had started uploading seventy gigabytes of emails and documents from the inboxes of some of the most powerful members of Nazarbayev's regime.

If some supporter of Ablyazov's cause had orchestrated the hacking, they had been clever to publish it online. It was an increasingly common trick in the big-money disputes of the internet age: hack or otherwise extract your opponent's private documents then, rather than presenting them before a court and risking them being struck out on the grounds of having been illegally acquired, stick them online first. That way your lawyer could tell a judge the information had simply been discovered on the internet. The Kazakhs inadvertently compounded the problem by suing in a US court to force Facebook to remove the Kazaword material. In doing so they confirmed that the leaked emails were genuine, only to lose the case on the First Amendment.

The Kazaword files were too voluminous to read in their entirety. But Peter, Bota and Iliyas fished around in them for anything related to Ablyazov. What they found left them gobsmacked. Among the hacked documents was a report, produced for the nationalised BTA Bank, totting up how much it had spent between 2009 and 2014 on lawyers, consultants, accountants, lobbyists, private investigators and propagandists to go after Ablyazov, his money and his public image. The total came to nearly half a billion dollars – about one and a half times the entire budget over the same period of the UK Serious Fraud Office, the agency that was investigating the Trio. That money had covered Hogan Lovells, Diligence and Portland, the engines of the bank's campaign to use the British courts to seize the fortune Ablyazov was said to have looted. But there were others, too, and the Kazaword files showed that their role was more clandestine.

One of BTA Bank's consultants was a middle-aged British emerging markets economist and occasional police source called John Howell. For Nazarbayev's regime, he had been one of the lobbyists who had for years urged the Brits to withdraw Ablyazov's refugee status. It queered the depiction of Ablyazov as a rank desperado. The lobbyists had had the good fortune to encounter a British home secretary amenable to their arguments. Theresa May was keen to give voice to the longstanding unease that parts of the Conservative Party felt towards foreigners. A 'hostile environment' would encourage immigrants deemed undesirable to leave, she declared. In early 2014, John Howell produced a memo on his efforts in the Kazakhs' cause. May, he reported, was in a state of 'considerable displeasure'. She had ordered 'a wider "clean-up" of asylum decisions that have been taken in recent years in respect of individuals who have abused the system and the rules'. As Howell reported: 'The Home Office and Border Agency are embarrassed about the grant of asylum to MA. They feel they have "egg on their faces". It is considered to be a problem for UK:Kazakh relations and there is a pro-Kazakhstan push by David Cameron who is keen to drive the relationship forward.' Cameron had indeed visited Kazakhstan the year before – the first British prime minister to do so. He signed contracts for British companies worth $1.1 billion.

As Peter digested the Kazaword documents, he learned that his adversaries had divined his strategy. FTI Consulting, an American-owned operation specialising in investigations and public relations, was one of the firms hired not by BTA Bank but by Reed Smith, the City lawyers retained directly by Nazarbayev's government. After Ablyazov had lodged an appeal against an initial French court approval of his extradition, FTI's consultants had given their view. 'Ablyazov's objective will be to win public opinion.' They recommended a counter-attack. It would involve a technique Peter had suspected in Rome, during the kidnapping: 'conditioning the information environment', he called it. FTI's consultants discussed using 'search engine optimisation' so Google results for Ablyazov would be more likely to say 'fraudster' than 'dissident'. And they proposed paying an ostensibly independent Swiss non-governmental organisation for an ostensibly independent report condemning Ablyazov.

It was clear that Nazarbayev's campaign against Ablyazov had been a bonanza for the private intelligence industry. The Kazaword files showed mercenary spooks firing off invoices for millions. One of the names stood out: Arcanum. It had been five years since Ablyazov and Bota Jardemalie had met Ron Wahid, shortly after they fled to London, and he had offered the services of his intelligence outfit. At the time, they had decided not to take him up. Bota had joked that he had probably run off to the Kazakhs, shopping whatever useful details he had managed to glean from them. She had not known that Wahid had been working for Nazarbayev all along. In the interim, he had recruited an assortment of superstar spies. Meir Dagan joined after eight years as head of Mossad – Arcanum had issued a press release that quoted him saying: 'It will be a privilege to work together with a special individual such as Ron Wahid.' Joseph DiBartolomeo arrived after a thirty-year career in the US Army that he ended as deputy commander of the special forces. His job title at Arcanum was to be 'Director of Special Operations and Irregular Warfare'. Another Arcanum press release had James Clad, formerly of the Pentagon, declaring it a 'distinct privilege to join Ron and his colleagues in their fast-rising global intelligence firm'.

Wahid was far less forthcoming about what exactly Arcanum did. He told people his team had 'above top secret' security clearances from the US government. But Arcanum also worked for private corporations and for dictators like Nazarbayev. It advertised its work as 'assessing transnational, regional and global threats', services that were mostly 'provided at the head of state and head of government level'. It conducted 'counter-terrorism operations'. It developed 'cyber and signals intelligence capabilities'. Wahid would say that Arcanum was far bigger than its competitors. He claimed its sister company, RJI Capital, was a merchant bank that had been involved in deals worth $20 billion, though discretion sadly prevented him from identifying the transactions. All that Peter, Bota or anyone else reading RJI's website could reliably tell was that Wahid was obsessed with an elite horseback ball game played with mallets, and that RJI sponsored British Polo Day, along with Harrods and Hackett. Its advert declared: 'We are often referred to as "masters of the game".'

Whatever it was that Wahid did, he seemed to be well paid for it. Arcanum had offices in Washington, London and a castle in Zürich. Wahid kept a private jet. In the UK he maintained a close-protection team, chauffeurs in Rolls-Royces and Mercedes Vianos, and an enormous house in Hampstead.

Peter Sahlas could see at least one source of Arcanum's income. The Kazaword emails contained only a few tantalising details of Arcanum's work for Kazakhstan, but they did show that it was lucrative. One from December 2012 mentioned total payments to date on one contract of $3.7 million. Then in June 2013, one of Wahid's lieutenants had emailed Kazakh officials about an Arcanum project called 'Raptor II'. The project's unnamed 'targets' were described as the subjects of a Kazakh request for legal assistance to the Swiss government who had been laundering money. 'Due to the sensitive nature of Arcanum's intelligence work,' the email read, 'and the importance of preserving the sanctity, protection, and confidentiality of our sources and methods, it is not feasible or advisable to provide additional detail in invoices that would be distributed within various departments of client.' To Peter it was as clear as day who these targets were: the Khrapunovs, their son Iliyas and his wife Madina Ablyazova.

The Raptor email referred to Arcanum having performed 'extensive analysis of factual intelligence ... including monitoring of Targets' activities and assets in Switzerland'. If Arcanum was not itself hacking and snooping, Peter concluded, it was part of an operation that was. Days after Ablyazov fled Britain in 2012, Madina had noticed a grey Toyota and a grey Peugeot following her around Geneva. She checked the family car and found a magnetic tracker underneath. She caught a woman filming her children when they were out for a walk. She, the Khrapunovs and their lawyers started to receive boobytrapped emails containing Trojan horse spyware so sophisticated that only two of forty-five anti-virus systems detected it.

Peter knew the Kazaword material was invaluable for his attempt to save Ablyazov from extradition. All the appeals so far had failed. By the summer of 2015, Ablyazov's legal team were waiting to learn whether Manuel Valls, the French prime minister, would sign the extradition decree. If he did so, Ablyazov would have to petition the *conseil d'état*. It had been Peter, right back at Tower 42, who had urged him to seize the narrative, to extract himself from a story of bankers siphoning off billions and depict himself instead as a hero in the saga of Kazakhstan's deepening dictatorship. Now it looked as though Peter would get his chance to tell that story. And perhaps that was why, at five minutes past midnight on August 27, 2015, he stopped being just one of the storytellers and became a character.

He was on a summer holiday with Cécile and their three children in Spain. They were getting older, the kids, and tonight they were up late chatting. Peter heard his Nokia chime in the next room. He left the conversation to check it. The message was from a number he didn't know.

Dear Peter Sahlas, please tell that bald headed cunt you work
for that we are bringing him and all his criminal shit down
around his ears, while he pumps iron in La Fleurie. For what
he did to my wife and daughter in Rome, be assured he has
got my very personal attention. And just to be clear, you
Quebec piece of shit, you are going to lose your shirt along
the way. Have a fun time, PR

Quite apart from the bizarre tone, there was something disconcertingly off about the world this midnight message described.
Its details were wrong by one remove, a parallax version of Peter's
reality. No one called Fleury-Mérogis 'La Fleurie'. That made the
prison sound like some hippy commune. Peter was from Ontario,
not Quebec. But the weirdest thing was the suggestion that
Ablyazov had caused something awful to befall the sender's wife
and daughter in Rome – an inversion of the kidnapping of Alma
and Alua.

Peter was not often rattled, but he was now. For the first time
since he took up Ablyazov's case, he feared for his own safety.
The message read as though it had been written by a gangster,
he thought. It was obvious to him that Kazakhstan was behind
this, that as one of the public faces of Ablyazov's case he had
been targeted for reprisals. He went back to his family and didn't
mention the message.

He let the whole of the next day go by before he replied.

'Hello, sure,' he began. That was his style: always be calmer
than your opponent. 'I will pass on your message. But who is it
from?'

The answer came back: 'Patrick Robertson. Have that name
etched on your collective memory.'

Peter had heard the name mentioned as one of Kazakhstan's
battery of consultants. He knew the rough outline of who Patrick
Robertson was. He was a Brit with a preener's beard who had

spent twenty-five years as what he called a 'strategic communications adviser'. His clients included the Chilean dictator Augusto
Pinochet and the disgraced British politician Jonathan Aitken.
He was well connected among the Conservative establishment:
Margaret Thatcher was honorary president of the Bruges Group,
the anti-EU organisation he had co-founded as a thrusting young
Tory in 1989. The website of World PR, Robertson's Panama-
registered firm, carried a quotation from an otherwise disparaging
article in the London *Evening Standard*: 'Patrick Robertson's
energy and entrepreneurial skill is phenomenal. He is a very
modern figure. He understands networking and the power of the
media. He has charm and a remarkable ability to make people
trust him.' Robertson lived in the Bahamas, but the website also
declared him 'a key player in Kazakhstan and Central Asia'.

Peter texted Robertson back to ask why he bore him and
Ablyazov such animosity.

'Don't piss around with me,' Robertson replied. 'I know
everything about what you do, to the tiniest detail.' He claimed,
again, that Ablyazov – 'your brave "oppositionist" warrior', he
called him – had 'fucked with my family'.

Peter rejoined: 'How or why on earth would my client do
anything against your family? He doesn't even know you …!'

Robertson did not address that. Instead he told Peter: 'We
have had people in your "organisation", if you can call it that,
for some time.' Peter's problem, he explained, was that 'You are
disarmingly naïve.' We have information on you, he added. Peter
should understand that Robertson's 'personal desire is to fuck
you so hard up the ass you forget what your name is'. But, he
added, 'I am a professional.' Peter could save himself by switching
sides. 'Time is running out. Make your choice, and let me know.
And don't bother to reply if you want to be a smartarse. So,
goodnight and fuck you, you arrogant piece of Quebec shit. Take
a reality check. Kind regards, Patrick.'

Had Robertson really infiltrated Ablyazov's team? Peter thought back to the previous year, to April 2014, not long after he'd started to act as the media spokesman of Ablyazov's campaign against extradition from France, as well as the bodyguard Pavlov's from Spain, and was, even though Alma and Alua had been safely returned to Italy, pushing to expose the full extent of the conspiracy behind their kidnapping. Someone called Ian Ferguson had rung him, a Brit who said he was a journalist making a documentary about Ablyazov. Peter agreed to have lunch with him in Paris. Ferguson seemed to know quite a bit about Nazarbayev's mercenaries. He mentioned Ron Wahid's name, and Patrick Robertson's. He offered to help Peter with security, saying he knew people, ex-MI6 and GCHQ, 'the best of the best'. When Peter agreed to meet them, they asked a lot of questions about his IT setup. They drafted a cyber security plan for him and called it 'Project Shadow'. Peter was suspicious. Neither Ferguson nor the purported cyber expert seemed to be who they said they were. Peter suspected ulterior motives, but stayed cautiously in touch with them over a few months. He had given Ferguson a number he used only for a handful of contacts. It was to that number that Patrick Robertson's messages had begun to arrive.

With all these characters, Peter considered it could be useful to keep talking, extracting what details he could of the operation against him. They all muttered darkly about the forces that were massing to crush Peter. Robertson was especially florid. He had a particular technique of projecting Nazarbayev's spies' tactics back onto Peter. 'If I don't address you with the professional courtesy that you believe you deserve, that's because a professional would not work for a criminal syndicate whose boss orders the ransacking of, and death threats to, the homes of women ans' – Robertson's messages often contained typos – 'children.' He wanted to meet, though he advised Peter that 'my close protection team' would observe from nearby. 'There is only one thing I want from you: to start negotiations on bringing you covertly onto our side of the fence, so as to bring you out from the encircling forces of law and order in several jurisdictions.' If Peter questioned the proposed arrangements for a meeting – which included a rendezvous on a beach in Miami, where they would hand over their phones to a barman and dress in shorts and T-shirts to demonstrate that they were not wearing wires – Robertson would get furious. 'Fuck off you pretentious cunt. You will get your comeuppance in good time.' He laid it out for Peter. Ablyazov was not a dissident, he was a 'thief on a giant scale' who had stolen from the Kazakh people and Western banks. Peter was both his lawyer and his 'propagandist'. So if Robertson was able to discover, 'through whatever process I elect to adopt, that you got paid from any one of your client's multiplicity of money-laundering accounts', he would 'personally ensure that you spend a very unpleasant time in prison. Think of cock up ass, and you will be on the right path. Now fuck off unless you want to come in and do the decent thing.'

An email in the Kazaword files shed some light on what Robertson was up to. It was from early 2014, around the time Nazarbayev's propaganda consultants were advising that the battle over Ablyazov's extradition from France would be shaped by public opinion. The email had been sent to senior Kazakh officials involved in the pursuit of Ablyazov from a sender called 'Peter Ridge'. That got Peter Sahlas' attention: Robertson used 'P Ridge' as his pseudonym on Seeking Arrangements, a site for rich people who wanted romantic company. The memo attached to the email was written in the distinctive font used by Robertson's firm, World PR. It proposed a project called 'Laurel 1', the production of a documentary called *Saint or Sinner?* The film would cover the activities of 'the Little Man': Ablyazov. 'This would be a focused documentary exploiting all the weaknesses of our target while outwardly having the appearance of complete balance.' It would be a 'major work', broadcast worldwide. 'But showing the documentary on television is *NOT* the main purpose of Laurel 1. The main purpose is to provide the perfect cover for a more sophisticated project called Laurel 2.'

As Peter read on, he felt sick. Laurel 2 was an 'intelligence gathering enterprise'. Robertson's memo explained: 'We propose covert operations of various kinds. The Little Man may not be the only target in these fields, as others close to him may prove of greater interest to us – family, lawyers, close friends, spiritual advisors, lovers, fiduciaries, PR consultants, tame journalists, senior staff, former staff, domestic staff and so forth.' The covert projects would include 'cyber assaults' on Ablyazov and those close to him, 'psyops' based on a profile produced by psychologists, recruiting 'agents of influence' such as journalists, academics and politicians, suborning Ablyazov's people wherever possible with 'inducements of all kinds', bugging and sabotage – 'the specialists we use are "the best of the best"' – as well as 'staff infiltration', liaising with 'common enemies' and 'media manipulation globally'. Robertson was evidently a practised fake newsman. He knew that, rather than go straight to a reporter with a smear, it worked better if you first planted your disinformation online, say in some anonymously written blog. Thus 'established', such allegations 'can legitimately be reported by the mainstream media'. They could say whatever they wanted about Ablyazov: 'perverted sexual proclivities, allegations of extreme criminality, jihadi sympathies'. In another email on Kazaword, the nationalised BTA Bank agreed to pay Robertson's firm $5 million. The contract said the job would be to make a documentary.

In October 2015, Peter told the French press that prime minister Valls had approved Ablyazov's extradition. The Russian request had taken precedence over the Ukrainian, so that was where he would be sent. The messages from Robertson stopped.

Peter felt that the perils of his work had crept into his home. Five times, there had been break-ins at the houses and offices of Ablyazov's team in France. He had to teach his children never to put anything with their names on it in the household rubbish. After he noticed a black van bristling with antennae outside his apartment block, he made sure only he knew the family Wi-Fi password. Learning the extent of the Kazakhs' mercenary intelligence operation made him shudder. But it was also giving him what he needed: material for the story to tell the *conseil d'état*.

And this story was gaining some local colour. Another hack yielded messages between the French magistrate who had handled the early phases of the extradition request and lawyers acting for BTA Bank. There was no legitimate reason why they should have been in touch: this was a matter between states. And days before the hearing, one of Ablyazov's French lawyers had received a startling letter. It was from Serge Tournaire, an investigating magistrate in the Parisian high court. As is customary in French criminal cases, Tournaire was writing to notify Ablyazov that he had been identified as a victim in the magistrate's current investigation. It was a case of bribery, money laundering, compromising state secrets and criminal association by the five alleged perpetrators. One of them was Bernard Squarcini. Under Nicolas Sarkozy, Squarcini had belonged to the president's inner circle, serving as head of France's domestic intelligence agency. These days he was in private intelligence. Tournaire was investigating whether he had improperly put his old contacts at the state security agencies at the service of new clients. Those clients included Nazarbayev's regime: Squarcini had joined the veteran spymasters on the payroll of Ron Wahid's firm Arcanum. His agents included the driver Peter Sahlas had hired to take him to and from his visits to Ablyazov in prison.

Ablyazov passed his days preparing political tracts and playing chess. If he was extradited, he expected to die. Maybe he would perish in a Russian prison; perhaps they would make it look like suicide, understandable for a proud man unmasked as a cheap crook. Or they might hand him over to Nazarbayev first. Yet as the day of the judgment approached, he seemed bafflingly confident. Ever since he had first challenged Nazarbayev in 1999, he had known it was likely that some part of his future would be spent incarcerated. During the months he spent in a Kazakh labour camp, he had been beaten and tortured. In France, conditions were rather better. If anything, his people on the outside felt the strain more. He sent word to them to find an expert capable of assessing the chess stratagems he was developing in prison. What the fuck, Bota would think, we're stressed out and you're sending us stuff about chess? Then she would feel bad for him because he was in solitary, developing attacks and defences with only himself for an opponent.

Ablyazov would explain his confidence like this: I am convinced that a political system ought to be the way it is in America and Europe. At some point in such a system the error that has been made vis-à-vis me would be corrected. That's how the system works. Even my guards are asking me, what's happened, have our judges gone insane? The prosecution was saying that Russia is our friend and ally, while everybody knows that there are all these political and economic sanctions against Russia, by France as well, and Russia is being accused of not adhering to human rights and engaging in aggression and torture. All the front pages of the French newspapers are showing how children are being bombed in Syria. He spent the day of the *conseil d'état* hearing packing.

Peter Sahlas was far more concerned. He had grasped during that terrible night in Rome that his version of events suffered from challenging what everyone in the West wanted to believe about their own institutions of state: that they were not for sale. And he was asking the judges to go against the position they had taken in every extradition case the court had ever heard, except one. In 1977 the matter of a Basque Spaniard living in France had come before it. Spain had requested that he be sent home to face charges of bank robbery. But the man had agitated against Franco's regime for years, and French law prohibited extradition if the motive for the request was political. The *conseil d'état* deemed that in this case it was, and the man was permitted to stay. Forty years on, the strategy that Peter and Ablyazov's French lawyers had devised to save their client was to persuade the justices to reach an identical conclusion. Peter had not forgotten his Fraenkel. He would have to show that although Nazarbayev's Kazakhstan might look on the surface like a normative state, a state of laws, underneath there lay a prerogative state, lawless and capricious, which had demonstrated what it did to those who betrayed the kleptocracy. Ablyazov was more than a client now. Peter was the family's hope. When they gathered, he would be given both his own portion of pilaf and that of the incarcerated head of the house, whose freedom it was his task to win.

The scenario that worried Peter most was that the Kazakhs and their agents in Europe might be able to repeat in France a manoeuvre they had almost pulled off in Spain. After the Spanish authorities had arrested Pavlov, Ablyazov's faithful bodyguard, a court had initially approved his extradition. Before the lawyers Peter had found for Pavlov could lodge an appeal, the Kazakh ambassador contacted a judge who had nothing to do with the case. With a Kazakh military plane on standby, the judge ordered that the extradition could be accelerated. Only at the last minute had Pavlov's lawyers discovered the ruse and averted it. Peter was determined not to be caught off guard this time. He had an emergency application to the European Court of Human Rights ready to go immediately should they lose at the *conseil d'état*. But that would only buy time; the prospect of that court reversing a French decision was slim. In truth, the hearing today, in the hallowed chamber of French justice, was where Ablyazov's fate would be settled.

The *juge rapporteur* stood and approached the wooden lectern. She had heard Ablyazov's French lawyer put the case as Peter had helped to frame it. Now she started to work through the arguments, discussing the trust between nations on which the practice of extradition rested. Then she slowed down and, enunciating clearly, said: 'Mutual confidence does not mean mutual naïvety.' Peter flashed a look at Madina, who was looking back at him. Their eyes widened. Peter knew then that the judges had believed them that France was being conned.

Peter went to the prison to meet Ablyazov when he was released that night. As he emerged, Ablyazov was thinking back thirteen years, to when his promise to Nazarbayev to stay out of politics had secured his release from a Kazakh prison. Back then, a friend had picked him up in a jeep. In the middle of the long drive to Astana they had stopped and walked out into the steppe. It was sunny and green and beautiful. Ablyazov's friend had asked him how he was feeling. He had replied: 'Well, I feel as though you and I have just stepped out to walk on the steppe, just a normal … I find it hard to imagine that half an hour ago I just stepped out of jail.' It was the same now. His cell had come to feel like a little home. When he walked out into the Paris night, the first shock was the flashes of cameras. His release was big news in France. The *conseil d'état's* decision was, as Peter put it, 'a slap in the face to the PM of France. It's a slap in the face to Putin. It's a slap in the face to the Kazakhs. Jurisprudentially, it's an earthquake.'

Back at the apartment the family had rented in Paris, Ablyazov decided to sing his getting-out-of-prison song. His wife Alma hated that song. It was tempting fate, or at least tempting Nazarbayev. Ablyazov picked up his guitar and sang it anyway.

The lyrics were dark Russian wordplay, about not having much luck dying, but being fortunate in love. Everyone pulled out their phones, and in moments the footage was on Facebook, the liberated dissident reunited with his family.

Peter was overjoyed. But he knew that this triumph in the forum of the law increased the risk that Nazarbayev's regime would resort to the means it had used against other enemies. He had visions of some Chechen sneaking through Paris with a contract hit to fulfil, and unsuccessfully asked the French Interior Ministry to post a couple of uniforms outside Ablyazov's block. 'We want the Kazakhs to think twice before they knock him off,' he reasoned. Meanwhile, he had to acclimatise his client to a new life as a free man. Peter took Ablyazov – who spoke even less French than he did English – around Paris on the Metro, and introduced him to his own wife and kids. There was no prospect of Ablyazov going home. Any tiny possibility of a deal with Nazarbayev had died in Rome. But Ablyazov had not given up on power. Far from it: he would speak of ousting Nazarbayev and taking over as interim ruler long enough to prepare Western-style democratic elections. On his release from prison, he had been struck by how everyone now played out their lives on social media. No longer did you have to risk being physically present to try to win a nation to your cause. All you needed was a phone.

35

The Future

Colchester, December 2016

Nigel Wilkins spent the Christmas of 2016 as he spent most Christmases: resigned to the disruption of his routine by the libraries closing for the holidays but content to leave London for Charlotte's place in Colchester. Nigel didn't like turkey, so as usual she cooked a chicken. Nigel wandered down to the pub. The day after Boxing Day, they went on an outing to the picturesque village of Stratford St Mary with some of Charlotte's friends.

Nigel had been banished from the City but resisted being silenced completely. He'd had another letter published in the *Financial Times*. The City's lobbyists, he argued, were exaggerating its importance to the economy as they demanded that the government maintain unfettered access for London's banks to the European market after Brexit. 'As to the City's contribution to the country's tax revenues, much of this has been offset by the scale of the public funds required to rescue the banks in the wake of the financial crisis. The City is also the home to institutions providing their expertise to companies and individuals wishing to minimise their tax contributions, often through the use of low tax offshore secrecy jurisdictions with close links to the City.'

Nigel had made another appearance in the *FT* a few months earlier, only in disguise. He had met a reporter from the newspaper during an event about corruption one evening at the Frontline Club in Paddington. Nigel and the reporter got talking afterwards. They arranged to meet again. One lunch became half a dozen. Nigel worked his way through the cocktail menu of the restaurant beside Shakespeare's Globe, across the river from the City, one per lunch. He recounted how he had stolen a load of documents from BSI's Cheapside office in 2008. Eventually, he showed the reporter a few of the documents, then some more, then all of them. Patiently, Nigel explained how the front companies worked, the dummy directors, the powers of attorney, the hold-mail instructions. In theory he was still bound by his severance agreement with BSI not to speak of the bank's affairs. But BSI had confessed to the Americans. It had been bought by a Brazilian bank and was about to be sold on to another Swiss one. And Nigel was sick of keeping secrets. Still, he and the reporter agreed that, in print, the whistleblower who had swiped the documents from the bankers' desks would go by 'Andrea'. At an Italian-speaking bank with UK and US operations, Andrea could have been a man or a woman, doubling the field of potential sources for anyone who might go on the hunt once the story was published. Nigel said the settlement he had signed with the Financial Conduct Authority meant that part of the story could not be printed: how the City regulator had fired him when he tried to alert his superiors to crime he believed was being committed under their noses. The reporter wrote a long article in May 2016. Nigel was pleased with it. But the reporter had not grasped the significance of Nigel's discovery. He had failed to follow the trails that began in the red boxes far enough.

The article caused no great waves when it came out. It did seem, though, to fit with a changing mood that Nigel found encouraging. A few days after it appeared, David Cameron convened an anti-corruption summit in London. During a reception at Buckingham Palace, Cameron told the Queen within earshot of a television microphone: 'We've got the leaders of some fantastically corrupt countries coming to Britain. Nigeria and Afghanistan, possibly the two most corrupt countries in the world.' One of those leaders, Muhammadu Buhari, was an aged military man with a reputation for greater integrity than his predecessors as Nigerian president. He responded to Cameron's remarks with a speech in which he did not dispute that previous rulers had looted Nigeria, the most populous nation in Africa and its biggest supplier of oil and gas to global energy markets. But he asked Western leaders to do their part – give the loot back. It was their countries that had accepted the stolen fortunes. 'Our experience has been that repatriation of corrupt proceeds is very tedious, time-consuming and costly,' Buhari said. By the end of the summit, Cameron had agreed to try to make it harder to shift dirty money through the City and the British crown dependencies and overseas territories that collectively formed the world's biggest financial secrecy network. He made some limited progress. A month later, he lost the Brexit referendum. The anti-corruption agenda, like his premiership and much else, promptly ceased.

At Christmas, Nigel felt good. He had noticed a news report that the City watchdog would undergo an inquiry into why it had ignored the warnings of a whistleblower from a property investment fund that subsequently collapsed. It was a template for his own case, he thought. Vindication lay out there still, somewhere in the mists of the future.

36

The Man With No Past

Washington, January 2017

The day before Donald Trump's inauguration, Sasha's private jet landed in Washington. Sasha was a titan of global business, a mining magnate, a multi-billionaire fixture on the Forbes list. The jet – a Gulfstream that could go 8,000 miles without refuelling – was not his only means of getting about, naturally. He had his yacht, the *Lady Lara*. She was the length of a football pitch and carried forty crew, but nonetheless a useful vessel for travelling like much of his money did: discreetly. The previous week she had been bobbing off the Seychelles, where the oligarch and his family were taking a holiday. At the same time, as it happened, Erik Prince, the mercenary founder of Blackwater and a good friend of the new US president-elect, was on the islands to meet one of Vladimir Putin's top moneymen. Whether the three had convened, and what they discussed, these details were where they belonged: out of sight of the public eye.

Sasha had left behind the Indian Ocean for Washington in January. The temperature was below zero, yet there were good reasons to be full of warmth and cheer. Sasha had been at Obama's inauguration in 2009. Today, though, was something else: a new era of hope was dawning. Trump embodied the money launderer's philosophy: the truth is what I say it is. Even this first day of his presidency had been too glorious to be circumscribed by reality. The crowds on the National Mall were about a third of the size they had been for Obama, and the media published aerial photographs showing as much. In doing so, they were guilty of 'deliberately false reporting', declared Trump's spokesman, Sean Spicer. 'This was the largest audience to ever witness an inauguration – period.'

All around the world, those who sought the privatisation of power were starting to capture sources of that power that even the most ambitious kleptocrat could scarcely have hoped would fall. But even as they were gaining control of the present, they had yet to win the battle to control the past. Sasha's secrets were refusing to lie quiet – especially the ones buried in Africa.

The mysteries of the Trio's African interests took human form in the hefty person of Victor Hanna. From his imposing build, his American accent and the fleeting moments when he mentioned his life before he entered the Trio's service, his colleagues at ENRC discerned scraps of his past. He had served in the US military, they believed, though they weren't sure which branch; one thought it had actually been the CIA. They believed he had some Egyptian heritage, or Australian, or both; might have had a law degree. There was scarcely a trace of him online. In ENRC's annual report there were mugshots of all the senior officers except him. When someone at a corporate gathering in the Gulf had taken a photograph of a group that included Hanna, Hanna had walked up to him, seized his phone and smashed it on the ground. Some of his subordinates found him smart and pleasingly direct. But he could grow ferocious too. If the company treasurer raised questions about one of the urgent transfers of money he demanded, he would reply by way of explanation that 'there are people starving in Africa'. One of ENRC's independent directors believed that 'everyone was petrified' of him.

The Trio had entrusted Hanna with the most sensitive part of their operation: Africa. If they were Queen Victoria, he was Cecil Rhodes. That was why, when Neil Gerrard widened his internal investigation into ENRC from Kazakhstan to Africa, he wanted to know everything he could about Victor Hanna. It was why, once Sasha had Gerrard fired and the Serious Fraud Office's investigators took up the case, they wanted to talk to him. In early September 2016, Hanna settled his bulk into a seat in one of the SFO's interview rooms just off Trafalgar Square. Two years had passed since he left ENRC, the Trio's corporation. But their bond was thicker than just business. Hanna had left his wife and children and married one of the Trio's daughters, Mounissa Chodieva. His fate and theirs were united.

When Neil Gerrard started looking into ENRC's African deals, he had gone to see a fellow City lawyer, Malcolm Lombers. Lombers had been retained by ENRC in 2009 when it was buying Camec, the mining company with assets in Congo and Zimbabwe. ENRC's managers in London, some of whom at the time still thought they were running a normal company, had asked him to check whether the acquisition would violate any international sanctions. Lombers told Gerrard he had been unable to get to the bottom of it – because Victor Hanna had refused to let him see the relevant documents.

Lombers did mention a name, one that Gerrard's people kept hearing. Tony Machado was a businessman involved in African mining ventures ENRC had acquired when it bought Camec, so much so, Gerrard was told, that he was an authorised signatory for some of those ventures' bank accounts. ENRC made payments into those accounts, so Tony Machado had access to company money. Gerrard wanted to know more about him. He asked Evgeny Boyarov, a Russian-born Brit who handled the financials for Hanna's African dealings. Boyarov was anxious. He said Hanna was very well connected and dangerous to defy. Boyarov had grown troubled about the purpose of payments Hanna was ordering, sometimes $1 million or more. He knew some of those payments were going to an account from which this Tony Machado could make withdrawals. One of Gerrard's people produced a photograph of Tony Machado. Is this him? Yes, Boyarov said, that's him. But the man in the photograph was not Tony Machado. The man in the photograph was Billy Rautenbach.

Rautenbach: the quick-tempered, rally-driving moneyman, a white Zimbabwean that the country's avowedly black nationalist leaders were more than happy to cut deals with. It was he who had brokered the transaction under which Camec would receive a Zimbabwean platinum prospect in exchange for sending Mugabe's regime $100 million just when it needed funds to steal the 2008 election. After Mugabe went ahead and terrorised the opposition into submission, the EU, like the US, had added Rautenbach to its list of regime 'cronies' subject to sanctions. The UK was a member of the EU, so for a UK company like ENRC, doing business with Rautenbach would be a crime. ENRC's bosses could say, quite rightly, that the pre-election platinum transaction had taken place before their corporation had anything to do with Zimbabwe. But Rautenbach held shares in Camec itself, payment for the mining interests in Congo that he had sold to the company. To buy Camec, ENRC would need to buy Rautenbach's shares. That would involve paying $124 million to a man subject to sanctions – impossible, surely. The British Treasury had the power to grant waivers to the sanctions. But none of the grounds for doing so appeared to apply. Nonetheless, after ENRC's people held discussions with Treasury officials, the deal was allowed to go ahead, for reasons the Treasury's spokesperson declined to explain.

That put ENRC in the clear – provided there were no further dealings with Rautenbach. But what Neil Gerrard was hearing was that ENRC money was still flowing to Rautenbach years later. Rautenbach and Hanna would meet in person. Sometimes Rautenbach came down to the ENRC office in Sandton, the plush district of Johannesburg, South Africa's commercial capital. Sometimes Hanna went up to Harare. The local staff would see the two of them driving off together in one of Rautenbach's cars.

Neil Gerrard concluded that Victor Hanna had been knowingly sending money to a designated Mugabe 'crony' in violation of sanctions that were meant to protect Zimbabweans from their rulers. And it wasn't just Zimbabwe. Gerrard heard that Hanna was showering money across Africa. Less than three weeks before Gerrard was fired, his team had interviewed Derek Webbstock, a senior ENRC employee in Africa. Webbstock said he had personally delivered cash bribes to the current and two previous presidents of Zambia. He had done so, he said, on Victor Hanna's instructions. At least, that was his story until he swiftly retracted it, after someone in the small team of ENRC directors overseeing Gerrard's investigation told Hanna what he had been saying.

Zambia was one of the calmer spots in Africa. Unlike its neighbours, it had never endured civil war, and the losers in its presidential elections accepted the results instead of summoning the mob. It was not immune to corruption, however. If Victor Hanna was indeed bribing Zambian presidents, perhaps it was to protect ENRC's asset in the country. The gigantic, royal blue Chambishi copper smelter rose above the baked earth and sleepy towns of the borderlands at Zambia's frontier with the chaos of Congo. ENRC had paid a prodigious sum when it acquired the smelter in 2010: $300 million. The rationale given to the investors who had bought ENRC shares on the London Stock Exchange was that, even at this price, buying a smelter would be cheaper than building one from scratch. Bankers at Credit Suisse, no less, supported the valuation. But Neil Gerrard discovered that they had done so based on assurances from within

ENRC that feedstock for the smelter would arrive from ENRC mines over the border in Congo. The Credit Suisse bankers had not felt the need to check these assurances. Gerrard's team established that the feedstock never materialised. What was more, Victor Hanna appeared to have intervened to increase the valuation. Could there have been another reason, Gerrard wondered, for such an expensive addition to Hanna's African operation. The $300 million price was forty-six times what the previous owner had paid for the smelter just seven years earlier. That previous owner was a company called International Mineral Resources. International Mineral Resources was a private company. It belonged to the Trio.

The smelter was real. The metals in the ground were real, as were the hands that wielded the drills that pierced the rock that contained them. But the story had been doctored to enable the extraction of hundreds of millions of dollars from ENRC, a public company, into the Trio's private hoard of money.

The Chambishi deal took to $1.4 billion the amount ENRC had paid to buy assets after the Trio had bought them first for much less. Then there were the transactions, struck on Hanna's patch, whose beneficiaries were concealed. Sometimes ENRC paid a giant sum for an asset worth practically nothing: $195 million to a company in the British Virgin Islands for a patch of Congolese wilderness that ENRC's own calculations valued at a few hundred thousand. Down in South Africa, in 2011, ENRC paid $295 million for a manganese prospect. The money went to a company with unnamed owners. Two years later, ENRC's annual report noted in a single paragraph on page 82 that the manganese prospect was now considered worthless. It was as though ENRC was a dual corporation, a cousin to Ernst Fraenkel's dual state. There was ENRC plc, a corporation with shares traded on the London market, bound by laws and regulations, producing accounts, making presentations to investors about its exciting prospects, and enjoying the protection of the law. Then there was its doppelgänger. Its purpose was not to dig ore from the earth, but to siphon money away into the black aquifer.

The Congolese had already lost more than most by the time Victor Hanna showed up. If you happened to have been born there, your life would be harder, sicker and shorter than if you had turned up somewhere not cursed by subterranean riches, or indeed almost anywhere else. During the early part of Congo's great war, Billy Rautenbach had helped to orchestrate the plunder of the country's natural wealth. He fell from favour and, though he clung to some mining concessions, lost his crown as the king of Congo's minerals. After Laurent Kabila's assassination in 2001, his son Joseph succeeded him as president. To play the role Rautenbach had played for his father – go-between connecting the Congolese kleptocracy to multinational mining corporations – Joseph selected a bearded, thickset Israeli named Dan Gertler. Gertler had demonstrated his usefulness by supplying emergency funds that the regime used to buy weapons. That had got him a diamond concession. But he wanted a slice of the real treasure, the metals under the red soils of the copperbelt.

The man who controlled access to that treasure was Augustin Katumba Mwanke. He had been the protégé of Bruce Jewels, the HSBC banker who had clashed with Rautenbach. Now, under Joseph Kabila, Katumba was a financial Rasputin, architect of a shadow state in which Congo's immense riches were harnessed to the private interests of the president and his entourage. In this endeavour, Katumba grew so close to Dan Gertler that he came to see him as a brother.

Soon, Gertler was able to boast that the 'landscape is in the making and I am shaping it – like no one else'. That was the message he sent in 2008 to Michael Cohen, the American moneyman who was pouring millions from the Och-Ziff hedge fund into African deals. 'What this bigger picture exactly looks like is yet to be determined, but it is your partner who is holding the pen.' And Gertler had other partners, more powerful still. Ivan Glasenberg's Glencore was one. Another was the Trio. They met Gertler's key ally, the presidential right-hand man Augustin Katumba Mwanke, at least twice to talk business, Neil Gerrard discovered. ENRC went ahead and bought Congolese mines and prospects. But not directly from the Congolese state, which owned them in the name of the Congolese people. No, first they were sold to Dan Gertler. Gertler would pay a modest sum for the asset, then ENRC would pay multiples of that sum to one of Gertler's front companies. Gertler, and anyone he chose to cut in, would make instant profits running to hundreds of millions of dollars, at the expense of the state entrusted with the care of the world's poorest population. And ENRC's shareholders on the London Stock Exchange lost too, because the company was paying far more than if it had bought the assets from the state directly. Once again, its purpose seemed to be to shift money from the open books of a public corporation to the closed ledgers of the financial secrecy system.

Neil Gerrard concluded of ENRC that 'the majority of its African business appeared to represent the proceeds of criminal conduct'. There was always a cover story, a paragraph or two of business jargon to justify the enormous expense. That was supposed to be all the City moneymen ever wanted: a tale they could agree to tell one another so that everyone could keep getting richer, so that more wealth could be extracted from the rest of society. But Gerrard refused to suspend his disbelief. Victor Hanna would provide explanations and Gerrard would puncture them. A payment of $35 million to a company linked to Dan Gertler was, one of Hanna's people explained to Gerrard's team, in fact sent to pay a tax bill. But a letter purporting to confirm that the funds had been received by the Congolese authorities for this purpose was dated before the money was supposed to have been sent.

When Gerrard started pushing for Hanna to be suspended, he was fired. But even though Gerrard had been got rid of, secrets continued to spill alarmingly from the Trio's control. The Serious Fraud Office's investigators picked up where Gerrard left off. When they interviewed Hanna in 2016, he told them their questions reflected a 'flawed' interpretation of corporate transactions that was based on his exchanges with Gerrard. But then came a hideous development. With great pride, the prosecutors of the US Department of Justice announced that they had for the first time succeeded in holding a hedge fund to account for violating the law against bribery abroad. The hedge fund was Och-Ziff, and the corruption in question related to Michael Cohen's and Vanja Baros's African adventure. Och-Ziff had copped a plea, paid a fine and agreed a statement of facts that the Americans now published. Most of the characters were anonymised. But the disguise was so half-hearted, so many identifying details remained, that it was the work of five minutes to decode. One section had a list of some of the payments made by an 'Israeli businessman' who was obviously Dan Gertler. The identities of the recipients were obvious too: Joseph Kabila, Congo's president, and his most powerful counsellor, Augustin Katumba Mwanke:

December 1, 2010 – $1 million – Kabila
December 3, 2010 – $2 million – Kabila
December 7, 2010 – $2 million – Kabila
December 9, 2010 – $2 million – Kabila
December 15, 2010 – $350,000 – Katumba
December 17, 2010 – $250,000 – Katumba
January 13, 2011 – $500,000 – Katumba
February 9, 2011 – $3 million – Kabila
February 9, 2011 – $1 million – Katumba
February 23, 2011 – $750,000 – Kabila

Gertler had been betrayed by someone who knew his deepest secrets – or who had been able to convince an American prosecutor that they did. Because Och-Ziff's chief moneymen decided to settle the case, no witnesses were ever required to give evidence in court. Kabila and Katumba could certainly have done with the millions. An election was drawing near, and stealing those cost money, even when much of the population was so hungry and traumatised that intimidation alone would mostly suffice.

Some of the money with which Gertler operated his bribery ring was alleged to have come from Och-Ziff. Some of it, the prosecutors suggested, had come from 'Mining Company 1'. This company, it was plain to see, was the Trio's corporation, ENRC. Neil Gerrard had heard something similar during his investigation: some of the millions Hanna authorised for deals with Gertler were denominated as bearer notes. That meant they could be passed on like cash to any ultimate recipient without leaving a trail.

Too many mouths were opening. But some were closing. Katumba died in a plane crash in 2012. In 2016 the charred corpse of Andre Bekker was found on the back seat of a burned-out Audi in a Johannesburg suburb. Bekker, a chipper Afrikaner who liked a pint, had been a mining geologist. He had assessed the value of a manganese prospect in the Northern Cape – the one ENRC bought for $295 million. Bekker knew the prospect was hopeless, that the valuation must have been inflated to push up the price. And he had started telling people as much.

Jim Gorman had died in the same city four years earlier. A Scot with a long career in mining, he had been Victor Hanna's number two. Lately he had been talking about a plan to hive off ENRC's Africa division. After a boozy night out with his colleagues, he took himself off to bed at the nearby hotel where they were staying. Normally, he would have been the first down to breakfast in the morning. When he didn't appear, his colleagues went up to his room. They found him there, lifeless. Gorman had had a bad heart. Maybe it had just given out of its own accord, those who knew him thought. Until they heard what had happened in Springfield, and started to wonder.

Gorman's replacement as Victor Hanna's deputy was James Bethel. Bethel worked closely with his old university friend and fellow South African, Gerrit Strydom. Both were in their forties and decided, in 2015, to leave ENRC. Bethel, for one, remarked that he had grown tired of Hanna's imperious manner. Then again, he had spoken of some business venture he and Strydom were cooking up with Hanna, outside ENRC. The main part of his job had been to run the operations in Congo. That was the centre of the corruption that Neil Gerrard believed he had started to detect when he was fired, and which the Serious Fraud Office's investigators were now apparently pursuing. The investigators had sent word to Bethel: they wanted to meet him. Strydom, for his part, had headed the ENRC subsidiary through which, Gerrard's people believed, payments to Billy Rautenbach had been funnelled.

Bethel and Strydom were bikers. In May 2015 they set off on a classic trail: Route 66. They flew to Chicago, picked up Harleys, and by May 6 had reached the town of Springfield, Missouri. They checked into a hotel, La Quinta Inn, taking separate rooms. On the third morning, they did not emerge. At 1 p.m. hotel staff opened the doors to their rooms. Strydom was lying naked on his bed. Bethel was on the floor of the bathroom in his underwear. Both were dead.

When the news reached SFO headquarters in London, the investigators on the ENRC case were alarmed. They scrambled to contact the Springfield police and ask them to secure the evidence: the men's phones, effects and so on. But the police were dealing with a representative of ENRC, who was assisting them. His name was Shawn McCormick.

McCormick had left BP shortly after his strange performance during the Kremlin's campaign against its Russian venture. He had returned to the region he'd covered for the US National Security Council, Africa, this time for his new employer: ENRC. During Neil Gerrard's investigation, he had been curious about what exactly McCormick did to earn his pay. Clearly he was one of Hanna's crew; Hanna would send him to debrief his underlings after Gerrard's team interviewed them. His contract was for the provision of services in 'Africa generally and in Zimbabwe in particular'. When Gerrard interviewed McCormick he was accompanied by a lawyer who, Gerrard would later learn, also represented the designated Mugabe 'crony' Billy Rautenbach. Neither the lawyer nor McCormick had clarified McCormick's job description to Gerrard's satisfaction. And now here McCormick was, representing the Trio's corporation in the wake of the sudden deaths of two men who had held senior positions in the ENRC unit at the heart of the suspected corruption. It was Shawn McCormick who the local police detective hoped might provide the codes to unlock the men's phones. Some codes did arrive, but if the US authorities ever checked them for evidence relating to the corruption investigation, no one told the SFO's investigators. The phones spent so long stashed in police storage that in time they, like their owners, died.

The bodies were taken for autopsy by the local coroner. His facility was poorly equipped. He lacked the necessary microscope kit to determine the nature of specks he detected in the men's cells. His office had a contract with a substandard local lab; when he sent off samples for toxicology tests, only partial results came back, and the report was not added to the police file. Another coroner turned up, a private one paid for by the Trio's corporation, ENRC. His name was Michael Baden, America's only celebrity medical examiner. He had made a career working on contentious deaths, from John F. Kennedy in Dallas to

Michael Brown, the young black man shot by the police in
Ferguson in 2014. From time to time, he would appear on Fox
News to opine on some case or other. Neither he nor the local
coroner could establish the cause of death, so they sent samples
to the Centers for Disease Control and Prevention, the federal
agency in charge of handling threats to public health. In London,
the SFO's investigators regarded the provenance of these samples
with suspicion. Had a chain of custody, which would have
ensured they were not tampered with, been maintained? No one
seemed to know.

The CDC's tests identified malaria in the samples. Its scientists
did not conclude that this was necessarily what had killed the
men. Nonetheless, six weeks after the bodies were found, the
Springfield Police Department announced the cause of death:
cerebral malaria. For some who knew the pair, that made sense.
They had been on a fishing trip together in a malarial stretch of
Zambia a couple of weeks before departing for the US. That was
about the usual length of time malaria took to develop, from the
mosquito bite, through the gestation of the parasites, to their
surge into the bloodstream and devastation of the organs. Then
again, Bethel at least had not mentioned being bitten; they had
both been feeling ill on the road but he had seemed perfectly
compos mentis on the phone a few hours before he died. And
there was another anomaly, one that only a trained eye could
catch. A malaria expert could tell you that a multitude of factors
affected the speed at which the disease developed over many days
as well as its severity, from the size of the mosquito's injection
to the state of the host's immune system. That meant that the
chances of two people contracting malaria at the same time and
then dying within hours of each other were effectively nil. Unless,
however, they had been bitten by the very same mosquito. Bethel
and Strydom had been fishing together: that could have happened.
Except that it hadn't: when the CDC tested the samples, they

found the parasites had different genotypes. They could only have come from different mosquitoes.

Malaria, it seemed, had not killed James Bethel and Gerrit Strydom. Which left the question: what had?

In London and Africa, colleagues of the dead men shuddered.

37

It's Over

Kensington, June 2017

The first curls of smoke crept out across the fourth-floor flat shortly before 1 a.m. The fire had started in the kitchen, in the corner with the old freezer. The flats were small, nothing like the palaces elsewhere in Kensington. In minutes it had reached the window. The cladding on the outside of the tower block was meant to have been made with zinc. But to save a few hundred grand, aluminium had been used instead. And only two measly slices of it, encasing polyethylene. The combination had never passed what was called a 'real-world' fire safety test. But it was permitted in the UK so developers would not be encumbered by excessive regulation. The senior official in charge of drafting building-safety guidelines had remarked a few years earlier that insisting on 'non-combustible' ingredients 'limits your choice of materials quite significantly'. When the flames reached the cladding, rivers of fire coursed up the outside of the building. A hellish candle licked the night sky. Some of the residents fled down the single stairway. Others obeyed the landlord's instructions: in case of fire, stay put. On the top floor, Rania Ibrahim dared not venture through her door. Like many of her neighbours in the tower, she was an immigrant. Three years earlier she had arrived from Egypt. She dreamed one day of moving to a little

Victorian house. Her husband was away. She was at home with her two small daughters. As the fire approached, she started to panic. She said a prayer. Then she said: 'It's over. It is here.'

Seventy-two of Grenfell Tower's residents died on the night of June 14, 2017. The remaining 250 needed shelter. But the local authority announced that finding them new homes would be tricky: there was a shortage. In fact, there was no such thing. Houses were plentiful. It was just that nearly 2,000 of them were empty. Much of the area belonged to front companies registered in the British Virgin Islands, Gibraltar or Jersey. The former Underground station once used as Winston Churchill's secret command centre, worth $87 million but unoccupied, belonged to Dmytro Firtash, the Ukrainian oligarch behind the natural gas scheme in which the Americans believed the Brainy Don had a hidden interest. The American billionaire Michael Bloomberg was another absent proprietor, as was the ruler of Dubai. The Grenfell survivors were shunted around temporary accommodation for months. Some were sent to live in a nearby block that was at high risk of catching fire.

When Charlotte Martin spoke to her friends in Kensington after the tragedy, many of them thought of Nigel Wilkins. He would have been in the thick of things, trying to establish who was responsible. This was his territory, had been ever since he bought his fourth-floor flat round the corner from South Kensington station all those years ago. All those campaigns for a council seat, all those battles with money-grubbing landlords, all those letters to the newspapers composed with an evening's single bottle of Old Speckled Hen. Now the evil he had perceived, the evil that was there in Hardy, the hoarding of plenty and the neglect of those deemed too many, that evil had taken monstrous, burning form. Nigel would have been able to explain the system that helped to light the fire. But he was not there.

Six months earlier, in January 2017, Charlotte had met up with him and been shocked by how he looked. It was a little more than a year since he'd settled with the FCA and begun his retirement, exiled from the financial world by the powers to whom he had tried to speak truth. He had seemed all right at Christmas, but had obviously lost weight since. He insisted he was fine. They arranged to see each other again soon. But on the appointed day, a Thursday in February, Charlotte received a call from Chelsea and Westminster Hospital. She arrived to find Nigel on an acute ward. He had brought his papers and his notebooks with him, but had a tube up his nose. His sarcoidosis had been weakening his lungs for years. Now he had contracted pneumonia. In the early hours of Sunday, Nigel had a heart attack. The doctors saved him, but his organs were failing. For six days he clung on. Then, as Charlotte sat beside him on a cold, grey Saturday, a doctor told her softly, 'His body wants to go now.'

The Story You Choose to Tell

Montreal, August 2017

Peter Sahlas moved back to Canada in August 2017. Mukhtar Ablyazov had been freed, Mikhail Khodorkovsky too. Soon a Montreal winter began, a brutal one. Late each evening, Peter would take his spade and attack the wall of snow that had risen by day outside his door. He knew he was still a target. Perhaps he always would be. At the *conseil d'état* he had won the climactic battle in the Kazakhs' long campaign to lay hands on Ablyazov by legal means. That left only other means. A scene would play out in his mind: he is on one of his trips back to Paris, a Chechen with a gun watches him approach … He worried that the terror of the world into which he had been drawn had intruded into his children's lives as they grew up.

He had done what Bota had asked of him. He had kept Ablyazov and his people from Nazarbayev's clutches. None of the Kazakhs' extradition requests or Interpol Red Notices had succeeded in capturing Ablyazov or his associates. Instead of handing over Ablyazov's bodyguard Pavlov to Kazakhstan, a Spanish court had ruled that he should be granted asylum. In Italy, Peter kept an eye on the prosecution of those involved in the kidnapping of Ablyazov's wife and daughter. It had left its mark on little Alua. She was in Rome with Alma; they had asylum there. Ablyazov was still applying for his in France. On the occasions when Alua got to see him during her school holidays, if anyone came to fetch Ablyazov for a meeting she would rush at them, kicking out to stop them taking her father away again. Italian prosecutors brought charges against those accused of involvement in the kidnapping, including three senior police officers and the judge who had signed off the deportation. The Kazakh diplomats invoked their immunity.

In Brussels, Bota Jardemalie was also granted asylum. But her life was changing in ways she had neither imagined nor wanted. She was starting to feel that she would never see her home again. She was as lively as ever in company, but the anxiety of being hunted crept into her being. The lifestyle of an accomplished international lawyer had given way to that of a fugitive dissident, her destiny tied to Ablyazov's. Her marriage fell apart. After the Zhanaozen massacre she had become more closely involved with activists and journalists back in Kazakhstan, as well as fellow exiles. She heard about Roza Tuletayeva, about what her torturers had done to her, and started posting online about injustice in her homeland. Torture was a taboo, especially when sexual degradation was part of the repertoire. But messages began to arrive from Kazakh women who said they had never before described what had been done to them.

The Kazakh authorities noticed Bota. Her parents, a well-to-do couple in Almaty, were called in for questioning. One day, she returned to her flat in Brussels and detected, with a shiver, the scent of a man's sweat hanging in the air. She could see from the leaked Kazaword emails the scale of the operation against her, Peter, Iliyas, Madina and the rest of Ablyazov's associates in the West. 'It's a repression machine,' she thought. 'When you put it in motion, it does not stop.' The Kazakhs had hired a team to find Bota: a Russian journalist and two former operatives of the German Stasi. They gave her the codename 'Boris' and plotted to smuggle her out of Belgium. The Belgian police rumbled them after they offered to pay off one of Bota's lawyers for information. In November 2019, a judge jailed them for two years.

But there were other ways to exert pressure on Bota, ways that no meddling Western court could hamper. Her brother Iskander Yerimbetov was arrested in Almaty in November 2017. His jailers told him they would arrest his father, arrest his breastfeeding wife. They would bring his young son in and rape him. They threw him in a cell with convicts instructed to soften him up. They beat him and throttled him with a cord. They said they would sodomise him with a broomstick, force needles infected with HIV under his fingernails. The interrogators told him he could stop this whenever he chose. Or rather, his sister could, if she returned to Kazakhstan and gave evidence against Ablyazov. Iskander was charged with having committed fraud by winning an aviation tender prosecutors declared overly profitable. Nothing in Kazakhstan's legal code appeared to make that a crime, but he was nonetheless convicted in October 2018, and sentenced to seven years' imprisonment. He was released a year later, after a brain aneurysm his lawyers believed was the result of beatings left Nazarbayev's authorities at risk of having him croak in their prison. They retained the right to send him back to jail if his health improved. Iskander told their mother that Bota should under no circumstances cut a deal with Nazarbayev's people. Even if she came home and agreed to turn on Ablyazov, they could hardly just set Iskander free after having denounced him in public as Ablyazov's launderer. Bota sat in Brussels, racked with anger and guilt.

The Kazakh courts were busy. Unable to secure Ablyazov's physical presence, they convicted him in absentia. In June 2017, six months after the *conseil d'état* had found in his favour, an Almaty court sentenced him to twenty years for leading a criminal group, abusing his office, embezzlement and financial mismanagement. In November 2018, another Kazakh court gave him a life sentence. It found that his early partner in BTA Bank, Erzhan Tatishev, had not in fact died in a hunting accident, but had been murdered on Ablyazov's orders.

In Astana, they realised their mistake. Marat Beketayev, justice minister and one of the senior members of Nazarbayev's regime charged with the pursuit of Ablyazov, grasped that the campaign had been poisoned – by money. A kleptocracy had gone after a man they said was a kleptocrat. Any spook, lawyer, lobbyist or PR could see there was a fortune to be made from that. And fortunes had been made. Half a billion dollars had gone out – more, probably. Some of that had bought results. Trefor Williams, the special forces sleuth with the James Bond posters, had found Ablyazov's offshore companies, then he had found Ablyazov. Williams thought it was mind-boggling that anyone – Peter Sahlas included – could look at all those front companies, see all the transactions that seemed to divert money from BTA to Ablyazov's personal interests, and conclude that he was anything other than a giant crook.

But that had not been the whole story. Others on the Kazakh dime had behaved like agents of precisely the lawless dictatorship Peter depicted in his version. That Patrick Robertson email talking of 'psyops'; Ron Wahid's attempt to play double agent; all the fouled-up plots to hack Ablyazov, his family and his people; hiring a couple of guys from the Stasi – the Kazakhs' many agents had inadvertently played exactly the parts Ablyazov had needed them to play. Because everyone in Astana knew that Ablyazov's scalp was the prize the khan most desired, his courtiers had set up freelance operations to catch or otherwise damage him. Even the Trio, doubtless mindful of the need to keep Nazarbayev sweet as they fought off the ENRC scandal in London, set the Israeli spooks of Black Cube to chase some dirt on Ablyazov.

The truth itself? That was secondary. To hold total power you didn't need your truth to beat your enemy's, but to destabilise the very idea of truth, neutering its power to challenge any narrative you might select. Beketayev, the young justice minister, understood that the foremost forum globally for establishing the primacy of your narrative was a Western court. Win there and every journalist could write it up without fear of being sued, every press release carried the weighty stamp of impartial justice. Now he was frustrated. He had served on ENRC's board as the representative of the Kazakh government's stake, witnessed the scenes of dysfunction and farce that allowed those who regarded Kazakhstan as a joke state to go on chuckling. In the pursuit of Ablyazov, he saw, the effect was more ruinous: it had, he claimed, let a thief who wanted to use stolen billions to overturn the established order go free. Hiring all those mercenaries with their grotesque plans to trap him and hack him and smear him and fuck with his head – maybe that would have gained Nazarbayev's regime some fleeting advantage. But in the long run, Beketayev concluded, too much of that stuff and you just look stupid.

In March 2019, Nursultan Nazarbayev stepped down from the presidency of Kazakhstan. Or rather, stepped up. He retained his position as Leader of the Nation, chair of the national security council and head of the ruling party. The successor he picked, Kassym-Jomart Tokayev, confirmed as the people's choice in the usual sham election, ordered that the Kazakh capital city, Astana, be renamed Nursultan.

One thing was different about the election. There were protests; police arrested hundreds. Ablyazov had helped to instigate them from France. He lived increasingly in a virtual world, juggling devices linked to social media accounts on which he denounced Nazarbayev. He took to giving visitors a business card that read simply: 'Mukhtar Ablyazov, politician'. He had never wanted money for the houses it could build, the comforts and the luxuries it could buy. 'Money,' he remarked, 'is a tool for achieving your ideas, for one's political objectives.' His belief that he would achieve his objective – removing Nazarbayev from power – did not waver. But although he was now free, his money was not. It was still hunted, harried and pursued from Moscow to Manhattan. In Kazakhstan, as in more and more of the world, kleptocrats held power; and kleptocrats could only be fought with money. Compared to Nazarbayev, Ablyazov reflected that he would always be outgunned: 'He owns an entire country.' By May 2020, Ablyazov was reduced to declaring himself broke. After he gave a deposition to BTA Bank's lawyers in which he claimed that he could not remember the name of a single frontman to whom he had entrusted his assets, whether he had employed any accountants since a London court froze his fortune in 2009, or even his own phone number, a judge in the US case against him lost patience. Ablyazov had accepted in the deposition that at the peak of his wealth he had $20 billion. Now he wrote to the judge pleading that he could not afford the $140,000 she had ordered him to pay towards his enemies' legal costs. What money he was managing to bring in came from 'like-minded Kazakhs who share my political goals of overthrowing the dictatorial and undemocratic regime of Kazakhstan'. Those Kazakhs risked imprisonment for supporting him, Ablyazov wrote, and Nazarbayev's surveillance was as constant as ever. So Ablyazov's backers avoided communicating with him by phone or email and instead came to see him in France. Ablyazov told the judge the coronavirus lockdown had prevented his benefactors bringing him money. 'I have no funds of my own,' he wrote, not even enough to hire a lawyer.

In Geneva, Iliyas Khrapunov was spending so much time fighting the Kazakhs' lawsuits that he was practically a self-taught lawyer himself. Judges in Switzerland ruled Kazakhstan's request for legal assistance in pursuit of Iliyas's parents unlawful. But in London the story was different. BTA Bank's lawyers demanded he appear before an English court to answer the allegations that he was helping Ablyazov shift his frozen fortune. If he left Switzerland, he risked being arrested on a Red Notice issued at Ukraine's request, then presumably carted off to Kazakhstan to face a fate like that of Bota's brother. The English judge was having none of it. When Iliyas refused to travel to London to be cross-examined he was, like his father-in-law before him, found to have forfeited his right to defend himself. That allowed BTA's lawyers to seek judgments against him unchallenged. A judge ruled that Iliyas held $500 million of the bank's money and must give it back. He appealed. In June 2020, a New York judge blocked BTA from pursuing that money in the US. But the case that had come to dominate his life showed little sign of ending. At weekends, Iliyas and Madina dropped their children off at the local Russian school, the same one attended by the offspring of Timur Kulibayev, Nazarbayev's billionaire son-in-law.

Peter Sahlas relished the victory he had helped to win in the *conseil d'état*, even if the Ablyazov who appeared on a Google search was still a crook. 'If he actually had billions or even millions of stolen dollars stashed away, you would think he would finally have been able to access those funds by now,' Peter reflected. 'He does not and he has not.' And anyway, that was not the battle Peter had been fighting. He had fought over the man, not the money. The triumph in Paris, he believed, 'was important not just for Ablyazov, but also for victims across Europe of repressive political regimes that have been developing a system of mechanisms to net their political opponents, rope them back in, and throw them into their torture chambers and gulags'. It was the other side that had deployed armies of spies and barrels of money. 'My tools,' Peter remarked, 'were the facts and the law.'

In Zhanaozen, Torekhan Turganbaev sat at home, feeling only anger and sadness, from morning to night. He remembered the Independence Day of 2011, the last day he saw his son Amanbek's face before the bullet struck it. That face now looked out, unageing, from a frame in Torekhan's reception room. He wished he had died instead of his boy. One evening he was asked whether he would ever know who killed him. 'It's impossible,' he replied, sitting on a sofa with brightly striped cushions. 'There is no law in Kazakhstan.'

The day after UN torture investigators publicly asked awkward questions about Zhanaozen, Roza Tuletayeva was released. She had spent nearly three years in prison. Some who knew her thought she had been changed beyond recognition by what she witnessed in the square and what she had suffered afterwards. When she spoke of those things she would cradle herself in her arms, as though for comfort. But her close friends were pleased to see that, after some time, she started to dance again at parties, even if it seemed to them that there was a part of her that was for ever hidden.

39

Alternative Facts

London, March 2019

When the past threatens to ambush you in the present, change the past.

In March 2019, lawyers for Sasha and his partners – through their corporation – filed a lawsuit in London against the Serious Fraud Office. This was the counter-attack. They had already secured their defences by invoking a venerated right, that of legal privilege. In 1576, a gentleman named Thomas Hawtry had been served with a subpoena to give evidence in a lawsuit brought by one Berd against one Lovelace. Hawtry objected: he was a solicitor, and had advised Lovelace on the case. The Master of the Rolls was informed, and it was decided that Hawtry should not be compelled to testify. A common-law right was established, shielding thenceforth advice of lawyer to client from disclosure to the other side. Now the Trio's corporation argued: had not Neil Gerrard been ENRC's lawyer while he did his investigating? And had not that investigation been undertaken to inform how ENRC might best avoid prosecution? There was a High Court judge, Geraldine Andrews, who didn't think so. She ruled in May 2017 that the SFO should have access to the records of Gerrard's investigation: for one thing, ENRC's representatives had assured the SFO that the company would cooperate. But this unfortunate setback was soon remedied, with a few more legal fees. In September 2018, the Trio's hold on their secrets was restored in the Court of Appeal. It was deemed 'obviously in the public interest that companies should be prepared to investigate allegations from whistle blowers or investigative journalists, prior to going to a prosecutor such as the SFO, without losing the benefit of legal professional privilege for the work product and consequences of their investigation'. If the SFO's top brass had been too soft in permitting delay after delay in order to keep alive the hope that ENRC would submit to justice rather than force the SFO to do its own investigating, well, that was their mistake.

The past thus wiped clean, the Trio could write their own version of recent history. In the years that had passed since Gerrard was fired in 2013, the SFO's investigators had been covering the ground Gerrard had covered first and even going further. As well as Victor Hanna, they interviewed Shawn McCormick. In September 2017 they interviewed Sasha himself. And there was a chance that the SFO could beat them at their own game, the game of secrets. Nazarbayev's pursuit of Ablyazov had grown so frantic, Ablyazov's continued absence from a Kazakh jail such a personal insult, so many years of dispatching expensive lobbyists to cajole the SFO brass had yielded so little, that word was sent to the British authorities: open a criminal case against Ablyazov and we'll give you what you want on the Trio. Sasha had once said that information was a weapon. If Nazarbayev's regime opened its arsenal of information to the SFO, even the Trio, with all their billions, would risk being routed. But only if they stuck to conventional information warfare, one side's facts in combat with the other side's facts. What about something more asymmetrical? What if the fight was not about what the Trio had done, but what the SFO had done? The Trio needed an alternative story, one in which the SFO itself was a character. And not just any character: the villain.

The Trio hired Hogan Lovells, the same City lawyers who had persuaded the High Court that Ablyazov was a thief, not a dissident. In March 2019 they filed a suit alleging that Neil Gerrard and the SFO brass had been in cahoots from the beginning to stitch up ENRC. Never mind that, as far as Neil Gerrard was concerned, the Trio's corporation had authorised him to talk to his SFO contacts as he set about trying to get ENRC a settlement. No, the tale went like this: with Richard Alderman, the SFO's bungling boss, Gerrard had devised a scheme to get hired by ENRC, leak to the papers that he was running an internal corruption investigation, then feed details to the SFO, which would in turn make menacing noises that ENRC should prolong Gerrard's investigation. There had been lucre in it for Gerrard and his firm: $25 million, ENRC had paid by the time Gerrard was fired. And Alderman would have a blockbuster case that he would struggle to screw up. As Gerrard's investigation went on, he found some of the funny business at ENRC was still going. Even better: a new law against bribery – designed to repair some of the reputational damage done when Tony Blair cancelled the Saudi corruption investigation – was passed in 2011. The SFO needed something other than small fry no one had heard of to net with it. Three billionaires from the former Soviet Union would do nicely. The Trio, their lawyers contended, were not conspirators but conspiratees.

The story took colourful narrative form in page after page. The account was subject to another form of privilege, the sort that said you could not sue the media for reporting documents placed before a court in public session. That meant everyone could write about it. Some of the little details ENRC had dropped into earlier filings against Gerrard and his firm. Once he had whetted the SFO's appetite for taking a bite of the Trio's corporation, the story went, Gerrard proceeded to a meeting at the Chelsea Brasserie in Sloane Square with a couple of ENRC consultants.

He approached them rubbing his hands and declared, 'Right boys, I'm in rape mode.' He went on to explain that he intended to 'screw these fuckers' out of millions. Again and again, Gerrard had what his former clients called 'unauthorised contact' with the SFO's bosses and its investigators on the ENRC case. In this account, there was skulduggery inside the SFO, too. A notebook belonging to its chief investigator, Kevin McCarthy, was missing. Evidently it had been suppressed or destroyed. And Dick Gould, one of the senior investigators overseeing the ENRC case, had maintained a clandestine arrangement with Gerrard, passing him details of confidential SFO investigations that he could use for his various corporate clients' benefit – so said the mysterious author of an anonymous letter posted to the SFO in the middle of 2012, just as Gerrard's investigation into ENRC was gathering momentum.

In 2019 the cast multiplied. Corporate spooks and mercenary propagandists had participated in the plot against the Trio and their company, including by tipping off the London *Evening Standard* about Sasha's SFO interview. The Trio's company sued them. Akezhan Kazhegeldin, the former Kazakh prime minister who had overseen the privatisations that created ENRC then fled into exile as a dissident, was involved as well, the Trio's lawyers claimed. They sued him, too, alleging that he had gathered confidential documents pertaining to the Trio's business and disseminated them to those for whose eyes they were not meant.

Among these interlopers in the Trio's affairs was Glenn Simpson, the *Wall Street Journal* reporter to whom Sugar had imparted the secrets of Nazarbayev's kleptocracy. Simpson had since departed the underfunded field of journalistic investigation for the richly funded one of private investigation. In 2015, Simpson's firm Fusion GPS was commissioned by a website controlled by a Republican moneyman called Paul Singer to research some of the candidates hoping to be the party's presidential nominee. Once Donald Trump won the nomination, Hillary Clinton's Democrats kept Simpson on, to examine Trump's strange connections with Russia. Simpson hired Chris Steele, formerly of MI6 in Moscow. Steele talked to his sources, and filed reports of what they said back to Simpson: the candidate's connections to the Russian oligarchs behind TNK-BP, the candidate consorting with Moscow prostitutes, the candidate compromised by kleptocrats from Putin down. Hillary, Simpson and Steele: soon they became lead monsters in President Trump's parallel reality.

Beyond their shared enmity for the likes of Glenn Simpson and anyone else who posed a threat to their information control, Sasha and Trump had plenty in common. They both consorted with people like Felix Sater, noted launderer, yet both were outraged whenever anyone questioned the origin of their own wealth. They had the same taste in operatives. Trump selected as his top intelligence official a propagandist called Richard Grenell. 'A lie gets halfway around the world before the truth even has a chance to get its pants on,' was the quotation, misattributed to Winston Churchill, atop his firm's website. The disinformation campaigns Grenell himself had orchestrated underscored the point. Before he served the president, he served private clients with a need for alternative facts – among them ENRC, the Trio's corporation.

As for enemies, Trump and Sasha's approach suggested they concurred with Nazarbayev: 'Those who agree with and accept his opinions and stick to the rules are in "his" group. Anyone who does not accept his opinion is one of the "others" and thus an enemy … If the enemy does not surrender, he must be destroyed.'

Neil Gerrard had been receiving anonymous death threats for a while when, one day in April 2019, he discovered that a high-quality, motion-activated video camera had been tied to a branch of a tree overlooking the entrance to the farm where he lived in Sussex. A cable ran from the camera to a shallow depression twenty metres away where, beneath some chicken wire and foliage, there lay a battery-powered router, a SIM card and a data storage device. Gerrard thought he knew who had set up the surveillance. A few months earlier, he and his wife had holidayed with friends on a Caribbean island. It was a private island, the kind of place where you could expect to be alerted by the authorities on nearby St Lucia if someone boarding a flight there said they were coming to visit you. The two men who said as much used the Gerrards' first names. But the couple went by their middle names. The pair were turned away. A couple of days later, a third man rolled up in St Lucia en route to the private island. He was rumbled too, and found to have a bagful of electronics that included a night-vision camera. Gerrard learned their names and their employer: Diligence, the same private intelligence firm from whose offices in Canary Wharf Trefor Williams had traced his Kazakh clients' quarry, Mukhtar Ablyazov.

ENRC made in profit in a week and a half what the SFO was given to spend in a year. The damages the Trio's company demanded in the March 2019 suit – $90 million – were double its annual budget. When Anna Machkevitch – like her father, a Damien Hirst collector – received an order from the SFO to hand over documents relevant to its investigation, she ignored it. Benedikt Sobotka, the boss of ENRC's successor company in Luxembourg, refused to come in for questioning. John Gibson, a chipper barrister who displayed a twinkling delight in legal duelling and had taken a large pay cut to join the SFO and lead the ENRC case, eventually grew weary. In September 2018, he returned to private practice.

Still, it was a never-ending effort, transforming the past and keeping it transformed. Look at Belgium. Sasha and his partners had thought, back in 2011, that their legal difficulties there were over. They had secured a deal to resolve the investigation into suspicions that they had laundered through Belgian real estate the proceeds of kickbacks that the Belgian company Tractebel was said to have paid them to help win Kazakh power contracts. It had been one of the longest-running cases ever to come before Belgian justice, the product of Sugar's botched intriguing back in the nineties. The cost of the settlement was peanuts: $30 million, less than two weeks of Rudny's profits. But once again, history would not rest. Across the border in France, the electorate's termination of Nicolas Sarkozy's presidency after a single term was soon followed by ever-expanding investigations into corruption and abuse of office during his reign. The investigators took an interest in a deal announced in 2010 while Sarkozy was hosting his Kazakh counterpart, Nursultan Nazarbayev, in Paris. Kazakhstan was to pay two billion euros for a consignment of French helicopters and locomotives. The investigators discovered dubious side-payments. They also came to suspect that there had been another quid pro quo: Nazarbayev would buy French if Sarkozy's people agreed to lobby Belgium for a favour. What Nazarbayev wanted – what his Trio needed – was a change in the law. For the financial crimes of which the Trio were accused, Belgian statutes forbade a settlement in which forfeiture was made without an admission of guilt. But admitting guilt was something the Trio could not risk: they had a London-listed company to think about. At the time – back before Neil Gerrard fucked everything up – Sasha was even contemplating taking over as chairman. No, they needed to emerge from Belgium as spotless as their magnificent mansions in Waterloo, Uccle, and Rhode-Saint-Genèse. And emerge they did, three months after the law was changed to remove the prohibition of settlements without admissions of guilt. When French investigative reporters discovered the lobbying behind the change in the law, they called it 'le Kazakhgate'. Still, it looked as though the usual playbook would be followed: some locals would go down, but none of the moneymen.

*   *   *

Of course, none of the manoeuvring in Belgium or in France, in Kazakhstan or in London would change what had actually happened. Least of all what had actually happened in Africa. There the Trio were reaping their rewards, not just the endless millions of dollars but the warm comfort, like a hot red sun over the copperbelt, of having picked the right allies to sustain.

After thirty-seven years in power in Zimbabwe, Robert Mugabe's departure in November 2017 could have been a destabilising affair, the kind of thing, emerging markets analysts were always warning, that disquieted investors. Yes, it was a coup. But those seeking reassurance that the country's investment climate would be unchanged needed to look no further than the soothing features of the man who had taken over: Emmerson Mnangagwa, the Crocodile. Soothing, at least, for Billy Rautenbach. It had been a fair while since that winter's day in July 2000 when he had rocked up at Victoria Falls and warned that if he were not retained in favour, he would reveal the secrets of the plunder operation that the Crocodile had mounted under cover of the war in Congo. But favour Rautenbach had retained. Lately, he had achieved something remarkable: he had become a prosperous white farmer in Zimbabwe. He was the biggest landowner in the country growing crops for ethanol – ethanol that, the government had decreed, must be mixed with every drop of fuel sold nationwide. The Crocodile's ascendancy – blessed by the people after an election of only moderate violence, far less than that he had overseen in Matabeleland – suggested that Rautenbach could rest easy on his rustic stoop. The EU had lifted its sanctions on him and others ahead of Zimbabwe's 2013 election to undercut

Mugabe's propaganda that foreign powers, not his own misrule, were responsible for his people's deepening poverty. In the event, voters were apparently more concerned about their physical well-being than such questions of high policy.

The Americans were more obdurate, but they too were persuaded, thanks to the good offices of Pierre Prosper. Ambassador Prosper, a former prosecutor, worked for the prestigious American law firm Arent Fox but retained the honorific from his stint as George W. Bush's envoy on questions of war crimes. ENRC had hired him for a while, when Neil Gerrard was conducting his investigation. It was Prosper who in 2012 had assured the SFO's investigators that no further examination of potential breaches of sanctions was required. Three years later he had a gratifying announcement to make on behalf of another client he had neglected to mention to the SFO: Billy Rautenbach. Ambassador Prosper had been holding discussions with officials from the US Treasury in Washington – a 'constructive exchange', he could now reveal. They had reached the 'correct conclusion' and removed Rautenbach's name from their sanctions list.

The Trio's middleman up in Congo, the Israeli billionaire Dan Gertler, found the Americans less amenable. After the Och-Ziff judgment revealed how Gertler went about turning Congo's minerals into fortunes for himself and President Kabila, the US Treasury imposed a new type of sanctions on him. In June 2017 his name was added to the list of rogues subject to the Global Magnitsky Act, a device named after the accountant who worked for the moneyman Bill Browder's Russian fund and was beaten to death in prison. After Magnitsky's murder, Browder had reinvented himself as an anti-corruption campaigner and lobbied for rich democracies to bar those deemed to have violated human rights from enjoying the pleasures and protections of the West. Any US assets of those named on the list were frozen. Gertler's deals, the Treasury stated, had siphoned off $1.36 billion from the Congolese state. Like any good player of the game of secrets, however, Gertler was able to do what Billy Rautenbach had done during his moment of crisis and turn it to his advantage. Ivan Glasenberg had foreseen Gertler's shaming. His vast trading house, Glencore, paid Gertler half a billion dollars to buy him out of their partnerships in Congo three months before the Magnitsky designation – then resumed paying him royalties running to millions, only now in euros. As for Kabila, if the restrictions on Gertler depleted his electoral warchest, it did so insufficiently to prevent the masterful manoeuvre he pulled off in January 2019. Three years past the end of his constitutional mandate, the votes were counted in an election to choose his successor. Kabila's chosen heir did badly; Martin Fayulu, an opposition candidate, won comfortably. But the electoral authorities announced a set of alternative facts, and Félix Tshisekedi, a rival opposition candidate, was declared the victor. The constitutional court endorsed the fake result. When Tshisekedi appointed one of Kabila's allies as prime minister, the stitch-up was complete.

The Trio's African mining interests were secure. And yet, from time to time, the past would threaten to bubble up to the surface. The former employer of Andre Bekker, the geologist found dead in the back of a torched car in Johannesburg after suspecting that hundreds of millions had gone astray in ENRC's acquisition of a South African manganese prospect, hired a private detective to look into his death. The detective, a dogged former South African police colonel called Clement Jackson, started to piece together what Bekker had known. When the Serious Fraud Office investigators on the ENRC case got in touch, he went to London and passed on the results of his enquiries. In Springfield, Missouri, the police initially announced that James Bethel and Gerrit Strydom had died of malaria. But they had not formally concluded that that was indeed the true explanation: they quietly kept the case open. By the middle of 2020, without any announcement, the FBI had taken over the investigation.

Whatever befell the deceased bearers of ENRC's secrets, their deaths struck fear into those charged with establishing the truth. After John Gibson left the Serious Fraud Office, Jon Mack took over as case controller on the ENRC investigation. On the morning of a court hearing into Sasha's daughter Anna's refusal to hand over documents, Mack collapsed. During the weeks he spent in hospital, Mack was convinced he had been poisoned. Though the doctors didn't confirm as much, he was so shaken that he dropped the ENRC case, leaving it to someone else to try to bring the seven-year investigation to a conclusion. The Trio's people grew confident that, were that ever to happen, it would take the form of a deal, with any punishment directed not at the Trio or their lieutenants but at the corporation itself, which could settle its debt to society by handing over a little of its money.

40

Quid Pro Quo

Washington, July 2019

Thursday, July 25, 2019 was a hot day in Washington. Not as hot as it sometimes got in summer, though, and less swampishly humid. Donald Trump made it known to the world that he had arisen with a tweet at 7.06 a.m. In the White House he had been watching the morning show *Fox & Friends*, and quoted the co-host, Ainsley Earhardt: 'Yesterday changed everything, it really did clear the President. He wins. It changed everything in favor of the President, who said all along this investigation is rooted in nothing.' The previous day Robert Mueller had testified before Congress about his investigation into Russian interference in the 2016 election and whether the winner, Trump, had colluded in it. 'The finding indicates that the president was not exculpated for the acts that he allegedly committed,' Mueller had said. He was asked about whether future campaigns might profit from foreign interference: Trump had benefited in 2016 from a Russian hack of senior Democrats' emails, and had recently declared on television that he would be open to receiving dirt on his rivals in the 2020 election from China, Russia, or indeed any country. 'I hope this is not the new normal,' Mueller replied, 'but I fear it is.'

Fox moved on to a poll it had done that found satisfaction with the economy. Trump tweeted about that. He did not refer to another of its findings. 'When Democrats are polled, the number one thing they're looking for in a candidate for 2020 is somebody who can beat Donald Trump,' the Fox host said. 'And right now, so many people go, well, the only person that kind of qualifies for that is Joe Biden.'

At 9.03 a.m. Trump picked up the phone in the White House residence for a call with Volodymyr Zelensky, a comedian who had been elected president of Ukraine in April. The two men started by saying how much they wanted to be friends. Zelensky mentioned that when he had travelled to New York, he had stayed at Trump Tower. He did not yet know that Trump had suspended $250 million in military aid to Ukraine, a country at war with an occupying force of Russian-backed separatists and Little Green Men.

Zelensky said he wanted to visit the White House. Trump's envoys had already let Zelensky's advisers know that any such visit would depend on the Ukrainian president having given Trump what he wanted. He would have to ensure that two investigations were opened in Ukraine. One would be into the role a Ukrainian company played in establishing that it was the Russians who hacked the Democrats in 2016. The other would be into Joe Biden's abuse of the office of Obama's vice president to block a Ukrainian investigation into his son's corrupt business dealings in Ukraine. The company that played a role in establishing that the Russians had hacked the Democrats was not Ukrainian. Joe Biden had not blocked an investigation into his son's business dealings in Ukraine, and there was nothing to indicate that they had been corrupt. But that was the sort of irrelevant detail valued only by those an aide to the previous Republican president, George W. Bush, once dismissed as the 'reality-based community'. Such fools had not understood that the world had changed. They had not understood how dirty money had changed everything – nor how it had transformed Donald Trump.

From the beginning, Trump had wanted to make money mean something other than what it actually meant. He inherited a fortune from his father; he wanted that to mean he was a self-made mogul. His property ventures and casino schemes kept going bust; he wanted that to mean they had been successful. Those of his financial records that became public showed enormous debts; he wanted them to prove him a gold-plated billionaire. Fortunately for him, at the turn of the millennium, just when it appeared that his mask had irreparably cracked, when the banks had lost patience and cut off the credit that sustained him, two developments, each an echo of the other, saved him. One was the advent of reality television. The other was the ocean of dirty money that flowed into the West.

In the spring of 2000, a new show in a genre that US broadcasters had largely neglected since *Candid Camera* aired on American TV. *Survivor* drew on a bastardised Darwinism: the idea that life at its essence was nothing more than a contest in which individuals kill or are killed. The contestants did not actually kill one another, of course: this was entertainment. They were simply eliminated one by one, through a series of challenges to feed and shelter themselves in the remote location to which the producers had consigned them, until only the victor remained. It was a huge hit: fifty-one million viewers watched the finale of the first season. Mark Burnett, the show's creator, was a Brit who had previously worked as a paratrooper, a used-clothing salesman and a Los Angeles nanny. 'The philosophy of *Survivor* is to build a world and destroy exactly what you've built for personal gain,' he said. It gave him an idea for a follow-up. It would be like *Survivor*, except the decisions of who to eliminate would be taken not by a tribal council of the contestants themselves but by a single, tyrannical judge. Burnett imagined a kingdom with a king on a throne saying, 'Off with your head.' The contestants would be 'so drawn to the horror of being excluded, of being killed' that the viewing would be 'magnetic'. Burnett took the show's title from a scene in Disney's *Fantasia*, The Sorcerer's Apprentice. He knew who he wanted as the sorcerer, the king. He had read the man's book, a largely fictional memoir presented as fact, *The Art of the Deal*.

In January 2004, the first episode of *The Apprentice* was broadcast. Over rollercoaster shots of the Manhattan skyline came the voice: 'My name is Donald Trump and I'm the largest real estate developer in New York. I own buildings all over the place, model agencies, the Miss Universe pageant, jetliners, golf courses, casinos, and private resorts like Mar-a-Lago, one of the most spectacular estates anywhere in the world.' It didn't matter that this account of himself was, as Trump's biographer put it, 'laced with a number of howlers'. Image was replacing deeds as the repository of identity. Mark Zuckerberg was putting the final touches to the online social network he would launch the following month. The Facebook age – in which you were whatever you said you were – was beginning. Still, Trump's voiceover revealed that 'it wasn't always so easy'. There had been a time when he had been in 'serious trouble'. He was billions of dollars in debt. 'But I fought back and won – big league.'

That much was true. In 2001, one of the tenants of Trump Tower had introduced himself. 'I'm going to be the biggest developer in New York,' Felix Sater told Trump, 'and you need to be my partner.' There was no need to discuss the criminal connections in either man's past: Trump's mobster associates or Felix's days as a pump-and-dump fraudster. What mattered was that Trump needed money and Felix was at liberty, thanks to his deal to spy for the FBI and the CIA. Felix and his partner, Tevfik Arif, were ideally placed to capitalise on the second great shift that would save Trump: the tide of dirty money.

The end of the Cold War had created an unprecedented opportunity to capture the wealth of nations. From Budapest to Beijing,
Almaty to Abuja, the nineties were spent in a violent contest to
do so. Then came the next task: to funnel that stolen wealth to
the West for safekeeping. For safekeeping and for another purpose:
to complete the process of turning power that had been turned
into money back into power. A global kleptocracy was born. For
a while you could just pump the money through banks: the
Brainy Don and others appeared to have done so on an enormous
scale at Bank of New York. But then, after 9/11, banks were on
orders to pay some attention to whose money they were handling,
lest they abet terrorism. Conveniently, there was another route
to the West that had retained its secrecy: real estate. The five
families had laundered their criminal proceeds through American
property for decades. Now the new kleptocrats followed them.

Felix and Arif knew the moneymen who had ventured into
the West from this new order. Sasha of the Trio, the Icelanders
with their purported Russian backers, the ex-Soviet New York
tycoon Tamir Sapir: these would be the partners of their real
estate company, Bayrock. They even knew those like Iliyas
Khrapunov, who had broken with the ruler under whom they
had grown rich but whose money was still inextricably bound to
the kleptocracy. Trump's role would be to rent out his name. As
the persona of *The Apprentice* had elided reality, that name had
been reinvented as a success. For a percentage, Trump would
append his personal brand to a skyscraper or a hotel. He would
make ignorance his business: what one of those who handled the
money called 'wilful obliviousness'. An architecture of shell
companies would keep the money incognito, and if anyone did
find out who it belonged to, provide plausible deniability for
those who had received it. The projects could go bust – they
usually did – but that wasn't a problem. The money had completed
its metamorphosis from plunder to clean capital.

There were laundering opportunities everywhere: David Murcia Guzmán pumped the proceeds of his black market peso scam through the Trump Ocean Club down in Panama. But the big money wanted to be in the greatest haven of all, North America. In 2008, the Trump SoHo opened. It had cost $370 million. Another $200 million half-hotel, half-condo tower in Phoenix, Arizona, was supposed to follow, but was never finished. Nor was the 24-storey tower in Florida. Still, both projects had usefully recycled plenty of money. The partners' horizons widened. Felix Sater set off for Moscow with two of Trump's children, Ivanka and Don Jr, to drum up a scheme for a Trump Tower in the Russian capital. For all their wilful obliviousness, Trump and his people showed a pretty clear sense of the sources of the funds: 'We see a lot of money pouring in from Russia,' Don Jr said in an interview published the day Lehman Brothers collapsed in 2008.

Felix Sater was a crucial conduit. For a while, he even enjoyed the title of 'Senior Adviser to Donald Trump'. His partner Tevfik Arif brought ex-Soviet moneymen to meet Donald. But they were by no means the only one. Ex-Soviet money had multiple pipelines into Donald Trump. Vyacheslav Ivankov, the brutal *vor* who was extracted from jail by the Brainy Don and came to New York: the luxury apartment he kept for himself was in Trump Tower. The five condos that the brother of the Brainy Don's US moneyman bought there: Trump sold them to him personally. The sixty-three politically connected Russians who spent $98 million on Florida property: that was Trump real estate. Dmitry Rybolovlev, a billionaire who prospered under Putin, bought Trump's mansion in Palm Beach for $96 million, more than double what Trump had paid for it a few years earlier.

In October 2007, Trump alighted from a limousine in Toronto and posed for the cameras holding a golden spade to mark the start of construction of a $500 million skyscraper. It would be built under the same terms as buildings Felix Sater masterminded. Trump would front the project. 'People really want to own what I do,' he declared in a publicity video for the Trump Toronto. The tower, he enthused, would be 'taller than other buildings'. Trump would get a cut for the use of his name, but the money would come from elsewhere. In this case, his backer was an awkward Russian-Canadian billionaire. He took a golden shovel too, and together they dug into dirt topped with letters spelling out 'TRUMP'. The focus was all on the Donald, in his greatcoat and powder-blue tie. But the partner looked delighted. His name was Alex Shnaider. How far he had come from the days when he was just a youngster in Ukraine being groomed for a career in money by his father-in-law, Boris Birshtein. Shnaider was estranged from Birshtein now, wanted nothing to do with a man who, according to another of his former employees, Patokh Chodiev of the Trio, 'stank of the KGB'. There was still some more transforming for Shnaider to do, however. By the time, five years later, that he and Trump again stood together and, to the sound of 'Fanfare for the Common Man', declared the Trump Toronto tower complete, Shnaider had sold the Ukrainian steel mill that had made his fortune. The transaction had brought in hundreds of millions for Shnaider – on the understanding that $100 million would be secretly diverted to representatives of Putin's Kremlin. The money came from a Russian state bank – it belonged to the Russian people, though the Kremlin treated it as its own. Once Shnaider got his share, he put up the final $40 million to finish the Trump Toronto. Trump then took his slice, and went on doing so for years as the building was completed, went bust and was sold off.

His business dealings with the billionaire who had sold a chunk of the Ukrainian steel industry to the Russians were not among the subjects Trump saw fit to raise in his call with Zelensky. But he did profess to think Ukraine a great country. Well he might:

it was the membrane between democracy and dictatorship, a faultline to be mined. So he cut to the chase. 'There's a lot of talk about Biden's son, that Biden stopped the prosecution. And a lot of people want to find out about that, so whatever you can do with the attorney general would be great. Biden went around bragging that he stopped the prosecution so if you can look into it – it sounds horrible to me.' William Barr would be in touch, as would Rudy Giuliani. The former was the US attorney general, the latter Trump's personal lawyer, but there seemed no distinction: both would be at work to tarnish the Democratic candidate shown by that morning's polls to be the biggest threat to Trump's extending by another four years his opportunity for privatising power. Trump didn't like to spell out quid pro quos. 'He doesn't give you questions, he doesn't give you orders, he speaks in a code.' So said the New York lawyer Michael Cohen – not the hedge fund moneyman, another Michael Cohen, one of Trump's fixers. But anyone listening would understand the deal the US president was offering his Ukrainian counterpart: help me make my narrative that my rival is corrupt and you will have your military aid, your White House visit. Fail to give me what I want and, well, choosing not to be my friend is choosing to be my enemy.

Because you couldn't simply lie. With dirty money, you couldn't just bring it in by the case and baldly state that it was clean; you had to give it a cover story, say in the form of a skyscraper with a famous name on top of it. If anyone challenged your story, you had to destabilise the truth. Maybe this had happened, maybe that had happened, who could say? An objective truth, reachable by honest enquiry? No such thing existed. Likewise, there could be no altruism, no acting out of an interest other than personal profit. The best strategy was projection: make it a battle of pot versus kettle. You claim I am corrupt? You've been paid off to say that. You're defending a man whose wife and child were kidnapped in Rome? Take care, that man went after my family – in Rome. You claim that I paid bribes in Africa? You cooked up that story to enrich yourself. You allege I trade in falsehoods, traffic in dirty money? Well they would say that, Lyin' Ted and Crooked Hillary. You say that there was collusion with a foreign power during the election? Absolutely: and we must know how Joe Biden did it. All the while, on social media, the greatest system yet devised for destabilising the truth, use one word more than any other: 'fake'.

At 9.33 a.m., Trump put down the phone. Within the hour, his people and Zelensky's were messaging to confirm that the investigations would go ahead and to arrange dates for the Ukrainian president's visit to the White House. At 11.19 a.m., Trump departed in the Beast, the heavily armoured presidential limousine equipped with emergency blood supplies and facilities to transmit nuclear launch codes.

The motorcade drove to the Pentagon, where Trump was to deliver remarks at the investiture of his latest defence secretary. He began: 'Thank you to all of the extraordinary patriots here at the United States Department of Defense, the world's largest building. I've heard for many years, the world's largest building.' He added: 'It is the greatest honour of my life to serve as your commander-in-chief.' As for Mark Esper, the new secretary – a former lobbyist who had declined to commit to recusing himself from decisions involving an old client that was still to pay him $1 million, the military contractor Raytheon – he was going to make all Americans very, very proud. 'They're right now very proud but they're going to be even more so as time goes by. People love our country more than ever, and our country is respected again. Remember that.'

He moved on to money, the 'billions and billions' he had added to the military budget and the weapons those funds were buying. 'Any battlefield will be a battlefield on which we win,' he said. 'Our first priority is always the safety and sovereignty of our nation and our citizens,' he went on. 'Here at home, we have deployed military forces to confront the grave national security crisis on our southern border.' Those bad hombres, those hordes of Latino rapists, here at last was a president with the courage to stand up to them. Such resolve, such solemn national vocation: this had restored America's dignity on the international stage. 'Around the world,' said Trump, 'America faces new threats and strategic rivals, it seems like all the time. We have met this competition with unmatched confidence, purpose, and resolve. We talk to all of them and they talk to us with great, great respect. They respect our country so much more than they have for many, many decades. Right now, they respect us more than they have in many, many years. And it's only going to get more so.'

The world was indeed growing more dangerous – and Trump was helping to construct a new global alliance suited to the times. It was an alliance of kleptocrats. Like the court of Nazarbayev, they might at times seem like rivals, even enemies. In truth they were united in their common resolve to advance the privatisation of power. And what progress they had made. With Trump's election, they controlled the three great poles of power. In the White House, a launderer, installed with the help of Putin's Kremlin. And in Beijing, Xi Jinping. They had prime access respectively to the great repositories of plunder: the world's biggest economy, the riches of the former Soviet Union, the one-party state containing a fifth of humanity. Naturally, a façade of decorum was required. Putin's billions technically belonged to his remarkably entrepreneurial close friends, such as the billionaire cellist. Xi's relatives, not the general secretary himself, held the business interests amassed as he rose through the Chinese Communist Party. At the time he took over the Party in 2012 they held stakes, hidden under layers of financial camouflage,

in companies with assets of $376 million, as well as $50 million
in Hong Kong real estate. And he used another form of subter-
fuge. Like Trump on Twitter, it was a strategy of projection, one
long favoured by those who had taken over a kleptocracy and
needed to assert their authority: the anti-corruption campaign.

When Xi came to power, the Party's good name had been
besmirched by revelations of the fortunes the previous leadership
had amassed. Relatives of his predecessor's prime minister, Wen
Jiabao, controlled assets worth $2.7 billion. Xi commenced a
campaign against corruption, promising to catch both the tigers
and the flies. A hundred thousand Chinese were indicted. The
tigers, big beasts of the Party, were certainly among those who,
like the Xis and the Wens, had enriched themselves magnificently.
They were also obstacles to Xi's consolidation of power. In closed
courts, they were condemned.

Such cunning appeared to inspire the next generation of kleptocrats – young talents Trump delighted in befriending. With his
appointment as crown prince of Saudi Arabia in 2017, Mohammed
bin Salman took day-to-day charge of the state with the largest
supplies of the commodity that is most readily transformed into
bribes: crude oil. Saudi Arabia, the only country where the ruling
family had gone so far as to name it after themselves, had for
years blackmailed the West into complicity by selling it oil, buying
its weapons and occasionally ratting out the jihadists it nurtured.
When MBS ascended to heir apparent, he had to realign the
spigots of dirty money. A purge began, dressed up as an anti-corruption campaign in the mould of Xi's. In November 2017
assorted princes, ministers and businessmen were confined to the
Ritz-Carlton in Riyadh, after which $107 billion was returned
to the national treasury. From that same national treasury, a few
billion could be pledged, during Trump's presidential visit to the
kingdom, to buy weapons manufactured in the swing states he
would need to carry for re-election.

Information control MBS found more challenging. He lacked Xi's totalitarian machine, could not simply censor from the internet stories about the Saudi ruling class's monetisation of their offices. His methods were thus more agricultural, closer to the way Boris Nemtsov was silenced. A murder squad including members of his Royal Guard lured the dissident commentator Jamal Khashoggi to the Saudi consulate in Istanbul, where they killed and dismembered him. The Turks and the CIA swiftly concluded that the crown prince had directed the operation. Trump published a statement on the White House website. There was some preamble about money: 'After my heavily negotiated trip to Saudi Arabia last year, the Kingdom agreed to spend and invest $450 billion in the United States. This is a record amount of money.' Trump declared that he had decided to reject calls to punish MBS for his complicity in the premeditated murder of a critic.

> Representatives of Saudi Arabia say that Jamal Khashoggi was
> an 'enemy of the state' and a member of the Muslim
> Brotherhood, but my decision is in no way based on that –
> this is an unacceptable and horrible crime. King Salman and
> Crown Prince Mohammad bin Salman vigorously deny any
> knowledge of the planning or execution of the murder of Mr
> Khashoggi. Our intelligence agencies continue to assess all
> information, but it could very well be that the Crown Prince
> had knowledge of this tragic event – maybe he did and maybe
> he didn't!

MBS would continue to enjoy American support as he reduced Yemen to misery in a proxy war with Iran. Obama wanted the Saudis to find a way to 'share the neighbourhood' with the Iranians and 'institute some sort of cold peace'; Trump tore up the nuclear deal that had begun that process. He could say he was just continuing longstanding American policy in the region. And yes, Washington had stood behind Riyadh for generations. But that was part of the genius of the new kleptocrats. They made skilful use of what Peter Sahlas called the presumption of regularity. If a state acted or spoke, that was presumed to be a legitimate act, an expression of sovereignty, as though countries themselves were unimpeachable persons. But the new kleptocrats were subverting the state, using its institutions against itself, to seize for themselves that which rightfully belonged to the commonwealth. Corruption was no longer a sign of a failing state, but of a state succeeding in its new purpose. Public policy, foreign policy, national security: these were for the kleptocrat what the front company was for the launderer. When it came to the single worst threat of sudden and massive violent death – the North Korean atomic weapons programme – Trump staged a pageant for Kim Jong-un, his 'Little Rocket Man'. Nothing was achieved, but both could prance for the world's cameras, statesmen about their business. As when Trump sat down with Putin unattended by witnesses, what really united the leaders was their shared purpose of privatising power. Kim's dynasty had even set up a secret government department devoted to the purpose: Office 39, which oversaw the regime's international clandestine commercial interests, including the export of slave labour.

After his speech at the Pentagon, Trump returned to the White House at 12.34 p.m. An official summary of his conversation with President Zelensky was released half an hour later: 'President Trump and President Zelensky discussed ways to strengthen the relationship between the United States and Ukraine, including energy and economic cooperation. Both leaders also expressed that they look forward to the opportunity to meet.'

Every American president had lied and dissembled, sometimes with good reason. Under Trump, there had been a subtle change.

The public record had become malleable. Like a string of bogus transactions concocted to hide a dirty money trail, it could be altered after the fact. The transcript of briefings from the White House podium, once sacrosanct, could now be quietly edited, like a Wikipedia page doctored by a dictator's PR firm. During his first appearance in his short run as White House communications director, Anthony Scaramucci embarked on a riff about the president's sporting prowess. 'I've seen this guy throw a dead spiral through a tire,' he rhapsodised. 'He sinks three-foot putts.' Golf: Trump's favourite occupation. He professed to have won a score of club championships (at his own courses). 'I've seen this guy throw a dead spiral through a tire,' read the official transcript of Scaramucci's comments that was published on the White House site, a record for posterity. 'He sinks thirty-foot putts.'

The rest of the presidential day was taken up with the affairs of state and periodic tweeting. Trump bigged up his daughter Ivanka's initiative to help American workers. His budget won in Congress, heralding the salvation of, among others, American military veterans.

All the while, unannounced, the real enterprise was progressing: dismantling obstacles to the privatisation of power. Of the teams appointed to government departments to cut back regulations, one in three had a conflict of interest. Perhaps that was the wrong term. It was not that the Trump administration had conflicts of interest – rather they were confluences. Its leader and its officers fused their interests with government policy, mining the offices of state for riches. Trump's wife Melania understood this. When the *Daily Mail* wrote a scurrilous piece about her past, she sued on the grounds that the newspaper had imperilled her 'unique, once-in-a-lifetime opportunity ... to launch a broad-based commercial brand in multiple product categories, each of which could have garnered multi-million-dollar business relationships for a multi-year term' for 'one of the most photographed women in the world'. By contrast, when it came to those duties of the state that simply served the collective interest – preventing nuclear catastrophe, say, giving advance warning of tornadoes, or arresting the spread of new viruses – the Trump administration had better things to do.

During the election campaign, Trump had refused to follow previous candidates and publish his tax returns: why would you just hand over the most precious currency of twenty-first-century power, the secrets of your money? After he won, he refused to divest his private companies, instead handing nominal control to his children, deploying them in the role of Xi's relatives, Putin's cellist, or, as members of the khan's court suspected, Nazarbayev's Trio. Visiting dignitaries could demonstrate their respect for the president by taking a suite at the Washington hotel he declined to sell. Or they could act more directly. The Turkish government of Recep Tayyip Erdoğan, an increasingly dictatorial kleptocrat, paid the former US general Michael Flynn $500,000 to lobby for its interests – while he was on Trump's campaign team. Jho Low, a colourful Malaysian businessman accused of embezzling billions from a state fund, sent millions of dollars to an American businessman called Elliott Broidy, one of Trump's fundraisers. The motives of those who threw money at Trump's courtiers were not always clear. Nonetheless, it was best to keep it quiet – like when BTA Bank hired Michael Cohen.

Under Kenes Rakishev, BTA's army of lawyers and private spies pursued Mukhtar Ablyazov with gusto. Having turned on Iliyas Khrapunov, Felix Sater was feeding them information. Unfortunately, following the trail of Iliyas's money to Felix Sater meant following it to Donald Trump. That was not a problem while Trump was merely some guy who played a successful busi-nessman on television. But then suddenly he was president. Having disturbed some of his secrets – filed in open court claims that the buildings that bore his name had been used in the greatest laundering scheme the world had ever seen – perhaps it would be wise to show some respect. Michael Cohen was Trump's bagman. He had no connection to or knowledge of the BTA Bank case. And yet in 2017, after Trump's inauguration, BTA paid him $300,000.

But Cohen would fall, a casualty in the game of secrets that swirled around Trump. He was convicted of paying hush money to a porn star who said Trump had cheated on one of his wives with her, and of lying to Mueller's investigators. BTA ditched him. When it emerged that it had been paying Trump's bagman, the bank's American lawyer claimed that Cohen had been retained for his ability to 'assemble a winning team' but BTA had promptly cancelled the agreement because Cohen 'did absolutely nothing of value'. Felix Sater found himself discarded as well. Or rather, having paid him handsomely – and, its representatives insisted, unwittingly through his front company – BTA's lawyers discovered that he had, through his Ohio shithole scheme, filched $20 million of the money they were gunning to seize from Iliyas. So Felix was added to the roster of defendants in BTA's American lawsuits, alongside Ablyazov, Iliyas and their associates. Trump had dropped Felix too. After Felix's criminal past had leaked out, he claimed back in 2013 that he barely knew the man who had been instrumental in crafting the dirty money model that had saved the failing Donald, wouldn't recognise him if he walked through the door. In office, he said as much again: Felix was little more than a stranger. 'It's very upsetting,' Felix remarked in 2018. 'But, you know, what am I going to do? Start calling him a liar?'

Before his election victory, Trump had told Michael Cohen that the campaign would be a significant 'infomercial' for properties branded with his name. While Trump angled for the Republican nomination, Felix was in Moscow, working on a plan for a Trump Tower there. In November 2015, he emailed Michael Cohen: 'Buddy, our boy can become President of the USA and we can engineer it. I will get all of Putins team to buy in on this, I will manage this process ... Michael, Putin gets on stage with Donald for a ribbon cutting for Trump Moscow, and Donald owns the republican nomination. And possibly beats Hillary and our boy is in ... We will manage this process better than anyone. You and I will get Donald and Vladimir on a stage together very shortly. That the game changer.' He wrote again later the same day: 'Donald doesn't stare down, he negotiates and understands the economic issues and Putin only want to deal with a pragmatic leader, and a successful business man is a good candidate for someone who knows how to negotiate. "Business, politics, whatever it all is the same for someone who knows how to deal."'

Once Trump was president and Mueller had commenced his investigation, the special prosecutor's team began to wonder whether Trump had been secretly seeking commercial advantage from Putin's regime while campaigning to be president. What might the Donald's side of the deal have been? Trump said he knew nothing of it. Michael Cohen told Congress as much. But he was lying: he had called Trump's personal lawyer again and again with news of his and Felix's pursuit of a deal for a Trump Moscow. After Cohen pleaded guilty to perjury, Mueller's team wrote to Trump to ask him to explain what had really gone on. But because the truth involved Trump's conversation with his personal lawyer, he could do what the Trio had done: he invoked privilege. That was as far as Mueller ever got.

Felix Sater had become a minor celebrity. One of his associates was in jail, another was president. Even though Trump kept on denying knowing him, Felix had high hopes for what the future might bring, once his old partner had done what he needed to in power and could seek his rewards. 'First thing I plan to do when Trump leaves office, whether it's next week, in 2020 or four years later, is march right into his office and say, "Let's build Trump Moscow."'

41

Normal Business

Worldwide, 2020

Najib Razak grew testy. The questions from the prosecutor were an insult to his station. Najib was the son of the country's second prime minister, the nephew of the third, and had held the post himself from 2009 to 2018, when Malaysians ejected him in the face of overwhelming evidence that, as one of them put it, 'The country is rotting.' About $4.5 billion of their money had been siphoned from a state development fund called 1MDB. So reckoned the American prosecutors who had taken an interest in the case because some of the loot ended up in the US. There it had, among other endeavours, financed the movie *The Wolf of Wall Street*, the tale of an epic swindler who ended up rich and content. Jho Low, the gaudy moneyman who had slipped millions to one of Donald Trump's fundraisers, was wanted in the US as the suspected mastermind of the looting. The Americans had described how Najib – identified as 'Malaysian Official 1' – made off with $700 million. And yet now, on January 22, 2020, as Najib sat before a Malaysian court and the prosecutor pressed him about how the money had come to be in his personal accounts, he retorted: 'I am not so stupid to do something like this, you know.' If justice was closing in on Najib, it was merely the only sort that is permitted in kleptocracies: selective justice. His vanquisher in Malaysia's May 2018 election, Mahathir Mohamad, was the very man who had groomed him for high office and whose own previous term as prime minister had itself been grievously corrupt. Justice in kleptocracies still carries her sword, but her scales are tipped and she has removed her blindfold.

In 2016 an enterprising hacker extracted the confidential files of a Panamanian law firm called Mossack Fonseca. Those files, the Panama Papers, revealed that 140 political leaders held money in front companies. From Australia to Argentina, Iceland to Rwanda, presidents, prime ministers and their advisers and confidants, intelligence chiefs, generals, ministers, legislators and central bankers had chosen to store their money not among their compatriots but within the global financial secrecy system. It was as though monetising public office was no longer an aberration but the purpose of seeking that office. And Mossack Fonseca was just one of the law firms specialising in corporate secrecy. As with every money-laundering scandal, we only saw the geyser that spurted from the black aquifer, not the immense caverns below.

At least there was recourse to the ballot box. Those exposed by the Panama Papers, other leaks or the efforts of unbought journalists, unbent coppers and unbunged judges could be swept away by the people they had vowed to serve, just as Najib was. Voters and parliaments have in recent years brought down governments and replaced rulers following major corruption scandals in Austria, Brazil, Israel, Poland, South Africa, South Korea and many other countries. Like Najib, those deposed thoroughly deserved their fate and the criminal prosecution that often followed. Like Najib, many of them would also be correct were they to argue that they have been the fall guys, sacrifices necessary for kleptocracies to maintain the illusion that they function to serve any interest other than those of whoever captures power. Around the world, corruption has become the primary mechanism by which power functions. The Najibs are just the ones who played the game of secrets and lost.

Najib and his fellow looters could not have bled all that cash away without some bankers. Goldman Sachs abetted the pillaging of 1MDB. Other 'wealth managers' helped, too. One, Yeo Jiawei, was a young hotshot operating out of the entrepôt of clandestine finance at the toe of Malaysia, Singapore. He copped four and a half years. A few days before he was sentenced in July 2017, the bank that had employed him had ceased to exist. It had been called BSI.

Like so many of the billions upon billions of dollars its bankers had shifted over 144 years, BSI itself vanished. First it had been caught helping Americans dodge taxes, then helping Malaysians drain the treasury. BSI's hands were too red even for the Swiss financial regulators to ignore. They approved its acquisition by another Swiss bank, EFG, on the condition that BSI be subsumed and its name discarded. But by then nine years had passed since Nigel Wilkins alerted the City authorities to what BSI's bankers were up to. There had been plenty of time for the most secretive money to slip away: to Switzerland, Monaco, the Bahamas, always primed to move again if sunlight edged too near.

It rained on Basingstoke cemetery the day of Nigel's funeral. His nephew remembered him playing 'The Entertainer' on the piano. His pals recalled the rude postcards he would send. The service was secular. For Nigel, this world was all that there was. Back at his flat, the clippings of his youthful hair were still displayed on a shelf. The thumbed, cracked Hardys still occupied the bookcase, near the red box files containing a thousand pages of the secrets Nigel had extracted from BSI.

Had those charged with policing money – those invested with the power Nigel lacked, the authority to override secrecy on behalf of society – followed the threads he had offered them, the threads that began in those red boxes, they might have found what they were looking at changing before their eyes. BSI was not a bank. It was a facilitator for a transnational kleptocracy, operating a short walk from the Bank of England. In the stacks of correspondence, contracts and client lists, they would have read the names BSI's bankers had gone to such lengths to hide so that money might be detached from its past.

Names like Behgjet Pacolli, a construction magnate implicated in bribing Boris Yeltsin who had smashed plates with President Nazarbayev and then enjoyed the contracts to build him a new capital at Astana. Other names matched those of ex-Soviet intelligence officers and oligarchs and billionaire oilmen, a former KGB spokesman, that Qatari prince known as a 'modern-day Medici'. Then there was Igor Pluzhnikov, a Ukrainian businessman and politician. He had been a BSI client until he perished in 2005. It was rumoured but never proved, amid a series of suspicious deaths following the Orange Revolution, that he had been poisoned. In Nigel's files was his own email signing off on the opening of a London account for the departed man's daughter, into which would pass $2 million of his fortune, enough to buy her British residency as an investor. Nigel had expressed unease about taking money from a politically connected client in a country 'with few checks against corruption', but had agreed that, in the absence of more specific concerns, he would not object to the request for an account.

Had he been sitting in Nigel's chair, Bob Levinson could have pointed out those more specific concerns. After years as its top man on Russian organised crime, he had by then left the FBI. But he was still chasing shifty characters freelance for the CIA, anti-corruption campaigners and the odd law firm. Wandering Bob and bloody-minded Nigel were kindred spirits, bloodhounds incapable of giving up the chase once they caught the scent of an expensively protected secret, even as they approached sixty. Levinson would have seen the name Pluzhnikov and recalled an intelligence report compiled in the mid-nineties by half a dozen security agencies that had pooled what they knew about a particular criminal network, one that made a point of working with gifted businessmen. The file recorded that Pluzhnikov had run the Ukrainian office of a multinational corporation engaged in the furniture, banking and hotel businesses, through which had passed the $4 million that purchased a swathe of the Hungarian weapons industry when it was sold off after the end of the Soviet Union. That qualified Pluzhnikov for a place on the list of seventy-odd individuals deemed to belong to the organisation of a criminal mastermind: Semyon Mogilevich, the Brainy Don.

Levinson was the best-known Seva-hunter around. He had appeared on a BBC *Panorama* programme about the Brainy Don. But even if someone at the tax office or the City watchdog had followed Nigel's leads, even if they had thought to call up Levinson for the benefit of his expertise, it would have been too late. By the time Nigel extracted BSI's files and alerted the British authorities, Bob Levinson had vanished. In February 2007 he had flown to Switzerland. He was investigating Seva's suspected connection to RosUkrEnergo, the shadowy corporate middleman in the East–West gas trade. He had nipped up to Toronto to see one of Seva's contemporaries from nineties Moscow, Boris Birshtein. In Geneva he met up with a couple of old detective contacts, fellow pursuers of Russian gangsters. The next month, he was in Dubai on the same trail. He also hoped to gather some intelligence on Iranian dirty money that he could pass to the CIA unit that had thrown him a contract. On March 8 he dashed off emails to two of his seven children – one had successfully fixed a computer with a screwdriver, the other was preparing to overcome her shyness with a speech to the whole school – and took the half-hour flight across the Persian Gulf to the tiny island of Kish, just off the Iranian coast. He expected to meet a contact whom he hoped would have some dirty money tips. He landed, took a cab to a hotel, then disappeared. In the years that followed he was heard from only in a brief video emailed to a friend by his nameless captors, pleading for help.

Pluzhnikov was not the only connection to the Brainy Don that appeared in Nigel's files. Page after page related to the services BSI's City bankers furnished to the Trio.

On January 23, 2003, a Mayfair private intelligence firm delivered report RA377-144 to BSI's office on Cheapside. The firm, Risk Analysis, was run by an MI5 veteran called Martin Flint. Fabrizio Zanaboni, BSI's senior private banker in London, had hired Flint to look into some new clients. They had arrived with a new recruit to BSI's City operation, the Tajik-born, Essex-educated banker Khofiz Shakhidi. Report RA377-144 concerned one of these new clients in particular.

Flint's spooks recorded their brief as 'discreet enquiries in Kazakhstan in order to verify the identifying particulars provided by the subject, and to confirm that he has no criminal record or associations, and that his financial assets have been honestly acquired from his business interests'. In recent years, they reported, the subject and his partners had controlled as much as 40 per cent of the Kazakh economy. They owned most of the country's chrome and aluminium industries, much of its transport and energy, a bank, a newspaper and other media outlets. A former Kazakh prime minister had accused the subject and his partners of money laundering. 'There may be some truth to these allegations about the way in which political and business activities are and were conducted in Kazakhstan,' Flint's team reported. Then again, the ex-prime minister himself had been accused of corruption. 'Officially', they went on, the subject 'has no records of criminal or fraudulent activity with law enforcement bodies in Kazakhstan, but his close associations with the (autocratic) government (compulsory for anyone who wants to succeed in Kazakhstan) render him vulnerable to allegations of this sort'. Indeed, 'the same could be said for most of the leading businessmen in the region'. Flint's team advised that the subject 'should not be seen as worse than any other'. Apart from that, it was just a case of checking the basics. Flint's team had confirmed the subject's birth in 1953 in an Uzbek village, that he had later taken Kazakh citizenship, that the passport number BSI had for him was correct, and that his name was indeed Alijan Ibragimov – the third member of the Trio.

That had been good enough for BSI's bosses. The names of the Trio and their relatives could be seen again and again in Nigel's files over the years that followed, in emails and internal reports, on client lists and credit card bills for thirty grand's worth of Monte Carlo jewellery. Moreover, the documents showed, BSI's bankers had helped Alijan Ibragimov run a nebula of front companies.

Next to the scrawny Sasha, Ibragimov was rotund, a chubby face beneath precisely parted, whitening hair. He wore tinted glasses and pocket squares. 'Everyone thinks he's the third wheel,' observed a spy who had worked for the Trio, 'but he's the mastermind.' Like Sasha and Chodiev, Ibragimov was an outsider in Kazakhstan, doubly so as a Uighur. From origins less auspicious than those of his future partners, he had grown wealthy in the quasi-capitalist barter trade that got things like locomotives and animal hides where they were wanted under Soviet rule. He was practical, a doer, less flashy than Sasha. And it was Ibragimov who was the Trio's master of incognito finance.

Nigel's files recorded how the BSI banker Khofiz Shakhidi worked hard to maintain convivial relations with the Ibragimov family. He flew to Kazakhstan for weddings, took young Shukhrat on for work experience in the summer of the financial crisis. In this endeavour and others, Shakhidi had a sidekick, a serious-looking man called Abdumalik Mirakhmedov. Both were Central

Asian by birth and alumni of the Essex University economics class of 2000. In Nigel's files Mirakhmedov's name appeared on several of the thick stack of contracts that BSI had signed with what they called 'promoters', whose task was to bring in rich clients in exchange for a cut.

Mirakhmedov embodied footloose money. He acquired citizenship of the Caribbean island state St Kitts and Nevis. He was entitled to at least 30 per cent of the profit the bank made on money he brought in, more when he was able to sign up specified barons of the post-Soviet kleptocracies. But lucrative though his work as promoter was, it was not Mirakhmedov's day job. That was in an office in St James's: ENRC headquarters. He was a senior manager in the department that sold the metals ENRC's miners dug from the ground. He was also married to the daughter of the boss at Rudny, the Trio's Kazakh iron mine. Mirakhmedov's signature appeared again and again in Nigel's files, commanding the movement of money along exotic tracks of the global financial system. One lot of documents showed him arranging for his company in the British Virgin Islands to receive $150,000 from a Latvian bank account controlled by an opaque company in the Marshall Islands, then to transfer the money on to a BSI account in Monaco in the name of another company he controlled, this time registered in Belize.

Precisely why someone would want to employ such elaborate secrecy to send a wodge of money to Mirakhmedov, senior ENRC manager and son-in-law to a still more senior one, was unclear. But a little digging could have established that Mirakhmedov had a hand in the decision to award ENRC contracts to a British firm of mining consultants, Alex Stewart International. And that the relationship between ENRC and Alex Stewart International was the subject of 'a possible US investigation'. And that, at around the same time, Mirakhmedov made an agreement to send a still bigger wodge of money – $290,000 – to a close relative

of the Trio, Alijan Ibragimov's son Dostan. Anyone who had dug
that far might be tempted to ask Mirakhmedov, yes or no, had
he ever taken money from Alex Stewart International. To which
his lawyers would reply that Mirakhmedov had only undertaken
'legal transactions related to the conduct of normal business'.
Certainly he had 'never taken a kickback or assisted in providing
kickbacks to others'.

A little more digging and a further set of financial Russian
dolls might have been unearthed. They had been buried by
another BSI client. When ENRC floated on the London Stock
Exchange in late 2007, Mehmet Dalman was appointed to the
board as a non-executive director, entrusted with protecting all
those who invested in the corporation. But through his web of
companies called Wealth Management Group, he was also
managing part of the tremendous fortune the Trio's Alijan
Ibragimov had amassed. That much was declared. It was an
obvious conflict of interest, and Dalman was supposed to cease
any role in serving Ibragimov personally. What the threads that
led out from Nigel's files showed was that Dalman's company
went on managing Ibragimov's fortune long after he joined
ENRC's board, for which Ibragimov agreed to pay him at least
a quarter of a million dollars. Still more money was to be paid
to a banker who had served as Dalman's nominee – BSI's Khofiz
Shakhidi. It was Dalman who became the final chairman of
ENRC as a London-listed company, his mission, according to
the business pages, to 'clean up' the scandalous corporation.

Nigel's files were a palimpsest: front company upon front
company upon front company. But beneath, still just discernible,
was the outline of a treasure map. Had anyone wanted to read
it, it would have pointed them towards the stashes where power
is hidden, disguised as money.

Nigel had understood that the kleptocrats of the world were
uniting. In his notebook, he pictured one node of their network,

BSI's home town in Italian-speaking Switzerland: 'Lugano. The cathedral on the hill – not a very busy confessional.' This was, he wrote, where the Russian and Italian mafia meet. But the kleptocrats were meeting everywhere.

In 2008, Robert Mugabe had been maintained in his dictatorship – the position from which he could dispense access to Zimbabwe's natural wealth – through violence funded by the deal-making of a pair of white Rhodesians, a former England cricketer, a Jewish Wall Streeter and his Australian underling. They had then cashed out to three Central Asian oligarchs through a transaction on the London Stock Exchange. In 2013, Mugabe had escaped the power-sharing he had been forced into because of the previous round of violence through a new round of violence, this time funded by a spot of business with an emissary from another axis of the transnational kleptocracy, China. Sam Pa, a Chinese businessman with at least seven aliases and a long relationship with the Communist Party's intelligence agencies, supplied the requisite $100 million, in exchange for secret access to Zimbabwe's militarised diamond fields. After the Crocodile replaced Mugabe in 2017, he imported Chinese facial recognition technology similar to that used to monitor Uighurs in Xinjiang province. And to that used in the Kazakh capital, previously known as Astana, now, after the father of the nation, as Nursultan. As they hoarded secrecy, the kleptocrats set about harvesting privacy. Covid-19 came as a gift. It was the perfect pretext to assume sweeping powers, expand surveillance states and empty public treasuries with even less scrutiny than usual.

They formed a new five families, these international kleptocrats: the Nats, the Brits, the Sprooks, the Petros and the Party.

The Nats, they declare themselves the saviours of besieged nations while overseeing the plunder of those nations. Drain the swamp, they cry, as they luxuriate in it. They have taken hold in central Europe, eastern Europe and Russia, with imitators on every continent: Bolsonaro in Brazil, Duterte in the Philippines, Erdoğan in Turkey, Netanyahu in Israel, Maduro in Venezuela, Trump in Washington. Left and Right: these are just their costumes. The mafia would admire the loyalty they inspire: at the Donald's impeachment trial for his Ukrainian favour-trading, Republican senators listened to cast-iron evidence that he had abused his office, then acquitted him. Those who resist them believe that, once they are gone, the institutions they have distorted will snap back to how they were. But like a parasite altering a cell it invades, so kleptocratic power transforms its host. Those who use their public office to steal must hold on to it not just for the chance of further riches but in order to maintain the immunity from prosecution that goes with it. When elections come around, losing is not an option.

The Brits, they continue their long fade from imperial power to global network of financial secrecy connected to the City of London and servicing new, private empires. Their new populist rulers take money and inspiration from the Ur of Kleptopia, post-Soviet Moscow. Nigel Farage salutes Putin. Boris Johnson enjoys the amity – and his party the seven-figure munificence – of Alexander Temerko, whose self-professed connections to the Kremlin's security agencies go back decades and on the wall of whose London office hang the British prime minister's autographed ping-pong bats. During the 2019 general election campaign, Johnson refused to publish a parliamentary report on Russian interference in British politics. The day after he won, he swung by a London party thrown by a billionaire veteran of the KGB's foreign intelligence arm.

The Sprooks – spooks and crooks in indistinguishable union – have a Moscow base too. Semyon Mogilevich, the Brainy Don, is said to be a guest of Putin's security services on the city's periphery, permitted to manage his criminal endeavours but, like Ramzan Kadyrov down in Chechnya, subordinate to the ex-KGB ruler. They are true globalists, however, the Sprooks. In Washington, in London, in Paris, the spirit of national security has given way to the profit principle. Sometimes intelligence officers don't even wait for their early retirement before taking on private clients. The Petros, they have a mechanism for setting the price they charge for the oil they steal from the countries they have invaded from within: they call it Opec. The Party, they are insatiable. Money, land, technology, its leaders in Beijing want it all; no resistance will be tolerated, certainly not from Hong Kongers quaintly attached to antiquated notions of freedom.

The Party, the Nats, the Brits, the Petros and the Sprooks are like the clans of the Cosa Nostra that came before them. On the surface they are rivals. But ultimately they are engaged in a common endeavour: to seize power through fear and the force of money, and then to privatise that power. As has been said of the British Establishment, they are a committee that never needs to meet. They have their Others, against which to unite populations whose interests they can make no credible claim to represent. Uighurs do nicely, or Mexicans, Muslims, refugees, Jews.

Perhaps what drives them all is fear: the fear that soon there will not be enough to go round, that on a simmering planet the time is approaching for those who have gathered all they can unto themselves to cut free from the many, from the others. There's only one side to be on if you wish to avoid destruction: theirs. You are with the Kleptopians or you are against them. The Earth cannot sustain us all. We are hoarding, we will be ready. Do you want to learn to love Kleptopia and be brought within the wall? Or would you rather be outside, in the wilderness that we used to call the commons, defenceless as the water rises? Choose.

If there is an antidote to kleptocracy, it is honesty, the sort of indomitable resistance to lies, obfuscation and bullshit that Nigel

Wilkins embodied. It is a struggle without end: the struggle for who gets to tell the stories by which we live.

On one page of his notebook, Nigel had set out why he had to steal the documents from BSI, and why he had to keep them. It seemed that his mind had drifted beyond questions of the law, of the rules. 'Can't think of much I have done that I am ashamed of,' he wrote, there on a sheet of paper that no one was ever supposed to read. He had also started to sketch an idea for a book. There were the beginnings of a pitch to a publisher: 'This book will expose the world's largest ever fraud.' He would explain why it mattered, all the money that could have paid for teachers to teach, doctors to heal, but had instead been ripped from the commonwealth. A title had come to him. It was the words the moneymen had used to silence him when he spoke up. 'Just normal business, Nige.'

NOTES

PART I: CRISIS

Chapter 1: The Thief

3 Nigel Wilkins: Much of Nigel Wilkins' story is drawn from the author's interviews with him in London in 2015 and 2016. Charlotte Martin shared memories of Nigel's life and death. Where details of his story come from another source that is not described in the text, the attribution is given in these notes

5 'Done because we are too menny': Thomas Hardy, *Jude the Obscure*, Oxford, 1895, p.355

Chapter 2: A Feast

8 made his way to the Banqueting House: Confidential interview

9 Alexander Machkevitch: A year and a half before this book was published, the author contacted representatives of Machkevitch and his fellow members of the Trio to ask to interview them. This request was ignored, as was another sent through a different route a few months later. In April 2020, the author sent the Trio's representatives a list of all the significant points in their story as it is told here, inviting them to correct any that might be inaccurate. A letter came back from a law firm saying that 'the accuracy of the information … is disputed' but making no attempt to refute or clarify any of the points

9 liken himself to the author: Lily Galili, 'A Kazakh oligarch trying to be a Jewish tycoon', *Haaretz*, October 27, 2002, haaretz. com/1.5145478

10 shoes encrusted with them: Interview with Iliyas Khrapunov, Geneva, 2019

11 'He has a tendency': Rakhat Aliyev, *The Godfather-in-law*, translated by James Addison White, Trafo (Berlin), 2009, p.127

11 outing to a restaurant: Aliyev, *Godfather-in-law*, pp.114–17. Behgjet Pacolli did not respond when the author sent fact-checking queries to him ahead of publication

13 a lot of ushers: Adam Jones and Christopher Thompson, 'PwC received £50m in fees from ENRC', *Financial Times*, May 3, 2013, ft.com/content/9d15e7f2-b3d5-11e2-ace9-00144feabdc0; 'In the City: Bilk float', *Private Eye*, May 3, 2013

14 claiming to the Belgian authorities: 'Tractebel réévalue ses positions kazakhs, gangrenées par des partenaires douteux', *L'Echo*, December 28, 1999, lecho.be/actualite/archive/Tractebel-reevalue-ses-positions-kazakhs-gangreneespar-des-partenaires-douteux/8627015; William MacNamara and Stanley Pignal, 'Case against three ENRC oligarchs settled', *Financial Times*, August 17, 2011, ft.com/content/95f8ecc4-c8dd-11e0-a2c8-00144feabdc0

14 bend the rules: Interviews in 2020 with James Leigh-Pemberton and Hector Sants, at the time the head of the Financial Services Authority

15 detained … Semyon Mogilevich: Andrew E. Kramer, 'Russian police arrest a suspected racketeer', *New York Times*, January 26, 2008, nytimes.com/2008/01/26/business/worldbusiness/26ruble.html; Luke Harding, 'Russia's most notorious mafia boss arrested in Moscow', *Guardian*, January 25, 2008, theguardian.com/world/2008/jan/25/russia.lukeharding

15 most powerful criminal: Mogilevich's close associate and fellow crime boss Monya Elson described him as 'the most powerful mobster in the world'. Robert I. Friedman, *Red Mafiya*, Berkley, 2002, p.203

16 accusing him of ordering murders: Misha Glenny, *McMafia*, Vintage, 2009, p.93

16 a severe reprimand: Mark Galeotti, *The Vory*, Yale University Press, 2018, p.221

16 Vladimir Putin: There was no reply to the author's fact-checking email to Putin's press secretary

16 an American and a Brit met late one evening: The account of Lough's meeting with McCormick and the events that followed are drawn from interviews with John Lough and Ilya Zaslavskiy, email communications between Zaslavskiy and McCormick and between Lough and McCormick, and parts of the FSB's case file on Zaslavskiy, including transcripts of Sergei Novosyolov's FSB

interview on March 26, 2008 and McCormick's the next day. Bob
Dudley declined to confirm or deny the details involving him. The
author put the significant points of this account to McCormick
before publication. He declined to respond to most of them.
Where he did offer an alternative version of events, it is recorded
either in the text or the notes

17 to keep staff numbers down, Lough would work as a consultant:
   McCormick claims Lough 'refused to move to Moscow'. Lough
   maintains that he was never offered a job based in Russia, nor was
   one ever discussed

18 'you are being watched by the FSB': McCormick told the author
   he recalled telling Lough he might be of interest to the FSB.
   McCormick said he had himself been stopped by FSB officers
   when flying into Moscow and they had mentioned Lough's name

19 nothing sinister should happen: McCormick claimed to the author
   that Lough had 'fabricated' this part of his account but declined to
   respond to Lough's detailed recollection of the episode

19 until we get to the bottom of this: McCormick insisted to the
   author that there were no caveats in Lough's assertion that it was
   not safe for him to return to Russia. But Lough had told Bob
   Dudley in an email that he thought he should lie low 'for a while'.
   Dudley had agreed. Lough also recalled meeting McCormick in
   Brussels on January 31, 2008 (two weeks before McCormick fired
   him) and saying he planned to stay out of Russia while TNK-BP
   worked out what was going on. In the meantime, Lough proposed
   working remotely for a couple of months. He does not recall
   McCormick objecting to that course of action at the time and
   McCormick declined to comment on Lough's account

20 being made redundant: McCormick claimed to the author that the
   termination of Lough's contract was 'mutually agreed'. Lough
   insists it was not. He is supported by McCormick's own testimony
   to the FSB, when he said Lough was 'very unhappy about my
   decision to dismiss him'

20 enveloped in McCormick's embrace: In 2014, Zaslavskiy emailed
   McCormick to confront him about his role in the TNK-BP affair,
   including his FSB testimony and the firing of Lough. On the
   latter, McCormick asserted that 'the person fired actually reached
   out and hugged me afterwards'. Asked by the author about the
   hug, McCormick said 'it was actually Mr Lough who reached out
   and embraced me at the conclusion of the meeting', using this to
   argue that Lough did not object to being fired

20 FSB officers stormed into: Tom Bower, The Squeeze, HarperCollins,
   2010, p.463

20 soon apparent to Zaslavskiy what was afoot: Zaslavskiy interview. The FSB's initial line of questioning concerned Lough and Dudley. Then in around July 2008 it developed into a direct suggestion that the alleged espionage was done at Lough's behest

20 Andrey Lugovoy: 'Report into the death of Alexander Litvinenko', The Litvinenko Inquiry, January 2016, assets.publishing.service.gov. uk/government/uploads/system/uploads/attachment_data/ file/493860/The-Litvinenko-Inquiry-H-C-695-web.pdf; 'Duma officials comment on TNK BP arrests', Associated Press video news report, March 21, 2008, youtube.com/watch?v=E_7k7gBlSu0

21 formally sent to TNK-BP by the Russian authorities: The judgment in Zaslavskiy's case, given on December 9, 2008, records that when FSB officers raided TNK-BP's office, they found a copy of the 'General Development Plan for the Gas Industry until 2030'. This, the court found, was classified and contained Gazprom's commercial secrets. However, the ruling also records that the document was accompanied by a cover letter from the Ministry of Industry and Energy of the Russian Federation to TNK-BP

21 billions of dollars: Alexander Kots, 'FSB catches energy spies', *Komsomolskaya Pravda*, March 20, 2008, kp.ru/daily/24067/307041 (in Russian)

21 told American diplomats: 'Update on GOR investigation of TNK-BP', US state department cable published by WikiLeaks, wikileaks.org/plusd/cables/08MOSCOW816_a.html

21 'the FSB suspects': Vera Surzhenko and Alexey Nikolsky, 'Lubyanka does not sleep', March 20, 2008, *Vedomosti* (in Russian), vedomosti.ru/newspaper/articles/2008/03/21/lubyanka-ne-dremlet

21 business cards of CIA officers: Asked about this by the author, McCormick neither confirmed nor denied that the cards were his

21 seventeen hours: McCormick later told Lough in an email that the interrogation had lasted seventeen hours. The official record of his testimony in Zaslavskiy's case file says it lasted three hours and ten minutes. It is possible there was another session that was not included in the case file. The author asked McCormick but he declined to clarify

22 conversed informally: Zaslavskiy and Lough say they spoke to each other in Russian, using the formal mode. The author asked McCormick, who confirmed he does not speak Russian, the basis of his assertion to the contrary. He declined to respond

22 He said Lough 'supervised' Zaslavskiy: On March 23, 2008, McCormick spoke with US diplomats in Moscow. This conversation is recorded in a cable subsequently published by WikiLeaks (wikileaks.org/plusd/cables/08MOSCOW816_a.html).

The cable reported that 'McCormick said Zaslavsky returned to the company to work in TNK-BP's Gas Division, where he worked under the supervision of two UK citizens, Alistair Ferguson (the section head) and John Lough, on what was called the "Gazprom project."' In 2011, Lough raised this cable with McCormick in an email. He asked whether the cable accurately reflected what McCormick told the diplomats. McCormick replied: 'Being more than 3.5 years ago, I don't recall every specific detail in the link provided. However, there appear to be some errors. For example, I believe that Ilya worked under supervision from within Alastair Ferguson's team (versus you) and would have made that point clear when asked.' The author asked McCormick why, in that case, four days after his conversation at the US embassy, he repeated his assertion that Lough supervised Zaslavskiy in his FSB interrogation, knowing this to be false. McCormick declined to say

22 Sergei Novosyolov: Novosyolov's signed evidence to the FSB, March 26, 2008. Novosyolov claimed in his FSB interview that John Lough had 'special status' in TNK-BP, did not report to the company's leaders and was secretive about his work, only communicating with a small group that included Ilya Zaslavskiy. None of this matches the accounts of others who were there at the time. Novosyolov is recorded as telling the FSB that Zaslavskiy had come to his office and confessed to having confidential information on Gazprom. Zaslavskiy told the author he did no such thing. The author wrote to Novosyolov to check the facts. Initially, Novosyolov claimed that he had never heard of John Lough or spoken to Shawn McCormick. The author sent Novosyolov a copy of his own signed evidence. Upon receiving it, Novosyolov's recollection improved. 'I have read the transcript of my interview ... and confirm that everything said there is correct,' he replied. One of the things Novosyolov is recorded saying in the transcript is that it was Shawn McCormick who told him that Bob Dudley recommended John Lough for a job. McCormick told the author that this was untrue: neither the purported recommendation, nor his telling Novosyolov about it, took place

23 years in prison: Surzhenko and Nikolsky, 'Lubyanka does not sleep'

23 Bob Dudley started to feel ill: Connie Bruck, 'The billionaire's playlist', *The New Yorker*, January 13, 2014, newyorker.com/magazine/2014/01/20/the-billionaires-playlist

23 say a few words: Tim Webb, 'The mining firm that found itself in a deep hole', *Guardian*, August 10, 2008, theguardian.com/business/2008/aug/10/lonmin.mining1

24 'It's so exciting': Interview with Kazakh businessman

Chapter 3: Tunnels

25 Cheapside: Peter Ackroyd, *London: The biography*, Vintage, 2001, pp.26, 180, 366

25 'creates much of the wealth': Tony Blair's speech to the Lord Mayor's Banquet, November 14, 2005, webarchive.national archives.gov.uk/20080909042558/http://www.number10.gov.uk/Page8524

25 'the world market is open': Imogen Foulkes, 'Swiss Gotthard rail tunnel – an engineering triumph', *BBC News*, June 1, 2016, bbc.co.uk/news/world-europe-36416506

26 collaborated with the Nazis: Gerald Posner, *God's Bankers*, Simon & Schuster, 2015, p.127; Arthur Spiegelman, 'Vatican bank dealt with Reichsbank in war – document', *Reuters*, August 3, 1997

26 a story that reversed the truth: Nick Shaxson, *Treasure Islands*, The Bodley Head, 2011, pp.49–51

26 increased tenfold: Gabriel Zucman, *The Hidden Wealth of Nations*, University of Chicago Press, 2015, p.14

27 amass a quarter of all increases in incomes: Martin Wolf, 'Inequality is a threat to our democracies', *Financial Times*, December 19, 2017, ft.com/content/47e3e014-e3ea-11e7-97e2-916d4fbac0da

27 grew to $7.6 trillion: Zucman, *Hidden Wealth*, chapter 2

27 double the single biggest reserves … half the global total: China's central bank put its reserves at $3.3 trillion in 2015, the year of Zucman's estimate. The IMF put global reserves at 9.4 trillion SDRs, or $13 trillion (IMF 2015 annual report, appendix I, imf.org/external/pubs/ft/ar/2015/eng/pdf/AR15_AppI.pdf)

27 $48 billion: BSI's results for 2006, web.archive.org/web/20070825092313/http://www.bsibank.com:80

27 father had worked for the bank: Fabrizio Zanaboni grievance procedure records, among the files Nigel took

27 three-quarters of a billion dollars: BSI internal correspondence and Fabrizio Zanaboni's biography on his website, fabportfoliomanagement.com/biographies.html

27 background report: Risk Analysis client vetting report for BSI, July 17, 2002

28 Frank Timis: Internal BSI documents copied by Nigel Wilkins. The London Stock Exchange would later levy a record fine against Timis's company for lying to its investors: Graeme Wearden, 'Record fine for company that misled investors over failed oil wells', *Guardian*, November 17, 2009, theguardian.com/business/2009/nov/17/regal-petroleum-oil-fine-aim

28 'Why would I': 'Confidential Disciplinary Investigation Report on Nigel Wilkins', prepared by Andrew Giles of the Financial Conduct Authority, August 6, 2014, pp.16–17

28 Khofiz Shakhidi: The author sent a list of fact-checking queries to Shakhidi via his companies but there was no response

28 'attempts to create a synthesis': Tolib Shakhidi's website, shakhidi. ru/main.mhtml?Part=2

28 poached Shakhidi: Confidential interview

29 Martin Flint: There are several public references to Flint's career in MI5, such as Robert Winnett and David Leppard, 'Whitehall hires former spies to nail honours leak', *Sunday Times*, January 18, 2004, thetimes.co.uk/article/whitehall-hires-former-spies-to-nail-honours-leak-g62plkcsd6n; Alastair Sooke, 'How to break into the world of spies', *Daily Telegraph*, June 19, 2004, telegraph.co.uk/news/uknews/1464921/How-to-break-into-the-world-of-spies.html

29 agreed that the London office could take them on: Confidential interview

29 read in *The Times*: Steve Hawkes and James Rossiter, 'Taxman loses out as property worth £200bn is registered in foreign havens', February 28, 2008, thetimes.co.uk/article/taxman-loses-out-as-property-worth-pound200bn-is-registered-in-foreign-havens-q6ws6x39rfw

Chapter 4: The Dual State

30 Peter Sahlas: Much of his story is drawn from the author's interviews with him, in London and Paris, between 2016 and 2019. Details not from these interviews that are not attributed in the text are referenced in the notes

34 Boris Nemtsov: Chrystia Freeland, *Sale of the Century*, Little, Brown, 2005, pp.38, 280

34 'a dictatorship of law': Neal Ascherson, 'Law v Order', *London Review of Books*, May 20, 2004, lrb.co.uk/v26/n10/neal-ascherson/law-v-order

34 Mikhail Khodorkovsky: The account of Khodorkovsky's life and fall draws on Chrystia Freeland's closely observed portrait in *Sale of the Century*, especially pp.114–21 and Chapters 8 and 14

35 'had come to power to create': Freeland, *Sale of the Century*, p.163

35 valued at $9 billion: Richard Sakwa, *Putin and the Oligarch*, IB Tauris, 2014, p.14

35 tax authorities produced a bill: Sabine Leutheusser-Schnarrenberger, Council of Europe human rights rapporteur, 'The circumstances

4348   KLEPTOPIA

surrounding the arrest and prosecution of leading Yukos executives',
November 29, 2004, paragraphs 10, 64, assembly.coe.int/nw/xml/
XRef/X2H-Xref-ViewHTML.asp?FileID=10730&lang=EN

36 written ambiguities into Russia's commercial legislation: Freeland,
Sale of the Century, p.176

36 Ernst Fraenkel: Jens Meierhenrich, 'An Ethnography of Nazi Law:
The Intellectual Foundations of Ernst Fraenkel's Theory of
Dictatorship', published as an introduction to Meierhenrich's 2017
edition of Fraenkel's *The Dual State*, Oxford University Press,
p.xxxv

37 'the ultimate piece of intellectual resistance': Jakob Zollman, 'The
law in Nazi Germany: Ideology, Opportunism, and the Perversion
of Justice', *German History*, vol. 32 (2014), p.496, quoted in
Meierhenrich's introduction to *The Dual State* (2017), p.xxvii

37 a regime whose defining attribute: Fraenkel's preface to the 1974
German edition of *The Dual State*, translated by Meierhenrich in
the 2017 English edition, p.xvii

37 unrelated works: Meierhenrich's introduction to the 2017 English
edition of *The Dual State*, p.xlix

38 a tip-off: Simon Ludwig-Winters, *Ernst Fraenkel: Ein Politisches
Leben*, Campus Verlag, 2009, p.127

38 Fraenkel and his wife fled: Meierhenrich's introduction to the 2017
English edition of *The Dual State*, p.xxxvii

38 sympathetic official at the French embassy: Fraenkel's preface to
the 1974 German edition of *The Dual State*, translated by
Meierhenrich in the 2017 English edition, pp.xviii, l

38 'The goals of the prerogative state': Peter Sahlas, 'The Dual State
Takes Hold in Russia: A Challenge for the West', 2006: a chapter
for an unpublished book

39 'volunteer to go to prison': Many of the details of Aleksanyan's case
are drawn from the judgment of the European Court of Human
Rights in Aleksanyan v Russia, December 22, 2008, hudoc.echr.
coe.int/eng?i=001-90390

40 Salavat Karimov: Vasily Aleksanyan's testimony to the Russian
Supreme Court, January 22, 2008, footage at web.archive.org/
web/20170221080246/youtube.com/watch?v=bNA4cY00i_g,
translation published by the Yukos defence lawyer Bob Amsterdam
at robertamsterdam.com/vasily_alexanyan_addresses_the_supreme_
court; judgment of the European Court of Human Rights, par 86.
Asked about the meeting with Karimov that Aleksanyan described,
a spokesperson for the Russian Office of the General Prosecutor
told the author in 2020: 'Investigator S. Karimov did not have a
meeting with V. Aleksanyan during the indicated period. Based on

this, the circumstances described in relation to this – non-existent – meeting cannot correspond to the reality'

41 an investigator on his case told one of his Russian lawyers that if he admitted his guilt and agreed to cooperate, he would be let go … made the offer a third time: Aleksanyan Supreme Court testimony; judgment of the European Court of Human Rights, pars 77 and 86. The spokesperson for the Russian Office of the Prosecutor General told the author that Aleksanyan's account of these offers 'cannot be considered truthful', without elaborating

42 'even the doctors': Aleksanyan Supreme Court testimony

42 captors decided otherwise: Judgment of the European Court of Human Rights, par 132

43 'our country is perishing': R. Pevear and L. Volokhonsky, trans, *Dead Souls*, Random House, 1996, pp.392–3, quoted in Peter Sahlas, 'The Dual State Takes Hold in Russia: A Challenge for the West'

Chapter 5: Silhouette

44 the silhouette: 'Tax Haven Banks and US Tax Compliance (Day One)', Permanent Subcommittee on Investigations, July 17, 2008, hsgac.senate.gov/subcommittees/investigations/hearings/tax-haven-banks-and-u-s-tax-compliance

45 transporting diamonds: Lynnley Browning, 'Ex-UBS Banker Pleads Guilty in Tax Evasion', *New York Times*, June 20, 2008, nytimes.com/2008/06/20/business/20tax.html

46 slipped him a note: Interview with Elise Bean, then staff director of and chief counsel to Levin's committee

47 American prosecutors: Joanna Chung and Haig Simonian, 'Ex-UBS employee charged over US tax fraud', *Financial Times*, May 14, 2008, ft.com/content/e3dba448-212b-11dd-a0e6-000077b07658

47 sensed what was coming: Bradley C. Birkenfeld, *Lucifer's Banker*, Greenleaf Book Group Press, Austin, 2016, p.195. He served thirty months in US prison. Upon his release the Internal Revenue Service paid him a $104 million reward as his share of the tax money recovered thanks to his revelations

47 'shells within shells': 'Private Banking and Money Laundering: A case study of opportunities and vulnerabilities', Permanent Subcommittee on Investigations, November 9–10, 1999, gpo.gov/fdsys/pkg/CHRG-106shrg61699/html/CHRG-106shrg61699.htm

Chapter 6: Mr Billy

48 Damien Hirsts: Nate Freeman, 'How Damien Hirst's $200 million auction became a symbol of pre-recession decadence', *Artsy*, August 24, 2018, artsy.net/article/artsy-editorial-damien-hirsts-200-million-auction-symbol-pre-recession-decadence

48 Billy Rautenbach: Details of Rautenbach's career, including his relationship with Emmerson Mnangagwa, come from interviews with associates and officials in Zimbabwe, Congo, South Africa and elsewhere; the archive of *Africa Confidential*; intelligence reports prepared by a security firm retained by HSBC after it learned about the alleged plot against Bruce Jewels; a telephone interview with Bruce Jewels in April 2020; Jason K. Stearns, *Dancing in the Glory of Monsters*, Public Affairs, 2012, chapter 19; Chris McGreal, 'The motiveless murder and Napoleon of Africa', December 16, 1999, *Guardian*, theguardian.com/world/1999/dec/16/chrismcgreal; and Robert Block's stories for the *Wall Street Journal* at the start of the second Congo war, including 'Zimbabwe's elite turn conflict in Congo into business bonanza', October 9, 1998, wsj.com/articles/SB907881277686053000. Ahead of publication of this book, the author wrote to Rautenbach with a list of the main facts set out here to ask him if any of them were incorrect. He declined to respond but his lawyers, BDK Attorneys of Johannesburg, did write to say: 'We remind you that in the various jurisdictions subject to which you might find yourself the laws of defamation, criminal insult, criminal defamation and a liability for defamatory conduct are alive and well. If you defame our client you will be subjected to the full might of the law, both criminal and civil, with regard to criminal insult and criminal defamation as well as an action for damages for defamation'

49 Emmerson Mnangagwa: Ahead of publication, the author repeatedly contacted Mnangagwa's spokesman, George Charamba, to ask if he wished to challenge any of the facts as set out in this account. There was no reply

49 tortured by the Rhodesians: Heidi Holland, *Dinner with Mugabe*, Penguin, 2008, p.35

49 massacred ethnic rivals: Holland, *Dinner with Mugabe*, p.199

49 opposition politician: Ibid., p.198

49 Mobutu: Michela Wrong, *In the Footsteps of Mr Kurtz*, Fourth Estate, 2001, pp.276–9; Martin Meredith, *The State of Africa*, The Free Press, 2006, pp.532–7

50 sixty-seven racks: Nick Davies, 'The $10bn question: what happened to the Marcos millions?', *Guardian*, May 7, 2016,

theguardian.com/world/2016/may/07/10bn-dollar-question-marcos-millions-nick-davies

50 stolen fortune: *Money Laundering and Foreign Corruption: Enforcement and Effectiveness of the Patriot Act*, Permanent Subcommittee on Investigations, July 15, 2004, hsgac.senate.gov/imo/media/doc/REPORT-Money%20Laundering%20&%20Foreign%20Corruption%20(July%202004).pdf

50 'revolutionary seriousness': Stearns, *Dancing*, p.84

51 'Mr Billy': McGreal, 'The motiveless murder'

51 sell the copper: 'Rhodies to the rescue', *Africa Confidential*, November 5, 1999, africa-confidential.com/article/id/1313/Rhodies-to-the-rescue

52 Elephant Hills: The account of the events at Victoria Falls is largely drawn from interviews that the ambassador and influential Zimbabweans including Nicholas Goche gave to a private spy working for HSBC, the records of which are in the author's possession. The author contacted Goche in April 2020 to ask him whether he wished to confirm or deny this account. Goche said he was 'retired from politics' and did not wish to

52 His protégé: Augustin Katumba Mwanke, *Ma Vérité*, published posthumously by EPI Nice, 2013, pp.60–1; Tom Burgis, *The Looting Machine*, HarperCollins, 2015, pp.34–5

53 trouble with the South Africans: McGreal, 'The motiveless murder'; 'Rautenbach denies murder allegation', South African Press Association, December 16, 1999; Victor Mallet, 'Businessman linked to Daewoo killing', *Financial Times*, December 16, 1999

53 preparing charges: Arrest warrant for Billy Rautenbach, September 26, 2000, Pretoria

54 sent him to London: Emiliya Mychasuk and Emiko Terazono, 'Och, what a protégé', *Financial Times*, November 15, 2007

55 emailed Cohen: Vanja Baros email to Michael Cohen, March 16, 2008. Och-Ziff's role in the Zimbabwe platinum deal was first revealed by the *Mail & Guardian* of South Africa. Craig Mckune, 'The investor who saved Mugabe', August 10, 2012, mg.co.za/article/2012-08-10-00-the-investor-who-saved-mugabe

56 Baros made his acquaintance: Scott Patterson and Michael Rothfeld, 'US investigates hedge fund Och-Ziff's link to $100 million loan to Mugabe', *Wall Street Journal*, August 5, 2015, wsj.com/articles/u-s-probes-och-ziff-africa-deal-tied-to-mugabe-1438817223

56 had they established what that money would be used for: Michael Cohen told the author that, at the time Och-Ziff made its

investment in Camec, he was told the proceeds would be used to develop copper assets in Congo

56 leaning on … Anglo American: 'Rich platinum claims change hands in hush-hush deals', US diplomatic cable published by WikiLeaks, May 23, 2008, wikileaks.org/plusd/ cables/08HARARE459_a.html

56 selected to receive this redress was Billy Rautenbach: Camec's announcement to the London Stock Exchange of its deal to buy the Zimbabwean platinum mine in April 2008 stated that the seller was Meryweather Investments Limited. Under the terms of the deal, Meryweather would end up holding 13.07 per cent of Camec's shares. In 2016, the US Securities and Exchange Commission, in its order against Och-Ziff, described the series of transactions that took place before Camec bought the mine. It said the Zimbabwean government seized the mine and then resold it to a 'holding company'. This company is clearly Meryweather, because it is described as selling the mine on again to a company that is clearly Camec. The SEC order does not name the owner of Meryweather. It describes it as being 'affiliated with' someone identified only as the 'Zimbabwe Shareholder'. This 'Zimbabwe Shareholder' is so called because he is Zimbabwean and came to hold shares in Camec. He is also described as having been expelled from Congo. There is only one person who matches that description: Billy Rautenbach. 'Acquisition of Platinum Assets', Central African Mining & Exploration Company Plc, April 11, 2008, investegate.co.uk/central-afr--min--38-exp--cfm-/rns/ acquisition/200804111130081641S; 'Order instituting administrative and cease-and-desist proceedings pursuant to section 21c of the Securities Exchange Act of 1934, and sections 203(e), 203(f) and 203(k) of the Investment Advisers Act of 1940, making findings, imposing remedial sanctions and a cease-and-desist order, and notice of hearing', Securities and Exchange Commission, September 29, 2016, sec.gov/litigation/admin/2016/34-78989.pdf; 'In the City', *Private Eye*, December 25, 2009. See also *Bribery in its purest form: Och-Ziff, asset laundering and the London connection*, Rights and Accountability in Development, January 2017, raid-uk. org/sites/default/files/oz_bribery_in_its_purest_form_full_report_ rev.pdf. Page 30 of that report mentions an Och-Ziff spreadsheet that came to light in a related legal dispute, in which Meryweather is marked 'BR', as in Billy Rautenbach

56 'It's your own fault': Chris McGreal, 'Beaten for voting the wrong way: how Zanu-PF is taking revenge in rural areas', *Guardian*, April 16, 2008, theguardian.com/world/2008/apr/16/zimbabwe

57 More than a hundred: Chris McGreal, 'This is no election. This is
a brutal war', *Observer*, June 22, 2008, theguardian.com/
world/2008/jun/22/zimbabwe1

Chapter 7: Shutdown

58 the London office would shortly be closing: Letter to BSI London
staff, June 24, 2008

58 offered Nigel $30,000: Letter from Alberto Mapelli of BSI to
Nigel Wilkins, undated

58 'I should be free': Nigel Wilkins email to Alberto Mapelli and
Karim Presti, August 19, 2008

58 Nigel was convinced that the reason: After receiving a private
warning from the Financial Services Authority in 2004, BSI
headquarters in Switzerland had downgraded the UK office,
shifting information about clients offshore but keeping bankers in
London. Nigel Wilkins believed that 'they did not want to keep
accounts in London but clients preferred contact through London
and lived in London a lot of the time'. When BSI headquarters
decided to close the London office altogether in summer 2008, he
wrote in his employment tribunal complaint: 'The business with
the firm's clients remained viable, especially those booked in
Switzerland and Monaco. The real reason for the closure (and
transfer of account officers to offshore centres like Monaco) was
the tightening up by the regulatory authorities in London
including the FSA and HM Revenue and Customs.' This analysis
was disputed by BSI in its correspondence with Nigel but given
weight by two documents in BSI's internal files. In one, BSI
executive Stefano Loffredi stated that, back in the summer of 2003
– that is, the year before the FSA's warning – the bank's strategy
was to expand private banking in London, not to cut it back. And
in his 2006 submission to the FSA in support of his authorisation
as head of BSI London, John Erskine mentions that the 2004 FSA
warning might be taken into account if the regulator contemplates
disciplinary action in the future – a possibility that would have
added impetus to BSI's retreat from London

59 a private warning: There are various references to this investigation
in Nigel Wilkins' BSI files, including a 2006 submission to the
FSA as part of his authorisation to practise finance in London after
returning from the Bahamas by John Erskine, the incoming head
of BSI's London office, describing the investigation in detail

59 'is being obliged': Nigel Wilkins letter to Karim Presti, September
11, 2008. This is a copy of an unsigned draft but the letter is

confirmed as sent by reference to it in Presti's reply of September 16

59 still taking clients' instructions: Nigel Wilkins email to Karim Presti, August 29, 2008

59 'My abrupt dismissal': Nigel Wilkins email to Karim Presti, October 2, 2008

Chapter 8: The Fallen Oligarch

60 'What the fuck?': Interviews with Bota Jardemalie, Brussels, 2017–2019

61 bumped into the chief banking regulator: Twelfth Witness Statement of Mukhtar Ablyazov in JSC BTA Bank v Mukhtar Ablyazov and others, High Court of Justice, London, November 25, 2010, pp.170–1

64 The fax contained: Ablyazov witness statement, p.173

64 seven times BTA's annual profits: BTA Bank's net income after tax for 2007, the latest available results before the nationalisation, was $538 million, bta.kz/en/investor/news/2008/04/17/124

65 withdrawn ten years of the company's accounts: Richard Brooks, 'Looting with Putin', *Private Eye*, September 7, 2018, private-eye.co.uk/pictures/special_reports/looting-with-putin.pdf

66 unfolded the narrative of his life: This account of Ablyazov's backstory draws on documents that grew out of Peter Sahlas's conversations with Ablyazov, including his witness statements in the civil litigation against BTA Bank, as well as the author's own interview with Mukhtar Ablyazov in Paris in April 2017 and Ablyazov's written account of his time in prison

68 In the prison camp: Mukhtar Ablyazov, *In the Red Zone*, unpublished account of his prison experiences

68 hand over a slice to Nazarbayev's people: Ablyazov witness statement, par 86

69 courtiers ... final warning: Ablyazov witness statement, pars 151–64, 198–204

Chapter 9: Top Secret

70 $5 trillion: Patrick Wintour and Larry Elliott, 'G20: Gordon Brown brokers massive financial aid deal for global economy', *Guardian*, April 3, 2009, theguardian.com/world/2009/apr/03/g20-gordon-brown-global-economy

70 BSI's bosses had agreed: Nigel Wilkins and BSI settlement agreement, March 30, 2009

Chapter 10: Paying Your Dues

72 The international warrant he had dealt with: The account of Rautenbach's dealings with Glenn Agliotti are drawn from two statements Agliotti made to South African prosecutors in 2006 and 2007 and the subsequent judgment delivered at the trial of Jackie Selebi in the South Gauteng High Court in 2010, which includes parts of Rautenbach's own testimony in the case

72 able to say he hadn't known that Agliotti would use the money to bribe Selebi: Mojalefa Mashego, 'Rautenbach says he paid money to Selebi's friend', *The Star* (South Africa), November 19, 2009

73 other charges: Madelain Roscher, 'Plea bargain agreement between NPA and Billy Rautenbach's company, SA Botswana Hauliers finalised', PR Worx, September 22, 2009, prlog.org/10350092-plea-bargain-agreement-between-npa-and-billy-rautenbachs-company-sa-botswana-hauliers-finalised.html

73 to buy Camec: 'Recommended cash offer', ENRC, September 18, 2009, investegate.co.uk/eurasian-natural-res--enrc-/rns/re-offer--recommended-cash-of/200909181229153109Z

73 a payout of $124 million: Camec's stock market announcement of the acquisition of the Zimbabwean mine stated that the seller, Meryweather Investments Limited – the company the US authorities described as 'affiliated with' Rautenbach – would at the end of the transaction hold 13 per cent of Camec, worth $124 million of the $955 million sale price (converted to dollars from the sterling amount of £584 million given in the market announcement)

Chapter 11: The Informant

74 Felix Sater: Sater has given accounts of his criminal and espionage careers in a plea for clemency submitted by his lawyers to Judge Glasser ahead of his sentencing, a submission to the House of Representatives intelligence committee in 2017 (documentcloud. org/documents/4406681-3851126-v1-Day-of-Revised-FS-StatementDOCX.html); to the judge who let him avoid jail for racketeering (United States v John Doe in the Eastern District of New York, transcript of sentencing by Judge I. Leo Glasser, October 23, 2009); and to two reporters from Buzzfeed (Anthony Cormier and Jason Leopold, 'The Asset', Buzzfeed News, March 12, 2018, buzzfeednews.com/article/anthonycormier/felix-sater-trump-russia-undercover-us-spy). The author has also interviewed

five people with direct knowledge of Sater and his exploits and corresponded with Sater himself over email

76 sprung him: Confidential report on Mogilevich and his organisation written after a meeting in November 1994 of a 'working group' of Russian, German, Italian and American law enforcement officials

76 credit-card fraud and extortion: Confidential FBI assessment of the threat from Eurasian organised crime, May 1996

76 alliances with the locals: Ivankov's operation combined with the Gambino family to make money from manipulating stock prices. Galeotti, *The Vory*, p.179

76 forged at a meeting in 1983: Ira Silverman and Alan A. Block, 'On the lam with an uber-mobster', *New Yorker*, November 14, 1994, newyorker.com/magazine/1994/11/14/on-the-lam-with-an-uber-mobster

77 Michael Markowitz: Selwyn Raab, 'Mob-linked businessman killed in Brooklyn', *New York Times*, May 3, 1989, nytimes.com/1989/05/03/nyregion/mob-linked-businessman-killed-in-brooklyn.html

78 labour camps … KGB: FBI Eurasian organised crime report; 'working group' Mogilevich report; Ralph Blumenthal and Celestine Bohlen, 'Soviet emigre mob outgrows Brooklyn, and fear spreads', *New York Times*, June 4, 1989, nytimes.com/1989/06/04/nyregion/soviet-emigre-mob-outgrows-brooklyn-and-fear-spreads.html

78 Evsei Agron: Friedman, *Red Mafiya*, chapter 2

78 gangsters' tankers would refill: Fredric Dannen, 'The born-again don', *Vanity Fair*, April 5, 2012, vanityfair.com/news/1991/02/john-gotti-joe-columbo-fbi-investigation-witness

78 honorary police commissioner: Ibid.

79 fleeing to Paris: Telephone interview with Ira Silverman, 2018

79 shot dead: Raab, 'Mob-linked businessman'

79 acting as an industry regulator: John Sullivan, 'After emigres began fuel scheme, traditional mob families moved in, officials say', *New York Times*, September 15, 1996, nytimes.com/1996/09/15/nyregion/after-emigres-began-fuel-scheme-traditional-mob-families-moved-in-officials-say.html

79 an extortion scheme: United States v Michael Sheferovsky, criminal information filed in the Eastern District of New York, October 26, 2000

79 the Oddfather: Selwyn Raab, 'Vincent Gigante, Mafia leader who feigned insanity, dies at 77', *New York Times*, December 19, 2005, nytimes.com/2005/12/19/obituaries/vincent-gigante-mafia-leader-who-feigned-insanity-dies-at-77.html

79 arrested in 1999: '19 defendants indicted in stock fraud scheme that was protected and promoted by organized crime', US Department of Justice press release, March 2, 2000, reproduced in Estate of Ernest Gottdiener et al. v United States of America, class action complaint, October 23, 2015

79 tap on his phone: Judge Denny Chin's amended memorandum decision in United States v Rosario Gangi et al. in the Southern District of New York, January 30, 1999, courtlistener.com/opinion/2519063/united-states-v-gangi

80 painted a piteous picture: Transcript of Sheferovsky sentencing hearing, June 20, 2006, at the Brooklyn courthouse

81 same prosecutor: Loretta Lynch, a future US attorney general

81 spin his story for the judge: Much of what Felix Sater told the judge is redacted, even in now unsealed court records. The account here is constructed from the sources given above

82 'Goodfellas meet the Boiler Room': '19 defendants indicted', DoJ

83 Danny Persico, whose uncle: Kenny Gallo, 'The Persico Life', *Breakshot Blog*, June 19, 2016, breakshotblog.blogspot.com/2016/06/the-persico-life.html

83 Carmine 'The Snake' Persico: Selwyn Raab, 'Carmine Persico, Colombo crime family boss, is dead at 85', *New York Times*, March 8, 2019, nytimes.com/2019/03/08/obituaries/carmine-j-persico-colombo-crime-family-boss-is-dead-at-85.html

84 reporter at the *New York Times*: Charles V. Bagli, 'Real estate executive with hand in Trump projects rose from tangled past', *New York Times*, December 17, 2007. nytimes.com/2007/12/17/nyregion/17trump.html

84 'I had to leave my company': Sater's departure from Bayrock was not so straightforward. There are two Bayrocks. One, Bayrock Group LLC, was founded by Tevfik Arif. Sater left that company after the *New York Times* exposé about his criminal past. Then there is Sater's Bayrock. This is Bayrock Group Inc. This is the company named in BTA Bank and Almaty's suits against Iliyas Khrapunov, Sater and their associates in the US District Court for the Southern District of New York, filed March 25, 2019. Asked to clarify when his business relationship with Arif ended – if it did – Sater told the author he left Bayrock 'not to hurt the company' but that he and Arif 'continued working till at least 2015'

86 Whitey Bulger: The gangster's story is set out in the exhaustive coverage by the *Boston Globe* and books such as that by his former henchman, Kevin Weeks, *Brutal*, William Morrow (2007), and by *Globe* reporters Dick Lehr and Gerard O'Neill, *Black Mass*, Harper (2001)

Chapter 12: The Real

88 loan Greece $146 billion: Gabi Thesing and Flavia Krause-Jackson, 'Greece gets $146 billion rescue in EU, IMF package', *Bloomberg*, May 3, 2010, bloomberg.com/news/articles/2010-05-02/greece-faces-unprecedented-cuts-as-159b-rescue-nears

88 someone from Her Majesty's Revenue and Customs had called: The author put the central points of the events involving Nigel to HMRC. A spokesperson said: 'We can neither confirm nor deny any of the statements you have put to us. This is due to strict rules which we have to follow with regards to intelligence sources'

89 'We did this just to make sure': Transcript of Nigel Wilkins' FCA disciplinary investigation meeting, July 23, 2014

PART II: CHRYSALIS

Chapter 13: Beginnings

93 'It is not clear': 'Lifestyles of the Kazakhstani leadership', cable sent by US embassy in Astana on April 17, 2008, later published by WikiLeaks, wikileaks.org/plusd/cables/08ASTANA760 _a.html

93 Boris Birshtein: Birshtein declined to be interviewed. The author put to him in writing the central points of the events involving him described in this book, Birshtein's alleged illicit payments in Ukraine and his relationship with Semyon Mogilevich, with a view to checking the facts. Birshtein's lawyer wrote back: 'I am instructed to advise that to suggest that this somehow constitutes "fact" checking is disingenuous as the content of the purported facts are more accurately described as fiction. To be clear, the "facts" and the narrative that you are apparently seeking to perpetuate are incorrect. My client will not be responding further.' The letter did not address any of the specific details the author had sought to check

95 twenty-eight-seat private jet ... diamond brooch: Jack Lakey and Cal Millar, 'Boris knows everyone ... Head of firm embroiled in Russian controversy moves with high, mighty', *Toronto Star*, August 23, 1993; Michael Dobbs and Steve Coll, 'Ex-communists are scrambling for quick cash', *Washington Post*, February 1, 1993, washingtonpost.com/archive/politics/1993/02/01/ex-communists-are-scrambling-for-quick-cash/00a47cf2-1f47-4051-90cd-844e3e35643b

95 'I'm for many years in business': Henry Hess, 'Canadian trader describes role in Russian scandal', *Globe and Mail*, September 13, 1993

95 settled in Toronto: Mark MacKinnon, 'Searching for Boris Birshtein', *Globe and Mail*, December 29, 2018, theglobeandmail. com/canada/investigations/article-boris-birshtein-investigation/

95 'I spent a lot of time': Leyla Boulton, 'The Soviet insider, the gold, and Kyrgyzstan's political innocents', *Financial Times*, 28 January 1994

95 'Boris always wanted more than money': Confidential interview

96 Anton Volkov: a pseudonym

96 accompany Gorbachev: Christopher Andrew and Vasili Mitrokhin, *The Mitrokhin Archive: The KGB in Europe and the West*, Penguin, 2000, p.723

96 Gorbachev gave orders: Dobbs and Coll, 'Ex-communists are scrambling'

96 business manager: 'Soviet Turmoil; New Suicide: Budget Director', Associated Press, August 27, 1991, nytimes.com/1991/08/27/ world/soviet-turmoil-new-suicide-budget-director.html

96 proposed a major expansion: Marius Laurinavičius, *Weaponizing Kleptocracy: Putin's Hybrid Warfare*, Hudson Institute, 2017, p.25, s3.amazonaws.com/media.hudson.org/files/publications/ WeaponizingKleptocracy.pdf

97 Leonid Veselovsky: Dobbs and Coll, 'Ex-communists are scrambling'; Mark Almond, 'Introducing KGB PLC', *Spectator*, July 10, 1993, archive.spectator.co.uk/article/10th-july-1993/9/ introducing-kgb-plc; Volkov interview

97 'friendly firms': Dobbs and Coll, 'Ex-communists are scrambling'

97 a memo: Ibid.

97 A billion dollars: Ibid.

97 $50 billion: David Wise, 'Spy vs spy', *Washington Post*, January 27, 2008, washingtonpost.com/wp-dyn/content/article/2008/01/24/ AR2008012402750.html

97 KGB men: Interview with former manager from Birshtein's company, Seabeco

98 Georgi Arbatov: *Newsweek* said Arbatov was to become chairman of a joint venture between his Institute of USA and Canada Studies and Seabeco. 'Arbatov, Inc', December 26, 1988. The Canadian magazine *Maclean's* quoted a Seabeco vice president saying Arbatov would 'act in an advisory capacity' to the joint venture. ('Cashing in on glasnost', January 16, 1989.) Birshtein has said he had 'no dealings of any substance' with Arbatov

98 codename Vasili: Andrew and Mitrokhin, *Mitrokhin Archive*, pp.275–8

98 The two had met: Dobbs and Coll, 'Ex-communists are scrambling'

98 'A lot of Russians': Ibid.

98 highly profitable: Ibid.

98 half a billion dollars: Ibid.; Diane Francis, 'Scandal Russian style: The man at the centre of Moscow's Watergate tells his story', *Financial Post*, September 18, 1993

98 $4 million went missing: Boulton, 'The Soviet insider'

99 Mikhas: The account of Sergei Mikhailov's relationship with Birshtein and criminal career is drawn from the author's interviews with Mikhailov in Moscow in 2018 and with Volkov, the former KGB officer; a confidential 1996 FBI report on Eurasian organised crime; confidential reports prepared in 2006 by Bob Levinson that were based on notes of interviews conducted in 1997 by US law enforcement officers with Semyon Mogilevich as part of a potential deal with the US government; Friedman's *Red Mafiya*, Glenny's *McMafia* and Galeotti's *The Vory*; MacKinnon, 'Searching for Boris Birshtein'; and Farangis Najibullah, 'Alleged Russian mobster uses "right-to-forget" law to break with his past', Radio Free Europe, June 1, 2016, rferl.org/a/alleged-russian-mobster-right-to-forget-law-break-with-past/27772535.html

99 a reception thrown by the Moldovan president: Birshtein has said he was introduced to Mikhailov not in Moldova but in Tel Aviv, then they met again at Birshtein's Zürich office. In total they met 'a handful of times' and Birshtein 'never had any business dealings' with Mikhailov

99 staying alive: Mikhailov interview

99 breezily deny: Mikhailov confirmed in his interview with the author that he goes by the name Mikhas. A person called Mikhas is widely acknowledged as the head of the Solntsevskaya brotherhood. But when asked whether he was the head of the Solntsevskaya brotherhood, Mikhailov said: 'No, for the simple reason that it does not exist'

99 bank accounts abroad: Levinson reports, Mikhailov interview

99 sponsored by IBM: FBI Eurasian organised crime report

99 drug trafficking, visa fraud, bribery, murder, money laundering and extortion: FBI Eurasian organised crime report; Levinson reports

99 drew on the *vory*: Galeotti, *The Vory*, p.146

99 *avtoritet*: Ibid.

99 introduced Mikhas to Alex Shnaider: Mikhailov in his interview with the author said he recalled meeting Birshtein's son-in-law,

Alex Shnaider, at a restaurant in Belgium. Birshtein, through his lawyers, has said he could not recall such a meeting. Mark MacKinnon, in 'Searching for Boris Birshtein', quotes Birshtein's son Alon saying Mikhailov came to the family home in Zürich

100 planning to invest: *Intelligence Online*, an intelligence newsletter, reported that Swiss detectives had found at Mikhailov's house in Geneva an agreement for him to pay $150 million to Birshtein ('Mikhailov between Mafia and KGB', March 27, 1997). Georges Zecchin, the Swiss magistrate on the case, said in correspondence with the author that while it was 'difficult to confirm facts of an investigation that took place 21 years ago ... the article must most probably have built on genuine information'. Birshtein has denied the existence of this contract. Asked about the agreement, Mikhailov told the author the agreement 'most probably' related to the gas project but ultimately the money was 'unfortunately' not paid

100 charged: Elif Kaban, 'Ex-Moscow police chief tells Swiss court he had to flee for his life', *Reuters*, December 2, 1998

100 was murdered: The author asked Mikhailov if he knew who had killed the witness, Vadim Rozenbaum. 'If I knew I would definitely share this information with law enforcement agencies ... I did not have this information. I wish I had'

100 in favour of Yeltsin's rule: Levinson reports

100 'economic genocide': Celestine Bohlen, 'Yeltsin deputy calls reforms "economic genocide"', *New York Times*, February 9, 1992, nytimes.com/1992/02/09/world/yeltsin-deputy-calls-reforms-economic-genocide.html

101 'corruption has penetrated': Jack Lakey and Cal Millar, 'Former Metro firm cited in Russian controversy', *Toronto Star*, September 2, 1993

101 the official said: Jack Lakey and Cal Millar, 'Russian scandal becomes as wild as any spy novel', *Toronto Star*, October 3, 1993

101 'octopus': 'The results of the work of the commission of Andrei Makarov' (in Russian), *Kommersant*, March 5, 1994, kommersant.ru/doc/72913

101 emblazoned in gold letters: MacKinnon, 'Searching for Boris Birshtein'

101 knowing Rutskoi: Boulton, 'The Soviet insider'; interview with Seabeco manager

101 'A country can't be rich': Boris Yeltsin, *The Struggle for Russia*, Random House, 2004, pp.226–7

101 'It's not a secret': Boulton, 'The Soviet insider'

Chapter 14: Big Yellow

104 Big Yellow: The account of how Diligence tracked down Ablyazov's stash of documents comes from the author's interviews with Trefor Williams, London, 2017–2019, and with another person involved, plus a recounting of the story that Williams gave to the French edition of *Vanity Fair*, 'Trouvez cet oligarque!', July 2014

105 visit a firm called Arcanum: Mukhtar Ablyazov and Bota Jardemalie interviews; interview with Ron Wahid, London, 2017

106 a third of the workforce of the US intelligence agencies were contractors: Julie Tate, 'CIA's brain drain: Since 9/11, some top officials have left for private sector', *Washington Post*, April 12, 2011, washingtonpost.com/world/cias-brain-drain-since-911-some-top-officials-have-left-for-private-sector/2011/03/25/AF3Nw1RD_story.html

106 'I've never seen rich people': Bota Jardemalie interview

106 knew Sugar had worked for the Trio too: Interviews with three people with knowledge of Arcanum's work. The work for the Trio was done through Arcanum's sister company, RJI Capital

107 the one Nazarbayev owned: Daniel Foggo, 'Kazakh leader "secretly owns" £50m home', *Sunday Times*, November 9, 2008, thetimes.co.uk/article/kazakh-leader-secretly-owns-pound50m-home-vsqfdjs37g0

107 serve as driver, translator and fixer: Interview with Madina Ablyazova, Geneva, 2019

107 risen from technician: Viktor Khrapunov, *Nazarbayev – Our Friend the Dictator*, Ibidem-Verlag, 2015, pp.18–19

108 Iliyas opened a note: Iliyas Khrapunov interview

110 'I am not coming to a party': Khrapunov, *Nazarbayev*, p.136

110 Tevfik Arif: The author sent a representative of Arif and his company, Bayrock, pre-publication fact-checking queries on all the salient points in this book's account of him. The representative initially disputed some of the facts off the record, then, presented with additional evidence, declined to make any further comment either off record or on it

110 investments worth millions: Contract for the sale of Bayrock's 50 per cent of the shares in Swiss Development Group SA to Iliyas Khrapunov, who already held the other 50 per cent, August 27, 2008

110 urgent message: Copy supplied by Peter Sahlas

111 not tolerated: Paul Starobin, 'Murder in Kazakhstan', *The Atlantic*, February 2006, theatlantic.com/magazine/archive/2006/02/murder-in-kazakhstan/304688; Ilan Greenberg, 'Top Kazakh aide quits in

crisis after killing of opposition figure', *New York Times*, February 23, 2006, nytimes.com/2006/02/23/world/asia/top-kazakh-aide-quits-in-crisis-after-killing-of-opposition.html

111 Rakhat Aliyev: Details of Aliyev's life are drawn from interviews with those who knew him as well as his statement in Hourani et al. v Mirtchev et al., and the judgment of Mr Justice Warby in Hourani v Thomson et al., UK High Court, March 10, 2017

111 'He would call me his son': Aliyev's statement in Hourani et al. v Mirtchev et al., par 17

112 opportunity presented itself: The account of Rakhat Aliyev's scheme to attack the Trio and Kazhegeldin is drawn from a 2003 report by Global Options Management, a Washington consultancy that advised Nazarbayev; a copy of communications from Eric Van de Weghe, a fixer with knowledge of the scheme; Steve LeVine, *The Oil and the Glory*, Random House, 2007, p.373; Ron Stodghill, 'Oil, Cash and Corruption', *New York Times*, November 5, 2006, nytimes.com/2006/11/05/business/yourmoney/05giffen. html; and interviews with two European former law enforcement officers and a former senior Kazakh official

113 mafia-style network: Some of the details of Aliyev's alleged crimes are set out in an internal note by Kanat Seydgapbarov, deputy head of the Kazakh Office of the Deputy Prosecutor General. This document was entered into evidence in Hourani et al. v Mirtchev et al.

113 lobbyists spread word: Letter from lawyers from Alexander Mirtchev, a consultant to Nazarbayev, to the *Washington Examiner* and the Human Rights Foundation, October 25, 2012

113 Sugar's lover: Seydgapbarov note

113 impaled on railings: Warby judgment, pars 33–61

113 a theory: Seydgapbarov note

113 evidence … was inconclusive: Warby judgment, par 79

114 refused the extradition request: Court order quoted in Aliyev declaration in Hourani et al. v Mirtchev et al., par 37, note 12

114 Sugar was convicted: Warby judgment, par 47; Aliyev declaration, par 35

114 assets were confiscated: Isabel Gorst, 'Kazakh leader's former son-in-law sentenced', *Financial Times*, March 26, 2008, ft.com/content/0f878542-fb54-11dc-8c3e-000077b07658; *An Atmosphere of Quiet Repression*, Human Rights Watch, December 2008, pp.34–5, hrw.org/sites/default/files/reports/kazakhstan1208web_0.pdf

114 some belonging to his allies: Mintewab Abebe, 'Kazakhstan held liable for expropriation of Hourani family's investment on second

round of ICSID arbitration', *Investment Treaty News*, December 21, 2017, iisd.org/itn/2017/12/21/kazakhstan-liable-expropriation-hourani-familys-investment-second-round-icsid-arbitration-caratube-international-oil-company-llp-devincci-salah-hourani-icsid-case-arb-13-13/

114 Sugar was sitting on the terrace: Aliyev, *Godfather-in-law*, pp.56–61

114 board a charter flight: Aliyev statement in Hourani et al. v Mirtchev et al., par 39; Sugar's use of the same trick against Kazhegeldin comes from the author's interview with a person with first-hand knowledge of the matter

115 'Project Super Khan': There are references to early Super Khan documents in Glenn Simpson's original 2008 story in the *Wall Street Journal* on Aliyev's revelations, Glenn R. Simpson and Susan Schmidt, 'Kazakhstan Corruption: Exile alleges new details', *Wall Street Journal*, July 22, 2008, wsj.com/articles/SB121667622143971475. A dispute over the authenticity of the Super Khan documents arose when Aliyev and his associates launched various counter-attacks against the Kazakh government and its consultants through Western courts. To support these lawsuits, Aliyev produced documents he said he had received from sources still loyal to him in Kazakhstan, including in the intelligence service (see Aliyev's declaration in Hourani et al. v Mirtchev et al.). One of these documents is purportedly a top-secret letter sent from the Kazakh prosecutor general to the Kazakh ambassador to the US on November 16, 2007, shortly after Nazarbayev turned on Aliyev. One of the enclosures to this letter is a thirty-three-page blueprint for curtailing the influence of any Kazakh oligarchs who might threaten Nazarbayev's plan to rule indefinitely. This undated blueprint resembles other Super Khan documents in tone, structure and the use of shorthand codes. Unlike some of the other Super Khan documents, it does not carry the branding of Global Options Management, the Washington consultancy that produced them. It further differs from the other documents setting out Super Khan strategies in that it identifies specific enemies to be targeted – Aliyev, as well as the Trio, Kulibayev and Ablyazov. If it is fake, it is nonetheless an accurate summary of the tactics that Nazarbayev has employed against Ablyazov and Aliyev, including seizing domestic and offshore assets and manipulating the Western legal system for domestic political ends. Its authenticity is hard to assess conclusively one way or the other. In the various court proceedings, the letter with which it was enclosed was persuasively shown to be a forgery, confected by Aliyev or someone acting on his instructions in an attempt to

strengthen a narrative of persecution. It is perfectly possible, however, that Aliyev was employing the classic espionage technique of mixing fake and legitimate documents. A former senior German police officer and a handwriting expert who examined the documents at issue made no pronouncement on the purported Super Khan blueprint attached to this letter (see the reports by Max-Peter Ratzel and Gideon Epstein, both submitted as evidence for the respondents in Hourani et al. v Mirtchev et al.). One of the other purported official Kazakh communications also shown to be a forgery was found to have been adapted from a genuine document that Aliyev obtained (see Max-Peter Ratzel's report)

116 assassinate him: Aliyev statement in Hourani et al. v Mirtchev et al., par 38

116 Sugar disclosed more: Interview with Ablyazov and his witness statement, pars 105–8

116 an offer: Ablyazov witness statement, pars 719–22

117 'We taxpayers': Tom Harper, 'Does this Kazakh banker know the secret of RBS's missing billions?', *Evening Standard*, April 12, 2011, standard.co.uk/news/does-this-kazakh-banker-know-the-secret-of-rbss-missing-billions-6391371.html

Chapter 15: Watchdogs

118 The Brink's-Mat trials: Stewart Tendler and Michael Horsnell, 'Brink's Mat: the bullion trail', *The Times*, July 8, 1988

119 shell companies and anonymous accounts: Simon Bowers, 'How Mossack Fonseca helped hide millions from Britain's biggest gold bullion robbery', *Guardian*, April 4, 2016, theguardian.com/news/2016/apr/04/brinks-mat-how-mossack-fonseca-helped-hide-millions

119 $1 trillion: testimony of Raymond W. Baker to Levin's hearings on 'Private banking and money laundering: a case study of opportunities and vulnerabilities', November 9–10, 1999, gpo.gov/fdsys/pkg/CHRG-106shrg61699/html/CHRG-106shrg61699.htm

120 'It's your turn, doctor': Kareem Fahim and Hwaida Saad, 'A faceless teenage refugee who helped ignite Syria's war', *New York Times*, February 8, 2013, nytimes.com/2013/02/09/world/middleeast/a-faceless-teenage-refugee-who-helped-ignite-syrias-war.html

Chapter 16: The Savarona

121 'help to redress': Paul Judge email, May 22, 2011

121 lowest governance rating: Clara Ferreira-Marques and Rhys Jones, 'Chairman of miner ENRC quits in fresh board shake-up', *Reuters*, April 23, 2013, reuters.com/article/enrc-board/update-2-chairman-of-miner-enrc-quits-in-fresh-board-shake-up-idUSL6N0DA4MN 20130423

121 MPs were asking questions: Rowena Mason, 'MP calls for Serious Fraud Office checks on ENRC', *Daily Telegraph*, April 9, 2011, telegraph.co.uk/finance/yourbusiness/bribery-act/8439251/MP-calls-for-Serious-Fraud-Office-checks-on-ENRC.html

121 'Our objective': Judge email

122 a yacht called the *Savarona*: an English translation of the indictment has been published online by a news organisation called *The Black Sea*, theblacksea.eu/_old/mirror/theblacksea.eu/RES/uploads/files/Savarona%20prosecution%20docs_ocr.pdf. It matches a Turkish version of the indictment provided to the author by one of the defence lawyers in the case

123 'I'm sorry to have to address it': Khrapunov, *Nazarbayev*, pp.138–40

126 entwined with organised crime ... one brother had a job: Craig Shaw, Zeynep Şentek, Ştefan Cândea, 'World leaders, mobsters, smog and mirrors', *The Black Sea*, December 20, 2016, theblacksea.eu/stories/football-leaks/the-football-leaks-family-world-leaders-mobsters-smoke-and-mirrors

126 channelled at least $10 million: Jody Kriss, Bayrock's erstwhile finance director, asserted this in his suit against Bayrock et al., filed in May 10, 2010 in the Southern District of New York

126 'sources of financing': 'Bayrock Group: Redefining real estate, investment and development', 2008, documentcloud.org/documents/3117892-Bayrock-Presentation.html. Tevfik Arif and Felix Sater would later claim that not a single dollar belonging to Machkevitch passed through Bayrock. But then, so much of Bayrock's funding was murky that it is hard to say with certainty where its money did or did not originate. Sater did confirm to the author that Machkevitch acted as a 'strategic partner' to Bayrock, making introductions and opening doors

126 the time at the Lanesborough: Iliyas Khrapunov interview. Arif did not dispute Iliyas's account. Sater claimed Iliyas had not been at this meeting and told the author that Machkevitch's appearance was just a coincidence. But he accepted that Machkevitch did help him and Arif with introductions

126 Russian funds behind them: The Icelanders were from FL Group. Jody Kriss, at note 46 to par 666 in his lawsuit against Bayrock, states that Arif and Sater told him 'the Russians behind FL were in favour with Putin'. Kriss repeated this claim in a 2017 interview with *Bloomberg*. Sater told the author that Kriss's statement is 'bullshit'; Putin's spokesperson told *Bloomberg* he had no connection to FL Group or to Bayrock. FL Group collapsed in the financial crisis. Since then circumstantial evidence has emerged suggesting large amounts of Russian money had been moving through Iceland's financial sector. See Timothy L. O'Brien, 'Hey, Mueller, you should check out Iceland', *Bloomberg*, June 23, 2017, bloombergquint.com/politics/hey-mueller-you-should-check-out-iceland

126 duly entrusted: Kriss suit, par 670

127 Arif was acquitted but his aide and a pimp went to jail: Recep Aktepe, 'Savarona'daki Fuhuş Davası Beraatle Sonuçlandı', *Habertürk*, April 15, 2011, haberturk.com/yasam/haber/621260-savaronadaki-fuhus-davasi-beraatla-sonuclandi; Mustafa Kozak, Savarona'daki Fuhuş Davasından Beraat Eden 5 Sanığa Hapis Cezası, *Sözcü*, February 22, 2016, sozcu.com.tr/2016/gundem/savaronadaki-fuhus-davasindan-beraat-eden-5-saniga-hapis-cezasi-1102662

Chapter 17: Off the Books

128 Project Maria: Dechert defence, par 83.1

129 shortlisted: ENRC's amended particulars of claim against Dechert and Neil Gerrard in the UK High Court, May 17, 2018, par 14; Dechert defence, June 7, 2018, par 40

129 Gerrard's brief: Dechert defence, par 83.1. Gerrard was originally at DLA Piper. In April 2011 he moved to Dechert, taking the ENRC case with him

129 to the oligarchs: Dechert defence, pars 6 and 76.4. This view is supported by ENRC director Ken Olisa in his farewell letter to the board of June 8, 2011: 'Although the founding shareholders had signed Representation Agreements committing them to support an independent board it soon became obvious that the original owners' informal historical links with Directors and senior management meant that their influence was ever present'

129 investigate some iffy paperwork: Herbert Smith's investigation report, September 25, 2007

130 written to the ENRC directors: Neil Gerrard's letter of March 29, 2011

131 $7 billion: Dechert presentation on Kazakhstan to the Serious Fraud Office, 2013, par 1.21

131 cleared $1 billion: ENRC annual report, 2011, p.28

131 ENRC generated two-thirds ... working age: Alain Lallemand, 'L'empereur du Kazakhstan: Enquête sur un trio venu de la république kazakhe qui fit trembler les polices de Belgique', *Le Soir* (Belgium), July 22, 2000, lesoir.be/art/l-empereur-du-kazakhstan-enquete-sur-un-trio-venu-de-la_t-20000722-Z0JGTU.html; Dechert report to the SFO on Kazakhstan, pars 1.27 and 1.31.c

131 'stank of the KGB': Lallemand, 'L'empereur'

132 state within a state: Richard Behar, 'Capitalism in a cold climate', *Fortune*, June 12, 2000 and the magazine's 'Update and clarification', July 12, 2004, archive.fortune.com/magazines/fortune/fortune_archive/2000/06/12/281972/index.htm#update

132 commended to his old comrade: Interview with former senior Kazakh official

132 'frightening speed' ... 'Going once, gone!' ... 'filthy cheap': Sander Thoenes, 'Kazakhstan's sale of the century', *Financial Times*, October 25, 1996. Thoenes also records the details of the privatisations involving the Trio and their backers, the Reubens. Lawyers for the Reuben brothers disputed the figures in Thoenes' story to the author but did not provide alternative numbers. See also Martha Brill Olcott, *Kazakhstan: Unfulfilled promise*, Carnegie Endowment for International Peace, 2002, chapter 5

132 'Do you want to keep working here?': Marc Champion, 'How a Trump SoHo partner ended up with toxic mining riches from Kazakhstan', *Bloomberg*, January 11, 2018, bloomberg.com/news/features/2018-01-11/how-a-trump-soho-partner-ended-up-with-toxic-mining-riches-from-kazakhstan

133 double-crossed: Charles Clover and William Hall, 'Aluminium "risk-taker" changes tack in Russia', *Financial Times*, April 11, 2000

133 'pantomime': Anthony Robinson, 'Kazakhs "seized company assets"', *Financial Times*, February 13, 1999

133 extracted a 'substantial payment': Press release jointly issued on the settlement of their dispute by Trans-World, the Trio and the other parties involved, February 20, 2000

133 One fortunate student: Dechert report on Kazakhstan, pars 6.1–6.93

134 visit a particular office: Dechert report on Kazakhstan, pars 3.47–3.51; Dechert defence, par 132

134 Soviet farm: Dechert report on Kazakhstan, pars 3.47, 4.2 and 5.12

134 the ENRC office: It was an office of SSGPO, ENRC's subsidiary at Rudny

134 use sophisticated data-deletion tools: Dechert report on Kazakhstan, pars 3.60–3.63

135 eight fatal incidents: Dechert report on Kazakhstan, 6.76–6.84

135 couldn't identify any favours: Dechert report on Kazakhstan, par 6.92

135 attacked in his hotel room: Dechert defence, par 134

135 deleted the previous day: Dechert report on Kazakhstan, par 3.60. The report also states that Farhad Ibragimov was later fired

135 four other employees: Dechert report on Kazakhstan, par 3.66

Chapter 18: God's Kingdom

136 'Terrorism/Extremism update': Shiv Malik, 'Occupy London's anger over police "terrorism" document', *Guardian*, December 5, 2011, theguardian.com/uk/2011/dec/05/occupy-london-police-terrorism-document

138 a report prepared for the bank: Report of Boston Consulting's CEE & Russia strategy workshop of May 14, 2008

Chapter 19: Fear

140 Roza Tuletayeva: The account of the events in Zhanaozen and what befell Roza and the other strikers is drawn from interviews with witnesses and survivors conducted by the author in Zhanaozen and Aktau in 2019. Additional details come from 'Striking Oil, Striking Workers', Human Rights Watch, September 10, 2012, hrw.org/report/2012/09/10/striking-oil-striking-workers/violations-labor-rights-kazakhstans-oil-sector

144 vanishingly thin: See, for instance, Agathe Duparc, Camille Chappuis, Marc Guéniat and Andreas Missbach, 'Vitol, the king of oil in Kazakhstan', *Public Eye*, November 2018, stories.publiceye.ch/vitolinkazakhstan/index.html; Jack Farchy and Nariman Gizitdinov, 'Shell said to drop plan to buy stake in Kazakh state oil company', *Bloomberg*, October 9, 2018, bloomberg.com/news/articles/2018-10-09/shell-said-to-drop-plan-to-buy-stake-in-kazakh-state-oil-company; and Isabel Gorst, 'Gazprom cosies up to Kazakh billionaire', *Financial Times*, July 1, 2011, ft.com/content/7412091a-c972-38bb-be7e-d6a366ce1313

146 Nurlibek Nurgaliyev: interview with Nurlibek Nurgaliyev, Zhanaozen, 2019

146 the head of a child: Communications with Galym Ageleuov, a Kazakh human rights activist who has documented the events of December 16, 2011 in Zhanaozen

146 Torekhan Turganbaev: Interview with Torekhan Turganbaev, Zhanaozen, 2019

148 her memory ... disturbed: Roza Tuletayeva gave an account of her traumatised memories at her trial

148 'Even if the workers': 'Kazakhstan: Oil Workers Convicted in Flawed Trial', Human Rights Watch, June 4, 2012, hrw.org/news/2012/06/04/kazakhstan-oil-workers-convicted-flawed-trial

149 'You are done ...': Roza Tuletayeva, testimony at trial, and her recollections later to an acquaintance

150 Bazarbai Kenzhebaev: Hugh Williamson, executive director, Europe and Central Asia division, Human Rights Watch, letter to Kazakhstan's prosecutor general, February 1, 2012, hrw.org/news/2012/02/01/kazakhstan-letter-prosecutor-general-regarding-december-events-zhanaozen-and-shetpe

151 The defendants... were divided into four groups: Defendant lists provided to the author by a lawyer who appeared at the trial

152 convinced her that it had all been her fault: Interview with Gulnara Zhuaspaeva, Almaty, 2019

152 Gulnara Zhuaspaeva: Gulnara Zhuaspaeva interview, Almaty, 2019

152 police interrogators approached: Gulnara Zhuaspaeva interview

153 'there was no evidence of a crime': 'Striking Oil', Human Rights Watch

153 sought to retract his statement: 'Kazakhstan: Oil Workers Convicted in Flawed Trial', Human Rights Watch

Chapter 20: Stability

155 a family dinner: Walter Mayr, 'The long arm of Kazakhstan's president', Der Spiegel, May 19, 2009, spiegel.de/international/world/ex-stepson-talks-in-family-feud-the-long-arm-of-kazakhstan-s-president-a-625720-2.html

155 'painted a picture': Simpson and Schmidt, 'Kazakhstan Corruption'

156 sent another $41 million: US v James H. Giffen, indictment, par 17, August 4, 2004, justice.gov/sites/default/files/criminal-fraud/legacy/2011/02/16/08-04-04giffen-second-superseding-indict.pdf

156 'direct jeopardy': Global Options Management 2003 report, p.55

156 'net the big fish': Global Options Management 2003 report, pp.11, 21–2

156 'the keys to the kingdom': Robert Baer, See No Evil, Random House, 2002, p.361

156 told his intelligence contacts: Opinion of the US Court of Appeals, Second Circuit, United States v Giffen, December 8, 2006, caselaw.findlaw.com/us-2nd-circuit/1487232.html

157 'The chief': Email from Massimov's aide Talant Muratbaev to Eduard Ogay, July 1, 2011. The author's emails sending fact checks to the press office of the KNB, the Kazakh intelligence agency Massimov now runs, went unanswered. A spokesperson for Kazminerals, the successor company to Kazakhmys, declined to provide any evidence that the company had not paid for the travel services its employees arranged for the Kazakh prime minister's family. He also declined to discuss whether, even if Kazminerals did not pay for the holiday, the company considered that employees working on company time for foreign officials might be of concern under anti-bribery legislation

158 leaked it … top brass wrote: ENRC amended claim, pars 60–61

158 Versace: Olcott, *Kazakhstan*, p.163

158 entire political party: Freedom House, *Nations in transit: 2004*, p.284, pdf.usaid.gov/pdf_docs/Pnadk499.pdf

158 'secret treasurer': Yulia Latynina, 'Looking with pride at mess in Kazakhstan', *Moscow Times*, January 12, 1999

158 had an interest: Aliyev, *Godfather-in-law*, p.144: 'Chodiyev [a variant spelling of Chodiev], who was one of the owners of the Eurasian Group, was Nazarbayev's partner in the aluminum business, and at that time controlled much of Kazakh industry'

158 Viktor Khrapunov … said the same: Khrapunov, *Nazarbayev*, p.140

158 'four partners': Confidential interview

158 suspected they were mere frontmen: Akezhan Kazhegeldin's defence to ENRC's lawsuit against him in the UK High Court, January 17, 2020

159 never entertain ambitions: Interviews with former Kazakh officials and influential figures. Sugar mentions this dimension to Nazarbayev's selection of favoured businessmen. Aliyev, *Godfather-in-law*, p.291

159 'It is a fact of life': Ablyazov twelfth witness statement, par 33

160 Irina Petrushova: Communications with Irina Petrushova and her declaration in Kazakhstan v Does 1–100 before the Superior Court of Washington for King County, April 2015; Michael Wines, 'Bruised, but still jabbing Kazakh heavyweights', *New York Times*, July 13, 2002, nytimes.com/2002/07/13/world/the-saturday-profile-bruised-but-still-jabbing-kazakh-heavyweights.html

161 Viagra supply: Joshua Chaffin, 'Kazakhstan's gatekeeper is a legal liability', *Financial Times*, April 14, 2003

161 $13 million a year: Andy Bloxham, 'Tony Blair helps Kazakhstan boosts its image in West', *Daily Telegraph*, October 22, 2011, telegraph.co.uk/news/worldnews/asia/kazakhstan/8843027/Tony-Blair-helps-Kazakhstan-boosts-its-image-in-West.html. A spokesperson for Tony Blair disputed the amount Kazakhstan reportedly paid Blair's company to work on a 'public sector reform' project but would not say what the correct figure was

161 British fighter jets to Saudi Arabia: See the *Guardian*'s long-running investigation that exposed the scandal of the arms deal, known as al Yamamah, theguardian.com/world/bae

161 questioned by the SFO: David Leigh and Rob Evans, 'Ex-chairman questioned in bribes inquiry', *Guardian*, December 22, 2005, theguardian.com/business/2005/dec/22/saudiarabia. internationalnews. See also Jonathan Calvert, Heidi Blake and Michael Gillard, 'Secretive deals that left Sir Dick sitting pretty', *Sunday Times*, February 3, 2013, thetimes.co.uk/article/secretive-deals-that-left-sir-dick-sitting-pretty-r0rk9zrxv65

161 next profitable course: Eric Ellis, 'Samruk: the outsider's inside story', *Euromoney*, January 8, 2008

162 Sir Dick assisted: See the acknowledgements in Jonathan Aitken, *Nazarbayev and the Making of Kazakhstan: From Communism to Capitalism*, Continuum, 2009

162 caught lying: Luke Harding and David Pallister, 'He lied and lied and lied', *Guardian*, June 21, 1997, theguardian.com/politics/1997/jun/21/uk.davidpallister

162 'He is a shrewd tactician ...': Aitken, *Nazarbayev*, p.248

162 made $1 million: Ibrahim Warde, 'Blair Inc', *Le Monde Diplomatique*, November 1, 2012. A spokesperson for Glencore declined to comment on the amount the company paid Blair for this work or how long he spent on it. A spokesperson for Blair disputed the figure but declined to correct it

163 fortune stood at $90 million: Luke Heighton, 'Revealed: Tony Blair worth a staggering £60m', *Daily Telegraph*, June 12, 2015, telegraph.co.uk/news/politics/tony-blair/11670425/Revealed-Tony-Blair-worth-a-staggering-60m.html

163 'blissful confidence': Tony Judt, 'The "Third Way" is no route to paradise', *New York Times*, September 27, 1998, nytimes. com/1998/09/27/opinion/the-third-way-is-no-route-to-paradise. html

164 'The turn of the twentieth century': Kazakhstan's embassy in Finland published an English translation of Nazarbayev's Cambridge speech: web.archive.org/web/20160810235850/kazembassy.fi/en/press-information/

speeches-statements/195-president-nazarbayev-delivers-speech-at-
university-of-cambridge.html. The description of the scene is
drawn from footage of the speech broadcast by Kazakh television
and posted on YouTube: youtube.com/
watch?v=V8M0M9CR8hI&feature=youtu.be

166 Vladimir Kozlov: Interview with Kozlov, Almaty, 2019

167 'one of the causes of the mass disorder': 'Striking Oil', Human
Rights Watch

168 awaiting trial: He was convicted and served five years in prison

169 privatisation of power: The author first encountered this term in a
brilliant analysis of the Angolan kleptocracy by Ricardo Soares de
Oliveira of the University of Oxford, 'Business success, Angola-
style: postcolonial politics and the rise and rise of Sonangol',
Journal of Modern African Studies, 45, 4 (2007), pp. 595–619,
gppi.net/media/Soares_2007_Business_Success.pdf

Chapter 21: Too Big to Jail

170 'pervasively polluted': 'HSBC Exposed US Financial System to
Money Laundering, Drug, Terrorist Financing Risks', US Senate
Permanent Subcommittee on Investigations, July 16, 2012, hsgac.
senate.gov/subcommittees/investigations/media/hsbc-exposed-us-
finacial-system-to-money-laundering-drug-terrorist-financing-risks

170 George Osborne … wrote: 'Too big to jail: Inside the Obama
justice department's decision not to hold Wall Street accountable',
Republican staff of the US House of Representatives' Committee
on Financial Services, July 11, 2016, p.43, financialservices.house.
gov/uploadedfiles/07072016_oi_tbtj_sr.pdf

170 HSBC settled: 'HSBC Holdings Plc and HSBC Bank USA NA
admit to anti-money laundering and sanctions violations, forfeit
$1.256 billion in deferred prosecution agreement', US Department
of Justice, December 11, 2012, justice.gov/opa/pr/hsbc-holdings-
plc-and-hsbc-bank-usa-na-admit-anti-money-laundering-and-
sanctions-violations

171 close permanently: Nate Raymond and Lynnley Browning, 'Swiss
bank Wegelin to close after guilty plea', *Reuters*, January 4, 2013,
reuters.com/article/us-swissbank-wegelin-
idUSBRE9020O020130104

Chapter 22: Sasha and Seva

172 Sasha Machkevitch descended: Dechert defence, par 401.2

172 'ensure that ethical UK businesses': ENRC amended claim, par 66;
Dechert defence, par 174.1. The Dechert defence's reference to
'extensive operatives' appears to be a misquotation of 'extensive
operations'

173 'If I don't deliver': ENRC complaint, par 88

173 homes of ENRC employees: ENRC complaint, par 66, Dechert's
defence, par 146.4.b

173 distract or delay: Dechert defence, par 16

173 'You will appreciate that': ENRC complaint, par 130

174 'board awareness': Dechert defence, par 258.2.c

174 saying Hanna should be suspended: Dechert defence, par 399

174 made all sorts of noises: For example, Christopher Thompson,
'Dalman in threat to quit ENRC board', *Financial Times*,
April 10, 2013, ft.com/content/b5af4c1c-a1fc-11e2-ad0c-
00144feabdc0

174 encountered Semyon Mogilevich: On August 9, 2016, the author
called Mehmet Dalman, the former chairman of ENRC, with
whom he had had some previous conversations, to ask what he
knew about Machkevitch's relationship with Mogilevich. Dalman
said he knew about it but that he was on a train. The author
spoke with him again on August 11, and discussed this
relationship. Dalman said: 'It's a name [Mogilevich] no one wants
to get linked with. During my time there [ENRC] I never met the
guy, but we always moved somewhere else … We knew they
[Machkevitch and Mogilevich] knew each other and they used to
physically meet … [asked where] in Monaco … I did not want to
know.' He also suggested a problem had developed between
Machkevitch and Mogilevich at some stage. Ahead of the
publication of this book, on April 18, 2020, the author contacted
Dalman again with some fact-checking queries, including questions
about whether Machkevitch knew Dalman was aware of his
relationship with Mogilevich, and whether Dalman had informed
the UK police or other authorities about it. Dalman's position had
changed but he declined to give any on-record comment.

Other sources attest to Machkevitch's relationship with
Mogilevich.

Scott Horton, a legal academic and attorney who has served as
an anti-corruption adviser and investigator for half a dozen
countries and a number of Fortune 500 corporations, told the
author that in the period 2005–7 he hired former FBI special

agent Bob Levinson, formerly the Bureau's top expert on Russian organised crime, to assist him in an investigation into energy contracts in Ukraine in which the involvement of Semyon Mogilevich was suspected (the RosUkrEnergo affair). Horton recalled that, in one of his conversations with Levinson about this investigation, Levinson discussed Mogilevich's business connections, noting that he understood based on materials he had seen during his time at the FBI that Machkevitch served Mogilevich as a principal 'money manager', and that the two had periodic meetings in the south of France.

Mark Galeotti, director of the Mayak Intelligence consultancy and one of the foremost experts on Russian organised crime, has for years maintained extensive contacts among the gangsters, law enforcement agencies and intelligence services of the former Soviet Union. He has advised the UK government, and given evidence to the Foreign Affairs Committee of the UK parliament and the Nato Parliamentary Assembly. He told the author: 'There's something of a consensus among my sources that Machkevitch is or was part of the Mogilevich network, his little black book, particularly in terms of moving money through London'

174 the Brainy Don: Two confidential documents in the author's possession recount what various security agencies knew about Semyon Mogilevich in the mid-nineties. One was the FBI's assessment of the threat from Eurasian organised crime, dated May 1996. The other is the report specifically on Mogilevich and his organisation written after a meeting in November 1994 of a 'working group' of Russian, German, Italian and American law enforcement officials. The report draws on information from FBI files, US intelligence, Czech intelligence and police, Ukrainian intelligence, the Italian anti-mafia police and Hungarian police. It also evidently formed the basis for some of the late reporter Robert Friedman's revelations about Mogilevich, including the chapter on him ('The World's Most Dangerous Gangster') in Friedman's book *Red Mafiya*. It is evidence of the accuracy of Friedman's reporting that, on a phone call intercepted by the CIA in 1998, Mogilevich put out a $100,000 contract on his life. Mogilevich denied doing so in a 1999 interview with the BBC's *Panorama* programme. Friedman went into hiding, then resumed his work. (He died of natural causes in 2002.) See Raymond Bonner with Timothy L. O'Brien, 'Activity at bank raises suspicions of Russia mob tie', *New York Times*, August 19, 1999, nytimes.com/1999/08/19/world/activity-at-bank-raises-suspicions-of-russia-mob-tie.html. The account here of the Brainy Don's career draws on the two law

enforcement documents, *Red Mafiya*, confidential reports produced by the FBI's Russian crime expert Bob Levinson from Mogilevich's interviews with US law enforcement in 1997, the transcript of Tom Mangold's interview with Mogilevich for 'The Billion Dollar Don', *Panorama*, 1999, news.bbc.co.uk/hi/english/static/audio_video/programmes/panorama/transcripts/mogalevich.txt, and the author's interviews with confidential sources who know Mogilevich's world and, in some cases, have encountered him personally

174 known Boris Birshtein: Bob Levinson recorded Mogilevich during a 1997 interview with US law enforcement officers referring to Birshtein as a 'close friend'

175 corruption of the Jewish state: See chapter 5 of Glenny, *McMafia*. The report by the working group of law enforcement officials that assembled in 1994 says Mogilevich moved drugs and money through Israel, which served as a haven for his organisation. It suggests that Mogilevich's source for the Israeli passports that he and many of his underlings acquired was Shabtai Kalmanovich, a KGB spy and businessman who would be assassinated in Moscow in 2009. Igor Fisherman, Mogilevich's top financial aide, took Israeli citizenship too. Sasha Machkevitch was named in the prosecution of an Israeli chief rabbi who took bribes to validate conversions as having paid $300,000 for his wife's conversion. Sharon Pulwer, 'Corruption trial of Israel's former chief rabbi begins', *Haaretz*, March 10, 2016, haaretz.com/israel-news/.premium-corruption-trial-of-israel-s-former-chief-rabbi-begins-1.5416101

175 front companies: Richard Behar, the *Fortune* reporter who had access to Trans-World's books and executives, found that in 1997 $3.5 million passed from a Trans-World account at Bank of New York to those of a front company called Benex. Between 1993 and 1998, another front company, Ilis Management, received $50 million from Trans-World. Behar concluded that Benex was a vehicle for shifting money out of Russia, Ilis for shifting money into Russia. US and Canadian investigators, respectively, identified Benex and Ilis as two of the companies used to launder money through YBM Magnex, Mogilevich's fake North American corporation. Behar, *Capitalism*

175 normal, legal business transactions: Lawyers for the Reuben brothers, writing to the author in response to fact-checking enquiries

175 jailed: Friedman, *Red Mafiya*, p.205

175 at the gym: Raymond Bonner, 'Reputed Russian mobster denies tie to laundering, and takes umbrage', *New York Times*, September 11,

1999, nytimes.com/1999/09/11/world/reputed-russian-mobster-denies-tie-to-laundering-and-takes-umbrage.html

175 A very talented businessman: Mikhailov confirmed in an interview with the author that he had done business with Semyon Mogilevich, whom he called 'a very talented businessman'. He mentioned 'international trade' they had done together. 'I remember we purchased a large batch of shoes from Belgium. We brought it to Russia and sold it.' He added: 'In the area where I was working with Mogilevich, it was absolutely legal.' Robert Friedman in *Red Mafiya*, pp.207–9, cited intelligence files saying that Mikhas held a stake in Arbat International, one of Mogilevich's key companies, served as deputy director of another, Magnex 2000, and that his wife managed a third. Friedman also reported that Mogilevich and the Solntsevskaya combined to fence art and antiques stolen from Russian museums and churches and to counterfeit top-end jewellery – claims that are to be found in the law enforcement report on Mogilevich. That report noted Mikhailov's 'reliance on Mogilevich to establish money-laundering channels for Solntsevskaya's criminal proceeds'. The author asked Mikhailov about some of these ventures. He would only say he had been a 'supplier' to Mogilevich. Asked what he supplied, he said: 'Spare parts.' Asked what the parts were for, he said: 'Here we are starting to get into business.' He would not elaborate further

176 FBI believed: 'Working group' report on Mogilevich

176 'formal token': Richard Dawkins, *The Selfish Gene*, Oxford University Press, 1976, p.244

177 British police took an interest: South East Regional Crime Squad report on Operation Sword, November 10, 1995

178 letter the home secretary sent: Operation Sword report; 'The Billion Dollar Don'

178 YBM Magnex: Friedman, *Red Mafiya*, pp.212–24; Alan A. Block and Constance A. Weaver, *All is Clouded by Desire*, Praeger, 2004, pp.158–62; the FBI's outline of Mogilevich's criminal activities in his 2009 entry in its top ten most wanted list, drawing on the indictments brought in the YBM Magnex case, archives.fbi.gov/archives/news/stories/2009/october/mogilevich_102109

179 Jacob Bogatin … David: 'Working group' law enforcement report on Mogilevich; Friedman, *Red Mafiya*, p.213

179 Seven billion dollars: Timothy L. O'Brien, 'Bank settles US inquiry into money laundering', *New York Times*, November 9, 2005, nytimes.com/2005/11/09/business/bank-settles-us-inquiry-into-money-laundering.html

179 Benex: Bonner, 'Reputed Russian mobster'

180 carrying a business card: Friedman, *Red Mafiya*, p.212

180 mutilations: Ibid., p.202

180 mortars and missiles: Ibid., p.211

180 in contact with an official from the criminal division of the Interior Ministry: A leaked entry dated 1986 from the Interior Ministry files describes Mogilevich's current criminal enterprise and past convictions and says he has been 'in contact' with an official

180 deal with German intelligence: Friedman, *Red Mafiya*, p.210

180 danced with Bob Levinson: Levinson's reports of the US law enforcement meetings with Mogilevich; Barry Meier, *Missing Man*, Farrar, Straus and Giroux, 2016, p.59

180 intelligence file disappeared: Friedman, *Red Mafiya*, p.211

181 in a bar nearby: Glenny, *McMafia*, pp.87–9; Friedman, *Red Mafiya*, pp.215–16; transcript of Tom Mangold's interview with Mogilevich for 'The Billion Dollar Don', *Panorama*, 1999

181 annual profits: Roman Olearchyk, Haig Simonian and Stefan Wagstyl, 'Energy fears highlight trade's murky side', *Financial Times*, January 9, 2009

182 his cable: 'USG concerns over Austrian banking operations', cable sent by US embassy in Austria on February 17, 2006, later published by WikiLeaks, wikileaks.org/plusd/cables/06VIENNA515_a.html

182 bearer shares: Andrew E. Kramer, 'Ukraine gas deal draws attention to secretive importer', *New York Times*, February 1, 2006, nytimes.com/2006/02/01/business/worldbusiness/ukraine-gas-deal-draws-attention-to-secretive.html

182 Seva's blessing: 'Ukraine: Firtash makes his case to the USG', December 10, 2008, later published by WikiLeaks, wikileaks.org/plusd/cables/08KYIV2414_a.html. The cable contains the ambassador's record of his conversation with Firtash: 'He acknowledged ties to Russian organized crime figure Seymon [sic] Mogilevich, stating he needed Mogilevich's approval to get into business in the first place. He was adamant that he had not committed a single crime when building his business empire, and argued that outsiders still failed to understand the period of lawlessness that reigned in Ukraine after the collapse of the Soviet Union'

182 dismissed the notion: Author's communications with Firtash's representatives, 2020. They said: 'Mr Firtash has stated many times, publicly, privately and on the record that he knew Mr Mogilevich but has never had any partnership or other commercial association with him'

182 discovered buried connections between Firtash's businesses and the Brainy Don's people: When the author asked Firtash's representatives about his apparent connections to Mogilevich, they wrote back that 'a thorough and detailed due diligence of Mr Firtash' conducted by his bankers at Raiffeisen, including an investigation by the private intelligence firm Kroll, 'confirmed that Mr Firtash did not have any links to criminals or criminal activities'. The author has, however, seen a draft section of the Kroll report, the findings of which Firtash's representatives did not dispute. It shows that Firtash's companies had several connections to Mogilevich.

Firtash's representatives confirm that, back in the 1990s, he supplied goods to the former Soviet republic of Turkmenistan. The government of Turkmenistan paid him in natural gas. Or rather, it gave the gas to a Russian company called Itera that belonged to a businessman, Igor Makarov, which piped the gas across Russia and sold it to Ukraine and Europe. Itera then paid Firtash for the goods he had supplied to Turkmenistan, completing the triangle. A group of companies was incorporated as a channel for this money, all with some variation on the name Highrock and all registered in places where ownership can be kept secret. It was among the Highrock companies that Kroll found the connections to Mogilevich.

Highrock Properties was the vehicle that would handle payments related to the barter trade: the goods Firtash supplied to Turkmenistan in exchange for the gas it gave to Itera. It was incorporated in the British Virgin Islands in 2000, then replaced with a company of the same name but incorporated instead in Tel Aviv. A holding company was also incorporated, which would own Highrock Properties, called Highrock Holding. Highrock Holding was incorporated in Cyprus in 2001.

Most of this incorporating was done by Olga Shnayder, Makarov's lawyer. According to the Kroll report, she served as a director of the British Virgin Islands incarnation of Highrock Properties and set up Highrock Holding. Kroll's investigators reported that she had also acted as a representative of Mogilevich. She had served as the founding shareholder of a company that owned Ritual Service, the upmarket Moscow undertakers Mogilevich had set up. (A *Wall Street Journal* reporter reached Shnayder, through the Ritual Service offices, only for her to deny that she was an owner of the company. She said it would be 'a violation of client-attorney privilege' to say whether Makarov or Mogilevich were her clients.) The last bit of incorporating – of the Tel Aviv Highrock Properties – was done by Zeev Gordon, an

Israeli lawyer. Gordon told a *Financial Times* reporter he counted Mogilevich as 'a client and a friend' and said he did not know whether or not Mogilevich was involved in Highrock.

The ownership of Highrock Holding, the entity at the top of the corporate pyramid that received the proceeds of the gas trade, was divided into three, according to the Kroll report. The flesh-and-blood owners of these thirds were hidden behind nominees. Firtash was able to provide Kroll's investigators with the names of the companies behind the nominees. One he controlled himself. One was another company incorporated by Olga Shnayder, the lawyer connected to Mogilevich. The director of that company, the Kroll investigators found, was Mogilevich's wife. The final third of Highrock Holding was owned by yet another company incorporated by Shnayder. The director of this one was a relative of a woman who shared an address with Mogilevich's wife.

Firtash told the Kroll investigators that 'it had widely been presumed that Makarov may have had commercial dealings with Mogilevich'. Moreover, the Kroll report notes that in 1999 Russian media had reported that Makarov's company Itera used Sergei Mikhailov as its agent on gas deals in Ukraine. Mikhailov, also known as Mikhas, was by then widely known as the leader of the Solntsevskaya crime gang and has since confirmed to the author that he did business with Mogilevich.

Nonetheless, the Kroll report records Firtash saying that, while he was in partnership with Makarov, he did not 'concern himself with the details of incorporation' of Highrock Holding and had not been 'in possession of the details' of who its owners were. In other words, Firtash himself asserted that he turned a blind eye to the identities of his partners in these companies, despite knowing that Makarov was widely presumed to be in business with Mogilevich, already a notorious organised crime boss.

Firtash has also said, in a 2006 interview with the *Financial Times*, that Makarov arranged the incorporation of the Highrock companies. But Makarov told the *Financial Times*' reporter that 'neither he nor Itera had ever had any economic interest in Highrock or undertaken any role in setting up Highrock or its parent companies'. (Makarov has also denied having a relationship with Mogilevich.)

These Highrock arrangements, under which the proceeds from the highly lucrative gas trade passed through companies in which Firtash shared ownership with Mogilevich's relatives and associates, were in place for nearly three years, according to the Kroll report: from January 2001, when Highrock Holding was incorporated, to

December 2003. That was when Firtash, after breaking with Makarov, completed the process of removing the other shareholders from Highrock Holding in order, his representatives said, to 'clean it up'.

Firtash undercut Makarov and supplanted him in the gas trade. Now he was running the barter end of it – supplying goods in exchange for Central Asian gas – as well as transporting and selling the gas himself. This he did through a new company, Eural Trans Gas. Firtash owned most of it. But from December 2002 until early 2004, the nominee for whoever owned a quarter of it was Zeev Gordon, lawyer and friend to Mogilevich. (Firtash and Gordon have both denied that Mogilevich was involved in Eural Trans Gas.)

In 2005, the management of the giant Russian state gas company Gazprom – led by Alexey Miller, a longstanding associate of Vladimir Putin – insisted that it be granted an interest in the gas transit trade that the owners of Eural Trans Gas controlled. Gazprom was cut in and the new venture was called RosUkrEnergo. Responding to the author's questions about Highrock, Firtash's representatives felt compelled to add that 'suggestions that Mr Firtash is somehow an agent of Mr Putin and the Kremlin are equally false'.

See Tom Warner, 'Key man in Ukraine gas dispute faces questions', *Financial Times*, July 13, 2006, ft.com/content/29f06170-12a2-11db-aecf-0000779e2340; Glenn R. Simpson, 'US probes possible crime links to Russian natural-gas deals', *Wall Street Journal*, December 22, 2006, wsj.com/articles/SB116675522912457466

183 'not of a particularly grave nature': 'Russia frees crime boss wanted by US', *Reuters*, July 27, 2009, reuters.com/article/us-russia-crime/russia-frees-crime-boss-wanted-by-u-s-idUSTRE56Q0JT20090727

183 'Through his extensive international criminal network': 'FBI top ten most wanted fugitive: Semion Mogilevich', October 21, 2009, archives.fbi.gov/archives/news/stories/2009/october/mogilevich_102109

183 arranging to exchange: Friedman, *Red Mafiya*, pp.210–11; Alain Lallemand, 'Le diplomate belge serait intervenu en faveur de Semion Mogilevich: L'ambassadeur Cahen a-t-il aidé un mafieux russe?' *Le Soir* (Belgium), September 4, 1999, lesoir.be/art/le-diplomate-belge-serait-intervenu-en-faveur-de-semion_t-19990904-Z0H6UA.html; 'Mogilevich's friends', *Intelligence Online*, November 18, 1999, intelligenceonline.com/threat-assessment/1999/11/18/mogilevich-s-friends,70281-bre

183 let it be known: Levinson reports

183 Russian spies: Alexander Litvinenko told an Italian inquiry into Russian organised crime what he knew of Mogilevich's relationship with Russian intelligence. Letter to the Mitrokhin Commission, undated, litvinenkoinquiry.org/files/2015/04/INQ018922wb.pdf. Another former KGB officer confirmed Mogilevich's role in an interview with the author. Litvinenko also made a tape in which he discussed Mogilevich's relationship with Putin. It became public after his murder. Lyndsey Telford, Edward Malnick and Claire Newell, 'Is this Alexander Litvinenko's beyond the grave attack on Putin?', *Daily Telegraph*, January 23, 2015, telegraph.co.uk/news/uknews/law-and-order/11364724/Is-this-Alexander-Litvinenkos-beyond-the-grave-attack-on-Putin.html. Yuri Shvets, a former KGB officer who claimed asylum in the US, described the origins of Putin's relationship with Mogilevich in an account that was submitted as evidence to the UK's inquiry into Alexander Litvinenko's death. 'Report on Igor Sechin', undated, litvinenkoinquiry.org/files/2015/07/INQ015691.pdf

184 Neil Gerrard be fired: Dechert defence, par 401.2

Chapter 23: The Loving Cup

185 'Employee of the Month': Email from James Borley, manager in the permissions department of the FCA's authorisations division, to his team, February 11, 2013

185 turn into the Financial Conduct Authority: The author put the central points of the events involving Nigel to the FCA. A spokesperson said: 'I'm afraid that we are unable to confirm or deny any of the facts that you're asking about'

186 ten thousand funds: Jeffrey Sachs, 'Reckless Caymans playing with fire', *Financial Times*, May 7, 2013, ft.com/content/ff5b2b4c-b34f-11e2-b5a5-00144feabdc0

186 returns were meagre: Miles Johnson and Dan McCrum, 'Hedge funds: California calls time', *Financial Times*, September 19, 2014, ft.com/content/6772a1b2-3ff2-11e4-a381-00144feabdc0

187 'Shoot first and ask questions later': Lindsay Fortado, George Parker, Martin Arnold and Caroline Binham, 'Martin Wheatley resigns as chief of Financial Conduct Authority', *Financial Times*, July 17, 2015, ft.com/content/61f867fa-2c76-11e5-8613-e7aedbb7bdb7

188 'greater accountability and transparency': Nigel Wilkins' campaign flyer for the City of London election of March 21, 2013

Chapter 24: The Presumption of Regularity

189 A woman in her forties: The account of the kidnapping is drawn from Alma Shalabayeva's statement of June 22, 2013, and the author's correspondence with her, and the author's interviews with Peter Sahlas, Madina Ablyazova and Iliyas Khrapunov

191 claimed he had helped Ablyazov concoct a failed terrorist plot: Ruling of the Spanish Supreme Court in Pavlov's case, February 23, 2015

195 Central African Republic diplomatic passport: Sahlas says Ablyazov told him later that he had met the president of the Central African Republic and agreed to serve as his counsel on economic reform, in which position he and his family were issued with diplomatic passports under aliases

195 law enforcement authorities: Interpol alert, Astana to Rome, May 31, 2013

196 doctored Ablyazov's Wikipedia entry: Portland said about this incident that 'the changes were carried out in order to correct inaccuracies ... designed to distort the truth about Ablyazov's fraudulent activities'. It said 'no attempt was made by Portland to deceive or to disguise the origin of these changes'. However, after its work was discovered, it trained its staff in 'the most up-to-date standards', including a visit from Wikipedia's founder

197 felt something inside herself collapse: Madina Ablyazova interview

Chapter 25: A Legit Shithole

198 Iliyas had always thought of Felix: Iliyas Khrapunov interview

198 Felix had called to offer help: Peter Sahlas interview

199 allegations were full of holes: Report by Professor Peter B. Maggs of the University of Illinois College of Law, commissioned by lawyers for the Khrapunov family and submitted as expert evidence in the Swiss legal proceedings triggered by the Kazakh allegations against the Khrapunovs

199 find a project and we'll do it together: Iliyas Khrapunov interview

199 real estate worth $2.5 billion: Bayrock presentation

199 electrocute his balls, cut off his legs and leave his body in the boot of a car: The business partner was Ernest Mennes and he made the allegations in a lawsuit against Bayrock and Sater that was public for a while then sealed. The suit was settled. Mennes told the author he and Sater now have an 'excellent relationship'. See Timothy L. O'Brien, 'Trump, Russia and a Shadowy Business Partnership', *Bloomberg*, June 21, 2017, bloomberg.com/opinion/

articles/2017-06-21/trump-russia-and-those-shadowy-sater-deals-at-bayrock

199 an old hotel at the far end of Lake Geneva: Bayrock presentation; Iliyas Khrapunov interview

200 he asked Felix: Iliyas Khrapunov interview

200 secured exemptions: Interview with Elise Bean, former staff director and chief counsel to Senator Carl Levin's Senate Permanent Subcommittee on Investigations, Washington, DC, 2017

200 flagged them as suspicious: Tom Burgis, 'US prime property is magnet for illicit wealth, warns Treasury', *Financial Times*, February 23, 2017, ft.com/content/3b1b583e-f9ea-11e6-bd4e-68d53499ed71

200 sixty-three Russians: Nathan Layne, Ned Parker, Svetlana Reiter, Stephen Grey and Ryan McNeill, 'Russian elite invested nearly $100 million in Trump buildings', *Reuters*, March 17, 2017, reuters.com/investigates/special-report/usa-trump-property

201 Pablo Escobar: Sergio N. Candido, 'Safe found at Pablo Escobar house in Miami Beach will be kept in bank vault – for now', *Miami Herald*, January 26, 2016, miamiherald.com/news/local/community/miami-dade/miami-beach/article56514733.html

201 dropped more than $1 million: US government forfeiture proceedings in the Jacksonville Division of the US District Court for the Middle District of Florida, against 4866 Yacht Basin Drive and other property, amended verified complaint, March 18, 2015, star.worldbank.org/corruption-cases/sites/corruption-cases/files/Toure_MDFLA_Amended%20Complaint_Mar2015.pdf, and settlement, February 1, 2016, worldbank.org/corruption-cases/sites/corruption-cases/files/Toure_MDFLA_Settlement%20Agreement_02012016.pdf. See also Burgis, *The Looting Machine*, chapter 5

201 fresh strawberries: TripAdvisor review, tripadvisor.co.nz/ShowUserReviews-g4153940-d6621406-r207257074-Pangea_Island_Market_Grill-St_Johns_Florida.html

202 a classic peso scam: See the indictment in United States v Murcia Guzmán et al., Southern District of New York, March 17, 2009

202 found a local fixer: Ned Parker, Stephen Grey, Stefanie Eschenbacher, Roman Anin, Brad Brooks and Christine Murray, 'Ivanka and the fugitive from Panama', *Reuters*, November 17, 2017, reuters.com/investigates/special-report/usa-trump-panama. Asked about dirty money passing through the Trump Ocean Club Panama, a spokesperson for the Trump Organisation told the author it 'was not the owner, developer or seller of units at the

Trump Ocean Club Panama. Our relationship, which has ended, was purely a brand and management agreement. Because we were not the owner or developer, we did not control unit sales nor did we deal with buyers on a regular basis'

203 recommended to his sister: Tom Burgis, 'Dirty money: Trump and the Kazakh connection', *Financial Times*, October 19, 2016, ft.com/content/33285dfa-9231-11e6-8df8-d3778b55a923

203 'legit shithole': Post on Reddit by clykins46, reddit.com/r/ deadmalls/comments/b50806/tricounty_mall_springdale_ohio/

203 received a bid: Almaty and BTA v Sater et al., complaint in the Southern District of New York, assets.documentcloud.org/ documents/5780579/BTA-Bank-v-Felix-Sater.pdf, pars 183–193

203 came from an account at FBME Bank: A spokesperson for FBME told the author that its bankers had not known the money to be Ablyazov's and 'no amount of due diligence that FBME could have done at the time would have ever revealed that those funds belonged to Ablyazov'

204 Neil Bush: SingHaiyi, 'About us – board of directors', singhaiyi. com/directors.html. The author asked Neil Bush by email about his role in Sater's deal and why the investors he represented paid one and a half times what Sater's backers paid. He wrote at first: 'I have never met nor do I know Felix Slater [a variant spelling of his name Sater has used] and the TriCounty Mall was bought out of a sheriff's auction not in a private deal. I am unaware of who the previous owner was or what they paid for the mall.' The author asked Sater about that. 'He is very mistaken. We had pleasant dinners. He especially liked the restaurant Solo in the Sony building in New York. It was the best kosher restaurant in New York at the time. And we even had dealings at another company around the same time called TXOil. I was an adviser there as well. Since we owned the debt on the [Tri-County] mall and set up the auction sale, how the hell could they [SingHaiyi] have bought it without a deal with us? And how did his partners from the Chinese company [SingHaiyi] he was on the board of come to New York and have dinner with me to conclude the deal at a restaurant called San Pietro? He introduced them to me. Everyone, especially presidential people and families, seem to forget me. I must not be very memorable.' To which Bush: 'I checked my email to refresh my memory. From correspondence with Sater apparently we had dinner the third week of Sept 2011, the one and only dinner, and he followed up by sending information on a project in Columbia [*sic*] and talking about a Kazakhstan oil project. I pursued neither of those deals. I don't think I could pick Sater out of a line up.'

204 considered himself entitled: Iliyas Khrapunov interview; confidential interview; Felix Sater's deposition in Almaty and BTA v Ablyazov et al., p.281

204 'I know about': Interview with Iliyas Khrapunov. Judge David Waksman of the UK High Court also believed Iliyas was moving Ablyazov's money, and said so in his judgment in BTA Bank v Mukhtar Ablyazov and Iliyas Khrapunov, June 21, 2018, hoganlovells.com/~/media/hogan-lovells/pdf/2018/approved-judgment-dated-21-june-2018-bta-khrapunov.pdf?la=en

205 persuaded his new father-in-law: Iliyas Khrapunov interview

205 Gennady Petelin: Iliyas Khrapunov interview; Almaty and BTA v Sater et al. complaint. Petelin, through his lawyer, declined to comment

205 split the profits: Iliyas Khrapunov interview; order and opinion of Judge Katharine H. Parker in City of Almaty et al. v Mukhtar Ablyazov et al., US District Court for the Southern District of New York, July 3, 2019, p.6

205 spotted … their quarry: Trefor Williams interview

Chapter 26: Risk Appetite

207 written warning: Occupational health assessment of Nigel Wilkins by Dr Geoff Earnshaw of Health Management Ltd, August 2, 2013

207 another written warning, a final one: Letter from Victoria Raffe, director of authorisations at the FCA, to Nigel Wilkins, July 18, 2013

207 'risk appetite … performance improvement plan': FCA's response to Nigel Wilkins' employment tribunal claim, April 30, 2015

207 'performance issues': Occupational health assessment by Dr M.J. Forbes of Health Management Ltd, June 18, 2014

Chapter 27: Doubles

209 still earning less: Chris Belfield, Jonathan Cribb, Andrew Hood, Robert Joyce, Living Standards, Poverty and Inequality in the UK: 2014, Institute for Fiscal Studies, July 2014, ifs.org.uk/uploads/publications/comms/r96.pdf

209 'We've got to make more cuts': Rowena Mason, 'Chancellor says more cuts on way in "year of hard truths"', Guardian, January 6, 2014, theguardian.com/politics/2014/jan/06/george-osborne-more-cuts-year-hard-truths

209 Sasha's celebrations: Event Concept promotional video, eventconcept.co.uk/case-studies/projects/60th-birthday-party

210 first time in ten years: William MacNamara and Alison Smith, 'Tensions deepen for ENRC as two directors dismissed', *Financial Times*, June 9, 2011

211 danger in that: Letter from Roger Ewart Smith, the Rothschild banker advising the Kazakh government on the buyout of ENRC, to Kairat Kelimbetov, June 14, 2013

211 Peter Mandelson ... made that very point: Peter Mandelson email to Kairat Kelimbetov, May 19, 2013

212 moodily concluded: 'Response of the Independent Committee of the Board of Eurasian Natural Resources Corporation plc to the Offer for ENRC by Eurasian Resources Group BV', August 8, 2013, investegate.co.uk/eurasian-natural-res--enrc-/rns/response-to-offer/201308081504283057L

212 business plan ... appoint the management: Roger Ewart Smith letter to Kairat Kelimbetov and other officials, December 9, 2013

212 on the hook: Rothschild presentation for the Kazakh government, October 17, 2013

212 'Everybody understands': Gil Shefler, 'Kazakh tycoon plans pro-Israel TV network to rival Al-Jazeera', *Jerusalem Post*, April 8, 2011

Chapter 28: The System

214 surge of relief: 'These issues have weighed heavily on my mind,' Nigel wrote to his superiors at the FCA on August 18, 2014, while they were investigating his conduct

215 moved to Monaco: The 2011–12 issue of *Banking & Finance Monaco* names Khofiz Shakhidi among the senior vice presidents of BSI Monaco, p.107, zyyne.com/pdf;6303

215 Bahamas: Shaxson, *Treasure Islands*, p.105; Nick Shaxson, 'The Bahamas tax haven – a (re-)emerging global menace?', Tax Justice Network, September 8, 2016, taxjustice.net/2016/09/08/bahamas-tax-haven-emerging-global-menace; interview with Bahamas private banker

215 a mother of four in Margate: Paul Hooper, 'Margate mum Emma Truscott jailed for receiving nearly £55,000 in illegal benefits', Kent Online, November 18, 2014, kentonline.co.uk/thanet/news/mum-jailed-for-55k-benefit-27124

215 offered an amnesty: Richard Brooks, *The Great Tax Robbery*, Oneworld, 2014, pp.201–5; Tom Burgis and Vanessa Houlder, 'HMRC: The taxman cometh', *Financial Times*, August 20, 2015, ft.com/content/3fa2fd16-42bd-11e5-b98b-87c7270955cf

216 James Bond: Nigel Wilkins email to intelligence officer at the Financial Services Authority, December 11, 2008

216 asleep at the wheel: Disciplinary Investigation Report, p.24

216 a $7 million reward: 'Who's the criminal?', *Economist*, February 14, 2013, economist.com/special-report/2013/02/14/whos-the-criminal

217 'areas of concern': Steve Slater, 'I'm the right person to fix HSBC, says CEO Gulliver', *Reuters*, March 9, 2015, uk.reuters.com/article/uk-hsbc-tax-politics/im-the-right-person-to-fix-hsbc-says-ceo-gulliver-idUKKBN0M51ME20150309

217 'I feel obliged to make a statement': Nigel Wilkins' email to James Anderson and Andrew Freeman of the FCA, June 24, 2014

PART III: METAMORPHOSIS

Chapter 29: Conquest

221 Little Green Men: Ray Furlong, 'The changing story of Russia's "Little Green Men" invasion', Radio Free Europe/Radio Liberty, February 25, 2019, rferl.org/a/russia-ukraine-crimea/29790037.html

221 'Take a look': Ibid.

222 'big connections': Sergei Mikhailov interview

222 'the accountant of the Communist Party': MacKinnon, 'Searching for Boris Birshtein'

222 $5 million: Charles Clover, 'Questions over Kuchma's adviser cast shadows', *Financial Times*, October 30, 1999. Birshtein has denied transferring any money to Kuchma or any of his aides. He was not convicted of any wrongdoing by the Swiss or Belgian investigations into these alleged payments and wider suspected money laundering

222 greasing Ukraine's KGB chief: Levinson reports on Mogilevich interview

222 'the real owner'. MacKinnon, 'Searching for Boris Birshtein'

222 Alex Shnaider: In an arbitration claim against his former partner Eduard Shyfrin brought on April 7, 2016 and later obtained by the author, Shnaider set out the events involving the sale of Zaporizhstal as described here. Further details are drawn from a witness statement given in response by Shyfrin on June 9, 2017, also obtained by the author. Both have denied wrongdoing. Shnaider has set out his position in a letter to the *Financial Times*, 'An article littered with "ifs" and "possibilities"', August 24, 2018, ft.com/content/63b2e102-a553-11e8-8ecf-a7ae1beff35b. Ahead of publication of this book, Shnaider's lawyers told the author that he had paid a law firm to investigate whether he had given kickbacks to Russian officials from the Zaporizhstal sale. The law firm

concluded that he had not, according to a summary of their report provided by Shnaider's lawyers, who declined to provide the full report other than under a non-disclosure agreement

223 mopped floors and stacked shelves: Michael Posner: 'The invisible man', *Globe and Mail*, May 27, 2005, theglobeandmail.com/report-on-business/rob-magazine/the-invisible-man/article18228210

223 set him up in business: Shyfrin witness statement

223 raid on their Antwerp office: Shyfrin witness statement; MacKinnon, 'Searching for Boris Birshtein'

224 fortune of $1.3 billion: 'The world's billionaires', *Forbes*, 2010, stats.areppim.com/listes/list_billionairesx10xwor.htm

224 affable Ukrainian moneyman: Interviews with Igor Bakai's associates, Kiev, 2018

224 monetise the gas trade: Askold Krushelnycky and Ivan Lozowy, 'Ukraine official "sacked for exposing government fraud"', *Independent*, September 7, 2004, independent.co.uk/news/world/europe/ukraine-official-sacked-for-exposing-government-fraud-40737.html

224 dacha … state railways … Monte Carlo: Tom Warner, 'Dubious dacha sale raises tricky questions over Ukrainians fleeing to Moscow', *Financial Times*, May 6, 2005

225 knew of Bakai: Shyfrin witness statement

225 putting up money … main rival: Shyfrin witness statement

226 cover for spies overseas: Erin Banco, 'Trump envoy Erik Prince met with CEO of Russian direct investment fund in Seychelles', *Intercept*, November 28, 2017, theintercept.com/2017/11/28/blackwaters-erik-prince-met-with-ceo-of-russian-direct-investment-fund

226 days doing business in the former Soviet Union were over: Shyfrin witness statement

226 paying the agreed $100 million 'commission': Shnaider would later argue in his arbitration claim that Shyfrin 'falsified the commission story as a means of syphoning off US $100m'. Shyfrin denied this. The arbitration was settled

Chapter 30: Privacy

228 They asked him why: 'Meeting Note: Nigel Wilkins, Andrew Freeman, James Anderson', June 25, 2014, in Disciplinary Investigation Report

230 banging your head against a brick wall: Nigel Wilkins' email to an administrator at the private health company contracted by the FCA, June 20, 2014

230 The *Economist* story: 'A whistleblower's woes', July 19, 2014, economist.com/schumpeter/2014/07/19/a-whistleblowers-woes

230 Kostas Vaxevanis: 'Greek bank list editor Costas Vaxevanis acquitted', *BBC News*, November 1, 2012, bbc.com/news/world-europe-20172516

230 Hervé Falciani: Patrick Radden Keefe, 'The bank robber', *New Yorker*, May 23, 2016, newyorker.com/magazine/2016/05/30/herve-falcianis-great-swiss-bank-heist

231 Antoine Deltour: Simon Bowers, 'World unites to decry prosecution of source behind LuxLeaks tax scandal', *Guardian*, December 23, 2014, theguardian.com/world/2014/dec/23/prosecution-source-luxleaks-tax-scandal-letter-luxembourg-auditor-antoine-deltour

231 killed with bullets: Neil Buckley, 'Gunmen claim life of Russia's bank reformer', *Financial Times*, September 15, 2006

231 an acquaintance: The author

232 do you have any evidence?: Disciplinary Investigation Report

232 'an inability on your part': Letter from William Amos and Greg Choyce of the FCA to Nigel Wilkins, September 29, 2014

Chapter 31: The Bridge

233 strolled past the Kremlin: Joshua Yaffa, 'The unaccountable death of Boris Nemtsov', *New Yorker*, February 26, 2016, newyorker.com/news/news-desk/the-unaccountable-death-of-boris-nemtsov. More details of the assassination are drawn from the account of Vadim Prokhorov, the Nemtsov family's lawyer, published by the Boris Nemtsov Foundation for Freedom, February 1, 2018, nemtsovfund.org/en/2018/02/investigation-into-boris-nemtsov-s-murder-brief-account-by-vadim-prokhorov. The author interviewed Prokhorov in London in 2018

233 'aliens among us': Michael Birnbaum, 'Before Nemtsov's assassination, a year of demonization', *Washington Post*, March 4, 2015, washingtonpost.com/world/europe/before-nemtsovs-assassination-a-year-of-demonization/2015/03/04/dc8f2afe-c11d-11e4-9ec2-b418f57a4a99_story.html

233 'end in catastrophe': Julia Ioffe, 'After Boris Nemtsov's assassination, "There are no longer any limits"', *New York Times*, February 28, 2015, nytimes.com/2015/02/28/magazine/after-boris-nemtsovs-assassination-there-are-no-longer-any-limits.html

233 toilet … had cost $75,000: Miriam Elder, 'Vladimir Putin "galley slave" lifestyle: palaces, planes and a $75,000 toilet', *Guardian*,

August 28, 2012, theguardian.com/world/2012/aug/28/vladimir-putin-palaces-planes-toilet

233 visiting Ukraine: Ioffe, 'After Boris Nemtsov's assassination'; Oleg Boldyrev, 'Nemtsov report exposes Russia's human cost in Ukraine', BBC, May 12, 2015, bbc.co.uk/news/world-europe-32703353

234 peculiar in the extreme: Vadim Prokhorov interview; Yaffa, 'The unaccountable death'

234 Adam Delimkhanov: Russian journalists and Kadyrov's opponents see Delimkhanov as a key figure in the Chechen regime's clandestine commercial interests. Nemtsov's friend and fellow dissident Ilya Yashin has described Delimkhanov's alleged role during the second Chechen war managing illicit sales of Chechen oil that generated funds for Kadyrov. See Yashin's report, *A Threat to National Security*, February 2016, Boris Nemtsov Foundation for Freedom, 4freerussia.org/wp-content/uploads/sites/3/2016/03/A-Threat-to-National-Security.pdf. In 2009, Kadyrov's political rival Sulim Yamadayev was killed in Dubai. During the trial of his murderers, a Dubai police officer testified that Delimkhanov had provided the killers with the gold-plated pistol with which they killed Yamadayev. As a result of his suspected involvement in the murder, Dubai police put Delimkhanov on the Interpol wanted list. (Awad Mustafa, 'Russian MP provided "golden gun" used in Dubai killing, court told', *The National* (UAE), February 2, 2010.) Delimkhanov has denied involvement in the murder. In 2014, the US Treasury imposed sanctions on Delimkhanov for involvement in transnational organised crime. ('Treasury targets leading figures and syndicate of transnational criminal organizations', US Treasury press release, July 2, 2014, treasury.gov/press-center/press-releases/Pages/jl2552.aspx). Repeated emails from the author to Chechen government press officers with fact-checking queries for Delimkhanov received no response

235 generous federal grants: Kathrin Hille, 'How Chechnya's Ramzan Kadyrov could destabilise Russia', *Financial Times*, August 28, 2018, ft.com/content/c8dadc00-a086-11e8-85da-eeb7a9ce36e4

235 this money and their own: Liz Fuller, 'Kadyrov's Chechnya appears exempt from Russian funding cuts', Radio Free Europe/Radio Liberty, July 30, 2017, rferl.org/a/caucasus-report-kadyrov-chechnya-exempt-funding-cuts/28648698.html; Yashin, *A Threat*

235 'powerful Chechens': Shyfrin wrote in his witness statement to the arbitration dispute between the two: 'Shnaider took to even more dangerous and extreme means of coercion by involving powerful Chechen individuals in our dispute.' A photograph in the author's

possession shows Shnaider meeting Kadyrov's lieutenant, Adam
Delimkhanov. During the dispute, Shyfrin's lawyers wrote to
Shnaider's with what they said was a photograph of a text message
sent to Shyfrin by a rabbi purportedly acting as a go-between for
Shnaider's representatives. The rabbi claimed that Shnaider had
approached Tamirlan Mezhidov, an aide to Delimkhanov
(identified as such in 'Dubai police accuse lawmaker in Chechen
exile's killing', Radio Free Europe/Radio Liberty, April 6, 2009)

235 come up under the wing of Timur Kulibayev: Interview with
Kenes Rakishev, Astana, 2017. Rakishev said Kulibayev 'was my
mentor and he teach [sic] me lots of things, good things'

235 the Russian cellist: Jake Bernstein, Petra Blum, Oliver Zihlmann,
David Thompson, Frederik Obermaier and Bastian Obermayer, 'All
Putin's men', *International Consortium of Investigative Journalists*,
April 3, 2016, icij.org/investigations/panama-papers/20160403-
putin-russia-offshore-network

235 Angry Birds credit cards: Rakishev interview

235 cryptocurrency venture: 'Kenes Rakishev issues letter to POG
shareholders', statement to the London Stock Exchange, June 21,
2018, investegate.co.uk/fincraft-holdings/rns/kenes-rakishev-issues-
letter-to-pog-shareholders/201806211348151750S

235 arrange for Western journalists: One of them was the author

236 'managing the president's family's money': Email of November 26,
2013 from Kai Martin Schmitz of the International Finance
Corporation to an executive at Net Element, a company in which
Rakishev had invested. Schmitz wrote: 'We enjoyed hearing about
the business and find this an interesting opportunity.
Unfortunately your investor from Kazakhstan is managing the
president's family's money and we cannot invest with them (due to
our mandate). I am sure they are the best investor to have in that
part of the world but we are not allowed to invest with people
with political exposure.' This and the others of Rakishev's emails
cited here were among those in the Kazaword leak

236 on Prince Andrew's Christmas card list: Christmas emails from
Prince Andrew to Kenes Rakishev in 2011, 2012 and 2013

236 arrange the deal: In July 2007, shortly before Timur Kulibayev
bought Sunninghill, Rakishev corresponded by email and held a
meeting with Amanda Thirsk, then deputy private secretary to
Prince Andrew, regarding the purchase of Sunninghill. The matters
they discussed included reviewing plans of the land, land-use
rights, security and interior design

236 $6 million over the listing price: Daniel Foggo and Jack Grimston,
'Kazakh tycoon's secret deal on Prince Andrew's house', *Sunday*

Times, February 22, 2010, thetimes.co.uk/article/kazakh-tycoons-secret-deal-on-prince-andrews-house-bsm5dbr6ch2. By way of explanation of the apparently inflated price, the *Mail on Sunday* later reported that 'a Royal source claimed that the explanation for the over-the-odds offer of £15 million for Sunninghill Park was that there was a higher offer in the background. Asked why that offer was not accepted, the source replied: "It was very protracted and contingent on financing and not as straightforward as the offer they actually went with."' Chris Hastings and Nick Craven, 'Prince Andrew tried to broker sale of Crown properties for Kazakh crony who later paid £3 million over the asking price for his marital home', July 2, 2016, https://www.dailymail.co.uk/news/article-3671807/Prince-Andrew-tried-brokersale-Crown-properties-Kazakh-crony-later-paid-3million-askingprice-marital-home.html

236 use his connection to Kenes: Guy Adams, 'Andrew, a secret deal and a very disturbing conflict of interests', *Daily Mail*, May 20, 2016, dailymail.co.uk/news/article-3601629/Air-Miles-Andrew-secret-deal-behalf-chums-disturbing-conflict-interests-jetsetting-Prince-afford-13million-ski-chalet.html. Asked about this episode in his 2017 interview with the author, Rakishev said: 'My friend called me and said, "Look, Kenes, can you organise something in Kazakhstan?" He's my friend. He's Prince Andrew. He's my friend, a close friend. My friend from the UK called me and said, "Kenes, one Greek company interested to hear, as a construction company. They want to build, they want to have contracts. Can you help me?" And I said, "Okay, because you are my friend, I will do something. What do I need to do?" "Can you organise for them, meetings?" I said, "Okay. I can organise. With whom, for example?" "With companies."' Rakishev said he organised the meetings but no contracts came of them and he was not paid for his efforts

236 'You should be shot': Yaffa, 'The unaccountable death'

236 'philanthropic help': A subsequently deleted post from Kadyrov's Instagram account, recorded on Kazakh news site Bnews. web. archive.org/web/20160722140135/http://bnews.kz/en/news/obshchestvo/chechnya_ready_to_give_any_support_to_kazakhstan_in_fight_against_radicals-2016_07_19-1282067

237 represented the interests of Kadyrov's prime lieutenant: Bela Lyauv, 'Galchev reconciled with a friend of Kadyrov', *Vedomosti*, April 12, 2010, vedomosti.ru/business/articles/2010/04/12/galchev_pomirilsya_s_kreditorom

237 'personal financial adviser': Olga Sichkar and Elena Kiseleva, 'The new creditor restructured Filaret Galchev', *Kommersant*, April 13, 2010, kommersant.ru/doc/1353661. The author contacted Krotov

and his associates ahead of publication with fact-checking enquiries but received no reply

237 joined the effort: emails between Krotov, a senior officer of BTA Bank, a senior officer at BTA's auditors EY and others relating to the bank's efforts to enforce the London judgments against Ablyazov by seizing assets in Russia

237 maintain that BTA had never formally engaged Krotov: Rakishev's communications, through his lawyers, with the author, 2020

237 anxious not to cross Kenes ... nonsensical ... 'not someone I want to be on the wrong side of': Interviews with two people with knowledge of the disputes among shareholders at Petropavlovsk, a London-listed Russian gold mining company in which Rakishev invested

237 the Clinton Foundation accepted: 'Our Supporters' page on the Clinton Foundation website, clintonfoundation.org/ contributors?category=%2450%2C001%20to%20 %24100%2C000&amp%3Bamp%3Bpage=7&page=7

238 lawyer declared himself highly suspicious: Alexander Weber and Boris Groendahl, 'Aliyev, Kazakh who fell out with leader, found hanging', *Bloomberg*, February 24, 2015, bloomberg.com/news/ articles/2015-02-24/aliyev-found-dead-in-vienna-cell-ahead-of-banker-murder-trial

Chapter 32: His Footprints Are Not Found

239 'You don't get changes': Gina Chon, 'Corporate America's inquisitor-in-chief', *Financial Times*, August 10, 2014, ft.com/ content/d13c9e52-1f47-11e4-9d7d-00144feabdc0

239 confided in a friend: Interview with Robert Barrington

240 noticed an announcement: 'BSI SA of Lugano, Switzerland, is first bank to reach resolution under justice department's Swiss Bank Program', US Department of Justice, March 30, 2015, justice.gov/ opa/pr/bsi-sa-lugano-switzerland-first-bank-reach-resolution-under-justice-department-s-swiss-bank

240 'These hundred banks': Janet Novack, 'Senate offshore tax cheating report skewers Credit Suisse and US Justice Department', *Forbes*, February 25, 2014, forbes.com/sites/janetnovack/2014/02/25/ senate-offshore-tax-cheating-report-skewers-credit-suisse-and-the-u-s-justice-department/#67ed332a1795

241 end of 'banker bashing': George Parker, Caroline Binham and Laura Noonan, 'George Osborne to signal end to "banker bashing"', *Financial Times*, June 5, 2015, ft.com/content/ eb8b6b1a-0b84-11e5-994d-00144feabdc0

241 removing the head of the FCA: Fortado, 'Martin Wheatley'; the *Financial Times* also published a letter from Nigel Wilkins commenting on Wheatley's departure, 'FCA chief's departure has exposed the extent of government interference', July 21, 2015, ft.com/content/235d0004-2bdc-11e5-acfb-cbd2e1c81cca

242 briefing memo: Nicholas Watt, 'UK seeking to ensure Russia sanctions do not harm City of London', *Guardian*, March 3, 2014, theguardian.com/world/2014/mar/03/uk-seeks-russia-harm-city-london-document

242 reached its settlement: Nigel Wilkins and the FCA settlement agreement, September 3, 2015

243 Macavity: T.S. Eliot, *Old Possum's Book of Practical Cats*, Faber and Faber, 1939

243 'a global policeman': Entry in Nigel Wilkins' notebook

Chapter 33: Winners

244 The clandestine deal had been agreed … with his front company: BTA and the Khrapunovs spent nearly two years fighting over this question in their New York litigation. The fight produced masses of documents, including BTA's 2015 deal with Sater's front company, Litco, and various confidentiality agreements slathering it in still more secrecy. BTA's lawyers at Boies Schiller maintained that they only discovered Sater owned Litco on the first day of his deposition as a witness in September 2018, whereupon BTA and Almaty cancelled their agreement with Litco, prompting Sater to bring an arbitration claim. On May 19, 2020, Judge Katharine H. Parker ruled that BTA's lawyers at Boies Schiller had not, contrary to the Khrapunovs' claims, broken the law that prohibits payments to witnesses. This was because, the judge concluded, no one at Arcanum had told the Boies Schiller lawyers that Sater owned Litco. The judge also found, however, that the Boies Schiller lawyers 'showed an incredible lack of curiosity' about whether Sater might have been Litco's owner

244 Wahid's people knew who owned it: Judge Parker found that Peder Garske, a lawyer, since deceased, who worked for Wahid's firm Arcanum, knew Sater owned Litco but that 'this information was not widely disseminated, if at all, within Arcanum'. She also said she was 'skeptical that [Arcanum's Calvin] Humphrey had no inkling that Sater owned Litco, given that some Litco invoices sent to him mentioned Sater and that he met with both [Sater's lawyer] and Sater'

245 'In the middle of the transaction': Sater deposition in Almaty and BTA v Ablyazov et al.

246 the US Treasury revealed: 'Notice of finding that FBME Bank Ltd., formerly known as Federal Bank of the Middle East, Ltd., is a financial institution of primary money laundering concern', Financial Crimes Enforcement Network, US Department of the Treasury, July 22, 2014, fincen.gov/sites/default/files/shared/FBME_NOF.pdf. The spokesman for FBME told the author that 'no evidence was ever produced of which accounts, if any, were used for money laundering. No evidence was ever shown in court and the basis for FinCEN's claims was supposition rather than fact. FBME's case is that the bank was scapegoated by the Cyprus authorities in order to draw FinCEN's attention away from widespread money laundering by the systemic banks on the island'

246 'frankly unbelievable': Judge Parker's opinion in Almaty et al. v Ablyazov et al., May 2020

246 Boies Schiller told it: Almaty and BTA v Sater et al.

247 Nicolas Bourg ... switched sides: Interviews with four people with knowledge of Bourg's change of allegiance, one of whom explained the incentive offered to him. See also Judge Parker's December 3, 2018, July 3, 2019 and May 19, 2020 rulings on the Litco question in Almaty et al. v Ablyazov et al.

247 Laurent Foucher struck the same bargain: Judge Parker December 2018 ruling

247 gave a statement: 'Declaration of Nicolas Bourg', May 2, 2016, submitted as evidence by Almaty and BTA in their Southern District of New York claim against Ablyazov et al. Iliyas Khrapunov maintains that Bourg's statement is inaccurate

247 Now Foucher had made himself useful for the other side: Interviews with three people with knowledge of Foucher's change of allegiance

247 given her the fright of her life: Notarised statement by Alina Zaharia, Geneva, November 1, 2016. Humphrey, through a lawyer for Arcanum, disputed Zaharia's account but declined to make any on-the-record comment

248 spoke in a methodical, precise way: Author's meeting with Calvin Humphrey

249 His taxi arrived: Ben Schreckinger, 'Inside Donald Trump's election night war room', GQ, November 7, 2017, gq.com/story/inside-donald-trumps-election-night-war-room

Chapter 34: Saint or Sinner

253 'To Mr Letta': Maurizio Molinari, 'L'appello di Ablyazov a Letta: "Volevano due ostaggi da usare contro di me, perché glieli avete dati?"', *La Stampa*, July 5, 2013, lastampa.it/esteri/2013/07/05/news/l-appello-di-ablyazov-a-letta-1.36069961

254 a case of extraordinary rendition: 'UN human rights experts urge Italy to seek return of illegally deported Kazakh mother and daughter', Office of the United Nations High Commissioner for Human Rights, July 18, 2013, newsarchive.ohchr.org/EN/NewsEvents/Pages/DisplayNews.aspx?NewsID=13559&LangID=E

254 lost his chief of staff: 'Italy storm over expulsion of Kazakh dissident's family', *BBC News*, July 17, 2013, bbc.com/news/world-europe-23340652

254 'the repercussions to us': Elisabetta Povoledo, 'Deportation of Kazakhs frays Italy's government', *New York Times*, July 18, 2013, nytimes.com/2013/07/19/world/europe/deportation-of-kazakhs-frays-italys-government.html

256 web page that appeared online: Memorandum of law of non-parties Respublika and LLC Media-Consult in support of motion for clarification of preliminary injunction order, in Kazakhstan v Does 1-100, August 4, 2015, eff.org/files/2015/08/04/respublika_mpa_clarification.pdf

256 suing in a US court: Complaint for damages and injunction relief, Kazakhstan v Muratbek Ketebaev in the US District Court for the Northern District of California, January 18, 2017, courthousenews.com/wp-content/uploads/2017/01/Kazakh.pdf

256 lose the case: David Greene and Karen Gullo, 'Kazakhstan's exploitation of flawed US law to censor Respublika finally ends, in cautionary tale about CFAA abuse', Electronic Frontier Foundation, January 19, 2017, eff.org/deeplinks/2017/01/kazakhstans-exploitation-flawed-us-law-censor-respublika-finally-ends-cautionary

256 half a billion dollars: Asset Return Consultants, BTA Bank, November 27, 2014; 'Changes to SFO funding arrangements', Serious Fraud Office, April 19, 2018, sfo.gov.uk/2018/04/19/changes-to-sfo-funding-arrangements

257 John Howell: Details of Howell's role emerge from the author's interview with Marat Beketayev in Astana in April 2017, and with another person with knowledge of his role, and memos written by the Reed Smith lawyers to whom he reported

257 He signed contracts: Helen Warrell, 'David Cameron leads trade mission to Kazakhstan', *Financial Times*, June 30. 2013, ft.com/content/17a0a358-e1a4-11e2-b796-00144feabdc0

257 FTI Consulting: Email from Chloe Carswell of Reed Smith to Marat Beketayev of the Kazakh justice ministry, February 21, 2014. The email was leaked on Kazaword and later also published by *Le Temps* (Switzerland), letemps.ch/sites/default/files/media/2015/06/16/3.0.1129743681.pdf. The expert at the Swiss NGO that FTI proposed to use for its project said he turned down the offer. Tom Burgis, 'Spies, lies and the oligarch', *Financial Times*, September 28, 2017, ft.com/content/1411b1a0-a310-11e7-9e4f-7f5e6a7c98a2

258 working for Nazarbayev all along: Interview with Ron Wahid

258 recruited an assortment of superstar spies: Arcanum press releases

259 Wahid would say: Interview with Ron Wahid

259 'We are often referred to': RJI Capital blurb on British Polo Day website, web.archive.org/web/20160405031043/https://www.britishpoloday.com/partners/rji-capital

259 chauffeurs: LinkedIn entry by former RJI Capital chauffeur, linkedin.com/in/mathew-macdonald-4059064b/

260 who these targets were: In an interview with the author, Ron Wahid did not deny that Operation Raptor was part of Arcanum's work on the Ablyazov case

260 Madina had noticed: Complaint by the Khrapunovs and their lawyers to the Federal Criminal Court of Switzerland, April 8, 2016; Madina Ablyazova interview

260 message was from a number: Notarised copy of Peter Sahlas's text conversations with Patrick Robertson

262 'strategic communications adviser': Website of Patrick Robertson's firm, World PR, worldpr.org/patrick-robertson-ceo.php

262 clients included ... Pinochet ... Aitken: Nick Hopkins, 'Two sides line up for action after Pinochet ruling', *Guardian*, March 23, 1999, theguardian.com/world/1999/mar/23/pinochet.chile; Nick Cohen, 'Aitken admits: "One more scandal and I'm finished"', *Independent*, June 18, 1995, independent.co.uk/news/aitken-admits-one-more-scandal-and-im-finished-1586933.html

262 disparaging article: Sarah Sands and Victor Sebestyen, 'The ruthless rise of Aitken's error-prone PR', *Evening Standard*, June 21, 1995

263 'Project Shadow': Peter Sahlas interview

264 email ... from early 2014: Email sent from 'Peter Ridge' via an intermediary to Marat Beketayev of the Kazakh justice ministry, January 31, 2014

264 Seeking Arrangements: 'Patrick Robertson Is on Seeking Arrangements', *The Dirty*, September 10, 2015, gossip.thedirty.com/gossip/london/patrick-robertson-is-on-seeking-arrangements/#post-2106189

265 agreed to pay Robertson's firm: World PR contract with BTA Bank, April 29, 2014

265 approved Ablyazov's extradition: 'L'extradition vers la Russie de l'opposant kazakh Moukhtar Abliazov a été validée par Paris', *Le Monde*, October 12, 2015, lemonde.fr/police-justice/ article/2015/10/12/l-extradition-vers-la-russie-de-l-opposant-kazakh-moukhtar-abliazov-a-ete-validee-par-paris_4788076_1653578.html

266 the French magistrate: Pierre-Antoine Souchard, 'Un ex-oligarque kazakh, un avocat français et des écoutes mystérieuses', *Le Nouvel Observateur*, April 2, 2014, nouvelobs.com/societe/20140402. OBS2348/un-ex-oligarque-kazakh-un-avocat-francais-et-des-ecoutes-mysterieuses.html; Agathe Duparc, 'L'oligarque kazakh Abliazov dénonce une justice française à l'écoute de Moscou', *Mediapart*, February 14, 2016, mediapart.fr/journal/international/140216/loligarque-kazakh-abliazov-denonce-une-justice-francaise-lecoute-de-moscou

266 startling letter: 'Avis à victime', Serge Tournaire to Mukhtar Ablyazov, December 5, 2016

266 inner circle: 'Portrait: Bernard Squarcini', *Le Nouvel Observateur*, June 27, 2007, nouvelobs.com/societe/20070627.OBS3999/portrait-bernard-squarcini.html

266 agents included the driver: Agathe Duparc, 'Des mails secrets de Squarcini relancent le scandale LVMH', *Mediapart*, November 14, 2016, mediapart.fr/journal/france/141116/des-mails-secrets-de-squarcini-relancent-le-scandale-lvmh

268 a Basque Spaniard: Thomas E. Carbonneau, *The Political Offense Exception as Applied in French Cases Dealing with the Extradition of Terrorists*, 4 Mich. Y.B. Int'l Legal Stud. 209 (1983), elibrary.law.psu.edu/cgi/viewcontent.cgi?referer=&httpsredir=1&article=1274&context=fac_works

268 manoeuvre they had almost pulled off in Spain: José María Irujo's reporting for *El País*, most recently '¿Quién robó el iPhone del opositor kazajo Alexander Pavlov?', October 31, 2014, elpais.com/politica/2014/10/31/actualidad/1414761557_416890.html

Chapter 35: The Future

271 letter published: Nigel Wilkins, 'City's importance is oft overstated', *Financial Times*, August 8, 2016, ft.com/content/ebe2a4ea-5a50-11e6-9f70-badea1b336d4

271 a reporter: The author

272 a long article: Tom Burgis, 'Dark money: London's dirty secret', *Financial Times*, May 11, 2016, ft.com/content/1d805534-1185-11e6-839f-2922947098f0

273 Muhammadu Buhari: Tom Burgis and Maggie Fick, 'Nigerian president hits back after Cameron gaffe', *Financial Times*, May 11, 2016, ft.com/content/3532d2de-1760-11e6-b197-a4af20d5575e

273 anti-corruption agenda … ceased: Author's interviews with British anti-corruption activists. See also Caroline Binham, 'UK drops out of top 10 in global anti-corruption rankings', *Financial Times*, January 29, 2019, ft.com/content/8d1a2474-224e-11e9-b329-c7e6ceb5ffdf

273 noticed a news report: Caroline Binham and Naomi Rovnick, 'City watchdog probed over property fund collapse', *Financial Times*, December 5, 2016, ft.com/content/36ed6802-bace-11e6-8b45-b8b81dd5d080; Nigel Wilkins, email to the author, December 13, 2016

Chapter 36: The Man With No Past

274 landed in Washington: Flight records for a private jet with the tail letters M-AAAL. This jet is widely held to belong to Alexander Machkevitch. See, for example, the reporting on Twitter by Juha Keskinen (@MacFinn44) and Super Yacht Fan's page on Machkevitch, superyachtfan.com/superyacht_lady_lara.html

274 bobbing off the Seychelles: Banco, 'Trump envoy Erik Prince'

274 on the islands to meet: Shane Harris and Karoun Demirjian, 'Congressional Democrats examine Erik Prince's statements on 2017 Seychelles meeting for possible perjury', *Washington Post*, April 20, 2019, washingtonpost.com/world/national-security/congressional-democrats-examine-eriks-prince-statements-on-2017-seychelles-meeting-for-possible-perjury/2019/04/19/b7f888da-62cb-11e9-9412-daf3d2e67c6d_story.html

274 Obama's inauguration: *Euro-Asian Jewish Yearbook 2008–2009*, Moscow, 2009, p.16

275 a third of the size: Tim Wallace, Karen Yourish and Troy Griggs, 'Trump's inauguration vs Obama's: Comparing the crowds', *New York Times*, January 20, 2017, nytimes.com/interactive/2017/01/20/us/politics/trump-inauguration-crowd.html?module=inline

275 'deliberately false reporting': 'Statement by Press Secretary Sean Spicer', US government, January 21, 2017, whitehouse.gov/briefings-statements/statement-press-secretary-sean-spicer

275 Victor Hanna: Before publication, the author sent Hanna a list of

all the significant facts in the account of him given here. His lawyers wrote back. They said that 'many' of the points 'do not deserve a response'. Others did, and here Hanna 'categorically denies the allegations of wrongdoing suggested'. The lawyers did not explain which points they were referring to in each case, and did not address any of them specifically

275 discerned scraps of his past: Telephone interview with former ENRC Africa mine manager Ron Honey, 2019; interviews with further colleagues of Hanna and others who have encountered him

275 except him: For example, ENRC's 2010 annual report, p.60, kase. kz/files/emitters/GB_ENRC/gbenrcf6_2010.pdf

275 smashed it on the ground: Ron Honey interview

275 'there are people starving': Dechert defence, par 349

276 'everyone was petrified': Dechert defence, par 329.1.a

276 a seat in one of the SFO's interview rooms: Suzi Ring, 'Ex-ENRC Africa boss interviewed by UK prosecutor in bribe case', *Bloomberg*, September 9, 2016, bloomberg.com/news/ articles/2016-09-09/ex-enrc-africa-boss-interviewed-by-u-k-prosecutor-in-bribe-case

276 he left ENRC: Ibid.

276 married ... Mounissa Chodieva: Interviews with an associate of Hanna's and with an adviser to ENRC

276 gone to see ... Malcolm Lombers: Dechert defence, par 204

276 Tony Machado: Dechert defence, pars 204.3, 215.3, 223, 306.3, 327.1, 364.4–5 and 390.4. The author sent a list of fact-checking queries to Machado before publication. He declined to respond to specific points, saying only that 'all of it is false', save that he and Rautenbach had indeed been 'associates'

276 Evgeny Boyarov: Dechert defence, pars 345 and 364.4. Ron Honey confirms Rautenbach used Machado's name as an alias

277 regime 'cronies': 'Commission Regulation (EC) No 77/2009 of January 26, 2009 amending Council Regulation (EC) No 314/2004 concerning certain restrictive measures in respect of Zimbabwe', European Commission, eur-lex.europa.eu/legal-content/EN/TXT/?uri=uriserv:OJ.L_.2009.023.01.0005.01. ENG&toc=OJ:L:2009:023:FULL; 'Treasury Designates Mugabe Regime Cronies', US Department of the Treasury, November 25, 2008, treasury.gov/press-center/press-releases/Pages/hp1295. aspx?mod=article_inline

277 held discussions with Treasury officials: ENRC's statement to the stock market in September 2009 announcing the proposed acquisition of Camec mentioned 'issues ... in relation to the possible application of international sanctions legislation'. It said

that 'these issues are being discussed with HM Treasury'. Campaigners at the British group Rights and Accountability in Development (Raid) spent years asking the Treasury what had transpired from these discussions. The Treasury spent years not telling them. Raid's campaigners recorded their efforts in the *Bribery in its purest form* report. They brought the case to the Information Tribunal but eventually despaired of receiving clear answers. A heavily redacted witness statement by Peter Maydon, head of the Treasury's Sanctions and Counter-Terrorist Financing Unit, made on June 26, 2015, refers to various exemptions the Treasury invokes to refuse Raid's request for information, including 'promotion or protection by the United Kingdom of its interests abroad'

277 declined to explain: A UK Treasury spokesperson told the author: 'I'm afraid we can't comment on individual firms or cases'

278 ENRC money was still flowing to Rautenbach: Dechert defence, pars 204.3, 215.3, 223, 306.3–4, 327, 338.1.a, 364, 381.2

278 Rautenbach came down to the ENRC office: Ron Honey interview; Dechert defence, par 390.4

278 driving off together: Ron Honey interview

278 personally delivered cash bribes: Dechert defence, pars 390, 398. The Zambian government spokesman had no comment on the allegation. The author sent a message to Webbstock but received no reply

278 Chambishi copper smelter: Dechert defence, pars 8, 18.3, 38.2, 59, 138, 215.3, 250.1.b, 326, 356.2, 362, 366.3, 381.3, 390.5

279 forty-six times what the previous owner had paid: Cynthia O'Murchu and Christopher Thompson, 'Cloud hangs over ENRC's purchase of Zambian assets', *Financial Times*, May 10, 2013, ft.com/content/83f06402-b806-11e2-bd62-00144feabdc0

279 took to $1.4 billion: Ibid.

279 patch of Congolese wilderness: ENRC bought the Dezita prospect in 2011 for $195 million (ENRC 2011 half-year results, August 17, 2011, investegate.co.uk/eurasian-natural-res--enrc-/rns/half-yearly-report/201108170700124917M). The seller was identified only as Legacy Industries Limited ('Acquisition of shares in Camrose Resources Limited and certain subsidiaries: Circular to ENRC Shareholders and Notice of General Meeting', ENRC, December 7, 2012). In ENRC's 2013 annual report (p.82, beta. companieshouse.gov.uk/company/06023510/filing-history) Dezita's value is written down by $145 million. Then in 2018, a Swiss court, ruling on a request from the UK Serious Fraud Office for some Swiss bank records related to its ENRC investigation,

revealed some of the SFO's evidence. ENRC, the SFO had told the Swiss, had paid $195 million to a British Virgin Islands company to acquire Dezita before having undertaken any assessment of its value. When it did have Dezita valued three years later, it was found to be worth at most $7.7 million, perhaps as little as $200,000 (or 0.1 per cent of what ENRC had paid). The Swiss judgment records another detail from the SFO's submission, namely that shortly before the acquisition, the price ENRC was to pay was reduced without explanation from $300 million to $195 million. The SFO suspected this happened in order to bring the price below the $200 million threshold at which ENRC's board would have had to approve it. (As is customary in Swiss proceedings, none of the companies involved is identified by name. But the acquisition discussed is described as one that took place in 2011 for $195 million. The only deal mentioned in ENRC's results for that year that matches that description is Dezita.) Ruling of the Swiss Federal Criminal Court, November 7, 2018, bstger.weblaw.ch/pdf/20181107_RR_2018_3.pdf

279 manganese prospect: According to ENRC's 2011 results (investegate.co.uk/eurasian-natural-res--enrc-/rns/final-results/201203210700267417Z), in December 2011 the company agreed to pay $295 million to acquire Erste Resources SA of Mauritius, which owned Rubio Holdings of the British Virgin Islands. Both of these offshore companies had been created in the previous six months in places where their ownership was concealed (Open Corporates, opencorporates.com/companies/mu/C103845; Panama Papers, offshoreleaks.icij.org/nodes/10154463). Rubio was the majority owner of a manganese prospect in South Africa called Kongoni. In the 2013 annual report, ENRC announced that it now considered the prospect worse than worthless. It wrote down the asset's value by $64 million more than it had paid for it, indicating that it was losing money just by owning it. The impairment was, the report said, 'due to downward pressure on prices'. Manganese prices had indeed fallen by a quarter since ENRC bought Kongoni and other companies that mined it also wrote down their operations' value (US Geological Survey, 2014 manganese report, s3-us-west-2.amazonaws.com/prd-wret/assets/palladium/production/mineral-pubs/manganese/mcs-2014-manga.pdf; for example, 'South32 reports $1.7B H1 loss on writedowns in manganese and coal', *Reuters*, February 24, 2016, cnbc.com/2016/02/24/manganese-writedowns-push-south32-to-17-billion-half-year-loss.html). But the bigger question, suggested by Andre Bekker's understanding of

Kongoni's unpromising geology, was why ENRC had paid so much for it in the first place

280 Dan Gertler: The author sent Gertler the main points of this account before publication, asking him whether any were incorrect. His lawyers claimed that most of them were incorrect without elaborating. The sourcing for each point is given below. See also Burgis, *The Looting Machine*, chapter 2

280 emergency funds: *Report of the Panel of Experts on the Illegal Exploitation of Natural Resources and Other Forms of Wealth of DR Congo*, United Nations Security Council, April 12, 2001, pars 50–51, reliefweb.int/report/democratic-republic-congo/report-panel-experts-illegal-exploitation-natural-resources-and

280 Augustin Katumba Mwanke: Burgis, *The Looting Machine*, chapter 2

280 see him as a brother: Augustin Katumba Mwanke's posthumously published memoir, *Ma Vérité*, EPI Nice, 2013, p.208

280 'landscape is in the making': Och-Ziff statement of facts, US Department of Justice, September 29, 2016, justice.gov/opa/file/899306/download, par 31

281 Glencore was one: *Equity in Extractives*, Africa Progress Panel, 2013, pp.48–58, annexes 1–2, reliefweb.int/sites/reliefweb.int/files/resources/relatorio-africa-progress-report-2013-pdf-20130511-125153.pdf; Bloomberg's extensive coverage, including Franz Wild, Vernon Silver and William Clowes, 'Trouble in the Congo: The misadventures of Glencore', *Bloomberg Businessweek*, November 16, 2018, bloomberg.com/news/features/2018-11-16/glencore-s-misadventure-in-the-congo-threatens-its-cobalt-dreams; Tom Burgis, 'Why Glencore bought Israeli tycoon out of Congo mines', *Financial Times*, March 13, 2017, ft.com/content/8c4de26e-0366-11e7-ace0-1ce02ef0def9

281 They met … Katumba: Dechert defence, par 381.4.a.ii

281 then ENRC would pay multiples: *Equity in Extractives*, Africa Progress Panel; Burgis, *The Looting Machine*, chapter 2

281 'the majority of its African business': Dechert defence, par 432.2.a

281 payment of $35 million: Dechert defence, par 324.3.c

282 When Gerrard started pushing for Hanna to be suspended, he was fired: Dechert defence, pars 21–23, 329, 392, 397, 400, 401, 404

282 'flawed' interpretation: Ring, 'Ex-ENRC Africa boss'

282 copped a plea: Och-Ziff deferred prosecution agreement, US Department of Justice, September 29, 2016, par 31, justice.gov/opa/file/899306/download

282 obviously Dan Gertler: The Och-Ziff statement of facts features a character called 'DRC Partner'. This person is described at par 12

as 'an Israeli businessman' who 'had significant interests in the diamond and mineral mining industries in the Democratic Republic of the Congo'. No one but Gertler matches this description, and further details in the statement of facts confirm his identity

282 identities of the recipients: At par 25, the Och-Ziff statement of facts describes a 'DRC Official 2', a former governor of Katanga province and 'closest aide' to 'DRC Official 1'. Katumba was Katanga governor before joining Kabila's court as his right-hand man

282 December 1, 2010 ...: Och-Ziff statement of facts, par 60

283 no witnesses were ever required: Och-Ziff's settlement with the US justice department says, 'Certain of the facts herein are based on information obtained from third parties by the [prosecutors] through their investigation and described to Och-Ziff'

283 'Mining Company 1': At par 35, the Och-Ziff statement of facts says: 'On or about August 20, 2010, Mining Company 1 acquired 50.5 percent of Company B.' On August 20, 2010, ENRC issued a statement to the London Stock Exchange that it had agreed to acquire 50.5 per cent of Camrose, one of Gertler's companies. 'Acquisition of 50.5 per cent of the Shares of Camrose Resources Limited', investegate.co.uk/eurasian-natural-res--enrc-/rns/acquisition/201008201532344192R

283 denominated as bearer notes: Dechert defence at par 301.4.c quotes an SFO investigator saying the use of these instruments had 'money laundering written all over it'

283 died in a plane crash: Jonny Hogg, 'Death of Kabila deal-maker leaves void in Congo', Reuters, February 13, 2012, reuters.com/article/congo-democratic-katumba/death-of-kabila-deal-maker-leaves-void-in-congo-idUSL2E8DD5L220120213

283 corpse of Andre Bekker: Reports by Clement Jackson on his investigation into the death of Andre Bekker

283 chipper Afrikaner: Interviews with Bekker's friends and associates, Johannesburg and by telephone, 2019–20

283 knew the prospect was hopeless: Interviews with Bekker's colleagues and others in the mining industry he spoke to; Clement Jackson investigation. Bekker had overseen geological assessments of the Kongoni prospect while working at its previous owner, Amari Resources

283 started telling people as much: Clement Jackson investigation; interviews with mining industry figures who spoke to Bekker

283 talking about a plan: Interview with a person with whom Gorman discussed this plan

284 found him there: Interviews with Gorman's colleagues and associates, Johannesburg and by telephone, 2019–20

284 decided ... to leave ENRC: Interviews with Bethel's and Strydom's colleagues and associates

284 he had grown tired ... spoken of some business venture: Interview with a person with whom Bethel had discussed these matters

284 investigators were now apparently pursuing: Interviews with two people with knowledge of the SFO's investigation

284 sent word to Bethel: Confidential interview

284 run the ENRC subsidiary: Strydom had been the general manager of Congo Cobalt Corporation (CCC), an ENRC subsidiary. Simon Goodley, 'Two former colleagues at mining giant ENRC found dead in US hotel', *Guardian*, May 15, 2015, theguardian.com/business/2015/may/15/former-colleagues-mining-giant-enrc-found-dead-us-hotel-business. The funnelling of money from ENRC to Rautenbach through CCC is described in the Dechert defence, pars 306.3-4, 327.1, 338.1.a, 345, 364.5, 381.2.a

284 they set off: The timeline of Bethel and Strydom's final days draws on confidential interviews and emails about the case between the authorities in Springfield and the Centers for Disease Control and Prevention (CDC), released in response to a freedom of information request

284 hotel staff opened the doors: Bethel and Strydom autopsy reports; CDC emails; Springfield Police Department incident report

284 Strydom was lying naked ... Bethel was on the floor: Report into the deaths prepared by Michael Baden

284 investigators on the ENRC case were alarmed: Confidential interview

285 what exactly McCormick did: In the Dechert defence, at par 257.4, McCormick is called 'a consultant engaged by ENRC in Africa at considerable expense but for obscure purposes'

285 to debrief his underlings: Ron Honey interview

285 'Africa generally': Dechert defence, par 381.2.b

285 McCormick's job description: The Dechert defence states at par 259 that, despite the documentary evidence of his contract, in his interview with Gerrard's team, McCormick denied that he had provided any services to ENRC in Zimbabwe. 'All questions posed to me were answered honestly and openly,' McCormick told the author

285 local police detective hoped: The author obtained emails between Brian A. Smith, the Springfield Police detective on the case, and Erica Mynarich of the local law firm hired by ENRC, Carver, Cantin & Grantham, released following a freedom of information

request. In one, Smith wrote: 'We will not be able to retrieve data from the phones unless the families are able to provide Mr McCormick with the pin codes.' In subsequent emails, Mynarich sends the phone codes to Smith; it is unclear whether McCormick or someone else retrieved the codes. McCormick told the author it was not he who obtained the codes. Indeed, he said he was not even aware they had been obtained

285 phones ... died: Confidential interview

285 the local coroner: Emails between the author and Jeff Harkey, at the time the Greene County medical examiner, 2019–20

285 partial results: The autopsy reports prepared by Dr Harkey note that, while the lab conducted some tests on the blood samples, 'Results of the toxicological tests on the urine and vitreous fluid, if any, were not reported.' Dr Harkey told the author that Dr Baden commissioned further 'heavy metals' toxicology testing, but Dr Harkey never saw any results

285 not added to the police file: Jasmine Bailey, public affairs officer for the Springfield Police Department, telephone conversations and emails with the author, October 2019

285 Michael Baden: Telephone interviews with Baden, 2019

286 could establish the cause of death: Harkey emails and telephone interviews with Michael Baden

286 regarded the provenance of these samples with suspicion: Confidential interview

286 chain of custody: The author's repeated questions to both Harkey and Baden about the chain of custody of the samples went unanswered. One message in the CDC emails suggests at least some of the samples were stored in a freezer at a local hospital, with no indication that they were secure

286 CDC's tests identified malaria: CDC emails

286 did not conclude: Email from Kelly Keating, staff pathologist at the CDC, to her colleagues, June 23, 2015

286 announced the cause of death: 'Cause of May hotel deaths confirmed', Springfield Police Department, updated on June 22, 2015, web.archive.org/web/20160315225535/https://www.springfieldmo.gov/civicalerts.aspx?AID=1139

286 been on a fishing trip: CDC emails; confidential interview

286 not mentioned being bitten: Confidential interview

286 feeling ill ... on the phone: Messages sent by the two men, copies of which were sent to the Greene County medical examiner's office and thence to the CDC, where they were mentioned in emails in the freedom of information release; confidential interview

286 malaria expert: Analysis of the author's material on the case by Sam Wassmer, associate professor of malaria pathogenesis at the London School of Hygiene and Tropical Medicine, 2020, lshtm. ac.uk/aboutus/people/wassmer.sam. Wassmer adds that, even in cases when two people are bitten by the same mosquito, it is likely that their immune responses would be different, leading to different progression times

287 different genotypes: Email from John Barnwell, head of the CDC's malaria laboratories, to his colleagues, June 24, 2015

287 colleagues of the dead men shuddered: Interview with Ron Honey and others of Bethel and Strydom's colleagues

Chapter 37: It's Over

288 The fire had started in the kitchen: The account of the Grenfell fire draws on the expert reports of Barbara Lane and Niamh Nic Daeid for the Grenfell Tower Inquiry, grenfelltowerinquiry.org.uk; David D. Kirkpatrick, Danny Hakim and James Glanz, 'Why Grenfell Tower burned: Regulators put cost before safety', *New York Times*, June 24, 2017, nytimes.com/2017/06/24/world/ europe/grenfell-tower-london-fire.html; Andrew O'Hagan, 'The Tower', *London Review of Books*, May 30, 2018, lrb.co.uk/v40/n11/ andrew-ohagan/the-tower; and Tom Symonds and Daniel De Simone, 'Grenfell Tower: Cladding "changed to cheaper version"', *BBC News*, June 30, 2017, bbc.co.uk/news/uk-40453054

289 Houses were plentiful: David Batty, Niamh McIntyre, David Pegg and Anushka Asthana, 'Grenfell: names of wealthy empty-home owners in borough revealed', *Guardian*, August 2, 2017, theguardian.com/society/2017/aug/01/names-of-wealthy-empty-home-owners-in-grenfell-borough-revealed

289 high risk of catching fire: Luke Barratt, 'Block of flats chosen to house Grenfell survivors found to have "high" fire risk', *Inside Housing*, August 14, 2019, insidehousing.co.uk/news/62729

Chapter 38: The Story You Choose to Tell

291 Spanish court had ruled: José María Irujo, 'Varapalo del Supremo al Gobierno al dar asilo a un opositor kazajo', *El País*, February 25, 2015

292 brought charges: *The State of the World's Human Rights*, Amnesty International, 2017, amnesty.org.uk/files/2017-02/ POL1048002017ENGLISH.PDF?xMHdSpNaJBUNbiuvt MCJvJrnGuLiZnFU, p.207; 'Shalabayeva indictments sought',

ANSA, February 28, 2017, ansa.it/english/news/world/2017/02/28/
shalabayeva-indictments-sought-3_ec0474a2-9d0f-458b-bff3-
fefb41394f6a.html

292 invoked their immunity: Judgment of Carla Maria Giangamboni
of Perugia in the kidnapping case, November 16, 2018

293 jailed them for two years: Louis Colart, 'Trois barbouzes
condamnés pour l'espionnage de la réfugiée kazakhe Bota
Jardemalie', *Le Soir* (Belgium), November 29, 2019, lesoir.
be/263653/article/2019-11-29/trois-barbouzes-condamnes-pour-
lespionnage-de-la-refugiee-kazakhe-bota

293 Iskander Yerimbetov: 'Opinions adopted by the Working Group on
Arbitrary Detention at its eighty-third session, 19–23 November
2018', UN Human Rights Council, January 30, 2019, ohchr.org/
Documents/Issues/Detention/Opinions/Session83/A_HRC_
WGAD_2018_67.pdf; Bota Jardemalie interview; author's
communications with Bota Jardemalie and with Yerimbetov's
lawyers

293 sentenced him to twenty years: 'Fugitive Kazakh banker Ablyazov
sentenced to 20 years in absentia, decries "farce"', Radio Free
Europe/Radio Liberty, June 7, 2017, rferl.org/a/kazakhstan-
ablyazov-20-years-banker-embezzlement/28533214.html

294 murdered on Ablyazov's orders: 'Fugitive Kazakh banker, Nazarbaev
foe sentenced to life in prison', Radio Free Europe/Radio Liberty,
November 27, 2018, rferl.org/a/fugitive-kazakh-banker-nazarbaev-
foe-sentenced-to-life-in-prison/29623588.html

294 grasped that the campaign: Marat Beketayev interview

294 Williams thought it was mind-boggling: Trefor Williams interview

294 set the Israeli spooks of Black Cube: Iliyas Khrapunov interview.
Two other people with knowledge of ENRC's operations told the
author that Black Cube worked for the company. The author
emailed Black Cube to ask the spies themselves but they did not
reply

295 sham election: Tamara Vaal and Mariya Gordeyeva, 'Nazarbayev's
handpicked successor Tokayev elected Kazakh president', *Reuters*,
June 10, 2019, reuters.com/article/us-kazakhstan-election/
nazarbayevs-handpicked-successor-tokayev-elected-kazakh-president-
idUSKCN1TB0JA

295 police arrested hundreds: 'Kazakhstan election: Hundreds arrested
in poll protests', *BBC News*, June 9, 2019, bbc.com/news/world-
asia-48574540

296 'Money … is a tool': Mukhtar Ablyazov interview

296 claimed that he could not remember: Judge Katharine H. Parker's
opinion and order in Almaty et al. v Ablyazov et al., July 3, 2019

296 $140,000 she had ordered him to pay: Judge Katharine H. Parker's opinion and order in Almaty et al. v Ablyazov et al., February 7, 2020

296 'like-minded Kazakhs': Mukhtar Ablyazov letter to Judge Katharine H. Parker in Almaty et al. v Ablyazov et al., May 7, 2020

297 having none of it: Waksman judgment

297 New York judge blocked BTA: Opinion and order of Judge Alison J. Nathan in Almaty et al. v Ablyazov et al., June 1, 2020

297 feeling only anger and sadness: Torekhan Turganbaev interview

298 UN torture investigators: 'Committee against Torture considers the report of Kazakhstan', UN Office of the High Commissioner for Human Rights, November 18, 2014, ohchr.org/EN/NewsEvents/Pages/DisplayNews.aspx?NewsID=15309&LangID=E

298 seemed to them that there was a part of her: Interviews with friends of Roza Tuletayeva

Chapter 39: Alternative Facts

299 one Berd against one Lovelace: Commonwealth Legal Information Institute case record, commonlii.org/uk/cases/EngR/1576/10.pdf; UK Supreme Court judgment in R (on the application of Prudential plc and another) v Special Commissioner of Income Tax and another, January 23, 2013, supremecourt.uk/cases/docs/uksc-2010-0215-judgment.pdf

299 a High Court judge: Court of Appeal ruling of September 5, 2018, in SFO v ENRC and The Law Society, bailii.org/ew/cases/EWCA/Civ/2018/2006.html, pars 50 and 171

300 'obviously in the public interest': SFO v ENRC judgment, par 116

300 interviewed Shawn McCormick: The SFO declined to comment on McCormick's interview. McCormick told the author he had been interviewed as a witness

300 interviewed Sasha himself: Mark Hollingsworth, 'SFO is stepping up its Kazakh miner probe', Evening Standard, September 15, 2017, standard.co.uk/business/sfo-is-stepping-up-its-kazakh-miner-probe-a3635861.html

300 dispatching expensive lobbyists: for example, in January 2014, Kazakhstan's lawyers at Reed Smith described in a note of a meeting with the consultant John Howell his efforts to encourage the SFO to open an investigation into Ablyazov

300 word was sent to the British authorities: Dechert defence, par 83.2.h and interview with a person with knowledge of the discussions. The mooted cooperation appears to have come to

little: the SFO did not open an investigation into Ablyazov and the Kazakh authorities provided little meaningful assistance to the SFO

301 a suit alleging: ENRC v the director of the Serious Fraud Office, particulars of claim, March 25, 2019

301 the Trio's corporation had authorised him: Statement to the author by a Dechert spokesperson on the allegations about Gerrard and his firm, Dechert, in ENRC's suit against the SFO: 'We stand by the work we did and look forward to the opportunity of defending it in open court. We note that the criminal investigation by the Serious Fraud Office into ENRC is continuing and deplore ENRC's attempt to discredit that investigation by seeking to publicise unwarranted allegations against Dechert and its personnel. We emphatically reject any suggestion of an improper relationship between Dechert/Neil Gerrard and the SFO or that there was any unauthorised disclosure of information to or from the SFO. The work we did during our investigation was with the authority and knowledge of the members of the independent committee of the board which was instructing us at the time. We shall in the ensuing court proceedings fully address these unfounded allegations'

301 leak to the papers: ENRC v SFO, particulars of claim, pars 11.6–11.8

301 feed details: 10.1 and 11.9. The author sent Alderman via the SFO an invitation to comment on ENRC's version of events but received no reply

301 $25 million: ENRC v Dechert, amended complaint, par 153

302 passed in 2011: The Dechert defence asserts at pars 83.2.e, 144.2.b.iii, 268.2 and 324.4 that illegal activity was taking place at ENRC after this date

302 'rape mode': ENRC v Dechert, amended complaint, par 9

302 notebook: ENRC v SFO, particulars of claim, 11.26–11.27

302 anonymous letter: ENRC v SFO, 12.16–12.17

302 Akezhan Kazhegeldin … Glenn Simpson: ENRC v Akezhan Kazhegeldin in the UK High Court, particulars of claim, July 24, 2019, globalinvestigationsreview.com/digital_assets/e8c14192-bbb4-4337-9aee-9a91ab58898c/ENRC-v-Kazhegeldin-Lawsuit-(July-2019).pdf

302 Simpson's firm … was commissioned: Kenneth P. Vogel and Maggie Haberman, 'Conservative website first funded anti-Trump research by firm that later produced dossier', New York Times, October 27, 2017, nytimes.com/2017/10/27/us/politics/trump-dossier-paul-singer.html

303 a propagandist: Josh Kovensky, 'Grenell's past foreign clients make him unprecedented choice to lead intel community', *Talking Points Memo*, February 26, 2020, talkingpointsmemo.com/muckraker/grenells-past-foreign-clients-make-him-unprecedented-choice-to-lead-intel-community

303 'A lie gets halfway' … among them ENRC: Archived version of Capitol Media Partners website, services page, web.archive.org/web/20120620093013/http://capitolmediapartners.com/?page_id=7, and clients page, web.archive.org/web/20120620093019/http://capitolmediapartners.com/?page_id=9. The author emailed Capitol Media Partners to ask what Grenell did for ENRC but received no reply

303 disinformation campaigns: Michael Ames, 'How Trump's new intelligence chief spread misinformation about Bowe Bergdahl', *Politico*, March 11, 2020, politico.com/news/magazine/2020/03/11/richard-grenell-smear-against-bowe-bergdahl-125157

303 he discovered: David Gerrard and Elizabeth Gerrard v Diligence, particulars of claim, September 6, 2019

304 Anna Machkevitch: Tabby Kinder, 'Court date for Hirst collector', *The Times*, June 15, 2019, thetimes.co.uk/article/court-date-for-hirst-collector-w2092w006

304 Benedikt Sobotka: Samuel Rubenfeld, 'UK drops prosecution of mining executive', *Wall Street Journal*, November 6, 2018, wsj.com/articles/u-k-drops-prosecution-of-mining-executive-1541532653

304 returned to private practice: 'Former SFO senior prosecutor joins Cohen & Gresser's London office', Cohen & Gresser press release, September 2018, sites-cohengresser.vuture.net/8/108/september-2018/jwg-announcement-final.asp?sid=4dd45e16-a2bc-42ee-a400-503821877dbe

305 kickbacks: William MacNamara and Stanley Pignal, 'Case against three ENRC oligarchs settled', *Financial Times*, August 17, 2011, ft.com/content/95f8ecc4-c8dd-11e0-a2c8-00144feabdc0

305 $30 million: Thierry Denoël, 'Transaction: ce que les Kazakhs ont réellement payé', *Le Vif*, June 21, 2017, levif.be/actualite/belgique/transaction-ce-que-les-kazakhs-ont-reellement-paye/article-normal-681331.html. This was the total in fines and forfeiture paid by the Trio and those of their relatives involved

305 'le Kazakhgate': Mediapart's long-running investigation, beginning with Yann Philippin and Alain Lallemand, 'Kazakhgate: comment l'Elysée de Sarkozy a manipulé le pouvoir belge', November 5, 2016, mediapart.fr/journal/france/051116/kazakhgate-comment-lelysee-de-sarkozy-manipule-le-pouvoir-belge

306 EU had lifted its sanctions: Peter Fabricius, 'EU begins lifting Zimbabwe sanctions', *Weekend Argus* (South Africa), February 18, 2012

307 no further examination: ENRC complaint, par 92.2, and Dechert defence, 233.8. The author put to Pierre Prosper the main points that relate to him in this account. He said they contained errors but that he was 'not at liberty' to correct them

307 gratifying announcement: Arent Fox press release, April 21, 2014, arentfox.com/perspectives/press-releases/ofac-removes-arent-fox-client-sdn-sanctions-list

308 buy him out: Burgis, 'Why Glencore bought'

308 resumed paying him royalties: 'Settlement of dispute with Ventora and Africa Horizons', Glencore, June 15, 2018, investegate.co.uk/article.aspx?id=201806150700055198R

308 stitch-up was complete: Tom Wilson, David Blood and David Pilling, 'Congo voting data reveal huge fraud in poll to replace Kabila', *Financial Times*, January 15, 2019, ft.com/content/2b97f6e6-189d-11e9-b93e-f4351a53f1c3

308 hired a private detective: Preston Haskell was an investor in Amari Resources, the owner of the Kongoni prospect before ENRC. He later hired Bekker to work at another mining company he owned, Auriant Africa. After Bekker's death, Haskell hired Clement Jackson to investigate

308 kept the case open … FBI had taken over: Author's emails with Jasmine Bailey, public affairs officer for Springfield Police Department, 2019 and 2020

309 Mack collapsed: Confidential interview

309 Trio's people grew confident that: Interviews with two consultants who work for the Trio, 2019

Chapter 40: Quid Pro Quo

310 July 25, 2019: Philip Bump, 'The day of Trump's call with Ukraine's president, minute-by-minute', *Washington Post*, November 26, 2019, washingtonpost.com/politics/2019/11/26/day-trumps-call-with-ukraines-president-minute-by-minute

310 a tweet at 7.06 a.m: Donald Trump's Twitter account, twitter.com/realDonaldTrump/status/1154347111145598976

310 testified: Julie Hirschfeld Davis and Mark Mazzetti, 'Highlights of Robert Mueller's Testimony to Congress', *New York Times*, July 24, 2019, nytimes.com/2019/07/24/us/politics/mueller-testimony.html

310 declared on television: Lucien Bruggeman, '"I think I'd take it": In exclusive interview, Trump says he would listen if foreigners offered

dirt on opponents', *ABC News*, June 13, 2019, abcnews.go.com/
Politics/id-exclusive-interview-trump-listen-foreigners-offered-dirt/
story?id=63669304

311 a call with Volodymyr Zelensky: White House transcript,
declassified and published (having been edited) September 24,
2019, whitehouse.gov/wp-content/uploads/2019/09/
Unclassified09.2019.pdf

311 not Ukrainian: Angel Au-Yeung, 'What we know about
CrowdStrike, the cybersecurity firm Trump mentioned in Ukraine
call, and its billionaire CEO', *Forbes*, September 25, 2019, forbes.
com/sites/angelauyeung/2019/09/25/what-we-know-about-
crowdstrike-the-cybersecurity-firm-mentioned-by-trump-in-his-call-
with-ukraines-president-and-its-billionaire-ceo/#798f635e1c55

311 Biden had not: For an example of the many debunkings of
Trump's claims about Ukraine, see Natasha Bertrand, 'How to read
Trump's wild phone call with Ukraine's president', *Politico*,
September 25, 2019, politico.com/news/2019/09/25/donald-
trump-ukraine-call-analysis-000039

311 'reality-based community': Ron Suskind, 'Faith, certainty and the
presidency of George W. Bush', *New York Times*, October 17,
2004, nytimes.com/2004/10/17/magazine/faith-certainty-and-the-
presidency-of-george-w-bush.html

312 make money mean something other: There are examples of this
throughout Timothy O'Brien's *TrumpNation*, Warner Business
Books, 2005

312 'The philosophy of *Survivor*': O'Brien, *TrumpNation*, p.16

313 'My name is Donald Trump': O'Brien, *TrumpNation*, p.17

313 'laced with a number of howlers': O'Brien, *TrumpNation*, p.18

313 'I'm going to be the biggest developer': Confidential interview

314 Trump's mobster associates: David Cay Johnston, 'Just what were
Donald Trump's ties to the mob?', *Politico*, May 22, 2016, politico.
com/magazine/story/2016/05/donald-trump-2016-mob-organized-
crime-213910; O'Brien, *TrumpNation*, pp.67–70

314 Tamir Sapir: Gary Silverman, 'Trump's Russian riddle', *Financial
Times*, August 14, 2016, ft.com/content/549ddfaa-5fa5-11e6-b38c-
7b39cbb1138a

315 'wilful obliviousness': Confidential interview

315 Trump Ocean Club down in Panama: Ned Parker, 'Ivanka and the
fugitive'

315 cost $370 million: Mike McIntire, 'Donald Trump settled a real
estate lawsuit, and a criminal case was closed', *New York Times*,
April 5, 2016, nytimes.com/2016/04/06/us/politics/donald-trump-
soho-settlement.html

315 supposed to follow: Monica Alonzo-Dunsmoor, 'City rejects high-rises on camelback', *Arizona Republic*, December 22, 2005

315 tower in Florida: Ryan Yousefi, 'Failed Fort Lauderdale Beach Trump project will finally open as Conrad hotel', *Broward Palm Beach New Times*, October 3, 2014, https://www. browardpalmbeach.com/news/failed-fort-lauderdale-beach-trump-project-will-finally-open-as-conrad-hotel-6455709

315 set off for Moscow with two of Trump's children: Felix Sater deposition in Donald Trump v Timothy O'Brien et al., April 1, 2008, p.132

315 'We see a lot of money pouring in from Russia': 'Executive Talk: Donald Trump Jr bullish on Russia and few emerging markets', *eTurboNews*, September 15, 2008, eturbonews.com/9788/executive-talk-donald-trump-jr-bullish-russia-and-few-emerging-ma

315 'Senior Adviser to Donald Trump': Felix Sater's LinkedIn profile, later deleted, said: 'Senior Advisor to Donald Trump, The Trump Organization, January 2010 – 2011 (1 year)'

315 to meet Donald: Trump's deposition in his lawsuit against Timothy L. O'Brien and the publishers of *TrumpNation*, December 19, 2007

315 luxury apartment he kept for himself was in Trump Tower: Friedman, *Red Mafiya*, p.113

315 sold them to him personally: James S. Henry, 'The curious world of Donald Trump's private Russian connections', *The American Interest*, December 19, 2016, the-american-interest. com/2016/12/19/the-curious-world-of-donald-trumps-private-russian-connections

315 that was Trump real estate: Layne, 'Russian elite invested'

315 more than double: Letter from Senator Ron Wyden to Treasury Secretary Steven Mnuchin, February 9, 2018, finance.senate.gov/imo/media/doc/020918%20-Mnuchin%202008%20Palm%20Beach%20Trump%20Sale%20Letter.pdf

316 'People really want to own what I do': CarinoAgencyPR, 'Trump International Hotel & Tower, Toronto – Ground Breaking Event!!', promotional video posted on YouTube, May 17, 2011, youtube. com/watch?v=2pgMtRmf7xo

316 brought in hundreds of millions: His share of the proceeds once they were divided between him and Shyfrin

316 put up the final $40 million: Shnaider's arbitration claim against Shyfrin

316 went on doing so for years: Trump's presidential financial disclosures

317 'He doesn't give you questions': Colleen Long, 'Cohen says Trump behaved "much like a mobster would do"', Associated Press,

February 28, 2019, apnews.com/88e83c32a9d54d82abe3ac52
bfad22e4

317 anyone listening: One official who became aware of the call's
contents blew the whistle to the heads of the Congressional
intelligence committees, triggering a process that culminated in
Trump's impeachment. The whistleblower's letter was later
published, washingtonpost.com/context/read-the-whistleblower-
complaint-regarding-president-trump-s-communications-with-
ukrainian-president-volodymyr-zelensky/4b9e0ca5-3824-
467f-b1a3-77f2d4ee16aa

317 projection: For instance, John Avlon, 'Trump's absurd projection
reveals his anxiety', CNN, September 24, 2019, edition.cnn.
com/2019/09/24/opinions/trumps-absurd-projection-reveals-his-
anxiety-avlon/index.html

318 'fake': Philip Bump, 'The expansive, repetitive universe of Trump's
Twitter insults', *Washington Post*, August 20, 2019, washingtonpost.
com/politics/2019/08/20/expansive-repetitive-universe-trumps-
twitter-insults/

318 messaging to confirm: Bump, 'The day of Trump's call'

318 Trump departed: Cheryl Bolen, White House pool report 1, July
25, 2019, publicpool.kinja.com/subject-in-town-pool-
report-1-1836697089

318 the Beast: Paul A. Eisenstein, 'Trump's new limo cost $1.5M and
comes with a fridge full of his blood type', *NBC News*, September
28, 2015, nbcnews.com/business/autos/trump-s-new-limo-cost-
16m-comes-fridge-his-blood-n912841

318 'Thank you to all': 'Remarks by President Trump at a Full Honors
Welcome Ceremony for the Secretary of Defense', White House,
July 25, 2019, whitehouse.gov/briefings-statements/remarks-
president-trump-full-honors-welcome-ceremony-secretary-defense

318 declined to commit to recusing himself: Edwin Djabatey and Kate
Brannen, 'What did we learn about Mark Esper and how he
views the world?', *Just Security*, July 17, 2019, justsecurity.
org/64956/what-did-we-learn-about-mark-esper-and-how-he-views-
the-world

319 held the business interests: 'Xi Jinping millionaire relations reveal
fortunes of elite', *Bloomberg News*, June 29, 2012, bloomberg.com/
news/articles/2012-06-29/xi-jinping-millionaire-relations-reveal-
fortunes-of-elite

320 controlled assets worth $2.7 billion: David Barboza, 'Billions in
hidden riches for family of Chinese leader', *New York Times*,
October 25, 2012, nytimes.com/2012/10/26/business/global/
family-of-wen-jiabao-holds-a-hidden-fortune-in-china.html

320 they were condemned: For one of the most spectacular examples, see Jamil Anderlini, 'Bo Xilai: power, death and politics', *Financial Times*, July 20, 2012, ft.com/content/d67b90f0-d140-11e1-8957-00144feabdc0

320 crude oil: Paul Collier, in chapter 3 of *The Bottom Billion* (Oxford University Press, 2008), describes how oil creates a power system he calls 'the survival of the fattest'. Leif Wenar, in *Blood Oil* (Oxford University Press, 2016), argues persuasively that the global oil trade amounts to handling stolen goods on a massive scale. See also Burgis, *The Looting Machine*, chapters 1, 3 and 8

320 returned to the national treasury: 'Saudi Arabia ends major anti-corruption campaign', *BBC News*, January 31, 2019, bbc.co.uk/news/world-middle-east-47065285

320 to buy weapons manufactured in the swing states: Ben Freeman and William D. Hartung, 'How the Saudis wooed Donald Trump', *The Nation*, May 10, 2018, thenation.com/article/archive/how-the-saudis-wooed-donald-trump

321 directed the operation: Shane Harris, Greg Miller and Josh Dawsey, 'CIA concludes Saudi crown prince ordered Jamal Khashoggi's assassination', *Washington Post*, November 16, 2018, washingtonpost.com/world/national-security/cia-concludes-saudi-crown-prince-ordered-jamal-khashoggis-assassination/2018/11/16/98c89fe6-e9b2-11e8-a939-9469f1166f9d_story.html

321 published a statement: 'Statement from President Donald J. Trump on standing with Saudi Arabia', White House, November 20, 2018, whitehouse.gov/briefings-statements/statement-president-donald-j-trump-standing-saudi-arabia

321 'share the neighbourhood': Jeffrey Goldberg, 'The Obama doctrine', *The Atlantic*, April 2016, theatlantic.com/magazine/archive/2016/04/the-obama-doctrine/471525

322 subverting the state: This idea is developed in Sarah Chayes, *Thieves of State*, Norton, 2015

322 Office 39: Tom Burgis, 'The secrets of Office 39', *Financial Times*, June 24, 2015, ft.com/content/4164dfe6-09d5-11e5-b6bd-00144feabdc0

322 official summary: Cheryl Bolen, White House pool report 6, July 25, 2019, publicpool.kinja.com/subject-in-town-pool-report-6-ukraine-call-1836700221

323 at his own courses: Michael Bamberger, 'President Trump won a 2018 club championship – without actually playing in it!', *Golf*, March 11, 2019, golf.com/news/2019/03/10/president-trump-club-championship-did-not-enter

323 'thirty-foot putts': Andrew Wyrich, 'White House changes press briefing transcript to make Trump's golf skills more flattering', *Daily Dot*, July 27, 2017, dailydot.com/layer8/scaramucci-trump-putts-quote-changed

323 periodic tweeting: Bump, 'The day of Trump's call'

323 one in three had a conflict of interest: Danielle Ivory and Robert Faturechi, 'The deep industry ties of Trump's deregulation teams', *New York Times*, July 11, 2017, nytimes.com/2017/07/11/business/the-deep-industry-ties-of-trumps-deregulation-teams.html?smid=tw-nytimes&smtyp=cur&referer=https://t.co/MaNefWxfzz

323 'unique, once-in-a-lifetime opportunity': 'Melania Trump's "once-in-a-lifetime" opportunity to profit', *The Economist*, February 9, 2017, economist.com/democracy-in-america/2017/02/09/melania-trumps-once-in-a-lifetime-opportunity-to-profit

324 preventing nuclear catastrophe, say, giving advance warning of tornadoes: Michael Lewis, *The Fifth Risk*, Norton, 2018

324 taking a suite: For example, David A. Fahrenthold and Jonathan O'Connell, 'Saudi-funded lobbyist paid for 500 rooms at Trump's hotel after 2016 election', *Washington Post*, December 5, 2018, washingtonpost.com/politics/saudi-funded-lobbyist-paid-for-500-rooms-at-trumps-hotel-after-2016-election/2018/12/05/29603a64-f417-11e8-bc79-68604ed88993_story.html

324 paid the former US general Michael Flynn: Peter Baker and Matthew Rosenberg, 'Michael Flynn was paid to represent Turkey's interests during Trump campaign', *New York Times*, March 10, 2017, nytimes.com/2017/03/10/us/politics/michael-flynn-turkey.html

324 sent millions of dollars to … Elliott Broidy: Kenneth P. Vogel, 'How a Trump ally tested the boundaries of Washington's influence game', *New York Times*, August 13, 2019, nytimes.com/2019/08/13/us/politics/elliott-broidy-trump.html. Broidy's lawyers have said he 'never discussed assisting Mr Low in any criminal matters and never lobbied to resolve the civil issues facing the financier'

324 disturbed some of his secrets: Burgis, 'Dirty money'

325 paid him $300,000: Erik Larson, 'Trump fixer Cohen paid by Kazakh bank for post-election work', *Bloomberg*, bloomberg.com/news/articles/2019-02-27/kazakh-bank-says-it-paid-trump-fixer-cohen-talked-to-prosecutor. Confirmed to the author by Kenes Rakishev's representatives

325 'assemble a winning team': Ibid.

325 lawyers discovered: Judge Parker's 2018, 2019 and 2020 Litco rulings

325 added to the roster of defendants: BTA v Sater et al.

325 wouldn't recognise him: 'If he were sitting in the room right now, I really wouldn't know what he looked like,' Trump said in taped testimony in 2013, thereafter repeatedly denying the true extent of their business relationship. Rosalind S. Helderman and Tom Hamburger, 'Former Mafia-linked figure describes association with Trump', *Washington Post*, May 17, 2016, washingtonpost.com/politics/former-mafia-linked-figure-describes-association-with-trump/2016/05/17/cec6c2c6-16d3-11e6-aa55-670cabef46e0_story.html

325 'It's very upsetting': Cormier, 'The Asset'

325 'infomercial': Robert S. Mueller III, 'Report on the investigation into Russian interference in the 2016 presidential election', volume 1, p.72, justice.gov/storage/report.pdf

325 'Buddy, our boy', Mueller report, vol. 1, p.71

326 invoked privilege: Mueller report, vol. 2, p.143, justice.gov/storage/report_volume2.pdf

326 'First thing I plan to do': Cormier, 'The Asset'

Chapter 41: Normal Business

327 'The country is rotting': Karishma Vaswani, 'Corruption, money and Malaysia's election', *BBC News*, May 11, 2018, bbc.com/news/business-44078549

327 wanted in the US: Byron Tau and Aruna Viswanatha, 'Jho Low, accused mastermind of 1MDB scandal, reaches DoJ civil settlement', *Wall Street Journal*, October 30, 2019, wsj.com/articles/accused-mastermind-of-1mdb-close-to-civil-settlement-with-doj-11572473653

327 'I am not so stupid': Sharanjit Singh, 'Najib: I'm not so stupid to do something like this', *New Straits Times*, January 22, 2020, nst.com.my/news/crime-courts/2020/01/558860/najib-i-am-not-so-stupid-do-something-you-know

327 If justice was closing in on Najib: As this book went to press in late June 2020, the verdict in Najib's case was expected in late July

328 140 political leaders: 'Panama Papers: The power players', International Consortium of Investigative Journalists, April 3, 2016, icij.org/investigations/panama-papers/the-power-players

329 abetted the pillaging: Nicole Hong, Liz Hoffman and Bradley Hope, 'Justice department charges ex-Goldman bankers in Malaysia 1MDB scandal', *Wall Street Journal*, November 1, 2018, wsj.com/articles/justice-department-to-charge-former-goldman-bankers-in-malaysia-1mdb-scandal-1541077318?mod=article_inline; Liz Hoffman and Aruna Viswanatha, 'Goldman Sachs in talks to

admit guilt, pay $2 billion fine to settle 1MDB probe', *Wall Street Journal*, December 19, 2019, wsj.com/articles/goldman-sachs-in-talks-to-admit-guilt-pay-2-billion-fine-to-settle-1mdb-probe-11576760406

329 Yeo Jiawei: Jake Maxwell Watts, 'Ex-banker sentenced to prison after pleading guilty to 1MDB-linked money laundering', *Wall Street Journal*, July 12, 2017, wsj.com/articles/ex-banker-sentenced-to-prison-after-pleading-guilty-to-1mdb-linked-money-laundering-1499852340

329 ceased to exist: 'EFG completes integration of BSI', *Finews*, July 4, 2017, finews.com/news/english-news/28006-efg-completes-integration-of-bsi

329 approved its acquisition: 'BSI in serious breach of money laundering regulations', press release by Finma, May 24, 2016, finma.ch/en/news/2016/05/20160524-mm-bsi/

329 to Switzerland, Monaco, the Bahamas: Confidential interview supported by documents in Nigel Wilkins' files setting out the plans for BSI client accounts after the closure of the London office and corporate filings from entities connected to BSI bankers in the Bahamas

330 not a bank: Nigel put it like this in his notebook: 'BSI – not a bank but a deeply corrupt organisation that facilitates money laundering and tax evasion'

330 bribing Boris Yeltsin: Sharon LaFraniere, 'Yeltsin linked to bribe scheme', *Washington Post*, September 8, 1999, washingtonpost.com/wp-srv/inatl/daily/sept99/yeltsin8.htm; 'Kosovo's New President Takes Office Amid Controversy', Radio Free Europe, February 24, 2011, rferl.org/a/kosovo_president_takes_office_controversy/2319676.html

331 Igor Pluzhnikov: BSI internal correspondence including Nigel Wilkins' email to John Erskine of April 20, 2007; 'working group' report on Mogilevich

331 Bob Levinson had vanished: The details of Levinson's disappearance are drawn from confidential interviews and Meier, *Missing Man*, pp.88–102

331 nipped up to Toronto: Levinson's emails with Boris Birshtein; confidential interviews

332 furnished to the Trio: For example, an email of September 20, 2006 from Khofiz Shakhidi to his superiors at BSI's London office refers to Machkevitch, Chodiev and Ibragimov as 'important clients'

333 'Everyone thinks he's the third wheel': Confidential interview

333 origins less auspicious: Interviews with former senior Kazakh official and businessmen who know Ibragimov

333 maintain convivial relations with the Ibragimov family: Khofiz
Shakhidi correspondence with his superiors at BSI London

333 Abdumalik Mirakhmedov ... 'promoters': promoter contracts from
2002, 2006 and 2007 with Mirakhmedov and his companies

334 senior manager in the department that sold the metals: *An
Introduction to Ferrochrome*, ENRC presentation, February 18,
2008. The presentation describes Mirakhmedov as General
Manager Beijing, ENRC Marketing, in which capacity he was
'product manager for iron ore responsible for the global strategy,
sales and marketing' and 'responsible for marketing of iron,
chrome and manganese ores in China'. His LinkedIn profile (as of
May 8, 2020) states that from 2010 to 2015, he was CEO,
ENRC Sales & Marketing. linkedin.com/in/abdumalik-
mirakhmedov

334 married to the daughter of the boss at Rudny: Confidential
interview confirmed in pre-publication correspondence between the
author and Mirakhmedov's lawyers

334 a hand in the decision to award ENRC contracts to ... Alex
Stewart International: Confirmed by Mirakhmedov's lawyers, who
told the author: 'His input into any decision-making in the
company was commercially justified and made on a legal basis'

334 'a possible US investigation': ENRC v Mark Hollingsworth in the
UK High Court, particulars of claim, October 21, 2019. At par
21.c.iii ENRC's lawyers refer to 'a possible US investigation
regarding payments which the Claimant [ENRC] was alleged to
have made to Alex Stewart International'. The author contacted
Alex Stewart International ahead of publication of this book asking
to discuss its ENRC contracts but received no reply

334 money ... to ... Alijan Ibragimov's son Dostan: Loan agreement
between Dostan Ibragimov as borrower and Mirakhmedov's
company Wealth Management Group Ltd of Belize as lender,
January 10, 2008. The copy of the agreement the author has seen
is signed on behalf of Mirakhmedov's company but not by Dostan
Ibragimov. The author invited Mirakhmedov to say if it did not
take effect and he did not

335 'never taken a kickback': Author's correspondence with
Mirakhmedov's lawyers, June 2020

335 managing part of the tremendous fortune the Trio's Alijan
Ibragimov had amassed: ENRC prospectus for its 2007 initial
public offering in London, p.185, preqveca.ru/placements/
memorandum/download/16

335 went on managing Ibragimov's fortune: A Companies House filing
shows Dalman was appointed as a director of ENRC on December

6, 2007 (beta.companieshouse.gov.uk/company/06023510/officers).
At that point, Dalman's company, WMG Advisors, was the
investment adviser to a fund, registered in the Cayman Islands,
called WMG Strategic Fund, in which Alijan Ibragimov had
placed some of his fortune. On April 9, 2008, the fund's name
was changed to Albion Investments. An offering memorandum by
Albion Investments lists Dalman's WMG Advisors as its investment
adviser. That was in June 2008, six months after Dalman took up
his position on the ENRC board. Albion Investments' annual
report of June 30, 2008 also names WMG Advisors as its
investment adviser. And then on October 16, 2008, ten months
after Dalman's appointment as a director of ENRC, an amended
and restated investment advisory agreement was signed in which
WMG Advisors was once more appointed as investment adviser to
Albion Investments, to be paid a $250,000 annual fee. Dalman
resigned as a director of the fund itself (but continued to own the
investment advisory firm WMG Advisers) on April 21, 2008,
replaced on the same day by the BSI banker Khofiz Shakhidi. But
this did not necessarily mean that Dalman was no longer involved.
In fact, Shakhidi had previously acted as Dalman's nominee – in
one of the very Wealth Management Group companies that
handled Ibragimov's fortune. This was the third kind of company
that is used in the offshore hedge fund setup that so troubled
Nigel Wilkins when he was at the FCA. There is the fund itself,
typically registered in some opaque tax haven, where the actual
money sits. Then the investment advisory firm, where the
financiers plot how best to multiply that money. This is registered
somewhere considered respectable, typically London (as with
WMG Advisors), but with the money in the fund safely beyond
the regulators' gaze in the Cayman Islands or wherever. Finally
there is the fund manager, the company responsible for the
day-to-day administration of the money in the fund, handling
bank accounts and so on. In this case, that was WMG
Management, incorporated on August 22, 2007, in Bermuda. The
registered shareholders were recorded as Shakhidi (5,880 shares)
and WMG Holdings of Jersey (6,120 shares). But the ultimate
beneficial owner is recorded, in a document obtained by the
author, as Mehmet Dalman, with a 100 per cent interest. In other
words, Shakhidi was fronting for him. After WMG Management
(Bermuda) changed its name to Albion Management (Bermuda)
on March 11, 2008, it remained the manager of the Albion
Investments fund that held Ibragimov's money. Shakhidi remained
chairman of Albion Management (Bermuda) until at least March

2009. Maybe longer – the finishing date of his tenure is confined to documents that are still secret. Dalman has said that it took so long to extract himself from his personal relationship with Ibragimov because of 'various legal, compliance and administrative tasks that needed to be completed'. When the author asked him about Shakhidi's role as his nominee, he did not respond

335 'clean up': For instance, Jim Armitage, 'ENRC plans to split off controversial African mines', *Independent*, May 7, 2012, independent.co.uk/news/business/news/enrc-plans-to-split-off-controversial-african-mines-7718759.html; Danny Fortson, 'ENRC pays $550m for copper in Congo', December 9, 2012, *Sunday Times*, thetimes.co.uk/article/enrc-pays-dollar550m-for-copper-in-congo-6k59bzr6gkw

336 Sam Pa: Burgis, *The Looting Machine*, chapters 4 and 10

336 facial recognition technology: David Gilbert, 'Zimbabwe is trying to build a China style surveillance state', *Vice*, December 2, 2019, vice.com/en_uk/article/59n753/zimbabwe-is-trying-to-build-a-china-style-surveillance-state; Chris Rickleton, 'Kazakhstan embraces facial recognition, civil society recoils', *Eurasianet*, October 17, 2019, eurasianet.org/kazakhstan-embraces-facial-recognition-civil-society-recoils

337 Alexander Temerko: Catherine Belton, 'In British PM race, a former Russian tycoon quietly wields influence', *Reuters*, July 19, 2019, reuters.com/investigates/special-report/britain-eu-johnson-russian; author's visit to Temerko's office

337 swung by a London party: Luke Harding and Dan Sabbagh, 'Johnson visit to Lebedev party after victory odd move for "people's PM"', *Guardian*, December 22, 2019, theguardian.com/politics/2019/dec/22/johnson-visit-to-lebedev-party-after-victory-odd-move-for-peoples-pm

337 a guest of Putin's security services on the city's periphery: Confidential interviews with two intelligence sources

338 said of the British Establishment: For instance in Nick Cohen, 'Political argument in Britain has stopped when we need it most', *Spectator*, October 18, 2017, spectator.co.uk/article/political-argument-in-britain-has-stopped-when-we-need-it-most

ACKNOWLEDGEMENTS

A great many thanks are owed to a great many people who helped in all manner of ways.

To Charlotte Martin for the hours she spent sharing her memories of Nigel Wilkins, so that this portrait could be true to the man.

To James and Amana Fontanella-Khan in New York, Christine Spolar in Washington, Julian Rademeyer in Johannesburg, Roman Olearchyk in Kiev and Max Seddon in Moscow for shelter, cheer and wisdom on the road.

To the tenacious Naubet Bisenov in Kazakhstan, Justin Glawe in the US, Burhan Yüksekkaş in Turkey, and in London two bright young stars, Avin Houro and Liam Travers.

To the rare talents Yinka Ibukun, Sarah O'Connor, Joe Burgis, Chinny Li and Francesca Jakobi, author of the brilliant *Bitter*.

To another splendid Nigel – McKeand – for sending the perfect line of Chekhov.

To those who have that thing we need more than ever – expertise – and gave it generously: Antony Goldman, Scott Horton, Mark Galeotti, Jens Meierhenrich and the distinguished thinkers at his conference on the authoritarian rule of law, Tom Warner, Elise Bean, Patricia Feeney and Anneke Van Woudenberg of

Rights and Accountability in Development, Tom Mayne, Richard Brooks, Michael Gillard, Richard Stovin-Bradford, Patrick Smith of *Africa Confidential*, Stefaans Brümmer, Sam Sole, Elisabeth Caesens and two generations of American intrigue, Gary and Ira Silverman.

To the *Financial Times* for the long sabbatical. The *FT* has not seen this book or endorsed its contents.

To Misha Glenny, who led the way.

And to all those who can't be named.

Any errors are the author's alone.

Sophie Lambert was, once again, there at the beginning, effervescent. Many others at C&W were invaluable, especially Emma Finn, the rights team and Luke Speed of Curtis Brown; so too was Sloan Harris at ICM.

The extraordinary Arabella Pike at HarperCollins never wavered in her confidence in this book, even when the threats were raining down. Tom Jarvis and David Hirst gave sage counsel. Jo Thompson kept the cogs turning. Helen Upton and Tracy Locke got the word out. Jennifer Barth in New York brought wonderful fresh perspectives. What a privilege to be the last beneficiary of Robert Lacey's legendary copy-editing before his retirement, with Iain Hunt seeing it home.

There has been much more to be grateful for, along the way. For glorious family, friends and neighbours. For the company of Delilah Burgis, who tells the best stories. And for Camilla Carson. There is no one, near or far, quite like her. No matter how early in the morning the chat starts, she abides. She'll pull a face, but this book is for her.

INDEX